THE LONG DEATH

THE
LONG
DEATH

The Last Days
of the Plains Indian

RALPH K. ANDRIST

WITH A NEW INTRODUCTION BY DEE BROWN

MAPS BY RAFAEL D. PALACIOS

COLLIER BOOKS
MACMILLAN PUBLISHING COMPANY
NEW YORK

MAXWELL MACMILLAN CANADA
TORONTO

MAXWELL MACMILLAN INTERNATIONAL
NEW YORK   OXFORD   SINGAPORE   SYDNEY

To Vivian—for many reasons

Copyright © 1964 by Ralph K. Andrist

Introduction copyright © 1993 by Macmillan Publishing Company, a
division of Macmillan, Inc.

All rights reserved. No part of this book may be reproduced or
transmitted in any form or by any means, electronic or mechanical,
including photocopying, recording, or by any information storage and
retrieval system, without permission in writing from the Publisher.

Collier Books   Maxwell Macmillan Canada, Inc.
Macmillan Publishing Company   1200 Eglinton Avenue East
866 Third Avenue   Suite 200
New York, NY 10022   Don Mills, Ontario M3C 3N1

Macmillan Publishing Company is part of
the Maxwell Communication Group of Companies.

Library of Congress Cataloging-in-Publication Data
Andrist, Ralph K.
    The long death: the last days of the Plains Indian / by Ralph K.
Andrist; with a new introduction by Dee Brown; maps by Rafael D.
Palacios.
      p.   cm.
    Includes bibliographical references and index.
    ISBN 0-02-030295-9
    1. Indians of North America—Great Plains—Wars.   2. Indians
of North America—Great Plains—History—19th century.
I. Brown, Dee Alexander.   II. Title.
E78.G73A55   1993   92-30050   CIP
978′.00497—dc20

Macmillan books are available at special discounts for bulk purchases
for sales promotions, premiums, fund-raising, or educational use. For
details, contact:

Special Sales Director
Macmillan Publishing Company
866 Third Avenue
New York, NY 10022

First Collier Books Edition 1969

First New Collier Books Edition 1993

10 9 8 7 6 5 4 3 2 1

Printed in the United States of America

Contents

IV
Give Me Eighty Men

V
The Great Road

VI
Ten Million Dead Buffalo

VII
Diversion in the Far West

VIII

The Road to the Little Bighorn

IX

The Last Small Wars

Maps

Introduction

Ralph Andrist was one of the first historians of the American Indian wars to perceive that the story should be told facing eastward toward the invading Europeans rather than facing westward toward the defending tribes. In this way he comes closer to an Indian viewpoint. Andrist was also among the first to see the wars as the holocaust they were. At the same time he recognized that the conflicts created nascent legends of red men and white men, of heroic persons and deeds that someday would match the epics of the Old World and become as enduring as Beowulf, the Siege of Troy, the medieval Crusades.

Andrist wrote much for radio, so that there is a crispness in his prose, a definite voice speaking clearly. He won awards for his documentary pieces, and between assignments he must have spent many hours researching for *The Long Death*, first published in 1964. The book still belongs in the top ten of its field. Although it went through several printings, copies have been very difficult to find in recent years.

Evidently the mounted warriors of the Great Plains first drew Andrist into the saga. From the Atlantic shore to the Mississippi River, the native Americans met intruders from across the seas peaceably at first, then when forced into defensive battles, they fought as foot warriors in forests and meadows. But as the European tide washed westward the forests ended, and there on the vast expanse of the Great Plains were bands of magnificent warbonneted horsemen with bows strung and quivers filled with arrows, the best light cavalry on earth. Somewhere in his career Andrist decided that he must tell *their* story.

To the Plains Indians the oceanlike sweep of grass under a tremendous dome of sky symbolized freedom. "I was born upon the prairie where the wind blew free," said the old Comanche, Ten Bears, "where everything drew a free breath." In the mid-years of the nineteenth century the Plains tribes were doubly shielded, first by an anomalous "permanent Indian frontier," and second by the fact that in the earliest contacts, the white invaders viewed the Great Plains as worthless, an unending tract of desert flatness that had to be crossed to reach the riches of the Rocky Mountains and beyond. The "permanent Indian frontier" was the creation of President Andrew Jackson and the U.S. Congress, who at first viewed the Mississippi River as a vague border beyond which all Indian tribes would live in peace. Pressure for settlement, however, quickly forced the line back to the 95th meridian, where it was about as effective as a curtain of cheesecloth.

Andrist has a knack for touching the salient keys that led inevitably to wars and near extermination of the Plains tribes. The end of the permanent Indian country, he says, began in 1842 when one hundred settlers and eighteen covered wagons took off across the Plains for Oregon. The track of their wagon wheels became the Oregon Trail, over which thousands of westward-bound settlers traveled during several successive years without the loss of a single emigrant's life to Indians. Discovery of gold in California increased the flow of travelers, and clashes between Indians and whites began to occur. A treaty signed at Fort Laramie in 1851 restored good relations, but a single incident three years later led inexorably to a series of bloody conflicts that did not end until a generation later at Wounded Knee.

In his direct style, Andrist tells of that incident, an emigrant's crippled cow straying into an Indian encampment near Fort Laramie where a Sioux slaughtered it for beef, and of how a hot-headed Lieutenant Grattan attempted to arrest the offender by needlessly firing rifles and then a cannon into the camp and starting a bloody fight. Beginning with that day, several young warriors who witnessed the incident lost their faith in treaties and resolved to resist further encroachments upon their hunting lands and their freedom.

After that came the massacres in Minnesota, which Andrist treats as Greek drama. (Minnesota was his home state.) And then he describes the revolting episode at Sand Creek in Colorado, sparing no details of the massacre's stark horrors—Black Kettle and the American flag that he trusted implicitly as a symbol of protection over his people—the infamous Colonel Chivington's order: "Kill and scalp all Indians, big and little; nits make lice."

In one skillfully constructed chapter, "Ten Million Dead Buffalo," Andrist shows the relationship between the Plains tribes and the buffalo, the food, shelter, and clothing dependency that had become a cultural and spiritual connection. Removal of the buffalo herds, encouraged by governmental policy, hastened the defeat of the tribes.

Sitting Bull, Red Cloud, Crazy Horse, and other leaders are brought to life in this book, each one becoming a symbol of universal tragedy. Brilliant exploits are followed by overconfidence, by deceptions and broken promises from their adversaries, by ultimate compromises and bitter betrayals.

Red Cloud is one of Andrist's favorite characters, and he uses him as an example of leadership transfixed. A dozen years after he, as a young Oglala Sioux, witnessed the Grattan incident at Fort Laramie, he was the spokesman for his people in a treaty meeting at the same fort. When he learned that a regiment under Colonel Carrington was preparing to march into the heart of the Indians' hunting country, Red Cloud defied the government commissioners, refused to sign the treaty, and led his followers north to defend their country. Under Red Cloud's direction, younger warriors such as Crazy Horse carried out a continual guerrilla war against the soldiers at Fort Phil Kearny, and eventually drew eighty soldiers into a skillfully planned ambush now known as the Fetterman Massacre. "He was the first and only Indian in the West," Andrist says, "to win a war with the United States." But the glory could not endure, as this book reveals in penetrating detail.

Andrist brings George Armstrong Custer into his narrative during the Hancock campaign in Kansas and keeps a close eye on the impetuous lieutenant colonel through his deadly winter assault upon Black Kettle's peaceful Cheyenne village in Indian Territory, the invasion of the Black Hills, and on to the Little Bighorn. Readers are unlikely to find a more effective depiction of the actions preceding and during the Little Bighorn battle than in this carefully crafted long chapter. The four accompanying maps by Rafael Palacios are superb, enabling readers to follow the text with ease. Custer experts (and they grow in number) may disagree with some of Andrist's rather positive statements, but the experts disagree among themselves, and Andrist's version is outstanding for its clarity.

In covering the last small wars in which the Plains tribes were involved, Andrist effectively uses the words of Chief Joseph of the Nez Percés to start bringing this great American tragedy to a close. The long death ends with the Ghost Dance and the massacre at Wounded Knee where the victims were buried together. This story, Andrist concludes, "has ended after many years, broken promises, and tragedies, at the edge of a mass grave in Dakota."

Dee Brown
Little Rock, Arkansas 1992

THE LONG DEATH

I

As Long as the Grass Shall Grow

THE last gunfire on the Great Plains between Indians and soldiers of the United States was exchanged on a bitterly cold day in 1890, the next to last day of the year. On that day, on Wounded Knee Creek in South Dakota, a forlorn and hungry band of Sioux, including women and children, was goaded and frightened into making a gesture of resistance to Army authority. When it was over, the Indian wars of the plains were ended, and with them the long struggle of all American Indians, from the Atlantic to the Pacific, to preserve some portion of their ancestral lands and tribal ways.

When the Civil War ended, a Union band played "Auld Lang Syne" at Appomattox, and many magnanimous words were spoken ("The men who own a horse or mule can take them home, General. They will need them to work their little farms.") But no band blared "Auld Lang Syne" into the frigid air at Wounded Knee Creek and there was no one who offered kind or noble words; when the frozen bodies were thrown into a common grave, not one of the ministers or priests who was in the area to lead the Sioux into the gentle religion considered it worth his trouble to bring God's presence to the bleak burial.

The condition of the Sioux, or of other tribes of the plains had not always been so low. Half a century earlier, the Indians had been almost sole possessors of the Great Plains. A few United States Army posts were stretched thinly along their eastern edge and a scattering of fur trading posts were lost in their enormous expanses, but these were the only permanent habitations of white men. The Santa Fe Trail cut across the southern plains, but its ruts were the only road made by wheels in the entire grasslands. No settler's fence hemmed in the smallest part of the vastness of the plains, no plow had yet cut a furrow through its hundreds of millions of acres of sod, no rancher's windmill stood anywhere against its sky. It was still a land of the Indian and the buffalo.

The entire region had been solemnly pledged to the Indians by the government in the years before 1840, to have and to hold forever. Even though the promise of the United States to Indian tribes had been proven worthless again and again, there were special circumstances that made many sincere men believe that here in the West, for the first time, an Indian treaty would actually be honored. But nothing was different. The usual encroachments by frontiersmen soon began, and steadily increased until the hardest-pressed tribes lashed back. Before long, the bright flames of open war were flickering up and down the plains, not to be completely extinguished for almost thirty years.

These Indian wars were different from the conflicts that had been waged for two centuries in the East. There were no dark ambuscades in shady forest glens but the drumming of horses' hoofs on prairie sod and battles in swirling dust under the open sky. The tribes of the plains were the first mounted warriors Americans had encountered in their westering, and the experience was to leave a profound impression on both history and legend.

The Indian of the plains has been glorified and romanticized until at last he has become *the* American Indian. In all the splendor of his eagle-feather warbonnet he sits on his horse on the bluff, watching the covered wagons roll down the valley far below; at last he raises his rifle above his head in the signal that brings a horde of whooping horsemen down on the stouthearted pioneers. The picture is seen through a pane of wavy glass, badly distorted. It is a stereotype built with the help of dime novels, nickelodeons, cliff-hanger movie serials, brewery-distributed cromolithographic fantasies of Custer's Last Stand hanging above a multitude of free-lunch counters, and similar methods of mass education.

However, while these dead warriors today ride the plains in tradition taller, swifter, and stronger than they ever did in life, they do not ride them alone. They share the sky and the horizon forever with the United States Cavalry which fought them, and by so doing made itself also a part of the legend of a world of bright and golden courage and endless space. But at the outset of this account, let there be no mistake: the wars of the plains were not clean, crisp little tableaux of cavalry with singing trumpets and snapping guidons meeting thundering charges of Sioux and Cheyenne warriors against a backdrop of grass bending in waves to the horizon and thunderheads piling up against a western sky. They were not that kind of conflict at all. As in all wars, men died unpleasantly, and often in extreme agony. Women and children suffered along with warrior and soldier, and the Army made it a part of strategy to destroy the enemy's food and possessions in order to leave him cold, hungry, and without the will to resist.

Striking at a foe by hitting his family does not quite fit in with the myth that all was bravery, sudden encounters, sharp clashes, and bright red blood—everything in primary colors. But it was effective strategy. In the end the Indian was defeated and confined to a reservation. He was no longer a hunter because the buffalo were gone; he had not learned to be a farmer. There was not much to do but sit in the sun and perhaps let a handful of dust trickle through his fingers and think how little it was to have left compared to the endless miles without a fence or a farm in the old days when the buffalo ran like a brown sea. It was too bad he did not appreciate that he would soon become a legend.

This, however, was the last scene in the long drama. There had been a time, in the years immediately following the Louisiana Purchase, when even the names of the Plains tribes were hardly known, while the possibility of fighting them seemed fantastic because no one, other than traders and trappers, had any reason to come in contact with them. Settlers had gone about as far as they could go. After two centuries, pioneers had at last come to the end of the great eastern forests, and the endless grasslands beyond stopped them as sharply as though they had come to the shore of an actual ocean. Pioneering technology, developed over more than two hundred years, depended on plenty of trees—for cabins and barns, for fences, for fuel, for a hundred other things. The sod shanty and breaking plow still lay in the future.

By 1825, it was pretty well established that the greater part of the

Louisiana Purchase was not of much account. Settlers had taken up homes wherever there were forests to be cut down (and there was enough such wooded land to produce three states—Louisiana, Missouri, and Arkansas) but the rest was largely grass and without much promise. Explorers had been even more pessimistic than the pioneers who took it as an article of faith that grassland was worthless. Lewis and Clark had seen a good bit of the plains and pronounced them "desert and barren." Zebulon Pike went across them in 1806 and made two predictions that later proved to be wildly wrong: that Pikes Peak, which he discovered, would probably never be climbed, and that most of the plains were too desert-like to be able to support a white population. He did think they had one benefit; they put a limit on the people of the United States who were "so prone to rambling and extending themselves on the frontiers . . ."

It was an 1820 pathfinder, Major Stephen Long, who summed up all the misconceptions in a phrase. He had gone up the Platte River and come back through Oklahoma on the Canadian River. He agreed with Pike that one of the few good things about the plains was that they would serve as a barrier to keep the American people from wandering too far and stretching the nation too thin. Otherwise most of it was worthless: ". . . we do not hesitate in giving the opinion that it is almost entirely unfit for cultivation, and of course uninhabitable by a people depending on agriculture for their subsistence." In fact, it was so worthless that Major Long labeled the entire Great Plains "The Great American Desert" and the name stuck. By 1825, every educated person knew that the country west of the 95th meridian was a barren wasteland, forever useless. The fable did not die easily; on the contrary it grew in later years as more and more people saw the plains for themselves and was as strong as ever between 1850 and 1860.

The plains were a long way from being a desert. The explorers were perfectly right; in the perspective of their times the plains were not suitable for cultivation, for the methods of cultivating them would not be developed for many decades. But it seems odd that any man with half an eye could have looked on the rich life of the grasslands and declared, in all seriousness, that they were a desert.

A few brief paragraphs of description of the plains are in order; this was the arena where most of the wars would be fought. Along the eastern part of this great open land of sky and grass, where rainfall was plentiful, were the true prairies, with grass taller than a man's head and a profusion of flowers in the spring, a fertile region where the Indian tribes were corn-raising farmers who gave the lie to whites who said the land was useless for agriculture. But farther west, between the 98th and 100th meridians (a line about through the middle of the Dakotas and Kansas although it wanders somewhat) the climate becomes more arid, and the tall, lush prairie grass is replaced by short types, mainly buffalo and grama grass, only a few inches tall but very thick and supported by a sod many feet deep.

The dry, short-grass portion of the grasslands was the Great Plains proper, a land of space and sky, in places dead flat, in others gently rolling, broken occasionally in its western portions by bluffs, out-croppings and canyons, by a range of hills or a nightmare region of badlands. It was, and still is, a land of extremes of climate: burning summer heat and bitter winter cold, prolonged drought and violent thunderstorms with cloudburst rains, deadly blizzards and explosive tornadoes—and some of the most magnificent days imaginable, with an infinity of blue sky filled with smoky puffs of clouds and the grass bending and rising before a western wind exactly like slow waves on a sunny sea.

It was a land full of wild life. Bands of pronghorn antelope were an abundant commonplace; herds of elk more than fifteen hundred strong were reported. Flocks of prairie chickens were so common they were mentioned only in passing by white men early on the scene; wild tur-keys broke the branches in their evening roostings on river bottom cot-tonwoods, and the high-bounding, long-legged, long-eared jackrabbits were everywhere. Even the lowly prairie dog excited the wonder of early white men by its sheer numbers; colonies of the burrowing crea-tures covered hundreds of square miles and contained tens of millions of animals. Wolves, coyotes, the grizzly bear on the western high plains, and numerous lesser creatures were predators on this rich and varied fauna. And, surprisingly, there were great horse herds, descendants of animals escaped from the Spanish colonies in the Southwest.

But all other animals seem insignificant in numbers compared to the buffalo. They moved in herds of tens and hundreds of thousands. They covered the plains farther than a man could see. Plainsmen, finding buffalo in their way, rode all day long through grazing bison and were still in the herd when the sun went down. One man told of traveling more than a hundred miles through one herd; another estimated the size of a herd at thirty by seventy miles. Many estimates have been

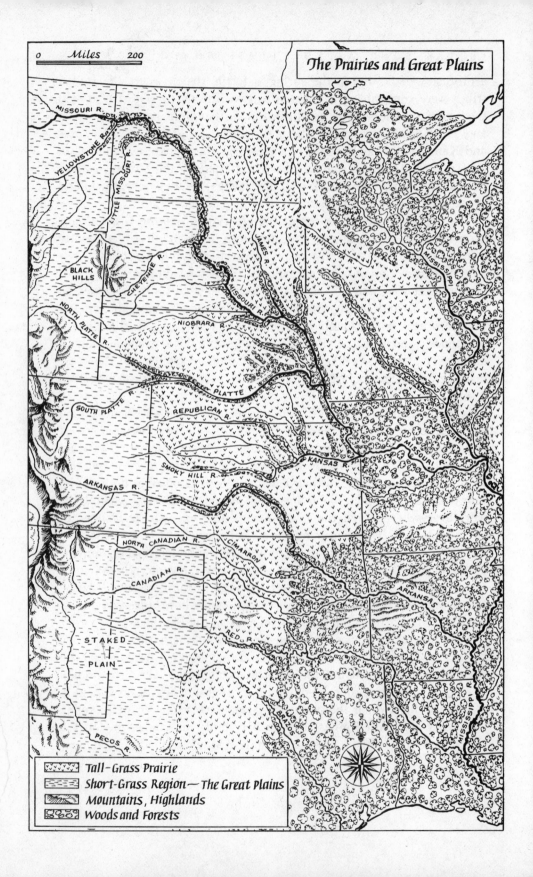

The Prairies and Great Plains

0 Miles 200

MISSOURI R.
YELLOWSTONE R.
LITTLE MISSOURI R.
BLACK HILLS
CHEYENNE R.
NORTH PLATTE R.
NIOBRARA R.
MISSOURI R.
JAMES R.
MINNESOTA R.
MISSISSIPPI
SOUTH PLATTE R.
PLATTE R.
REPUBLICAN R.
SMOKY HILL R.
KANSAS R.
MISSOURI R.
ARKANSAS R.
NORTH CANADIAN R.
CIMARRON R.
CANADIAN R.
ARKANSAS R.
STAKED PLAIN
RED R.
BRAZOS R.
RED R.
MISSISSIPPI R.
PECOS R.

Tall-Grass Prairie
Short-Grass Region—The Great Plains
Mountains, Highlands
Woods and Forests

made of the total number of buffalo on the plains; they are so far apart as to prove only that no one really knew. But there is basis for conservatively estimating that fifteen million buffalo, at the least, were cropping the short grass of the Great Plains in the early part of the 1800's, before the great slaughter began.

And finally, there were the Plains Indians, virile peoples who had learned to come to terms with the land and had built an existence based on the horse and the buffalo. The plains had not been hard and pitiless to them. The rigors of daily life were enough to eliminate the weak and the misfits but living was pleasant enough, and there was plenty of leisure so that they were able to create, in a very few generations, the unique Plains culture which became so characteristic of all the tribes. For the Plains culture was very recent. The Indians did not obtain the horse until the Pueblo Revolt of 1680 forced the Spanish to flee and abandon their jealously guarded animals. After that, it took several generations for horses to be traded from tribe to tribe; not until almost 1800 were the northernmost tribes of the Great Plains mounted. In such a short time was the most dynamic and picturesque of modern Indian cultures created.

Nevertheless, in spite of game, grass, and Indians, it was still The Great American Desert as far as the United States was concerned. And what does a nation do with millions of acres of useless land? John C. Calhoun, Secretary of War under James Monroe, had the answer: use it as a huge Indian reservation. Make the Indians already there move over a little, transport the remaining tribes east of the Mississippi out to the plains where they would learn to hunt buffalo—and the Indian problem would be taken care of for all time.

The plan was not as callous as it might appear, because the remaining eastern tribes were in need of rescue. Government policy toward them had temporized and trimmed its sails to the winds of frontier clamor. Tribes were forced to cede land and move farther west, only to be pushed on again when the tide of settlement caught up with them. By 1825, the frontier had reached or crossed the Mississippi and there was no farther place to push the eastern Indians except out onto the open grasslands. To leave them to be surrounded by white settlers would have condemned most of them to pauperization and extinction by disease, hunger, drunkenness, and lack of purpose. Calhoun was probably completely sincere in his aims.

The first step was to get some of the western Indians to move over.

The Kansa and Osage tribes, people of the tall-grass prairies who farmed as well as hunted buffalo, agreed in 1825 to give up all their lands—present Kansas and northern Oklahoma—except for two reserves for themselves. Then government commissioners went patiently to work getting eastern tribes to agree to move into the West.

It was not a simple matter of calling out the troops and forcing Indians to move. There were certain prescribed forms to be gone through. The government had always been completely correct in its relations with Indian tribes, treating them as though they were independent nations. Under this pleasant fiction, treaties were negotiated with them and drawn up in formal language in the same form as treaties with foreign nations, and, like all treaties, had to be ratified by the Senate before becoming effective. Because Indian treaties were so negotiated, there are still defenders of the government's purity of method and purpose who will argue that the United States has never taken land from Indians without their consent. This is, with a handful of exceptions, entirely correct, but it overlooks the conditions under which consent was granted. It was given by tribes which had just been broken in wars. It was given by peoples who had been threatened or cajoled into signing, or misled about what they were agreeing to. It was often consent granted by a minority of the tribe's leaders who had been subverted or liquored up; the commissioners were never squeamish about hailing the voice of a few as the voice of all if that was the best that could be had. So, when the Indians gave up their land by their own consent, they were usually consenting with a knee in their groin.

All this was to be changed now. In the past, each time an Indian tribe had ceded its tribal grounds and accepted other lands in their place, it received the solemn assurance that the new lands were its own, to have and to hold forever—"as long as waters run and the grass shall grow" was one of the phrases the government liked to use in its treaties. Later, when the frontier had caught up with the Indians again, there was another treaty of cession to be negotiated with more promises in more poetic language. But this move, the commissioners assured the very skeptical Indians, would be absolutely the last.

The task of moving the tribes west went slowly until Andrew Jackson became President. Jackson had been a frontiersman when Tennessee was the Far West, and his first fame had come as an Indian-fighting general. His attitude toward Indians was unclouded by sentiment and was founded on the firm frontiersman's conviction that no Indian had the slightest right that any white man was under any moral or legal obligation to respect. So, when Congress passed a bill in 1830 permitting the exchange of Indian lands east of the Mississippi for lands in the West, no crystal ball was needed to predict the results, even though there was nothing mandatory about the measure. It was, in fact, designed mainly for use against southern tribes which showed no interest in removal.

Most tribes signed removal treaties without causing difficulties. Almost all had been moved before, some of them several times, and they no longer had either the will or the ability to resist. There were a few exceptions. The Indians of New York refused to exchange their trees and lakes for grass and sky, and because no one was seriously clamoring after their small lands, they made good their refusal. The darkest tragedy of the removal was the treatment of the so-called Five Civilized Tribes in the South: the Cherokees, Creeks, Choctaws, Chickasaws, and Seminoles. The Cherokees refused to give up their reservation in Georgia which they had made into a progressive Indian state within a state (portions of the reservation extended into three neighboring states, but the heart of the Cherokee nation—and of the conflict—lay in Georgia). When a Supreme Court decision affirmed their right to the reservation, the state of Georgia ignored the ruling and, by a series of unprincipled laws, overthrew Cherokee tribal law and turned the Indian lands over to white squatters and speculators. President Jackson, when appealed to for help, blandly replied that he was helpless to force Georgia to comply with the court decision. The Creeks, Choctaws, and Chickasaws were similarly served by Mississippi and Alabama. The troop-escorted removal of the tribes was called the Trail of Tears by the Indians; several thousand died of exhaustion, hunger, and sickness on the long trip into the West.

The Seminoles alone of the Five Tribes fought removal by resort to arms. They retired to the depths of the Florida swamps, forcing the United States Army to fight a "Seminole War" lasting from 1836 to 1842. American tactics did not add many bright pages to Army annals; the most effective method used to capture Indians was to lure small groups in for a parley under the supposed sacred immunity of a flag of truce and then seize them. Seminoles were taken a few at a time and sent West—at a cost of 1,500 soldiers killed and $20,000,000. When the Army finally called off the war there were still a few hundred in the swamps but four thousand had been sent on the Trail of Tears.

The Five Civilized Tribes were given lands that make up the present state of Oklahoma excepting the Panhandle. There they quickly adjusted to new surroundings, organized their courts and governments again, and became an important factor in the Indian Country.

One flare-up of violence occurred in the north in 1832 when Black Hawk, an elderly chief of the Sauk tribe, led about four hundred warriors and a thousand women across the Mississippi to return to their lands along the Rock River in Illinois. White squatters, with military help, had forced them out the year before. This time the results were disastrous as four thousand soldiers and militia converged on the Indians and jubilantly pursued and killed women and children as well as men. Black Hawk got his band back to the Mississippi; there they were almost annihilated when a steamboat of soldiers appeared as they were trying to cross back to the west side. The soldiers lined the deck and, overcome with the joy of killing Indians, spared few. Black Hawk was taken prisoner. Never one to pass up an opportunity, the government forced the confederated Sauks and Foxes to cede a strip of land fifty miles wide on the Iowa side of the Mississippi as punishment.

By 1840, the boundary of the permanent Indian Country was complete. Starting at the edge of the Republic of Texas, it ran north along the western boundaries of Arkansas and Missouri, then east along the northern edge of Missouri to within fifty miles of the Mississippi, north through the Territory of Iowa on a line fifty miles from the Mississippi (that fifty-mile strip was the price the Sauks and Foxes had had to pay for the Black Hawk War); then to the Mississippi which it followed far up into Minnesota before cutting east across Wisconsin on an irregular line to Lake Michigan. It gave the Indians the supposedly worthless grasslands, as well as some forest land in Minnesota and Wisconsin which apparently was considered too frigid to be valuable to white men. A number of forts guarded this long line of frontier; General Edmund Gaines, commanding in the West, proposed in 1838 that the forts should all be built of stone since they were going to be permanent.

Only about twelve thousand Indians remained in the East of all the vigorous tribes that had once been there. More than ninety thousand had been carried across the Mississippi, to join, in something less than perfect amity, the almost quarter of a million already living there. It was fully believed that at last the Indian would be able to work out his own destiny, hunting buffalo and living to the sweep and rhythm

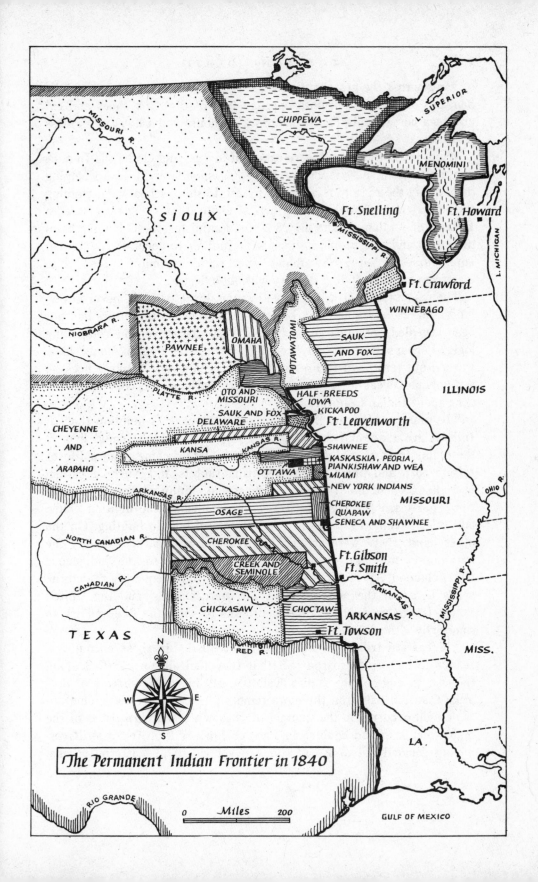

The Permanent Indian Frontier in 1840

of wind across the grass while his savage heart slowly wakened to the benisons of civilization, until one day he would put on shoes and exchange a nomad's life for regular working hours and a house with glass windows.

While the buffalo herds were expected to feed and clothe the Indians and make them self-supporting, the government was to lend a helping hand along the road to civilization by establishing schools and training the natives in farming and other arts of civilization. Congress created a Bureau of Indian Affairs in 1832 to administer these helping-hand programs and to handle relations with Indians in general; the Indian Intercourse Act of 1834, among other things, prohibited any white man from entering Indian country without a license.

The whole thing, at this remove in time, has a dreamy, never-neverland kind of quality about it, but at that time, when the future had not been revealed, it appeared to have a very attractive and compelling logic. Perhaps if they had been left alone, the Indians could have worked out their own future, although it seems very unlikely because a number of weaknesses showed up very early in the concept of the permanent Indian Country.

The planners, for one thing, had made the easy assumption that all Indians are alike, and that because a Crow or Arapaho could live off the plains in easy contentment, an Indian lately come from a life of raising corn and pumpkins and snaring rabbits and catching catfish in Indiana could immediately do the same. Many of the Easterners could not learn the high degree of horsemanship, the hunting skills, and other techniques necessary for successful buffalo hunting. On the other hand, there were enough hunters and apt learners among the immigrants to make inroads on the buffalo—or so the indigenous tribes claimed. At the same time, the Plains tribes frequently raided the cattle herds of the newcomers. There were clashes, and the United States Dragoons rode out onto the plains to show the flag and try to smooth over the difficulties.

The eastern tribes did not always fare badly in these encounters, thanks in large part to the fact that they had all been settled along the eastern edge of the Indian Country and had better access to firearms than did tribes on the more remote plains farther west. One notable fight occurred in the summer of 1854 when southern tribes of the plains met in grand council on Pawnee Fork of the Arkansas River, having decided the time had come to get rid of all eastern Indians.

The entire Kiowa and Comanche tribes were there, the Kiowa Apache, one band of Arapahoes, two of Cheyennes, and the main body of Osages. Old traders who were present estimated that there were 1,200 to 1,500 lodges, which would mean about 2,400 to 3,000 warriors.

From this camp a war party of about fifteen hundred set out to sweep the plains clear of the eastern interlopers. In eastern Kansas they got their chance when they came on a party of Sauks and Foxes with a few Potawatomies, about one hundred men in all. The Easterners took shelter in a ravine and, with their rifles, put up a fire that kept the Plains Indians from coming even close. With a few exceptions, the Plains warriors were armed with bows and arrows, deadly weapons and equal or superior to the rifles of their day at short range but useless at a distance. In the end the chastened extermination force retired, even leaving their dead on the field, an admission of complete defeat because Plains Indians went to great risks to recover slain warriors to prevent the mutilation by the enemy which would prevent the dead heroes' entry into the spirit world as whole, vigorous fighting men.

However, antagonisms between tribes were not the greatest problems in the Indian Country. Tribes always had been fighting, and with Indian agents on hand and Army forces on the border, there was every probability that most conflicts could be nipped before they really got going. The serious threats to the security of the plains were those created by white men.

The worst assault of the white man on the integrity of the Indian was made with alcohol. The Indian Intercourse Act strictly forbade the sale of alcohol to tribesmen, but it took a strong-principled trader to resist the lure of the tremendous profits which a brisk trade in firewater brought in. It was easy to get the stuff into Indian Country because the few soldiers stretched along hundreds of miles of frontier could not possibly enforce the ban. Traders had a more or less standard formula for the near-poison they mixed up when time to do business arrived. A keg of cheap whiskey was diluted with water, a great deal of water. Pepper, and sometimes tobacco juice and other condiments, were added to give it a real bite. Despite its rather low proof, the Indians were highly susceptible to the violent mixture, probably as much because of the other horrors in it as the amount of alcohol. Profits were sky-high; the going rate for a fine buffalo robe was usually about two drinks of half a pint each. After a native had had several drinks, some traders shoved their profit margin even higher by switching to whiskey with more water in it, pretty certain the Indian no longer would notice the difference.

The results were completely predictable. During the debauch that followed, drunken rows flared into stabbings, women wailed, adulteries were committed without discretion, and initial euphoria sagged into soddenness so deep the victims lay in their own vomit. Indians who had developed a craving for alcohol awoke from such bouts with a horrible headache and nothing else, having traded away all their robes and obtained no necessities in exchange. Many traders opposed the use of alcohol as a short-sighted policy that would debauch the Indians and ruin future trade for quick present profits. But as long as some did it, all had to meet the competition.

More than alcohol, the white man's diseases so weakened the Indians that they had already partly lost the war long before any hostile shots were exchanged with the United States Army. As early as 1801, a Pawnee war party returning from New Mexico brought smallpox with them. It spread from their tribal grounds on the lower Platte all the way to Texas; some of the Plains tribes were said to have lost half their people, although there was no one to keep accurate statistics. An 1816 smallpox outbreak hit the Comanches and Kiowas on the southern plains especially hard.

The worst of the smallpox epidemics began in 1837 on the upper Missouri, the infection brought there by steamboat passengers. The Mandans, a farming people and one of the most advanced tribes of the plains, were almost wiped out; of their fifteen hundred people only thirty-one remained. Their neighbors and allies, the Arikara and Hidatsa, were cut from four thousand to about half that many. The disease spread north and west to the Crows, Assiniboines and Blackfeet; six to eight thousand of the Blackfeet were believed to have perished.

Attempts had been made to stop the spread of the epidemic by sending runners ahead with warnings, telling each camp to isolate itself, but the disease continued to spread among the wandering tribes. No one, not even the government, knew much about the tribes on the Great Plains in 1837; no one cared much. Everywhere people tried to flee the disease, abandoning tepees and the dead in them. For several years the lodges stood gaunt against the sky until the buffalo-hide covering rotted away to shreds flapping in the wind and the skeleton of poles at last settled back to earth.

The smallpox did not run its course in one summer. The Sioux escaped the worst of it, but some camps became infected, and probably four hundred Sioux died. In the spring of 1838 a war party of Pawnees took several Sioux prisoners; the captives carried the disease and an estimated two thousand Pawnees died as the sickness spread through their villages. They carried it south during the year to the Osage, who, after suffering terrible losses, in turn passed it on when some Osage visited the Kiowa and Comanche in the winter of 1839–40. The latter two tribes, when they found the smallpox was with them again, fled onto the northern Texas plains in an attempt to escape. At last the epidemic wore itself out, after taking no one knows how many lives.

Other epidemics, other diseases struck the plains. Venereal disease, that bright forerunner of culture and civilization, became common. Ailments such as measles, minor childhood upsets to the whites, were deadly to natives who had built up no immunity to them. There were many Indians killed by white men who never heard the sound of a gun.

Thus, any picture of the Indian Country as a region primeval and unreached by white men was largely illusion. The land remained untouched by a plow and unfenced, the wind blew across endless miles of grass, and the buffalo grazed in the majesty of their millions. But things had changed; nothing would ever be as it was. An additional hundred thousand Indians had been shoved, willy-nilly, onto the grasslands, to tax what had been a balanced economy. Disease had decimated some of the finest peoples of the West at a time when they would need their strength most. And liquor-bartering traders were sapping the moral fiber of large numbers of Indians.

In 1842 came the event that hurried the end of the permanent Indian Country. One hundred settlers in eighteen covered wagons took off across the plains, marking out a road that would evermore be famous as the Oregon Trail. It was not much of a showing—the grass had probably sprung back and obliterated the wheel tracks before two weeks had passed—but it was the proverbial cloud no bigger than a man's hand. The next year a thousand came, driving five thousand head of cattle with them, and from then on the trail was never empty during the traveling season.

The United States still ended at the Texas border and the crest of the Rockies, but the country laid claim, as did Great Britain, to the enormous Oregon country which extended from the Rockies to the Pacific and from the northern edge of California far up into Canada.

In 1818, the two countries had made a very sensible agreement to occupy the region jointly until they could come to an understanding on how to divide it. Nothing had been settled when word began to be passed around in the United States that the newest Promised Land was out in the Willamette Valley in the Oregon country in the very Far West—and the rush of land-hungry Americans was on again.

The Oregon Trail began at Independence, Missouri, a river port on the Missouri where the wagon trains made up and waited before they started in the spring for the grass to get green enough to feed the animals. It ran about three hundred miles northwest to the Platte River, then along the south side of that stream and of its fork, the North Platte, and finally followed the tributary Sweetwater River to South Pass where it crossed over the Continental Divide. More than half the trip, and by far the hardest part, still lay ahead, but at South Pass the trail had left the permanent Indian Country. In reaching that point, it had angled across present Kansas, Nebraska, and Wyoming, the heart of the Great Plains. It was a route almost certain to cause future troubles.

The emigration to Oregon continued and swelled, and in 1847 was joined by another migration. The Mormons, after running head-on into the harsh realities of intolerance during years of attempting to found religious communities in Missouri and Illinois, headed west for the Great Salt Lake country to have another try away from meddling neighbors. Their route started at Council Bluffs, Iowa, and followed the north side of the Platte and North Platte as far as the American Fur Company post, Fort Laramie, in eastern Wyoming; there it crossed over and joined the Oregon Trail. This was the Mormon Trail; it paralleled the Oregon Trail on the opposite site of the Platte River across most of the plains.

During these same years, political events completely changed most of the conditions on which the concept of the Indian Country had been built. Texas was annexed in 1845, the entire Oregon country south of the 49th parallel became uncontested American territory in 1846, and in 1848 the peace treaty ending the Mexican War extended the southwestern part of the country to the Pacific. The Indian Country was no longer a region out at the end of nowhere, a useful buffer between the United States and foreign nations; now it had become a barrier dividing the country. Modifications would have to be made in the pledges made to the Indian tribes. It remained to be seen whether the

United States would make those changes in good faith and with fairness to the Indians.

Gold was discovered in California in 1848; the next spring the parade of the forty-niners joined the covered wagons of the emigrants on both the Oregon and Mormon Trails. All that had gone before was nothing compared to the unending lines of wagons that moved across the plains from horizon to horizon during the traveling months of late spring and early summer. Wagon followed wagon so closely, often with the noses of horses or oxen almost against the tailgate ahead, that for miles all but the lucky earliest starters of the morning spent the day in clouds of choking dust.

The tremendous stream of westering humanity, plodding along day after day across the rutted sod, fouled the land and drove away the buffalo and other game. The way was littered with discarded tools, clothing, furniture, broken-down wagons, food of all kinds, thrown out as equipment broke down and baggage was discarded to compensate for the reduced pulling power of weakening animals. Animals gave out and died; the fresh smell of spring grass was blotted out by the corruption of rotting flesh. Hunters from the wagon trains ranged far out onto the plains after buffalo and antelope. The buffalo became nervous at the constant smell and activity of humans and began to stay well to the north and south of the Platte during the travel season; eventually they were divided completely into a northern and a southern herd.

Cholera swept along the overland trails in 1849, brought by the forty-niners and Oregon-bound emigrants, and at once spread to the Indians. To the Kiowa it was the most terrible experience of their existence, much worse than the smallpox nine years earlier. Close to half the Pawnee died; the survivors refused to bury the dead and bodies partly eaten by wolves lay within a short distance of the Pawnee Agency. The western Sioux were convinced that the disease had been deliberately introduced among them by white men in order to exterminate the Indians—to such a state had Indian trust in white motives fallen.

None of the throng of emigrants wanted anything to do with the plains. There was still the Great American Desert, an expanse to be crossed and left behind as quickly as possible. But in their crossing, they played hob with the land and the people along the way. The Pawnees, whose range centered on the Platte valley and included much of present Nebraska and a good piece of Kansas, had already been reduced to a shadow of their former powerful estate, without a shot being fired. They lived with hunger because the buffalo shunned the Platte River valley and the vicinity of the overland trails; they did not dare go out onto the plains after the herds because there was always the chance of a clash with their enemy, the Sioux, and they were too reduced in numbers to hold their own. As a result, they were reduced to begging, petty thievery, and once in a while, when conditions were right, an attack on an unprotected emigrant wagon.

The Sioux and Cheyenne farther west were not so drastically affected but they were grumbling. The emigrants took the best campsites; their hunters killed or drove away the game; there were arrogant men among them who treated the Indians in a manner calculated to cause trouble. There were even occasional young fools who tried to demonstrate what great Indian-killers they were by taking pot-shots at passing braves— fortunately without notable results in most instances. The two tribes did not resort to violence, but they did begin to demand payment for the use of the trails.

It was important to maintain a right of unobstructed passage over the Oregon Trail, to obtain treaty rights guaranteeing the free use of the road. At the same time, the government decided to make a bigger sweep than a simple right-of-passage agreement: nothing less than a fixing of limits to the territories of all the Plains Indians. Such a move, it was explained, would help reduce intertribal conflicts.

The first council—which had nothing to do with the Oregon Trail— was held on the Minnesota River, in July, 1851, at Traverse des Sioux, where the eastern Sioux Indians signed away all their lands in Iowa and Minnesota except for a twenty-mile-wide reservation along the upper Minnesota River. For this empire they were to receive $68,000 annually for fifty years. Of this amount they were immediately bilked of a fair portion by being hoodwinked into signing over their first annual payments to traders for debts they supposedly owed, totaling $210,000. The thing was a fraud; there would be other frauds and swindles so that in the end the Sioux got almost nothing while Minnesota suffered the most tragic interlude in her history.

However, the main treaty-making was on the northern plains, where the Oregon Trail passed through. There the heaviest burden of making ready for the council was borne by Thomas Fitzpatrick, known as Broken Hand to the Indians. He had been one of the greatest of the mountain men until he gave up fur trading when men began wearing high hats made of silk instead of beaver and took the rich cream from the fur business. For a period he had guided wagon trains through the mountains he had explored—he was the discoverer of South Pass, through which the Oregon Trail passed—until the government had appointed him Indian agent for the upper Platte and Arkansas in 1846. He was a good agent in a service that was becoming notorious for its bad apples, because he knew his people and had a conscience about them. Now, in 1851, he had runners all over the plains calling a council of all the tribes of the northern plains at Fort Laramie.

The result was the greatest meeting of Indians in the history of the plains; the estimates run variously between eight thousand and twelve thousand persons present. The council had been set for September 1 but the Cheyennes, Arapaho, and the Brule and Oglala bands of the Sioux were there even before July was over. Fort Laramie was now an Army post, having been purchased from the American Fur Company two years before to protect the Oregon Trail. A couple of hundred dragoons were on hand and more arrived during the council but they were there more as a symbol of the might of far-away Washington than for any practical purpose, because they could have been overwhelmed in minutes by the thousands of Indians.

The council almost did turn into war with the arrival of a Shoshone contingent, mountain tribesmen whose annual buffalo hunts out onto the plains had made them bitter enemies of the Plains tribes. As the Shoshones galloped up, magnificent horsemen led by their great chief Washakie, a Sioux whose father had been killed by a Shoshone war party, spurred his horse forward and, whooping, charged alone against the line of mounted Shoshone braves, seeking the bright answer to some private vision of glory. Washakie and his men raised their weapons, the Sioux warriors stirred to support their wild-eyed friend, but the clash that could have turned the council into a murderous melee was prevented when an interpreter raced out on his horse and threw the avenging young Sioux to the ground.

The tribal delegations continued to come in, Crows, Assiniboines, Atsinas, Arikaras, most of them with women, children, dogs, and horse herds; with a few exceptions the tribes were nomads who took everything they owned with them whenever they moved. The combined horse herds totaled many thousands and soon had the grass cropped down for acres. The camps, a forest of tepees rising thickly from acres of meadows around the fort, soon began to put forth a mighty stench until at last the harassed officers ordered that the encampment should be moved to Horse Creek, thirty-seven miles to the east.

The council was being delayed pending the arrival of wagon loads of food and gifts which were always distributed at such affairs; at last the Superintendent of Indian Affairs, David Mitchell, ordered the council to get down to business and let the gifts come when they would (it turned out that the Army, in its age-old way, had mislaid them at one of the Missouri River steamboat landings). The parley was held in a large tent, one of the most colorful such meetings ever held, with great men from great tribes sitting, rank on rank, in the full glory of their ceremonial regalia. The council lasted twenty days, being purposely drawn out to permit the Army to locate and bring the gifts.

The council had been held mainly to get the Indians' promise not to molest travelers on the Oregon Trail; this promise they gave, recognizing the right of the United States to establish the road and to build forts to protect it. Also, the commissioners got the tribes to agree to observe a general peace among themselves and to accept definite boundaries to their lands. The matter of boundaries was a difficult one. Even settled agricultural tribes have seldom agreed on the lines separating them unless it was a natural barrier such as a large river; among free-roaming Plains tribes in an open land with few natural bounds and limits, the boundaries of a tribe's land shifted with the strength of the war parties that rode along them. Nevertheless, with perseverance, the Indian leaders assembled in the tent were able to agree on definite borders for their hunting grounds.

In return for these concessions, the Indians were to be paid $50,000 a year for fifty years, the annuity to be in the form of food, various goods, and—what the wandering tribes must have agreed without enthusiasm to accept—domestic animals and agricultural implements. When the treaty came up for ratification, the Senate decided the commissioners had been too generous and reduced the term to ten years, with the possibility of extension for another five.

Thomas Fitzpatrick arranged a similar council with the Comanches and Kiowas at Fort Atkinson on the Arkansas River in present Kansas state. The two tribes, far-raiding, warlike, and closely allied, were the principal nomadic tribes of the southern plains; their main hunting range was from the Arkansas River south into the Texas Panhandle. They agreed to the right of the United States to lay out roads and to set up posts and forts to protect them—this had reference mainly to the Santa Fe Trail. They also promised not to make raids into Mexico in the future. In return, they were to receive annuities in goods worth $18,000 a year for ten years, with a five-year extension if the President in Washington decided they had merited it.

An attempt was made to get the Indians to give up their captives, but this proved impossible. Few or none of the captives wanted to leave. The tribes not only replenished their horse herds by raids into Mexico; they had kept up their own numbers in the same way. Young captive boys and girls had been accepted as full members of the tribe; the girls had grown up to be wives and mothers of Comanches and Kiowas, while some of the boys had developed into leading warriors of the tribe. Few of them, men or women, wanted to go back to being Mexicans.

The two tribes complied with the treaty quite faithfully except for the clause about raiding into Mexico. Along with this, they had a hard time accepting that New Mexico had become part of the United States, a difficulty in comprehension which caused frequent annoyance to American authorities. There was also a curious situation in regard to relations between the Comanches and Texas, although it had nothing to do with the Fort Atkinson Treaty. The Comanches, although their name has become synonymous with bloodthirstiness, actually remained at peace with the United States most of the time, but they hated Texans with a bitter hate. The Republic of Texas had followed a policy toward its Indians that made the United States appear benevolent by comparison, and the Comanches had suffered heavily. They had a special grudge as well; during a council between Texans and Comanches, a disagreement had occurred, upon which the Texans had turned on the outnumbered Indian chiefs in the room and killed them to a man. Long after the annexation, Comanches made a distinction between Americans and Texans.

The permanent Indian Country was dying fast; already the frontier that was to have divided it forever from the white man's world had bulged and given way along a great section under pressure from land-hungry settlers. The myths about the worthlessness of grasslands were evaporating; pioneers had learned that tall-grass prairie land, at least, was tremendously fertile. The Indians had been pushed off almost all the prairie land of Minnesota and Iowa—part of the original permanent Indian Country—by the weary old method of land cession treaties, and bigger things were ahead.

The government's solemn promise to most of the eastern tribes that they would not have to move again had to be broken in 1854. After long wrangling, free and pro-slavery forces had agreed to the creation of two territories on the Great Plains, but along what would be their eastern boundaries lay a solid tier of Indian reservations, most of them the homes of eastern tribes who had moved there a couple of decades before with full assurances that there would not have to be any more moves. George W. Manypenny, Commissioner of Indian Affairs and a man with a conscience, visited these tribes in 1853 to go through the dreary business of telling them that they would have to move once again. The treaties, with a few small exceptions, were signed in 1854; the tribes gave up thirteen million acres of land. Most went on small reservations elsewhere; a few remained on reserves that were a small portion of their former lands.

That same year Kansas and Nebraska Territories were organized and the permanent Indian Country came to an end. Much larger than the present states of Kansas and Nebraska, the two territories together included almost all that had remained of the Indian Country, from the southern boundary of Kansas to Canada, and from the Missouri to the Rockies. Only the land belonging to the Five Civilized Tribes in Oklahoma still remained without any organized state or territorial government. It was considered quite certain that this land, which was soon labeled the Indian Territory, was too worthless ever to be wanted by white men, and that the Indians living there could possess it indefinitely without being molested.

Thomas Fitzpatrick served as Indian agent for the upper Platte and Arkansas River country until 1854 when he died while on a trip to Washington. Only the year before he had made a final trip through his huge territory, and found that the effects of the traffic endlessly crawling westward on the Oregon Trail had been disastrous to the Indians of the area. "They are in abject want of food half the year," he wrote in his final report. "The travel upon the road drives the buffalo off or else confines them to a narrow path during the period of migration, and the different tribes are forced to contend with hostile nations in seeking support for their villages. Their women are pinched with want and their children are constantly crying with hunger. . . . Already, under pressure of such hardships they are beginning to gather around a few licensed hunters . . . acting as herdsmen, runners, and interpreters, living on their bounty; while others accept most immoral methods with their families to eke out an existence."

The year of Fitzpatrick's death, the peace between the United States and the Plains Indians was seriously broken for the first time. The event occurred four years after the great peace council of Fort Laramie and only ten miles from the spot where it had been held; the cause, as is usually the case, was trivial and in this instance was the lame cow of a Mormon emigrant. Whether the cow had strayed or been abandoned is a subject on which opinions differ. At the time, there were several thousand Arapaho, Cheyenne and Sioux camped above Fort Laramie awaiting the distribution of their annuity; a hungry young Brule Sioux came on the lame cow in the brush of the river bottom, killed her, and, with his friends, made what feasting was possible on her meager flesh.

Somehow, word of the fate of his cow got back to the owner whose wagon train was camped near the fort resting its animals and making ready for the long trip still ahead. He stormed into the fort demanding that the Army make the Indian or Indians responsible pay for the cow The Brule Sioux youth who had butchered the animal, learning that trouble was afoot, took refuge in the camp of Chief Conquering Bear whom the government had named supreme chief of the Teton Sioux.* Although the Sioux did not have such a position in their own social and political organization, the government, in its dealings with Indians, always felt a compulsion to have a top man to talk to.

Conquering Bear hurried in to Fort Laramie to take care of matters; he offered to pay $10 for the cow. The owner demanded $25. The animal was certainly not worth $25, or even $10 to its owner; there were still hundreds of miles to go over mountain, desert, and alkali flats to the Mormon country, hard enough for a whole animal to travel, and impossible for a lame one. It was said that the owner had abandoned his cow and then had showed up again when there seemed a possibility of realizing something from it. Conquering Bear stated the obvious: $25 was not only too much but beyond the resources of those who had eaten the stringy flesh of the trail-worn cow. He returned to his camp.

The United States Army has, without favoritism, included in its officer corps men ranging from geniuses down to incompetent fools lacking the slightest rudiments of judgment. Young Lieutenant Grattan

* There were three main divisions of the Sioux. The Teton Sioux were dwellers on the plains and the true nomads of the tribe; they were by far the most numerous and were further divided into the Brule, Hunkpapa, Two Kettles, Blackfeet Sioux (not to be confused with the Blackfeet proper), Sans Arcs, Miniconjou and Oglala bands. On the prairies of eastern South Dakota was the Yankton division, divided into the Yankton and Yanktonai bands, and easternmost of all were the Santee Sioux in Minnesota, whose component bands were the Sisseton, Wahpeton, Mdewakanton and Wahpekute—who will be heard from, very vehemently, later.

who was sent out from the fort to obtain satisfaction for the dead and
digested cow was one of the latter. He took a detail of thirty men and
a drunken interpreter, added two cannons for extra authority, according to most reports fortified himself with whiskey against the rigors of
his assignment, and marched his men off after making stirring statements about conquering or dying.

The Sioux camp contained many lodges of Brules and Oglalas and
a few Miniconjous, a gathering formidable in strength but peaceful
in spirit. Grattan, with no attempt at diplomacy, deployed his men,
wheeled his cannon into position, and arrogantly demanded payment
for the cow or surrender of the Sioux who had killed her. Conquering
Bear remonstrated, an argument followed, and Grattan opened fire
with his cannon, killing several Indians and mortally wounding Conquering Bear. The soldiers were set upon instantly by the shocked and
infuriated Sioux; one alone escaped alive but so badly wounded that
he lived only long enough to carry the story back to Fort Laramie.
Knowing that retribution would be swift, the Sioux at once struck
camp and headed to the northeast, taking the wounded Conquering
Bear along on a horse travois. He died of his wounds and his body was
placed on a scaffold, as most Plains Indians disposed of their dead, by
the Niobrara River.

The killing of Grattan and his command, no matter how much it had
been provoked, demanded vengeance, so the next summer Colonel
William Harney with 1,300 troops marched from Fort Leavenworth to
deal out summary justice. He happened on the band of Little Thunder
camped at Ash Hollow on Blue Creek just off the North Platte. Little
Thunder's band had had nothing to do with the attack on Grattan and
his detail. They had not had anything to do with the killing of the
Mormon's cow. But the United States Army subscribed to the curious
theory of collective responsibility: if any band of Indians committed a
crime or a depredation, any Indian who came within reach could be
punished. Colonel Harney opened fire on the Sioux camp with artillery.
The Indians fought back as best they could, and bravely, after recovering somewhat from the surprise, but were almost wiped out, losing 86
killed and several wounded. Many of the killed and wounded were
women and children.

Harney gathered up a sad procession of captives, including the
wounded, and drove them all the way to Fort Laramie. He was so
elated by his victory that he had his gunners try to shoot the top off

Chimney Rock, a landmark to travelers on the Oregon Trail. The Sioux were upset and frightened by Harney's expedition, and a young Brule named Spotted Tail, along with several others, gave himself up to accept punishment for the Grattan fight. They were taken to Fort Leavenworth in chains; when Spotted Tail was released a year later he had been so impressed by the unlimited number and powers of the white man that he was thereafter convinced that it was futile to contend with them. He became one of the most ardent peace advocates among the Indians.

The Army showed an unfortunate tendency to continue Colonel Harney's tough policy. On several occasions, when young braves on the plains met detachments of cavalry on patrol, they approached after making the peace sign as they had been doing for years, only to be shot at by the troopers. After a few such incidents, the word got around, and small Indian hunting parties no longer rode up to troops to make friendly talk and beg tobacco.

The northern Cheyennes, whose roamings took them near the Oregon Trail, were the victims in several of these unprovoked shootings, and, not unreasonably, began to feel that the Army was deliberately trying to incite war. There was a considerable element among them that was all for getting the jump on the whites by attacking first and in force, while the Americans in Kansas were absorbed in the Slavery-Free Soil conflict which had the state torn and prostrate.

There were incidents; Indians attacked wagon trains and trappers, the Army administered punishment by attacking the first group of unsuspecting Indians it came across, whereupon the Indians retaliated in turn by jumping the next poorly defended wagon train they met up with. After one such chain of events in May, 1857, in which punishment always fell on innocent parties, Colonel E. V. Sumner was sent out to knock heads together and teach the northern Cheyenne some manners. Sumner trailed a large band of Indians across western Nebraska and Kansas, finally catching up with them in Kansas on the Republican River. There, but for a strange happenstance, might have begun the wars of the plains.

The American Indian was a person whose fate was determined by signs, omens, and magic. If the signs and the magic were favorable, he went into battle convinced he was invincible. If they went awry, he would often refuse even to face the enemy because he knew in advance that all was lost. This day, three hundred Cheyenne horsemen were absolutely certain of victory as they waited for Sumner to attack. Their medicine man had assured them that washing in a certain lake would make them proof against the bullets of the white soldiers, and they had washed.

But the incredible happened. Colonel Sumner ordered his men to charge with sabers, why, no one knows, for it was probably the only full-fledged saber charge ever made on the plains. To the Indians, it meant only that their bullet-proofing magic had been circumvented and all was lost in advance. They turned and ran with the cavalry in hot pursuit. They fled so fast and so far that they lost only four men (their own figures), while the soldiers lost two killed and several wounded. Sumner burned the Cheyenne village and then continued his march to further intimidate the Indians; there were no further encounters.

So, only by unlikely coincidence was a major battle avoided. The Indians became more resentful, the whites a bit more overbearing. Naked and open war was avoided for a few more years, but real peace was gone. When 1861 came, Regular Army troops were withdrawn to fight more important battles elsewhere. When the columns disappeared beyond the eastern horizon it did not mean a return to old days and old ways for the tribes of the grasslands because state and territorial militias took over, frontiersmen volunteers whose personal credos usually included a firm conviction that there were few higher achievements than killing Indians.

But the plains were vast. The conical tepees clustered tranquilly beside a hundred creeks and river campsites with the smoke from the cooking fires rising above them. The buffalo herds continued to come in numbers that shook the earth and covered its face for miles, and the white man still looked on the plains as an expanse to cross as quickly as possible. With all the changes that were being wrought, there were still things that remained comfortingly familiar, especially for peoples living well off the white man's trails.

These pleasant continuations of an older day had only a short course to run now, a couple of years for some tribes, perhaps a dozen or more for others. For each one the moment would come when the old way was irrevocably lost—and for some, that moment was already at hand.

II

Massacre in Minnesota

1. "LET THEM EAT GRASS"

IN 1862, the Sioux in Minnesota had two things to show for a little more than a half century of treaty-making with the United States: a reservation 10 miles wide and 150 miles long on the Minnesota River, and a deep and smoldering resentment over years of having been swindled.

This is not to say that the Indians were plotting an uprising of any sort. But deep frictions and hard feelings were there, and the amazing thing about Minnesota in the harvest season of 1862 is that so few people seemed to consider trouble even within the realm of possibility. It may be that there were settlers here and there who felt that it would be a good precaution to keep a rifle handy, but if such were the case, there was nothing in the events of August 18 to indicate it. When catastrophe came, no people could have been caught more completely by surprise.

There had been incidents; it was not an easy summer for the Indians. Ordinarily, the Sioux went on their annual buffalo hunt out into Dakota Territory early in July, but this year they had put it off from day to day, waiting for the arrival and distribution of their annuity, until August had arrived and they had neither buffalo meat nor the food that was part of the annuity. The annuity was paid in money, goods, and food. Only the money had not arrived; the food and goods were on hand at the two agencies on the reservation—and the sight of the filled warehouses must have been a constant irritation and temptation to the Indians. On August 4, the Sioux at Upper Agency, the westernmost of two, had finally had enough of waiting, and let grumbling turn into action. They moved against a warehouse containing food.

There were a hundred soldiers at the agency, two companies of a Minnesota volunteer regiment. Like the Indians, they had been waiting for the payment of the annuities, their job to maintain order when several thousand Sioux would be assembled in one place. The Indians acted quickly; several hundred of them ringed Lieutenant Timothy J. Sheehan's company and very effectively kept it from doing anything. At the same time, other Indians broke down the door of the warehouse and began carrying out sacks of flour. It was not a warlike move; the Indians were only after food and made no threatening gestures as they kept the soldiers aside.

However, they did not get Lieutenant Thomas Gere's company boxed in so efficiently, and Gere, only nineteen years old but a young man of mature judgment and resolution, quickly ordered a howitzer swung around and trained on the warehouse entrance. Then, as the Indians hesitated and drew back out of the field of fire, a sergeant with a squad of men took control of the door. In the meantime, Lieutenant Sheehan was arguing with the Indian agent, Major Thomas J. Galbraith (all Indian agents bore the honorific "Major"), asking him to issue the food portion of the annuity. Galbraith had the irrefutable argument of all bureaucrats, that it had never been done that way; money, food, and goods had always been issued together. Besides, he said, any concessions would make the Indians difficult to control.

After Sheehan was able to convince him that the Indians were not exactly easy to control at that moment, Galbraith had a token issue of flour and pork made, which cooled tempers for the moment. The next day a council was held with Sioux leaders; the Indians agreed to return to their villages and wait for the money if the goods and food were given them, and the agent ordered it done.

The incident at Upper Agency was a transient one, a matter of hungry people, short tempers, and bad judgment. It was dramatic, but the Sioux had older and greater resentments whose roots had grown deep and fed in a bitter soil of bad faith and broken promises during a couple of generations. Their dealings with the United States had included some very souring experiences.

To begin at the very beginning, the Minnesota Sioux were Santees, one of the three great divisions of the tribe. Once, all Sioux had lived in the lake and forest country of Minnesota until, during years of grim, no-quarter struggles in deep northern forests, they were slowly pushed onto the prairies to the south and west by the Chippewas. The Chippewas were the only people ever to defeat the Sioux decisively; they did it during years when they had the one-sided advantage of firearms.

Once out on the prairie, the Sioux obtained horses, prospered, multiplied, became the dominant tribe of the northern plains. The Teton Sioux, largest division of the tribe, moved west onto the high plains and became horse-and-buffalo nomads. The Yankton Sioux stayed farther east, with a range centering near the Missouri River in present South Dakota. Easternmost of all, the Santee Sioux remained closest to the land from which their ancestors had been expelled by the Chippewa.

The range of the Santee extended over an area that included not only the Minnesota prairies but large adjoining parts of Iowa, Wisconsin, and the Dakotas. It was not unbroken grassland, but contained numerous clumps and areas of woodland, and was rippled by many lakes and marshes. It was a rich land and a beautiful one. Settlers thought so, too, and began moving in; the government followed the frontier, as it always did, by forcing the Indians to cede the land.

In all land cession dealings, the white men were able to avoid any temptation to be honest and honorable, and carefully arranged that the Sioux came out the small end of the funnel each time with nothing left but resentment. At a treaty signed in Washington in 1837, the Sioux gave up all their lands east of the Mississippi, but the money they got in return was turned over to traders for debts supposedly owed by the Sioux. At the great council at Traverse des Sioux on the Minnesota River in 1851, the Indians signed away all the rest of their lands, more than 30,000,000 acres in Iowa, Dakota Territory, and Minnesota for $1,665,000—about a nickel an acre—keeping only a reservation extending 10 miles on each side of the general course of the Minnesota River, and from its source 150 miles downstream. There was to be a cash annuity for fifty years but those good friends of the Indians, the traders, always alert for the soft clink of coin against coin, had arranged for the signing of separate "Traders' Papers" immediately after the treaty by which the Sioux agreed to turn over their cash annuities for several years until more huge debts which had somehow piled up were paid off. Long before that happened there were more claims; the Sioux received nothing for all their lands.

Even the reservation they kept was halved in 1858 when the Senate decreed that they should keep only the part south of the Minnesota River, a shoestring strip 10 miles wide and 150 miles long. They were granted compensation for the north half, but at once a swarm of white claimants demanding pay for shadowy services descended on the money like blowflies on a dead buffalo. The nature of the services was never quite specified, but it ran into large amounts for some individuals. There were also traders with debts to be paid off—there were always traders to be paid off. Once again the Sioux got little or nothing, except another reason to feel bitter.

By 1862, the traders had been able to establish a foolproof credit system. They sold goods to the Sioux on credit, chargeable against the Indians' cash annuity. At annuity time, when the pay tables were set up, the traders were on hand. As each Indian stepped forward, the traders called out their claims and were paid. The Indian received what was left, if any. No accounting was demanded; it seems to have occurred to no Indian agent that it was part of his duty to his wards to ask for one. But, to repeat, a lot of fancy work was being done with Indians' money.

Leaders among the Sioux had a strong suspicion that there was a lot of water in the traders' accounts, and they wanted the traders barred from the pay tables. At the same time, they wanted to eat their cake, too; they depended on credit, and especially so that summer, with the buffalo hunt delayed and the annuity not yet paid. The Indians at Upper Agency had obtained temporary relief by forcing the distribution of the food and goods, but nothing of the kind had happened at Lower or Redwood Agency to the east. There the Indians continued to buy on credit until the traders became worried that they might have difficulty collecting, especially if the Sioux were successful in getting them barred from the pay tables. Some of them went to Fort Ridgely across the river to ask whether they could depend on the Army's help if there were trouble. The commanding officer, Captain John Marsh, gave them cold comfort with the tart observation that the Army was not in the collection business.

On this, the traders immediately cut off all further credit. When protests were made that many of the Sioux would suffer actual hunger as a result, one of the traders, Andrew Myrick, retorted, "Let them eat grass."

The date was August 15, 1862. Myrick's words were repeated among the Sioux—with sullen satisfaction by the most ardently anti-white factions. However, it was going to have little effect on events. The shape of the future at that moment was in the hands of a small hunting party of Sioux who were a long distance north of the Minnesota River and the reservation, in an area known as the Big Woods. Unfortunately, the hunting was bad, and two days later the party were patting in their moccasins through the dust of a prairie road in Acton Township in Meeker County on the way home. Such hunting parties passed by often because the Indians were under no constraint to remain on their reservation, and if any settler saw it passing, he probably paid it little attention.

But this group was in a bad humor. It was returning empty-handed and it was hungry. As the men proceeded, sullen and wrangling by turns, one of them came on a nest of eggs in the tall grass by the side of the road, the gift of a hen from a farm well off the road. The finder began to gather in this godsend to hungry men, was warned by another that the eggs belonged to a white man and that taking them could cause trouble, expressed his disdain of all white men in return, and punctuated his sentiments by smashing the eggs. The disputation grew acrimonious and took a dangerous turn: from who was afraid of a white man it turned to who was afraid to kill a white man. Eventually, four young men had taunted each other into a position where it was difficult to find a middle ground between killing a white man or admitting to being a coward. The rest of the hunting party goaded them until it was even more difficult to find a line of retreat, and then went ahead, leaving the four to consider the folly of intemperate remarks.

However, they had traded dares and there was no backing down without loss of face. Probably with a hope all around that one among them would offer an honorable way out, they turned off the road into the farmyard of Robinson Jones whose house was also post office and an inn of sorts which offered rooms and meals to travelers. Jones was at home; so was his fifteen-year-old daughter and an infant son. The four Sioux were boisterous but they hesitated to consummate their purpose; Jones, on his part, had no qualms about walking out after a period of arguing with the young Indians, taking his daughter with him and leaving the Sioux in full possession of the house and the sleeping boy. He merely announced that he was going to join his wife who was visiting at the neighboring farm of Howard Baker, not much more than a stone's throw away.

In a short time the Indians followed Jones to the nearby farmyard where Mrs. Jones, Mr. and Mrs. Baker and an emigrant couple with their covered wagon were enjoying the bright Sunday weather visiting in the yard. When the four young Sioux arrived, there was probably a certain amount of fluttery excitement on the part of Mrs. Viranus Webster, the emigrant woman, but the Indians only proposed a shooting at targets, a challenge quickly accepted. The white men shot first and, without reloading, stood back to see how the young Indians would do. Here was a measure of how complacent the Minnesota settlers had become, because it is basic frontier doctrine to reload a gun at once.

The settlers had a brief moment to realize their error—or perhaps time was too short for them to comprehend what was happening. The Sioux, instead of firing at the targets, swung their guns on their hosts, and killed the three men, and Mrs. Jones and the daughter. Then, their bravado evaporating, they took horses and fled without completing the bloody and senseless deed by killing the other two women.

They had approximately forty-five miles to go to reach home, which was the village of Chief Red Middle Voice. It was after dark when they arrived, and reported to Red Middle Voice what they had done. The chief probably heard the news with some secret satisfaction. He hated the white men and he was a troublemaker—as a matter of fact, his village was made up of malcontents, dissidents, and general bad apples who had been asked to leave other villages. Red Middle Voice called in his nephew, Chief Shakopee, no lover of the settlers either, for advice. The two knew there was going to be trouble and elected without hesitation to stand behind the four young murderers. The important thing was to marshal tribal support. They sent messengers through the night to summon leading men to an immediate council at the house of Little Crow, the Sioux chief who wielded the most influence.

A brief explanation of the geography of the situation becomes almost essential at this point. The Minnesota River has its source in Big Stone Lake on the western border of the state and flows southeast for about two-thirds of its length before making a sharp elbow and running northeast till it meets the Mississippi. The Sioux reservation lay along

Scene of the 1862 Sioux Uprising

the south side of the river for its first 150 miles, from Big Stone Lake almost to the village of New Ulm. About twenty-five miles upriver from the lower or southeastern end of the reservation was Lower Agency, also called Redwood Agency because the Redwood River flowed into the Minnesota nearby. Another thirty miles upriver beyond Lower Agency, and also overlooking the Minnesota, was Upper Agency —or Yellow Medicine Agency, so named from Yellow Medicine River which enters the Minnesota below the bluffs on which the Agency perched.

The agencies were busy communities with government offices and warehouses, churches and missionary schools, traders' stores, and other activities. It was not caprice, inefficiency, nor an Indian Bureau swindle that had caused two agencies to be built only thirty miles apart to serve one tribe. There were four bands of Santee Sioux, too many Indians to have their problems handled by a single agency. Upper Agency was responsible for the Wahpeton and Sisseton bands; Lower Agency took care of the problems of the Mdewakantons and Wahpekutes.

A few of the Indians had adopted permanent dwellings built by the government, either story-and-a-half brick houses or frame houses. Most still lived in tepees, tepees covered not with buffalo hide but with government-issue canvas. About a hundred families among them were doing their best to live as whites; they cut their hair short; the men wore coats and trousers; they went to school and church, farmed, and buried their dead. The majority remained Indians, wore their hair long, kept the breech clout, blanket and leggings, exposed their dead on scaffolds, and sent out war parties to fight the Chippewas to the north.

Red Middle Voice, Shakopee, Little Crow, and other Sioux who took part in the midnight council at the home of Little Crow were Mdewakantons and Wahpekutes whose villages were all in the vicinity of Lower Agency. It would have been desirable to have representatives from the Wahpetons and Sissetons but Upper Agency was thirty miles away and the matter could not wait. The council was an acrimonious one, hopelessly split on what course should be followed. Some argued persuasively—with any amount of historical precedent to back them up—that it would do no good to turn the four murderers over to the whites for punishment because all Indians would be punished indiscriminately anyway; the thing to do was to attack first. There would never be another time like the present, they said; Indians who passed through settled country on hunting trips toward the Big Woods re-marked that they saw nothing but old men, women, and children because all the fit young men were away in the war. On the other hand, a strong peace faction whose spokesmen included Wabasha, Wacouta, and other respected chiefs, argued eloquently the futility of bloodshed. Voices rose, taunts were hurled, threats made in the hot, crowded room.

Little Crow spoke last. He began by ridiculing the war faction with its talk of killing or driving out all the whites. He had visited some of the cities of the white men; he had seen their numbers and their power. Crushing defeat lay at the end of the war trail. Then, when the war leaders were shouting and threatening him, he dramatically reversed himself to announce that, if they wanted war, he would lead them. The meeting broke up in complete pandemonium. The news was passed to the groups of young men who had gathered outside and there was more whooping and shouting. Plans were made for an attack at daybreak, August 18, only a few hours away.

Little Crow had been very much of a disappointment to his father— also Chief Little Crow, as was his grandfather—because he had been the Sioux equivalent of a playboy and had showed no aptitude nor interest in leadership. Some of his tribesmen accused him of a notable lack of enthusiasm for the hazardous little raids against the Chippewa, preferring to spend his time bringing comfort and companionship to wives whose men had gone after scalps. He did not extend his circle of friends greatly by such good works, and one time, in a shooting scrape, a bullet shattered both wrists, leaving them crooked and weakened. (He was also said to have had a double set of teeth, though how this prodigy was arranged is not made clear.)

Then he abruptly ended his wastrel life, took four wives—sisters— simultaneously (which was cause and which effect remains unknown), and settled down to assume the responsibilities of leadership, which he did with surprising vigor and ability. Of recent years he had been gradually becoming something of a white man's Indian; he wore trousers, lived in a wooden house, did some farming. Major Galbraith, the Indian agent, had talked to Little Crow on the fifteenth, only two days before the murders and had promised to build him a bigger and better house if he would use his influence to bring the young men of the tribe to "habits of industry and civilization." The chief had agreed to do all he could and had picked out the site for the house. And the day of the murders he had attended services at the Episcopal chapel at the agency. He was not a Christian but he had been very attentive, and the missionary priest was hopeful of making such an important catch in his fishing for souls.

But to gain favor with whites was to lose it with a very large segment of his own people. The Sioux began calling him a "cut-hair" and a tool of the whites. He felt the chill breeze very keenly when, in the election for the speakership among the Lower Indians, a position of great prestige which he had long held, he was defeated. At the midnight council, he had been forced to make a choice between responsible leadership and the loss of his remaining prestige. When he found the Sioux meant to fight regardless of his warnings, he had decided that it was better to lead a lost cause than become a nobody.

Lower Agency was the target of the first attack. The council had broken up very late; the chiefs had had to hurry to get their warriors assembled and moved to the agency. There they were split up into groups and quietly put into positions around every building where there were white men and women. This was no war-whooping raid.

Early risers at the agency were surprised to see Indians around even before full morning light but they were not apprehensive. The Sioux waited until the agency began stirring; the smoke of breakfast fires was already rising out of several chimneys before they fired their first shot. The first victim was James Lynd, clerk in the store of trader Andrew Myrick, who was killed as he came to the door, probably still a little heavy with sleep. Lynd was a former state representative but the Sioux knew him better as a man who had fathered children by several of their daughters, and they undoubtedly put a bullet into him with considerable satisfaction. Myrick was upstairs. He could have had no illusions about the chances of a man who had said, "Let them eat grass." Leaping out the window, he ran for the shelter of a clump of brush but a bullet cut him down in flight. The Indians pulled a handful of prairie grass and stuffed it into his dead mouth.

Another trader, François La Bathe, was killed in his store, and three clerks were shot down in a third store. Three men in charge of the barn left off feeding horses and walked out to see what all the shooting was about; they were killed as they walked into the open air. Thirteen men were killed at the agency and another ten while fleeing; no women were slain but ten were taken captive. The Sioux could easily have wiped out everyone if they had only kept their mind on their bloody business but they were soon diverted by the treasures that became available as they broke into buildings. Killing was soon almost forgotten in favor of looting while white survivors took advantage of the opportunity to escape.

No one at the agency knew the dimensions of the uprising; most were in some state of shock. But there was no doubt where the nearest chance of security lay: at Fort Ridgely across the river and downstream, about fifteen miles away. The agency stood on the prairie; from it a road led down the river bluff to the river bottoms, passed through the trees and brush and across the river, climbed the opposite bluff to the prairie again, and continued to Fort Ridgely.

The road crossed the river on a small ferry which was the bottleneck on this morning of August 18. When he might easily have escaped on one of his early crossings, the ferryman continued to ply back and forth, taking refugees across until some Sioux left off looting long enough to notice what was happening down below and put a stop to it. The ferryman, Hubert Millier but almost unknown to Minnesota history by any name other than Old Mauley, was shot and mutilated, but by then he had taken most of the refugees across. Up above, at the agency, flames were rising from burning buildings and Sioux warriors, in a delirium of excitement, were alternately war-dancing and adding to their stacks of plunder. The white women captives were not enjoying their part in the victory celebration.

2. MURDER ON THE PRAIRIE

Not all the Sioux attacked the agency. Bands were ranging the prairies, raiding the farms of settlers, and the paths of two or three of them intercepted the straggling parade of refugees on foot and in wagons and buggies on their way to Fort Ridgely. Seven more were killed during this flight. Old friendships did not necessarily mean anything. Philander Prescott was an interpreter who had lived at peace among the Sioux for forty years—since long before there had been settlers in Minnesota—and had an Indian wife; he was shot when a war party caught up with him as he headed toward the fort. On the other hand, there were instances aplenty where Sioux warriors allowed whites to escape, or gave them warning of impending attack, because of past friendship or simply "because he was a good man."

Disaster came in many ways on the prairie that day. Teen-age Mary

Schwandt worked for a man and his wife, both government school-teachers, whose home was off the agency. When word came that the Indians were killing and burning, Mary found a place in a wagon with two other young girls and three men, who headed for New Ulm. Half-way there they were cut off by a band of Indians. The men were shot at once; one of the girls, Mary Anderson, was also hit in the back when the three made a futile attempt to escape into the tall grass of a slough. The girls were taken captive, and were raped many times during the period they were held by the Sioux, even Mary Anderson, till she died of her wound and mistreatment. Indians of the plains and prairies, unlike those of the East, had no taboo about taking sexual advantage of women prisoners, and a white woman taken captive could expect the proverbial fate worse than death.

At about the same time Mary Schwandt was traveling across the prairie, her father was shingling the roof of his new house on the opposite side of the river when a party of Sioux rode up. Probably the first intimation of disaster he had was in the split second when he saw a rifle raised and aimed at him; then the gun fired and he rolled off the roof and fell to the ground. His wife, his sons aged five and seven, his married daughter and son-in-law, and the young son of a neighbor were slain before the warriors passed on to other deeds of bravery. One son, eleven, ran into some brush, escaped, and made his way to Fort Ridgely to relate the story.

There were unknown numbers of settlers who died with just as little warning as these people, as the war parties, usually in groups of about ten or twenty men, criss-crossed the prairies. The settlers made virtually no attempt to fight back that day; if any of them fired a gun there is no record of it. The American frontiersman of tradition, keen-eyed and ever alert, with rifle always within reach, apparently did not exist on the Minnesota prairie. The Indians had given no cause for alarm for a long time—and no one remains perpetually keyed up when no danger is in sight. Besides, many of the settlers were immigrants, chiefly German, who knew little of Indians and probably owned no guns.

Other families were wiped out, or nearly so, in the small settlement called Middle Creek where the Schwandts died. A Justina Boelter who lost her husband, father-in-law, and sister-in-law escaped into the bushes with her small child where she lived on berries and raw vegetables which she dug up from gardens at night. She watched helplessly as the child died of starvation; finally, not knowing and not caring any longer whether Indians were around, she crawled back to her own home where she was found by soldiers nine weeks after the day of the outbreak, still alive, but just barely. Her husband, in his death throes, had inflicted one of the very few casualties on the Indians that first day of the uprising; he had almost bitten off the thumb of Cut Nose, one of the most murderous of the Sioux.

Other Indian bands south of the river rode at least as far as Milford Township in Brown County, twenty miles from the Sioux villages, where almost fifty German settlers lay dead by night, while another eight died as far away as Nicollet County on the north side of the river below Fort Ridgely, thirty miles and more east of homes of the Sioux. The Indians were ranging far.

Pillars of smoke from burning farms rose here and there against the sky, although the Sioux did not make it their common practice to fire buildings before riding on (it was commonly believed that they were saving them for their own use later). The word "massacre" has been loosely used and misused, but what occurred in Minnesota was a massacre in the true sense of the word. No one knows how many settlers were killed that first day, but it may have run into the hundreds. There were not usually witnesses left to come in and report the time and manner of their families' and friends' going.

The vanguard of the miserable parade of refugees plodding its way to Fort Ridgely reached its destination during the middle of the morning, bringing stories of terror and death that were not always coherent. Few, if any, of the survivors had a very good idea of what had happened; for most it was a nightmare alley of impressions: of hitherto friendly Sioux suddenly shooting, of seeing someone pitch and fall and struggle to rise and then go down limply with his skull crushed by a club, of running to get away.

Out of these impressions Captain John Marsh, commanding, gathered for certain only that there had been an outbreak of violence by the Sioux at Lower Agency; he erred tragically in not considering that he might have an entire war on his hands. Captain Marsh turned command of the fort over to young Lieutenant Thomas Gere, and set out at once for the agency with a force of forty-eight men, including himself and a civilian interpreter. On the way, the detachment continued to pass refugees, several of whom warned Marsh that this looked like a major outbreak and not just the actions of a few radical malcontents. Captain Marsh was a brave man, as his record at the first Battle of Bull Run proved, but he had never fought Indians. So, without hesitating, he led his command down the road onto the river bottom to the ferry, where they were hemmed in by trees and brush.

The only Indian in sight was on the other bank, a man named White Dog who worked at the agency and was considered completely civilized. Through the interpreter, he invited them to come across and assured them everything was perfectly all right. The body of Old Mauley, the ferryman, lying in sight suggested that all was not quite all right, and Marsh hesitated to put his men on the ferry. While the parleying was going on, Sioux warriors were crossing the river upstream and sneaking through the thickets; several even got into the ferryman's shack.

The ambush caught the soldiers with devastating surprise, a hail of bullets and arrows from the bushes on both sides of the river. A number of Marsh's men died in the first minute or two—several in the first volley. The Captain got the rest out of the most exposed position on the ferry landing and into grass and willows; then, looking for a way of retreat, Marsh decided that the best plan would be to cross the river well below the ferry where there appeared to be no Indians on the opposite side, and return to the north side somewhere near the fort. He attempted to find a place to ford, apparently stepped into a hole, and drowned. From then on, it was a case of every man for himself, but most of those still alive were well enough hidden in the thickets by then so that the Sioux had no great stomach for going in and routing them out. The coming of twilight enabled most to escape from their hiding places to straggle back across the prairie, the last reaching the fort well past midnight. Only twenty-three returned of the forty-eight who left in the morning.

As for the Sioux, they had lost one man at the ferry, apparently the only Indian killed anywhere in a day that saw so many whites die. The Indians were jubilant; the defeat of Marsh's force convinced them that they could handle any white soldiers without the least trouble.

The distance between Lower and Upper Agency was about thirty miles; word of the uprising crossed that distance in a matter of a few hours. The Sisseton and Wahpeton bands soon received overtures to join the war; they debated long and finally took the somewhat less than forthright position that they would not join in the fighting but would not refuse their support. It was not that they had any more

love for the Americans than the Lower Sioux; they just wanted to see
how things developed before going out on a limb. Many of their young
men went off to join Little Crow and share the excitement and glory,
but Little Crow had hoped for much more. It was the first great blow
to his expectations.

Indians at Upper Agency did loot traders' stores, killing one man
and mortally wounding another in the process, but there might have
been an outbreak of much worse violence that would have put the
Upper Sioux into the war willy-nilly, if it had not been for a Christian
Indian, John Other Day. Other Day and his white wife gathered most
of the whites into a brick warehouse in the evening, and he and a small
group of Wahpeton friends guarded them through a tense night. At
daybreak the next morning (August 19), he led sixty-two people across
the Minnesota River, carrying the young and the feeble in five wagons
and buggies, and after three days of travel got them safely to Hutchinson.

On Tuesday, the nineteenth, the Indians were still ranging ahead of
the news that they were on the warpath. When settlers at Sacred Heart
Creek settlement on the north side of the river learned that Indians
had committed murders at nearby farms, thirteen families gathered,
took counsel, and rejected a proposal that they make a stand at one of
the farms that possessed a large and heavy log house, well suited for
defense. Instead, they set out by wagon for Fort Ridgely, but were
overtaken by a party of Sioux who told them that the Chippewa were
on the warpath and that their only safe course was to return home
under the protection of the Sioux (the Sioux included Chief Shakopee
who had been the first to argue for war, and Cut Nose, he who had had
his thumb almost bitten off by a dying settler the day before; the two
were among the worst that the Sioux had to offer). The settlers turned
around; they had guns, but they had stowed them in the bottom of one
of the wagons instead of carrying them, and the Indians kept carefully
between the men and the wagon. When they reached home, the Indians
suddenly opened fire, killing twenty-five; all the men, and some of the
women and children. The women and children not slain were taken
prisoner.

One woman, Justina Kreiger, was left behind when the Sioux rode
off with their captives. She had seen her husband murdered but there
was no time for grief; she had waited till the Indians' attention was
distracted and then pushed the eleven children in her wagon toward

a roadside thicket. The escape was detected and several Indians ran up and began clubbing the running children. One of those killed was Justina's, but seven got away and eventually were saved. Mrs. Kreiger jumped from the wagon and attempted to follow the children into the bushes but a shotgun blast knocked her down and put seventeen pellets in her back. The Indians left her lying for dead and moved on, but events would prove that there was an amazing amount of life left in her body yet.

Across the prairie on this second day of the uprising, as on the first, settlers were being murdered in reprisal for all the grudges the Sioux had against the government of the United States. They died, in most cases, with the way of their going unknown because only Indians stood over the bodies, although occasionally their fate became a matter of record because one of the intended victims managed to escape and report the fate of the others. But on Tuesday, August 19, everything else that happened on the Minnesota prairie country was of minor importance to what was occurring at Fort Ridgely.

3. THE GATE TO THE VALLEY

On that second morning of the uprising, Fort Ridgely was the hope of the entire southwestern part of the state. At the same time, it was almost as vulnerable as any point within range of the Sioux horsemen. Captain Marsh had led the major part of its defending force into ambush at the ferry, and only twenty-three of his forty-eight had stumbled back. Yet those twenty-three hollow-eyed, beaten men doubled the force available to defend Ridgely. Lieutenant Tom Gere had been left in command of twenty-two men on duty and seven on the sick list. With the defeated survivors of Marsh's detachment, he had approximately fifty soldiers. He also had about two hundred refugees to take care of; they had continued to trickle in long after dark that first night of the uprising and were there to give him something to worry about when he woke up early on Tuesday morning.

On the Indians' side, Little Crow well understood the strategic value of Fort Ridgely. If it could be taken, the farms and villages of the older and more populous lower Minnesota River valley would lie open to Sioux attacks. But Little Crow could not order an attack, he could only propose one, and at the moment, the young Sioux warriors were more interested in the sport of ranging over the country, raiding and looting farms. They voted against attacking the fort.

In withholding their attack, the Indians made a priceless gift of time to the defenders. On Tuesday morning, the gate to the lower valley stood almost wide open. During the day, while Sioux warriors made raids that could have no real effect on the war, the gate slowly began to close. On Monday morning, First Lieutenant Timothy Sheehan had left Fort Ridgely with his company of the 5th Minnesota Infantry after having been on detached duty to oversee the annuity payments at Upper Agency, and was on the way back to their regular post at Fort Ripley up north in Chippewa country. The last thing Captain Marsh had done before setting out on his tragic march to the ferry was to send a messenger after Sheehan, recalling him. The messenger caught Sheehan already forty miles out, and Lieutenant Sheehan, being a soldier of decision, turned around at once and marched his company all night to reach the fort about Tuesday noon where, as senior officer, he took over command from Gere.

Lieutenant Gere had also put in a call for help. As soon as the first survivors of the ambush at the ferry came in with the story of the catastrophe, he realized this was a matter for much larger forces and higher authority. He prepared a terse report outlining what he knew of the events of the day: the attack on the agency, the killing of settlers, and the defeat of Marsh's command. This, together with a request for reinforcements without delay, was addressed to the commanding officer at Fort Snelling; the message was handed to Private William Sturgis who had saddled the best horse at the fort; Sturgis disappeared down the New Ulm Road into the darkness to begin a long and grueling ride, 125 miles in 18 hours.

Private Sturgis's message initiated large-scale operations against the Indians, but he also sent some immediate help to the garrison. As he galloped down the lower Minnesota River valley, at St. Peter his path overtook that of a group of about fifty recruits also on their way to Fort Snelling to be mustered into the Union Army. It was late at night but Sturgis was playing Paul Revere as he went through the river towns and villages, and the recruits were wide awake in a minute.

They had been signed up in an enlistment drive by Major Galbraith, the Indian agent, who had brought in about fifty boys, many of them half-breed youths who had been hanging around the agency with nothing to do. Most of them had come from Renville County which lay directly across the river from Lower Agency; Sturgis, in his few brief moments, could tell them that refugees had been coming in from that direction all during the day before he left. Galbraith himself was taking the recruits to Fort Snelling; now he scouted around, arousing the sleeping village, located fifty old Harpers Ferry muskets in storage and got them released, found powder and lead, and put his men and local volunteers to work casting bullets. After remarkably little delay, they were on their way at 4 A.M., swinging along the dusty dirt road toward Fort Ridgely where they arrived on Tuesday afternoon. The unit quickly named itself the Renville Rangers; for a while it was looked at with some suspicion because of the Sioux blood of so many of its members but all feelings of doubt disappeared as soon as the Rangers were seen in action.

There was one other small and very ironic addition to the fort's garrison that same Tuesday when a stagecoach carrying four armed guards stopped on its way to Lower Agency. When the driver and guards learned the situation, they decided to stay and help fight Indians, but first they carried a strongbox into the commanding officer's quarters for safekeeping. It contained $71,000, the annuity money then about two months overdue. Had it come only three or four days earlier it is very possible there would have been no massacre.

By Tuesday afternoon, Sheehan's refugee list had risen to about 250. Of these, some 25 men had presented themselves as ready and willing to fight. The number of soldiers under his command—using the term soldiers advisedly for some were raw recruits—had become about 180 by the time the day ended. His total force, then, was more than 200; with it Sheehan should ordinarily have been able to hold off a force of tribesmen several times his defending force.

The only flaw was that Fort Ridgely was not designed for a hard defense. It sat on the north side of the Minnesota, on the prairie but only a short distance from the bluffs that overlooked the valley. Ravines led back from the bluffs, growing smaller until they petered out in the prairie. One such ravine cut into the western edge of the fort, another ran along most of its northern side, still another lay to the east. They were filled with trees and thick brush and provided perfect cover for an enemy to approach unseen. The river bluffs, too, were wooded; at the same time they were too far from the fort to be defended and not steep enough to bother an enemy on foot. Only to the northwest was there unobstructed prairie.

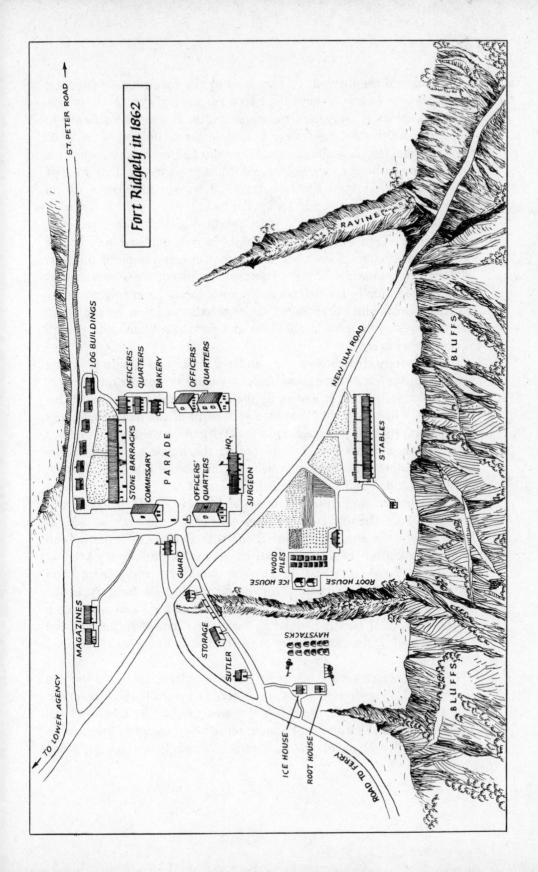

The heart of the fort was its parade, a square about ninety yards on a side, about which were built the barracks, officers' quarters, commissary, headquarters, surgeon's quarters, and bake house. Scattered to the north, south, and west were various other buildings, some near, some far: stables, magazines, ice houses, warehouses, hospital, quarters for civilian employees, root house, and granary, as well as long rows of cordwood and hayricks. Where nature had not supplied cover for an enemy, these structures made up for the lack.

By Wednesday, Little Crow had assembled a large war party. The morning was spent by the Sioux warriors in working their way up the ravines that brought them close to the central quadrangle of the fort. Although four hundred or more men were involved, the operation was conducted so quietly the defenders were not aware an enemy was near till Little Crow himself appeared on horseback on the open prairie to the northwest, riding back and forth and waving a blanket as though asking for a parley.

It was purely a diversion, for suddenly some two hundred yelling warriors broke out of the ravine on the opposite side of the quadrangle. They drove in the picket line easily, gained an excellent advanced line by seizing a line of small log houses just north of the quadrangle, and at one point pierced the inner defenses at a gap between two buildings where three warriors got through before the break was closed in a bloody, snarling little fight in which the three were killed, along with one soldier killed and two wounded.

A year before, an artillery unit of the Regular Army had been stationed at Fort Ridgely but had been withdrawn for war service. It had left behind a number of guns, along with Ordnance Sergeant John Jones to look after them. Jones must have found it dull merely keeping his big guns free from rust, because he obtained permission to train some of the men of Company C of the 5th Minnesota Infantry in the handling and firing of artillery. Enough men had been given a chance at Jones's special training squad to form three gun detachments and this Wednesday, the twentieth of August, their training was being put to good use.

After the attack on the north had been repulsed, another from the south got close enough to put the gunners at an artillery piece under rifle and arrow fire. But the return fire was too hot for them and the Indians drew back, with grape shot from the cannon speeding them on their way. Five hours of almost continuous attack had accomplished nothing for the Sioux except that they had run off the fort's horses and cattle. The artillery had been a complete and unpleasant surprise to Little Crow, but he was not dismayed and made plans for a more vigorous assault the next day.

However, a very heavy rain fell that night and into the next afternoon, and the Indians did not attack. The defenders used the time to strengthen protecting works in the gaps between buildings of the quadrangle; there were very few shovels so breastworks were made of sacks of oats and cordwood. The day was not lost for Little Crow, either. All day, braves drifted in to join his forces. Many of them came from the Upper Reservation even though the Sissetons and Wahpetons continued officially neutral in the war. By Friday, as many as eight hundred warriors may have been ready for the fight, although the number was probably somewhat less.

Once again the Sioux spent the morning—Friday, the twenty-second —getting into position, working their way up the ravines and along the river bluff. At one o'clock in the afternoon they attacked, opening fire from all directions. They quickly seized the large post stables south of the quadrangle and only about eighty yards away, a protective position as good as that of the defenders. The artillery changed the odds, however; shells set the stables on fire and the Indians were driven out.

Stubbornly, the Sioux attacked here and there, probing for a weak spot, but each time were repulsed. Then they withdrew completely to regroup their forces in the shelter of a ravine to the southwest. But the charge never got organized. Two of the fort's three cannon were wheeled around to the threatened side; as the Sioux began to come out of the brushy ravines, double charges of canister exploded among them and cut them down. It took the last heart for fighting out of them; after gathering their dead and wounded they moved away, giving up all hope of taking the fort.

". . . the soldiers fought so bravely we thought there were more of them than there were . . . ," Chief Big Eagle recalled many years later. "We thought the fort was the door to the valley as far as St. Paul, and that if we got through the door nothing could stop us this side of the Mississippi. But the defenders of the fort were very brave and kept the door shut."

It had been a costly defeat for Little Crow, an estimated one hundred dead and many wounded, while the whites lost only three killed and thirteen wounded. The fort itself was stronger than ever; material damage had been limited to the burning of a few scattered buildings and the stolen horses and cattle.

However, there was more than one way to skin a cat. On the opposite side of the river from Fort Ridgely and about twenty miles downstream was New Ulm. Thirty miles farther to the southeast was Mankato, just about at the elbow where the river swings to the northeast and flows toward Fort Snelling and its meeting with the Mississippi. The northeast-flowing reach below Mankato was the lower valley on which the Sioux had their eyes fixed, a well-settled stretch with many villages and farms. Little Crow, who fancied himself a strategist, reasoned that if Fort Ridgely could not be taken, it could be by-passed if the Indians moved down the south side of the river. But first New Ulm would have to be captured to eliminate any threat in their rear.

Most of the Sioux warriors did not know whether Little Crow's strategy was sound or not. Most of them did not care one way or the other. But they were eager to strike at New Ulm where they had not been willing at first to attack Fort Ridgely. Young warriors in their teens and early twenties might not understand strategy but they could understand a village filled with more loot than they could haul away in wagons.

New Ulm was a community settled largely by Germans. It was growing rapidly, and in 1862 had a population somewhere near nine hundred. But for five days refugees had been pouring into the town until the population was more than doubled; many were wounded; many numb with grief and horror. Except for its riverfront, the town was almost without natural defenses. From the bottomlands on which it lay, the land rose in a couple of natural terraces to the prairie to the south; an attacking foe would come down from higher ground undeterred by any obstacles except those the defenders might put in its way.

On the other hand, as the Sioux moved to attack on Saturday the twenty-third, New Ulm had the powerful advantage of a determined defending force. As soon as word of the uprising reached the nearer towns of the lower valley, they sent help to New Ulm. On Tuesday, the day after the outbreak, Mankato had already sent a hundred men and a company came from South Bend. Militia units hurried out, the St. Peter Guards, the Le Sueur Tigers and others who had some small military training, along with volunteers who had nothing much except the will to help; in some instances they actually came without guns, possibly expecting—who knows—to throw rocks at the Sioux. The men from South Bend did not stay to fight, however; a rumor that the Winnebagoes in a small reservation about ten miles south of South Bend were about to go on the warpath sent them hurrying back to protect their own. The story was without foundation; the Winnebagoes had already been harried and moved about so much that all they wanted was to be left alone.

Charles Flandrau, justice of the Minnesota Supreme Court and former Indian agent among the Sioux, had been elected to command the St. Peter unit; at New Ulm he was put in top command by a vote of all officers. Popularity contests are not ordinarily the best way to ferret out military talent, but this was one case where it could have done worse. He posted his forces outside the village, making use of the protection offered by the natural embankment where the land rose from one terrace to the next. In the business district, near the river, he barricaded six blocks as an inner bastion in case a last-ditch stand became necessary, and there he put the crowd of some 1,200 refugees and noncombatants.

Flandrau's first move, though, proved to be a tactical error. He sent a group of seventy-five militia across the river by ferry to reconnoiter. The detachment was cut off by Sioux from returning by the ferry and was forced to retreat far down the river before it could find a place to recross. It did not get back to New Ulm that day at all; as a result, it missed the battle completely, thereby costing the defense about a quarter of its badly needed strength. The white forces actually taking part in the battle were about 250, the Sioux probably twice as many.

Pillars of smoke from burning farms and haystacks announced the coming of the Indians well in advance. When the Sioux forces at last appeared on the rim of the valley, it was as a great mass, but as they came down the slopes they fanned out, groups of horsemen swinging to right and left until they enveloped the entire land perimeter of the town by the time they were almost within rifle shot of the defense lines. There were an estimated five hundred of them; watching them come on in a seemingly inexorable advance was doing unpleasant things to the nerves of the defenders, so that when the warriors broke into a sweeping charge, yelling as they came, the militia broke and ran.

Once their panic had spent itself, they settled down to businesslike fighting, but the lapse had been costly, for by then they were inside the village itself, and it had become a matter of house-to-house fighting. When foes could not be driven from a house with weapons, they were burned out. Flandrau had a number of houses put to the torch even before the fighting reached them to deny their cover to the Sioux; the Indians, in their turn, started fires on the windward side of the village and burned out blocks of houses.

In the midst of a small inferno of smoke, flames, yells, curses, the crack of rifles, and the thud of arrows, the fighting went on, hardly a battle but dozens of separate deadly fights, usually for possession of strong points. A stone windmill was a prize much coveted by the Sioux but a band of militiamen inside doggedly refused to give it up. The post office, a brick building, was another fortress of the defenders that gave a good account of itself and refused to be taken. Flandrau's men were gradually constricted toward the barricaded downtown area; a large group of Sioux began gathering for a heavy assault to take the inner fortifications before the militia could get themselves sorted out and a defense organized. Flandrau, with considerable trepidation in view of the way his men had fled at the first Sioux charge of the day, ordered sixty of his men against the Sioux. It was surprise against planned surprise. Flandrau's worries about his men were baseless; they made an irresistible, cheering charge that broke and scattered the assembling Indian force.

The repulse marked the real end of the battle; thereafter the Sioux leaders were unable to exhort their men to any real effort. There was fighting till after sundown but the heart was gone from it, and some long-distance shooting the next morning, but the Sioux were finished and New Ulm was saved. The village, though, had not come off easily. Of its defenders, 26 were dead and more than 60 wounded. Only 25 of its houses stood; 190 were in ashes. Ammunition was almost gone; food was running low. The noncombatants were crowded into a small area under intolerable conditions. Flandrau took counsel with his lieutenants and decided there was no choice but to abandon the town and run whatever risks there might be in leaving the protection of its defenses.

On Monday, the children, the aged, and the wounded were put on 153 wagons, and with everyone else walking, the procession headed for Mankato, thirty miles away. The militia kept a close guard but no Indians appeared. Mankato was reached in one day; the volunteers returned to their own towns and became civilians again on the instant.

As for the Sioux, they had withdrawn to the northwest after their repulse. They did not stop at their villages around Lower Agency but had packed up their tepees and taken their captives and moved on until they were among the Wahpetons and Sissetons. It was not an admission of defeat, but they knew the white soldiers would probably soon be after them, and that it would be best to get their families and captives out of the probable area of fighting.

All the Sioux had not taken part in the attacks on Fort Ridgely and New Ulm; many groups of warriors had searched the prairies in ever-widening arcs to find farms where no warnings had reached and to intercept fleeing settlers before they could reach security. On Wednesday, the twentieth, while Fort Ridgely was undergoing its first attack, a raiding party struck the isolated settlement of Lake Shetek in the southwestern part of the state fifty miles south of Upper Agency. The settlers, after attempting to flee by wagon, ran into the tall dead grass of a dry slough where they tried to hide while the Indians on higher ground at the margin fired at leisure into every movement of the dry reeds. The Sioux treacherously shot several emerging settlers after a surrender agreement, clubbed two or three children (the women seem to have been mainly responsible for this), and took the rest of the women and children captive. Surprisingly, only fifteen were killed out of fifty members of the community, and a good number escaped—in the case of several of the men, by cowardly abandoning women and children and running.

Many remarkable things happened and prodigies were performed during the uprising; one of them during the Lake Shetek killings. A family named Eastlick suffered tragically in the episode: the husband was killed instantly, the wife, Lavina Eastlick, received four gunshot wounds and was clubbed over the head with a rifle until the stock broke; two of her children were beaten and died during the next twenty-four hours of their injuries and hunger and exposure as thundershowers beat down on the dismal scene. But two of her children escaped unscathed, and eleven-year-old Merton obeyed his mother's dying request that he take care of his eighteen-month-old brother Johnny. Somehow this young boy managed to lead and carry his baby brother for fifty miles during the next several days, finding enough berries to keep them going. Help finally came in the form of his erstwhile dying mother who had at last found new strength to rise up and start out in the direction of civilization. As she stumbled on her way she was picked up by the mail carrier, who either did not know what was happening, or took the slogan about the mail going through with more than ordinary seriousness. Mother and two small sons were reunited and won through to safety. Also saved was the Eastlick boys' Uncle Tom who had come out of the slough to attempt truce talks and had sunk back riddled with buckshot. He had bade Merton a tearful farewell but, like the boys' mother, at last had wearied of lying cold and wet, bleeding to death, and had also risen up out of the slough grass and headed eastward to safety. He survived for many garrulous, story-telling years.

There is no point in giving the complete calendar of raids and killings—nor is it possible because no one knows when or how many of the settlers were slain. By the twenty-third, a week after the first attacks, a raiding party had reached almost to the Iowa border, killing thirteen at a Norwegian settlement on the Des Moines River in Jackson County. At almost the same time, and in exactly the opposite direction, the commanding officer of Fort Abercrombie on the Dakota side of the Red River of the North received news of the uprising and was advised to take appropriate action. He sent word to the scattered settlers in that far northwest area to come in to the fort. Three men in Wahpeton on the Minnesota side of the river decided to hole up in the village's primitive hotel and take their chances; they were all found dead when white men at last returned to Wahpeton. The driver of the mail coach to St. Paul got no warning; he was killed and the mail scattered over the prairie.

Fort Abercrombie was no more built as a fortification than was Fort Ridgely; it was a mere collection of buildings without any stockade or protective works. Its only advantage over Ridgely was that there were no ravines or other cover; an enemy had to approach in the open over flat prairie. The fort's garrison, Company D of the 5th Minnesota Infantry, was eighty-four strong; eighty refugees had crowded in with them. Captain Vander Horck, commanding, strengthened the defenses as much as possible, using cordwood to build breastworks.

An attack by a small force of Sioux came on August 30; a much larger one on September 3 was repulsed leaving three of the defenders wounded. The Indians made their main effort on September 6, attacking at dawn and directing their main assault at the fort stables. The defenders had the tremendous advantage of artillery, three howitzers

—which were brutally effective on the dead-flat Red River Valley prairie where an anthill is an eminence; artillery fire broke up groups of warriors every time they attempted to assemble. Even so, one of the defenders was killed, two wounded, one of them mortally, in the days' fighting. The Sioux did not attack again but their sporadic presence in the area kept the garrison in a state of apprehension for more than a month until a relieving force finally arrived from Fort Snelling, two hundred miles away.

4. THE STATE UNDERTAKER AND HIS GRAVEDIGGERS

While these hundreds of individual dramas of violent death, terror, flight, and stout resistance were being played out on the prairie frontier, preparations were going ahead for full military action against the Indians. When Private Sturgis ended his long ride and brought the first news of the uprising to Fort Snelling, Governor Alexander Ramsey in St. Paul, a few miles away, was immediately informed. The Governor at once went out to the fort to see how many men were available (most were recruits waiting to go to join the Union army), then took the ferry across the Minnesota to the old fur trading village of Mendota to call on his personal friend and political foe, Henry Sibley, whom he immediately commissioned a colonel of militia and put in full charge of all operations against the Indians.

Sibley had been the first governor of Minnesota and Ramsey's immediate predecessor. He had been a fur trader for years, knew personally many of the leaders among the Sioux, was well acquainted with the habits of the Sioux, and had a good insight into their ways of thinking. But as far as fighting Indians was concerned, he was completely without experience.

Sibley started briskly, putting four companies of the 6th Minnesota Infantry the next morning on a steamboat which took them a little more than twenty miles up the river to Shakopee, whence they marched for two days to reach St. Peter on Friday, the same day Fort Ridgely was standing off its second attack. There was no reassurance in the stories pouring into the lower valley, with refugees hourly bringing new tales of horror which seldom suffered from understatement. Sibley became convinced the fort had fallen; he believed it highly possible that the entire Sioux nation with seven thousand warriors was moving in from the Great Plains and that fifteen hundred warriors might at that moment be waiting just over the horizon.

Men from St. Peter where he waited were even then out beyond that same horizon defending New Ulm. They had gone without asking about the number of Indians they might meet, but Sibley was not imbued with the same spirit. He sent messages back to Governor Ramsey complaining about the rifles and demanding Springfields, asking for more men, saying he needed more supplies. Ramsey sent the Springfields at once, dispatched supplies, filled six more companies of the 6th Minnesota and sent them. Sibley was carrying on a recruiting drive of his own among the excited people of the valley, enlisting militia and impressing farmers' horses and wagons into service. Finally, with a force of 1,400, including 300 of what might, with courtesy, be called cavalry, he set out for Fort Ridgely on Saturday morning, the day of New Ulm's agony.

The mounted troops pushed ahead and traveled all day and night to reach the fort where they were greeted as deliverers. Sibley and the main force showed no similar tendency to make haste. When evening forced them to make camp, they were only six miles from St. Peter, an advance so tortoiselike one wonders what the force could have been doing most of the day. It speeded up somewhat thereafter, reaching the fort a day and a half after the mounted troops.

Sibley sent the refugees back to safety in the lower valley with an escort, then cautiously reconnoitered for Indians. None appearing after three days of search, he sent a detachment of about 160 men under Major Joseph R. Brown down the road toward Lower Agency. It was accompanied by a number of civilians, most of them in the grim hope—or fear—of finding the bodies of missing relatives or friends.

The detachment moved slowly because it found sixteen bodies to bury on its way to the Agency. It camped overnight on the river bottoms; the next morning one section of it buried twenty men of Marsh's command at the ferry. In the ruins of Lower Agency, the body of trader Andrew Myrick was identified by his brother Nathan who had accompanied the detachment for just that purpose; Nathan knew precisely why his dead brother's mouth was stuffed with grass.

On the north side of the river, they came on a living being—although one so emaciated, so unkempt, so crusted with dirt and dried blood that at first they did not know whether she was white or Indian. They had chanced on Justina Kreiger, the first part of whose story has already been told, how she had been shot and left for dead when Shakopee's raiders had intercepted a band of settlers fleeing toward Fort Ridgely. Two Indians had later returned after dark to look for plunder among the bodies; one decided to take the dress from Mrs. Kreiger's body and slit it with a sweep of his knife. The blade cut a four-inch slash in her body but she did not flinch; then the Sioux changed his mind and went away. The woman survived her cruel wounds, and for twelve days had wandered on the prairie with no food except a few wild berries. She was too weak to give much information to the soldiers, so they wrapped her in blankets and laid her carefully in one of the wagons.

On their second night, they made camp on the prairie on the north side of the river near Birch Coulee, a deep, wooded ravine that runs several miles through the prairie to the river bluffs. Major Brown had been explicitly directed not to camp near timber or any uneven terrain. He should not have needed such instructions. He was married to a half-Sioux woman; he had been an Indian agent; he had lived among the Sioux most of his life. Yet, like the rankest greenhorn, he placed his camp only about 200 yards from the trees and brush of the coulee, and south of a swell in the prairie that made it impossible to see anyone approaching from the north.

The complete absence of any sign of Indians had convinced Brown and his officers that all was well. What they did not know was that a large force of Sioux led by Chiefs Mankato and Big Eagle was going down the south side of the river to pick up plunder they had left behind when they withdrew from their villages, and possibly even to have another try at New Ulm. The detachment had not seen any Indians, but the Indians had seen them and during the night had crossed the river and quietly surrounded the soldiers' camp.

The Sioux plan had been to kill the sentries noiselessly with bow and arrows, then fall on the sleeping camp and annihilate the soldiers. The scheme went awry when a sentry saw a movement in the grass in the first faint gray light and fired at it. The shot woke the camp but there was little margin against disaster for, with their original plan upset, the Sioux attacked at once. A number of soldiers were shot and killed in the first moments as they tried to shake off sleep and get their bearings in a world that was exploding in a chaos of Indian yells, gunfire, neighing horses, and soldiers' curses.

Major Brown and his officers set about rallying the men and improvising a defense. Wagons were heaved on their sides to form a barricade of sorts, all except the one in which Justina Kreiger lay. After the first overwhelming element of surprise was gone, the Sioux were checked for the moment and drew back. There is nothing more open and exposed than a piece of prairie, and the beleaguered soldiers did what they could to make it more hospitable, improvising protection with dead horses, chunks of tough sod laboriously cut out with knives, with anything, in fact, that came to hand.

The Sioux knew exactly where the defenders were. The warriors, on the other hand, could stay out of range, crawling forward through the tall grass to fire for a while and withdrawing again before the soldiers could pinpoint them. As the sun climbed higher, thirst and heat tortured the men lying on the ground inside the defense line; the Sioux, when fighting began to weary them, could go back into the shade of the trees of Birch Coulee for something to eat and perhaps a nap.

The gunfire was heard very plainly at Fort Ridgely only fifteen miles away, a distance that should have been an easy march of five hours or less. After discussing its meaning with his officers, Sibley ordered Colonel Samuel McPhail to take a strong force of 240, including artillery, to investigate. The relief force was sighted by Sioux scouts long before it reached the battlefield, and a small band of braves on horseback was sent out to meet it.

The Sioux were few, but noisy and active. They galloped about, whooping, shooting, dashing in first from one quarter and then another. Colonel McPhail halted his force and had his artillery fire a few rounds at the elusive Indians, upon which they slowly withdrew, making derisive gestures. Then the timid Colonel took up a strong defensive position and sent word back to Sibley that he was outnumbered and almost surrounded and needed help.

At Birch Coulee, the hard-pressed soldiers had heard McPhail's cannon and had taken immediate heart, but the hours passed and nothing happened except that the sun grew hotter, their thirst became fiercer, and the moans of the wounded became more urgent. McPhail was sitting and waiting for help and looking uneasily over his shoulder for Indians, while Sibley was coming to his rescue with all the precipitate speed of a glacier.

Colonel Sibley, with one thousand men and artillery, finally reached McPhail at midnight. With the hard muscle of 1,250 men and strong artillery, the combined forces might have been expected to push on with full speed. Instead, there was an unaccountable delay of three hours before anyone moved. Finally, at three o'clock in the morning, the force got under way. Birch Coulee was only three miles away; while there was little firing at that time of night, the sporadic shots could be heard very plainly at that distance and it would seem a time for haste. Yet it took until eleven o'clock—eight hours—to cover the last three miles. Then the besieging Sioux simply withdrew, and the thirty-one-hour ordeal of the detachment was ended.

Thirteen were dead, another three so badly wounded they would soon die. Forty-four were seriously wounded but would live. Among the casualties were some of the civilians who had gone along to find the bodies of relatives and friends. All who came out of the circle of makeshift defenses were dazed with fatigue and suffering from hunger and thirst. The wagon in which Justina Kreiger lay still stood upright but its wood had been literally torn to splinters in places by rifle bullets. When they looked to see what violence had been done to her body, they found not a shattered corpse but a woman very much alive. "They seemed perfectly astonished to find me alive," Mrs. Kreiger related afterward. "The blanket on which I lay wrapped in the wagon was found to have received over two hundred bullet holes in the fight." Yet not a bullet had pierced her flesh, although five had grazed her in so superficial a manner as hardly to have left a mark on the skin.

The Birch Coulee battle ended on September 2. On that same day, another force of soldiers was moving toward battle without knowing it. More than a week earlier, Governor Ramsey had answered appeals from Meeker County settlers on the edge of the Big Woods by sending a company of the 10th Minnesota Infantry, commanded by Captain Richard Strout, to protect and reassure the people there. Strout and his men had been moving through the settlements and letting themselves be seen as much as possible, to show that all was well. But all was not going to remain well; Little Crow was moving into the same area.

When Mankato and Big Eagle had started down the south side of the river, Little Crow with another band had headed northeast to raid settlements toward the Big Woods. His warriors agreed wholeheartedly with the plan for it would take them into country untouched by the war and ripe for looting. But Little Crow was still thinking in terms of grand strategy; he had no way of knowing the other Sioux force had been diverted at Birch Coulee, and he began talking about swinging behind the army in a great arc to join Mankato and Big Eagle, catching Sibley in a giant pincers movement.

His warriors wanted only the uncomplicated pleasures of raiding and plundering. If the chief was interested in strategy, he was welcome to it. When he became insistent, approximately two-thirds of them seceded from his band. The two bands went along separately, but on parallel roads that brought them into Acton Township, where the murders that had started the whole bloody string of events had occurred only a little more than two weeks before. That night they made separate camps, while not far away Captain Strout with sixty-four men was making a bivouac near Acton Post Office.

The next morning Strout set out with his company. He had been warned there were Indians in the vicinity and he had skirmishers out, so he was not caught by surprise when he ran into Little Crow's warriors. There was a brisk exchange of shots. One soldier fell mortally wounded but the Indians were beginning to give way after a short fight when the second group of Sioux came up in back of the company. Undismayed, Strout detailed men to face about and fight off the new attack. A lake lay on the company's left; the Indians extended their lines to cut off escape on the land side completely. Strout ordered a bayonet charge that opened the road, then quelled a panicky attempt by his own teamsters to abandon the company and make a frenzied dash for safety.

Captain Strout formed up his company for a fighting retreat and started down the road, holding off the outnumbering Sioux as they went. But, having been almost an exemplary leader thus far under the most difficult circumstances, Strout somehow let control of his men slip away from him. Panic began to spread; the march became a headlong and utterly disorderly flight which continued all the way to the village of Hutchinson, twenty-five miles to the southwest, with Indians riding on the flanks for miles and shooting into the terror-stricken soldiers. Three soldiers were killed during the flight, three fatally wounded, many more less seriously hurt. Nine horses were lost and most of the ammunition and rations. The dead were left where they fell. It was a disgraceful rout, especially after the brave beginning of the battle, and led to a second flight of settlers from the counties north of the Minnesota River.

After the disaster at Birch Coulee, Sibley returned to Fort Ridgely.

His lack of aggressiveness and slowness were raising a tremendous amount of criticism. Newspaper editors, sharpening their similes and metaphors in St. Paul far from any danger, called him a "snail" who "falls back on his authority and dignity and refuses to march," and the "state undertaker with his company of grave diggers." Although communications were not the best, Sibley received the papers from the state capital no more than three days late, so he knew what they were saying about him. Still he delayed, but now he had a rationale for his delay: he did not want to make any move that would endanger the lives of the prisoners in the hands of the Sioux. He carried on a form of negotiation with Little Crow by means of messages left in forked sticks thrust into the prairie; Little Crow used a half-breed prisoner who wrote a somewhat shaky English as his amanuensis. This channel of communication was also adopted by Wacouta and Wabasha, the peace chiefs who had opposed war ever since the midnight council; they put up messages asking how they could come in with their people and be sure they would not be harmed.

Negotiations were getting nowhere and the army at Fort Ridgely was beginning to suffer from slack discipline, desertions and the other ills of sitting around and doing nothing. At last, on September 18, one day short of a month from the afternoon when Governor Ramsey had made him a colonel and told him to save the state from the Sioux, Sibley led his forces out to do battle. He commanded exactly 1,619 men, a very potent force, especially since it included strong artillery units. He did suffer one major handicap, the lack of cavalry. The horsemen who had come with him to the fort had long since gone home to their own trades and businesses, leaving Sibley without any mounted troops.

The force crossed the Minnesota and moved upstream on the south side toward the Indian camps; in four days of cautious advance it traveled forty miles to Wood Lake, with the Sioux camps still twenty miles ahead. While the soldiers bivouacked near Wood Lake, the Sioux prepared their final battle, an ambush to catch the army when it took up its march again in the morning. It was a sound plan, which was simply to conceal seven hundred or eight hundred Indians in tall grass, and other cover on both sides of the trail the army column would follow. When the column was on its way and strung out over several miles, it would be attacked simultaneously from both sides and cut into disorganized fragments that could be wiped out easily.

Luck was not with the Indians—it seldom was. Among Sibley's forces was a group of real veterans, men from the 3rd Minnesota who had been taken prisoner and paroled by the Confederates, and were back in Minnesota until they could be formally exchanged and go back to fighting rebels again. In the meantime, they were lording it over the recruits in the Indian-fighting army, and this morning were about to demonstrate the possibilities of adding variety to an Army mess by foraging. A dozen of them had obtained four teams and wagons and had started across the prairie to raid the gardens of deserted Indian villages near Upper Agency. Their course took them directly toward the grassy clump where two or three Sioux were lying, waiting for the Army to get under way; the Indians had no choice except to shoot or be run over.

One of the soldiers was killed at once. His battle-wise comrades jumped out of the wagons and withdrew, firing as they went, giving the rest of the men of the 3rd time to come up and form a line of battle. The Sioux, with all hope of surprise gone, came out of hiding and moved in to attack; in turn the scrappy Renville Rangers hurried up to support a threatened flank of the veterans of the 3rd. Sibley, help-lessly watching a battle develop without having a thing to do with it, became concerned at the exposed position of the 3rd and the Renville Rangers, and two or three times sent orders for them to fall back on the main body of the Army. The cocky veterans paid no attention to him, and after a brisk battle, the Sioux gave way and ran. Just as very few of Sibley's forces had a chance to get in the fighting before it was over, so only a fraction of the Sioux were near enough to reach the battlefield. The main engagement lasted a very short time; desultory firing kept up for possibly as much as two hours on the outer fringes. This, in Minnesota history, is the Battle of Wood Lake, and Colonel Sibley was promoted to brigadier general for winning the great victory.

However, it had been a bitter fight for those who were engaged. Seven soldiers were killed or mortally wounded, another thirteen wounded. Counting the Indian casualties was, as usual, an inexact science because the Sioux carried off their dead if humanly possible, but they had been driven back so sharply that they had abandoned fourteen bodies. Chief Mankato died in the battle, although his body was carried away. Sibley was quite shocked to learn that all the Indian dead had been scalped and gave his troops a stern lecture about acting like civilized gentlemen. There was some attempt to blame it on the savage instincts of the half-breeds among the Renville Rangers, but no one was very convinced.

The Sioux now realized the hopelessness of their struggle and began a flight into Dakota Territory. Not all ran. The Wahpeton and Sisseton bands had remained officially neutral even though large numbers of their young men had joined the fighting, and most of them felt they had nothing to fear. A considerable number of the Lower Reservation Indians had also remained apart from the fighting and refused to join the exodus. There were some, too, who had fought through the uprising and believed that they were too unimportant to be noticed if they remained and kept their mouths shut.

The Sioux were camped about twenty miles above Wood Lake. A large army and a beaten foe did nothing to speed Sibley. He went into camp for another two days at Wood Lake, probably to contemplate his victory, and then took another two days to march the twenty miles to the Indian camp. His explanation for his leisurely advance was still that he did not want to endanger the lives of the captives. However, they were almost slain while he dawdled; their preservation was due in little part to his efforts.

Little Crow, making ready for the retreat west, debated the massacre of the captives as a last gesture of defiance at the soldiers closing in. Other leaders whose hands were bloodied were all for it; those whose consciences were clear were against a step that would turn the whites irrevocably against all Sioux. While the arguing went on, Chief Wabasha quietly moved his tepees next to the camp of the captives, indicating that he was taking them under his protection. Little Crow had no wish for a civil war right then; he forgot about a general killing and moved on out into Dakota. When Sibley at last appeared, deporting himself like a conqueror, as a contemporary observer described his arrival, the captives were perfectly safe in the custody of friendly chiefs and Sibley was doing his posturing principally for Sioux who had supported him from the beginning.

There were 107 white and 162 half-breed captives in the camp, which was quickly named Camp Release. Almost all were women and children; the Sioux had shown little mercy toward adult males, and none at all toward those of all-white blood. The Sioux women had made some effort to dress up the captives a little before the arrival of the soldiers but they were still a pathetic band, ragged and hungry and showing in their haunted faces the mental strain they had undergone. Some of the

younger women had been badly misused; others among the captives
seem to have been treated about as well as the conditions of an Indian
camp at war could give them to expect. "There were some instances of
stolidity among them," Sibley wrote, "but for the most part the poor
creatures, relieved of the horrible suspense in which they had been left,
and some of the younger women freed from the loathsome attentions to
which they had been subjected by their brutal captors, were fairly
overwhelmed with joy." But the attentions of the brutal captors were
not universally loathsome. Sibley, writing to his wife, mentioned one
married woman who had become infatuated with the Indian who had
captured her. Some of the women remained with the army to be witnesses against the Sioux but the rest of the captives were sent back to
Fort Ridgely and then to the settlements.

5. "HAVE MERCY UPON US, O JEHOVAH"

To Sibley, his mission from that point on was one of vengeance, the
speedy hanging of many Sioux. Detachments scouted the surrounding
country, bringing in Indians, until eventually they had collected about
two thousand. The only flaw with plans for mass executions to make the
Minnesota frontier happy was that the really big fish were far out of
reach in Dakota Territory. Most of those Sibley had rounded up were
there because they had no reason to run. However, he did have about
four hundred who looked like prime suspects.

A court was organized which had no close counterpart in either civil
or military jurisprudence; after a brief warm-up period to establish
working procedures, it became so efficient that it could try and sentence
a man to the gallows in as little as five minutes. It was not considered
necessary to prove actual killing or other crime; taking part in a
battle, or even presence at the scene of a battle were ruled to be pun-
ishable by death.

In the latter part of October, with hard frosts biting down on the
prairie at night and the growing possibility that before long an early
snowstorm might pin an unprepared army in an empty region, Sibley
took his prisoners and his troops to Lower Agency, where the trials
continued in the only building that had escaped the torches of the Sioux.
The work of justice was finished in the first week in November. Almost
400 men had been tried; 306 of these were sentenced to hang for

murder, rape, or, in most instances, simply for taking part in a battle. Another 16, with tempered justice, were given prison sentences for robbery.

Those who were considered free of any culpable act—approximately 1,700 and mostly women and children—were taken to Fort Snelling; the convicted men were taken in irons two days later to a prison stockade at Mankato. The first group was set upon by enraged citizens as it passed through the village of Henderson on the lower Minnesota; no Sioux raider had come within miles of Henderson, nor did it occur to the villagers that the Indians passing through were almost entirely those who had remained friendly during the uprising. The townspeople were now admirably valiant in defending their homes and one especially intrepid soul snatched an infant from its mother, fatally injuring it.

The condemned men had even worse misfortune; they passed through New Ulm on the day the bodies of those killed in the defense were being taken from temporary graves in the streets and reinterred in the cemetery. Villagers, especially the women, set upon the Sioux with everything from hot water to scissors and pitchforks. The infantry guard had to use bayonets to drive back the angry, clamoring townsfolk; several soldiers were injured along with more than a dozen of the prisoners.

Even though the nation was more concerned with the Battle of Antietam in mid-September than with an Indian uprising on an obscure frontier, there were great protests in the East at the idea of executing more than three hundred Indians. Minnesota settlers, looking over the wreckage of a very considerable portion of their state, felt no such compunction, and wanted a vengeance as ruthless as possible. There were rare exceptions, and one of the foremost was the Right Reverend Henry Whipple, Episcopal Bishop of the Missionary District of Minnesota. Bishop Whipple went to President Lincoln himself to plead the Indian's cause; the uprising, he said, was the result of years of lies, broken promises, and being shamelessly cheated and victimized. Lincoln was convinced, although Whipple was virtually ostracized in Minnesota. The Minnesota Sioux, the President decreed, had been fighting a war, and therefore those who had done nothing beyond fighting in its battles were to be treated as any other prisoners of war. The records were gone over; the work of Sibley's court collapsed. Using the new criterion, the list of condemned men was reduced to forty who had committed murder or rape. One of these was later pardoned, another died a natural death before the day of execution.

The thirty-eight were hanged at Mankato on the day after Christmas, 1862, on a single scaffold built in the form of a hollow square. They met their deaths bravely, though far from stolidly. They kept up a death chant, a monotonous "Hi-yi-yi-yi, Hi-yi-yi-yi" through most of the proceedings, and although hanging is an odious way of death to an Indian, they made no objection to the placing of the noose or other preparations until the hoods were drawn over their heads. This, though, was too ignominious for many of them; they tried to object but the traditional ritual of legal life-taking had to be gone through in its entirety.

At the last there was a great deal of weaving and twisting around among the condemned as they worked to get their tied hands in a position to grasp the hand of a neighbor in a final handclasp. For two or three seconds there was absolute silence, not only among the troops drawn up around the scaffold but also in the surrounding crowd of spectators. Then three taps on a drum, at the third the executioner cut a single large rope which sprung all traps, dropping all thirty-eight men into eternity at the same moment. It did not go entirely without a hitch. A rope broke and the body of one man, Rattling Runner, dropped heavily to the ground under the scaffold. He was quite plainly dead or dying, but a new rope was attached and his body was hoisted again, to dangle yet a while for the edification of the spectators.

The hangman was a man named William Duley who had escaped during the massacre at Lake Shetek. The bodies of three of his children were still lying on the frozen prairie—would, in fact, not be buried until the following October when a military expedition would reach the spot and gather the bleached bones—and his wife and two other children, according to somewhat unclear records, were still captives of the Sioux who had taken them on their retreat toward the Missouri River. Duley, on his day of vengeance, did not know whether they were dead or alive. He was a very willing executioner.

It was discovered afterward that one of the men put to death was the wrong one; it was possible that other mistakes had been made. Sibley's court had operated at such high speed that it had kept only scanty records; it was difficult or impossible to transliterate many Sioux names very closely into the English alphabet which lacked some of the necessary sounds—and no one had been very careful at the time anyway because it seemed silly to go to much trouble for an Indian who was being sentenced to death. However, it created problems later when it turned out that many of the Indians were not going to be dead in a hurry after all—and it was not the white jailers who paid for the inevitable mistakes that were made.

The bodies were buried in a shallow mass grave on a sandy flat by the river, but they did not rest quietly there even during the night. A number of doctors from surrounding towns had come to the hanging with something more in mind than an interest in watching human beings sent to death; after dark they dug up the bodies and drew lots to decide how they should be assigned. The doctors were interested in turning them into articulated skeletons, almost a necessity for a physician in that day of few medical schools. A skeleton was a ready reference book he could turn to for help when a balky plow horse left a farmer with a tricky fracture; it was also an important training aid because likely youths became doctors by "reading medicine" with an established physician and it had no substitute for demonstrating bone anatomy.

Among the doctors was a William W. Mayo from Le Sueur. He had been at the New Ulm battle and had attended wounded all during the uprising; in the drawing of lots he had gotten the body of Cut Nose, the same battle-shy cutthroat who had been the companion of Chief Shakopee on his raids; he had refused to flee although he well knew what would happen to him at the hands of the Americans. Two of the young men Dr. Mayo first taught anatomy with the help of the skeleton of Cut Nose were his own sons, William and Charles. Later—much later—father and sons went on to establish the Mayo Clinic at Rochester, Minnesota, which soon became world-famous. It thus becomes a matter for interesting philosophical discussion whether Cut Nose, through his bleached and wire-hung bones, had thus expiated any small part of his vast guilt.

The men who were reprieved from the gallows by Lincoln, almost 270, were still technically prisoners of war. They were kept in the Mankato prison during the winter, where they were gentle and tractable prisoners, and almost all of them became Christians. In the spring they were put on the steamboat *Favorite* and sent down the Mississippi to Rock Island, Illinois, where a prison camp for Confederate soldiers was located. As the steamboat passed the flats below Fort Snelling where their families, along with the other Sioux, brought down from the Upper Reservation, had been penned in a stockade during the winter, the prisoners aboard sang the hymn "Have Mercy Upon Us, O Jehovah."

At Rock Island, they were no trouble at all; they were soon permitted to come and go freely, and began working as farm hands and doing odd jobs in the neighborhood. At the end of three years they were allowed to join their families who in the meantime had been sent to a reservation in Dakota Territory. Their people had not had it easy since they had passed them at Mendota and saluted them with a hymn; the government had put them on a barren reservation, ignoring completely that many of the deported Sioux had had nothing to do with the uprising. The reservation had been so poor, however, that even the government had taken notice and had given them something better.

Minnesota had got rid of almost all her Sioux—and nearly with a clear conscience, because if some of them had made war, it stood to reason that all should be made to pay, even those who had remained friends of the whites during the hostilities. There were, however, about twenty-five whose services to the settlers had been so outstanding that they, with their families, were permitted to remain. Their descendants are still there, farmers in large part, most of them living around the two agencies which still are in operation, as hard-working citizens as the state could wish.

Payment of annuities to all Santee were stopped for four years, 1863–66, with no favors granted to bands that had been neutral or had aided the whites. The funds so saved were used to pay off settlers' claims for damages, although a committee set up to take a hard look at some of the claims reported that most of them had been greatly exaggerated, and also that much of the looting of abandoned houses had not been done by Sioux warriors at all but by white men willing to take advantage of another's misfortune.

Nevertheless, the uprising depopulated a large strip of frontier. An estimated 30,000 fled their homes and had retreated, some to the lower Minnesota Valley, some as far as the Mississippi, some all the way back to homes in the East, never to return. Twenty-three counties were devastated and left almost completely without humans, a region 50 by 200 miles. More than a year later no one had returned to nineteen of those counties; in the other four only a portion of the former population was cautiously returning.

No one knows how many died in the uprising. For years 737 was accepted as reasonably close to the truth; more recently experts have, by some legerdemain, counted the dead again and one says there were 644 dead, another that 490 died. The truth is, it was impossible to tell. With new families arriving daily, there was no way of knowing how many people were on the frontier when the Indians struck; there is no way of knowing how many of those who were presumed to have abandoned their farms and fled east actually were slain out on the prairie. Settlers were killed or crawled to die in lonely thickets or in the tall grass of marshes; it was a year or more before other white men returned to the vicinity and by that time what had been human was reduced to bones and tatters of cloth with grass and prairie flowers growing through them. It might be years, if ever, before a plow turned up the grass-veiled bones, and by then who could say whether it was victim of the massacre or possibly an Indian killed in a battle between Sioux and Chippewa fifty years before?

The spring following the outbreak, a punitive army headed into Dakota Territory to chastize the Sioux. It went in two columns, General Sibley leading the southern one of 3,300 men, which set out from the upper end of the former reservation, Brigadier General Alfred Sully in command of the other, with a strength of about 3,000, which headed across the prairies from up in the Red River Valley. The strategy was to catch the tribesmen in a pincers, but it was a pincers so ponderous in its closing that the nimble, fast-moving Indians, even with their families and baggage, were able to sidestep, and only a couple of inconclusive brushes occurred.

Little Crow attempted to enlist the aid of the western Sioux, but without success although the presence of the troops bumbling around west of Devil's Lake was not doing anything to calm the western bands. The Santee chief then went to Canada on the strength of a vague and pathetic legend that the British were so grateful for help given by the Sioux in the War of 1812 that they would return the favor whenever their aid was needed. The legend was tied up with a cannon supposedly captured during the war and held by the British for the Sioux, the sort of story told around tepee fires by old men until it becomes hazy and distorted. There was, of course, no cannon and no promise.

There was blood on the prairie in Minnesota again in 1863 as small bands of warriors cut in behind the punitive army and killed thirty settlers in scattered raids. One band was audacious enough to camp overnight on a hill within sight of St. Paul. Late in the summer, a farmer named Chauncey Lamson and his son came undetected on an Indian man and youth picking berries in a clearing on some brushy land, and in an unheroic engagement, shot the man from ambush. The youth escaped. The body was taken to Hutchinson four or five miles to the south, but when no one could identify it, it was thrown into the offal pit of a slaughter-house.

A month later, a sixteen-year-old Indian youth was captured. His name, he said, was Wowinapa; he was the son of Little Crow, and had been with his father when the one-time powerful chief was shot down while picking berries. Little Crow, according to his son, was not in Minnesota for revenge but only to steal a few horses. Wowinapa was permitted to join the few Sioux who were still in the state, and in time, this son of a great war chief became the man who founded the Young Men's Christian Association among the Sioux in Minnesota.

White man's justice caught up with Chief Shakopee, who had wanted war but had been interested only in murder and rapine. He was captured near the Canadian border (some accounts say he was kidnaped from Canada where he had taken refuge, others that he had been lured across the border), and brought to Fort Snelling where he was hanged late in 1865. There is a legend that, as Shakopee stood on the gallows on the river flats below the fort, the whistle of the first railroad locomotive in the valley echoed between the limestone river bluffs. Shakopee gestured. "As the Indian goes out, the white man comes in," he said. It is a fine story, very symbolic. The only thing wrong with it is that it did not happen.

III

Nits Make Lice

1. PIKES PEAK OR BUST

THERE was no breathing spell on the plains after the Sioux uprising. The times of peace were over because there were too many white men around by then, coming into friction with the Indians too often and at too many places. Emigrants, settlers, railroad builders, buffalo hunters, prospectors, a hundred kinds and types were moving into or across the one-time Indian Country. Virtually every one of them found Indians in his way, and hardly anyone considered that any native had any rights that needed to be respected. The result was foregone. There would be fighting until the tribes were finally subdued and pushed off the land.

Even while the Santee Sioux were raiding on the Minnesota frontier, the next war was in the making. In Colorado and western Kansas, the Cheyenne and Arapaho were being slowly pushed toward a conflict they would do their best to avoid. However, there was no escaping what had become inevitable almost the day the first white man appeared in their country.

The Cheyennes and Arapahoes lived on the high plains between the Platte and Arkansas Rivers. They had been closely confederated for no one knows how long, probably since soon after they came out on the plains and became mounted buffalo-hunting peoples. The Cheyennes were a farming tribe in Minnesota when the first explorers came; the original home of the Arapahoes is not known except that it was east of the Missouri and may also have been in Minnesota. Forced out onto the plains by the Chippewas and Sioux, they both became horsemen, formed their close alliance, and after several generations of warfare with the Sioux, Crow, and other northern tribes, gradually moved south of the Upper Platte River.

It was the Cheyennes who were the leaders in the confederation; they had a stronger tribal organization and a more highly developed culture, and the easy-going Arapahoes were usually content to follow where their Cheyenne partners pointed the way. Both were brave opponents in war, the Cheyennes especially fought with a courage and dash that often bordered on fanaticism. No other tribe, except the much more numerous Sioux, did so much to delay American occupation of the plains; it is said that no other tribe lost such a large part of its people fighting the whites.

In 1835, trader Charles Bent persuaded a large hunting party of Cheyennes to make a decision of great importance to the entire tribe. Three years earlier, in 1832, Bent, with his brother William and Ceran St. Vrain, had established the trading post known as Bent's Fort on the Arkansas River and the Santa Fe Trail near the site of present La Junta, Colorado. It was to the partners' benefit to have friendly and industrious Indians in the area as a dependable source of buffalo robes for trade, so Bent proposed to the Cheyennes that they move to the Arkansas River region. About half the tribe, with about the same proportion of the Arapahoes, agreed to make the change.

From that time on, the tribes were divided into Northern and Southern Cheyennes and Arapahoes. The Southern bands, in the wars ahead, would usually be allied with the Comanches and Kiowas; the Northerners, who roamed in the region of the upper Platte, fought with the Sioux.

When the great council was held at Fort Laramie in 1851, the chiefs who were trying to set the boundaries of tribal hunting grounds agreed that the Cheyennes and Arapahoes were firmly established on the vast tract of high plains and foothills between the North Platte on the north, the Arkansas on the south, the Rockies on the west, and, roughly, about the 101st meridian on the east. This, their hunting range, included large parts of four existing states, but chiefly eastern

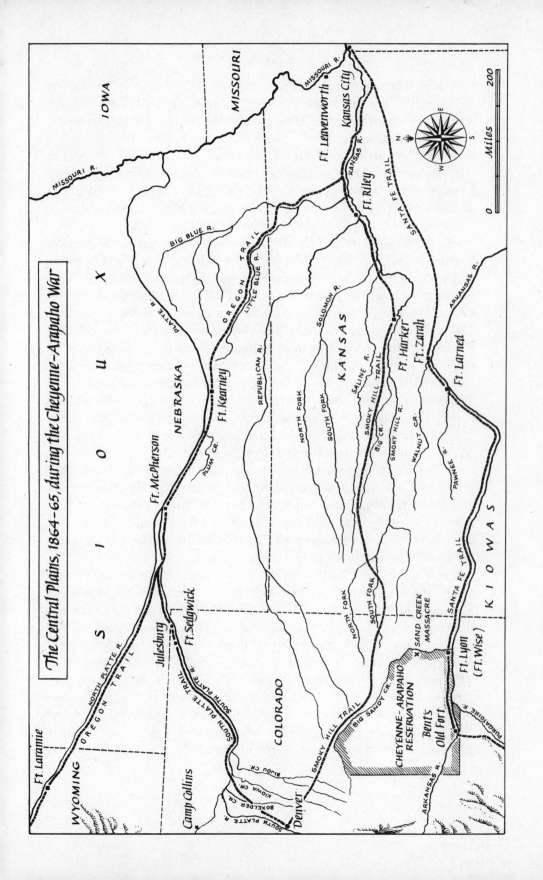

The Central Plains, 1864–65, during the Cheyenne–Arapaho War

Colorado. The two tribes, however, held no rigid monopoly on hunting in the region. The Sioux often came down from the north after buffalo, while the Comanches and Kiowa crossed the Arkansas from the south. This was no cause for friction; the Cheyenne had buried the hatchet with the three tribes and put an end to old enmities with them. The Utes to the west were a different matter; they remained traditional enemies; when they came down onto the plains to hunt buffalo there was always a bitter fight if they met warriors of the Plains tribes, and there was frequent raiding back and forth for scalps.

The hunting grounds of the two tribes was rich in game, the heart of a grazing land over which the buffalo herds flowed northward in spring and south in the fall in their great seasonal rhythms. The Oregon Trail lay on its northern edge and the Santa Fe Trail was a thin line on its southern border, but between it was free of white travelers and the various blessings of civilization they brought. On its western side, the Rockies rose in a towering wall unbroken by any passes feasible for emigrant wagons. All in all, there seemed no reason why Americans would either want to settle on the land or beat a path across it.

It was, of course, too pleasant a situation to have lasted long, and it began to crumble with the finding of gold in the Rocky Mountains in the general region across which the long shadow of Pikes Peak fell. There had been rumors of gold for years, but in 1858 a party of white and Cherokee prospectors went out and had a good look. When they found gold, the news was trumpeted back to the Missouri River cities, amplified with every mile, bringing on the hysteria that the word "gold" always causes. No one paid any attention to the rest of the story that came later: pickings had been so slim that all but thirteen of the original seventy prospectors had quit and gone home.

The Panic of 1857 had set an army of unemployed loose, and Cherry Creek at the foot of the mountains offered the miracle that would end all their troubles. Many headed west in 1858 even though the season was drawing on, and passed a miserable winter in cold, leaky shacks. The next spring, though, brought the real flood of gold hunters. As in every gold rush, the ratio of fools and incompetents was high. They came with pack mules, in wagons, on foot with packs on their backs, even pushing handcarts and wheelbarrows. "Pikes Peak or Bust," the banners on the sides of their covered wagons said, and they got laughs on the way out, but the laughter became hollow, because for too many it was a matter of going bust. Many of them turned around within two or three months and started back across the plains, putting up new signs on their wagons, "Busted, by Gosh."

While the homeward parade was going on, another strike was made, and the word went out that the North Fork of Clear Creek, not Cherry Creek, was the place to find wealth beyond all dreaming. The tide reversed, another gold rush was on. And once again most of the rushers found little gold; they chased rumors up and down the flanks of the Rockies but before the summer was over, many of them were heading east once more.

The gold rushers, with all their running back and forth, had driven a trail right down the middle of the Cheyenne domain, along the Smoky Hill River midway between the Platte and the Arkansas. The buffalo avoided the long lines of men in wagons and men on foot (there were almost a hundred thousand in 1859) moving under their banner of dust, and the Indians found it difficult to live on their once-fat land.

At first the tribesmen had been friendly. Little Raven, leading chief of the Arapahoes, went into Denver when it was a new mining camp to promise the prospectors his people would remain at peace. An Arapaho camp sat near the shacks of miners; the Indian men would go out hunting or after Ute scalps while the miners went to work in the gold diggings. This friendly arrangement came to an end when a gang of miners headed for the Arapaho camp while the men were gone and raped some of the women.

Such incidents quickly dispelled early good will. After the first couple of frantic years of gold rushing, mining became a big-capital business and the surviving camps became communities where wives and school-teachers displaced most of the fancy ladies. And north and south, along the foothills, ranchers and farmers were settling in the more fertile and well-watered valleys. There was no place for the Indians on the western part of their own lands any more; they did not fit into the new scheme of things.

A government report, drawn up later when a great many were dead and beyond all caring, agreed that the use of the Smoky Hill Trail was probably based on sound legal right since the Fort Laramie Treaty had reserved the right of transit over Indian lands for travelers. But. far beyond crossing these lands, the travelers "took possession of them for the purpose of mining, and, against the protest of the Indians, founded cities, established farms, and opened roads. Before 1861 the Cheyenne and Arapaho had been driven from the mountain regions down upon the waters of the Arkansas and were becoming sullen and discontented because of this violation of their rights.

"The Indians saw their former homes and hunting grounds overrun by a greedy population thirsting for gold," the commissioners continued in their report, becoming lyrical in their indignation as they warmed to their subject. "They saw their game driven east to the plains, and soon found themselves the objects of jealousy and hatred. They too must go. The presence of the injured is too often painful to the wrong-doer, and innocence offensive to the eyes of guilt. It now becomes apparent that what had been taken by force must be retained by the ravisher, and nothing was left for the Indian but to ratify a treaty consecrating the act."

There were, as the report indicates, people who sympathized with the Indian. Unfortunately, most such were in the East where they could do little beside send up clouds of words of protest, while the frontiersmen who believed that the only good Indians were dead were right on the spot where they could put their ideas into practice. The treaty which the report mentions was signed by the two tribes at Fort Wise * on the Arkansas River on February 18, 1861. They gave up their huge range for a triangular tract lying—except for an inconsequential portion —between the Arkansas River and Big Sandy Creek which flows into the river from the northwest (the stream was almost always called simply Sand Creek, even though there is another stream of that name in Colorado; the Indian reserve was invariably designated the Sand Creek Reservation). It was a miserable piece of land, not only a patch on the former range in terms of size, but sterile, sandy and useless. It was so poor that only a few of the chiefs present at Fort Wise could be induced to sign the treaty, and some of those who did sign claimed later that they had been fast-talked into believing the agreement meant something other than what the government claimed it did.

* The person who attempts to learn more about Fort Wise may well walk into a nomenclatural ambush where he will be shot down from all sides. In 1849, William Bent, by then sole proprietor of Bent's Fort and its trading business, blew up the adobe post with gunpowder for reasons that are only poorly explained by tradition, and moved forty miles down the river where he built Bent's New Fort, a stone structure. In 1859, the government leased the New Fort, built barracks, and christened it Fort Wise in honor of the governor of Virginia. In 1861, governors of Virginia no longer being held in high esteem, the name was changed to Fort Lyon in honor of Union General Nathaniel Lyon who had been killed in battle in Missouri. To further compound confusion, high waters endangered the fort so that New Fort Lyon was built upstream in 1866, on the site where the present Fort Lyon stands today.

The Indians did not stay on the new reservation much of the time—they would have gone hungry if they had—but continued to roam freely, managing to remain peaceful even though they were being crowded more and more by the growing number of white men who traveled the plains. It was rather extraordinary, the way the two tribes continued to abide by their promises, given at Fort Laramie, to refrain from making war, especially since they—and especially the Cheyennes—were proud and warlike peoples. This is not to say that the plains were any place for a Sunday School picnic; there were plenty of young braves who were tired of forbearance and could not always be depended on to pass by a chance-met white man without lifting his scalp if it could be accomplished without too much risk. But, with minor exceptions, they kept the peace.

Most of the exceptions, at first, were the result of actual want. By 1863, both tribes were suffering greatly from hunger, and were afflicted with a variety of diseases to which malnutrition and lowered resistance had made them easy prey. Their agent, Samuel G. Colley at Fort Lyon, had reported that winter that no buffalo were to be found within 200 miles of the reservation, and precious little game of any kind. The Indians had made a number of attacks on wagon trains, but not for scalps; they had robbed the wagons of the food and, in almost every case, left the men unharmed. Colley, with as little understanding of the desperation of hunger as of grammar, wrote in his report, "Most of the depradations committed by them are from starvation. It is hard for them to understand that they have no right to take from them that have, when in a starving condition."

Major Colley was not going to be of much help to the Indians in the days ahead, although occasionally he appeared to be stirred by a feeling of mission and responsibility. His son, Dexter, was a trader, and it was commonly believed, and fairly well established, that Major Colley diverted a good portion of annuity goods to son Dexter, who later sold them back to the Indians.

Fortunately, times improved somewhat for the tribesmen after this hunger year, although their relations with the Americans did not get better. The beginning of the incidents that led to war appears to have come April 11, 1864 when a rancher named Ripley rode into Camp Sanborn on the South Platte River trail, northeast of Denver, with an excited report that Indians had driven stock from his ranch on Bijou Creek. It is very possible they had. On the other hand, men who had been around the country said that every time a horse or cow strayed out of sight, a greenhorn lost his head and blamed it on the Indians; a few of the more cynical pointed out there was no proof Ripley ever had any stock.

The next morning, Lieutenant Dunn with forty men was sent out with orders to find and disarm the Indians and recover the stolen stock. Ripley went along as guide. The detachment eventually came on a party of Indians driving some horses Ripley claimed were his. The soldiers had no interpreter along, and Dunn was too impatient for much parleying by sign language; he demanded that the horses be handed over. The Indians willingly agreed (later, much later, after all the damage was done, a less impatient Colorado officer talked to some of the Indians involved, who said the horses were not stolen but strayed beasts they had found; this may or may not have been so), but when the Indians came up to shake the soldiers' hands, the latter began trying to snatch their weapons away. It was a foolish move. Arrows were flying in an instant; the detachment found itself involved in more than it had bargained for. Two soldiers were killed, two mortally wounded, another two less seriously hurt. Lieutenant Dunn was certain his men had killed a dozen Indians, but there was no proof that even one had died.

The Colorado authorities apparently felt that they had a small Indian war on their hands now, or at least, could build the situation up into one. There had never been any doubt about official policy; Governor John Evans had advocated war with the Plains Indians from the time he took office. A few days after Dunn's fight, Major Jacob Downing was sent to Camp Sanborn to handle Indian-fighting operations. He did not have long to wait for action; on April 18 word came that Cheyennes had driven settlers from a ranch on the South Platte. Downing took sixty men and went in hot pursuit. The only trouble was that, although the company rode more than fifty miles east along the river, it found no Cheyennes, no deserted ranch, no evicted settlers.

Having found nothing, Downing, with consummate logic, decided on a campaign to punish the Indians for their outlawry. He made a new start from Camp Sanborn with forty men, and at a place called Cedar Canyon found a Cheyenne village to punish. Then, as this fearless knight later described it: "We commenced shooting. I ordered the men to commence killing them. . . . They lost . . . some twenty-six killed and thirty wounded. . . . I burnt up their lodges and everything I could get hold of. . . . We captured about one hundred head of stock, which was distributed among the boys."

The distribution of the horses helps to explain one of the powerful forces that moved many of the "boys" to take the field against Indians, not only in Colorado but in other arenas. Such divisions of spoils often made the boys over-eager to start trouble so that there might be some tangible benefits to show for their time and trouble. The troops in Colorado during the Civil War were entirely volunteers, local boys with all the frontier contempt for the rights of the red man, and many of them hoping to reap some reward.

The scattered actions continued. Colonel John Chivington, commanding all Colorado Volunteers, had ordered Lieutenant George S. Eayre with an independent battery of artillery out early in April to pursue Indians who reportedly had stolen a couple of hundred head of cattle from a government contractor. The Indians denied the theft, but no one listened. No one knows; perhaps they took the cattle, perhaps they did not. Lieutenant Eayre with fifty-four men and two twelve-pound howitzers headed east, across the line into Kansas where he came on a village that had obviously just been abandoned by its frightened people ahead of his coming; he destroyed tremendous quantities of dried buffalo meat, powder and lead, robes, and various equipment and utensils and burned down tepees. Fifteen miles farther on he found another empty village which he treated in the same fashion.

Eayre returned to Denver to replenish his supplies, commandeered a dozen or more wagons from their astonished owners in the street, and returned to Kansas again, bearing orders, so it is claimed, to "kill Cheyennes whenever and wherever found." On May 16, about fifty miles northwest of Fort Larned on the Arkansas, he found a large camp of Cheyennes—not deserted this time. He was met by Chief Lean Bear, who rode out with his son to greet the soldiers. There are two versions of many of the episodes of this conflict; there is only one of what happened next. The soldiers let the two Indians approach, hands upraised in the universally understood peace sign until they were within point-blank range; then they were gunned down.

The results were more than Eayre had bargained for. The Cheyennes began buzzing like angry hornets around the Colorado troops, who lost four dead and three wounded in the resulting battle. Incredible as it may seem, the retreat of the soldiers was facilitated by Black Kettle, leading chief of the Cheyennes, a staunch peace man, who managed to get his warriors under control enough so that Lieutenant Eayre and his command could withdraw to Fort Larned. Eayre immediately sent word of a great victory back to Denver; he was also asked by higher military authority in Fort Leavenworth to the east how he happened to be so far out of his own military jurisdiction.

After Eayre's exploit, Cheyenne Dog Soldiers raided several ranches on Walnut Creek generally north of Fort Larned. Each Plains tribe had several military societies, partly social, partly charged with police duties on the hunt and in various other circumstances. The Dog Society was considered the strictest in discipline of these groups among the Cheyennes; its members also had a reputation as young firebrands. Yet, after spending a night raiding, the Dog Soldiers had killed only one man. Clearly, the Cheyennes still had not quite got the hang of fighting white men.

Lieutenant Eayre, hurrying back without his command to make his report to Colonel Chivington in Denver, met an unlikely person on the way: William Bent, trader, good friend of the Cheyennes. Much had happened since that time, at the old Bent's Fort, when he had persuaded half the Cheyennes and Arapahoes to move down to the Arkansas. He had married a Cheyenne, Owl Woman, and fathered two daughters and three sons, and when his wife had died, he had married her sister, Yellow Woman. He loved the Cheyennes, their blood was in his wife and his own children, and now he listened as Eayre told how he had shot down Cheyennes with no more feeling than he would have squashed a bug.

Whatever Bent's personal feelings he must have submerged them. Shortly thereafter, an Indian rider found him on the plains and gave him a message from Black Kettle. The Cheyennes were upset and worried about Eayre's attack, the chief said; they did not know why he had done such a thing, and they would like Bent to come and talk to them about it. Bent did. Then he went on to Fort Lyon to talk to Colonel Chivington and tell him that the majority of the Indians still wanted peace. The Colorado military leader replied that things were now out of his hands and that he was without the authority to make peace. Besides, he was not interested because now he was making war and meant to continue.

Bent tried again. He pointed out the consequences of a general Indian uprising. There would be attacks along the Oregon and Santa Fe trails. With the soldiers available, it would be impossible to protect all settlers in Kansas, Colorado, and Nebraska in Cheyenne country. Many would be killed. Chivington replied callously that he could not worry about the settlers; they would have to find ways of taking care of themselves. Bent went away half-believing he had heard wrong. The primary role of a frontier military leader was to protect the settlers; here was a military leader who was interested only in killing Indians, and the devil take the settlers.

Colonel John M. Chivington, an elder of the Methodist Church, was a huge man, over six feet tall and more than broad in proportion, weighing at least 250 pounds, little of which was fat since he was enormously barrel-chested. Chivington was a native of Ohio where he had taken up the ministry; he had preached his way westward across half a dozen states before reaching Colorado. In Denver he had been presiding elder of the First Methodist Episcopal Church in the camp, and had gone preaching in neighboring camps, where his size probably saved him much trouble in an era when a minister often had to defend his doctrine with his fists. But whatever his skills in exegesis may have been, he somehow never got even within shouting distance of the real meaning of the religion he was trying to preach, as events abundantly proved.

Chivington's reputation as a military leader, on the other hand, was built on a sound foundation of performance. When he had been offered a chaplain's commission in the 1st Colorado Volunteer Regiment, he had asked instead for a fighting commission. In the one Civil War campaign of consequence west of the Missouri, he had very competently handled volunteer troops in a manner which had contributed considerably to the decisive Union victory over Confederates attempting to invade New Mexico. His political enemies afterward claimed that his lack of interest in a peaceful settlement of the trouble with the Indians was due to his desire to add more luster to his standing as a military hero. Chivington, they said, was planning to go into politics, and in the West, about the best vote-getting record a candidate could have was a period of defending the frontier against the bloodthirsty redskins.

What Chivington and a great many like-minded Indian-fighters needed was a good atrocity to stir people up; they got it on June 11, 1864, when a settler named Ward Hungate, his wife, their four-year-old daughter and an infant child were murdered, their ranch burned, and their stock run off on Box Elder Creek only twenty miles east of

Denver. It was a vicious crime, and when the bodies, scalped, mutilated, and swollen by sun and exposure, were brought into Denver and
put on exhibit, the result was completely predictable. Four young
Arapaho warriors had carried out the senseless raid, but it was accepted
as proof that all Indians were murderers and cut-throats.

2. "KILL AND DESTROY— WHEREVER FOUND"

Governor John Evans of Colorado Territory was beginning to sense
that the mood of the Indians was growing sullen and that big trouble
might be brewing, something beyond the ability of his own Colorado
Volunteers to handle with a few free-ranging attacks on Indian camps.
On June 24 he issued a proclamation that called on the Plains tribes
in the region to report to certain forts and to make their camps in
their vicinity to avoid "being killed by mistake." As evidence that they
were friendly, the Southern Cheyennes and Arapahoes were to go to
Fort Lyon, the Comanches and Kiowas to Fort Larned in Central
Kansas, the northern bands of the Cheyennes and Arapahoes to Camp
Collins in northeast Colorado, and all Sioux in the area were to go to
Fort Laramie. There was to be food and protection for the Indians
who showed their good will and friendliness by gathering at the forts,
harsh punishment for those who remained on the warpath.

The purpose of concentrating the friendly Indians around the forts,
he said, was so that they "should not fall victims to the impossibility
of soldiers discriminating between them and the hostile, upon whom
they must, to do any good, inflict the most severe punishment." The
proclamation was made known to the leading chiefs of the tribes with
the help of Indian agents, traders, and friendly Indians but the response
was not overwhelming. The soldiers had not been showing much interest of recent months in "discriminating between the friendly and the
hostile," and it probably seemed unwise to the Indians to concentrate
around the forts. A couple of small bands came in, but that was all.

William Bent, in the meantime, was doing his best to try to patch
up a peace, and was actually making some headway, doing the work
that should have been done by Indian agent, Major Colley. Of course,
Bent had considerable incentive. Three of his children were somewhere
in the Cheyenne camps. George and Charles were living—and would

soon be fighting—as warriors. Julia was tending a cooking pot beside a tepee; she had married a man like herself, the half-breed son of a trader married to a Cheyenne woman. William Bent had sent all his five half-breed children except Julia back to Westport (very long-since swallowed by Kansas City) to be educated, but as they grew older, these three had felt more at home with their mother's people.

Whatever his incentive, Bent worked hard. He arranged discussions at Fort Larned between the Cheyenne chiefs and the Army officers in charge—which were very nearly wrecked at the very beginning by the commanding officer, Captain Permeter, a rum-pot who antagonized the Indians by his arrogant manner. Bent, however, had smoothed things over and had moved on to expand his peace missions when a large band of Kiowas, led by Chief Satanta, had camped near the fort to hold a scalp dance.

Satanta, in the next few years, was to be one of the more troublesome antagonists of the United States government. Yet only months earlier, in April, a government physician out vaccinating the Plains tribes against smallpox had found the Kiowa a friendly people, and Satanta a hospitable host. The chief spread carpets in his lodge for his guests to sit on, and had painted boards about three feet by twenty inches, ornamented with brass tacks around the edges, on which he had his meals served. When meals were ready, he announced them by blowing on a French horn.

But Satanta was as touchy as hot gunpowder. Now, three or four months after the physician had found him such a pleasant dinner companion, the Kiowa chief and a cousin left the scalp dance and rode toward the gate of Fort Larned, for reasons now unknown. The fort command had directed that Indians not be permitted to approach within a specified distance of the fort; as often happens in such cases, no one had told the Kiowas that such a limitation existed. A sentry warned Satanta and his cousin off but they could not understand what he was trying to tell them. When he raised his gun as a warning, Satanta accepted it as a challenge and whipped two arrows which laid the sentry low (the records do not inform us whether this young man performing a simple duty died as a result). In the confusion that followed, the Kiowa ran off the post's string of horses which were grazing in a meadow well away from the fort, and hastily moved out, safe from pursuit by the horseless troopers.

The Kiowas claimed that it was the first time they had clashed with

United States troops. It would not be the last, and over the next ten years or so, Americans who encountered Satanta were not to find him a genial, French horn-tooting host.

Shortly after the Kiowas had run off the fort's horses, Chief Left Hand with his band of Arapahoes came to Larned. Left Hand very much wanted to keep the peace; he had come to offer his services to help recapture the stolen horses. But as he rode up to the fort to give his offer of assistance in running down Satanta's band, a very jittery sentry guard shot at the Indians with an artillery piece. Their aim was as shaky as their nerves and they did not come near the Arapahoes, but Left Hand's friendliness had been shot full of holes.

In this manner, with a few incidents, Bent's attempts to bring peace back to the plains were completely shattered.

Convinced that the whites had no desire for peace, the Indians met in a great council on the Solomon River in Kansas to talk things over. Present were both northern and southern divisions of the Cheyennes and Arapahoes, as well as the bands of Sioux from the Platte River region. The northern tribes shied away from giving any promise to join in a general war, although the idea of raiding settlements and wagon trains appealed greatly to the young men. They could be depended on to give substantial help when the time came.

And the time came during the first part of August, about the tenth of the month, when war parties struck more or less simultaneously along the entire length of the main trails. The booming stage and freight business of Ben Holladay, transportation king of the plains, came almost to a halt, unable to continue in the face of the mounting debit of drivers' scalps on Cheyenne lances. The stage stations were attacked and burned along both the Smoky Hill Trail and the northern road, which followed the Platte River (on the Oregon Trail) to the forks of the river, and then went along the South Platte to Denver. Isolated farms were burned, settlers killed, small parties of emigrants on the trails wiped out. At Plum Creek on the Platte Trail the Indians caught a party of thirteen in ten wagons; nine were murdered, two women and two children taken captive, the wagons looted and burned. At Ewbank Station a family of ten was killed and mutilated. Ben Holladay's general superintendent stated that for 370 miles every ranch but one was "deserted and property abandoned to the Indians."

Holladay was still claiming damages from the government fifteen years after the war. In view of the magnificent deliberation with which the Federal government operates on such matters, that in itself means nothing, but the supporting affidavits are interesting. Driver George Carlyle related how he had come on the bodies of the nine victims of the Plum Creek massacre lying amid the burned-out remains of their wagons and had interrupted his trip to help bury them; he told how every ranch between Fort Kearney on the Platte in mid-Nebraska and Julesburg on the South Platte in northeast Colorado had been abandoned—and in most cases, burnt to the ground; he described his wild flight of twenty miles, whipping up the horses on his stagecoach to stay ahead of pursuing Indians.

The Cheyennes are known in Western history as fearless foemen, but during this war they appeared to exercise caution and restraint. There were none of the headlong, reckless charges so typical of the Cheyenne in battle; they moved in small bands to attack a stage station when the chance for surprise was good, waited along the trails for wagon trains and stagecoaches, and did not move if they saw that their prospective prey was better guarded than they had planned on.

There were no really notable battles. Indians fell on the advance guard of troops moving along the Pawnee Fork of the Arkansas River west of Fort Larned and almost wiped them out; east of the fort they struck a government wagon train, killing fourteen teamsters. In all, about two hundred whites lost their lives during the summer, most of them ranchers and travelers. Denver was never in any danger for the Indians did not come within miles of it, but it had its scares—and its hysterical moments. One night, the entire population was sent racing in panic to the two sturdiest stone buildings in town when a wild-eyed horseman galloped into town with the news that the Indians were coming. The buildings were turned into forts with women and children on the second floor; at one building, two men stood ready with axes to chop away the supports of an outside stairway the moment an Indian appeared. Nothing happened; no Indians showed up anywhere near. However, if Denver did not suffer from Indians, it did have some troubles with food shortages. Most of its provisions came across the plains on Ben Holladay's wagon trains; after that route was cut food supplies dropped alarmingly. For a while flour was selling at $25 for a hundred pounds.

During this time, the Cheyennes and Arapahoes were not the only Indians making war. A number of Sioux were taking part along the Platte, while the Kiowa and Comanche were raiding in the south into

Texas, driving off hundreds of horses and mules and killing many settlers. The Comanches were taking full advantage of both sides' preoccupation with the Civil War to indulge some of their old hate of Texas and Texans.

Governor Evans, in the meantime, had been keeping the telegraph wires hot to Washington. Not one for understatement, the Governor shrilled that all tribes, from the Canadian border to Texas, had formed an alliance for war and would soon be screaming down on the whites the length of the plains. When a report was brought to him that a man and boy were said to have been killed by Indians a few days earlier south of Denver, he whipped off a message to Washington: "Extensive Indian depredations, with murder of families, occurred yesterday thirty miles south of Denver. Our lines of communication are cut. . . . Large bodies of Indians are undoubtedly near to Denver, and we are in danger of destruction both from attacks of Indians and from starvation. . . ."

However, Evans failed to move anyone in the seats of the mighty in Washington. His plea for Federal troops was answered with what amounted to "Don't you know there's a war on?" and he was no more successful in attempts to get Colorado's own 2nd Volunteer Regiment returned from Missouri where it was serving with the Union Army. He did obtain approval for raising a third regiment to serve for one hundred days only against the Indians. The Governor also issued a proclamation "authorizing all citizens . . . to go in pursuit . . . also to kill and destroy as enemies . . . wherever they may be found, all such hostile Indians."

In all the sad and brutal record of these months, almost the only voices heard were those who, like Evans, could think only in terms of "kill and destroy." It was not unique to Colorado; these were the same voices that were raised everywhere on the plains, and in all our relations with our Indians, from the Atlantic to the Pacific. But while Evans and Colonel Chivington were making plans for military action and killing, William Bent was having still another try at ending hostilities. Major Colley, who should have been trying to make contact with his Indian wards, was sitting at the agency at Fort Lyon after having done a Pontius Pilate washing of hands in a letter to the Governor in late July: "There is no dependence to be put in any of them. I have done everything in my power to keep peace. I now think a little powder and lead is the best food for them."

In late August, Bent sent a letter to the elder chiefs, proposing that they approach the white leaders with overtures for ending hostilities. Bent's plan was upheld in tribal council at which the young hotheads were voted down, and identical letters, written by Bent's son George who was in camp as a warrior, were sent to Major E. W. Wynkoop, commanding officer at Fort Lyon, and to Colley, the Indian agent.

Cheyenne Village, August 29, 1864

We received a letter from Bent wishing us to make peace. We held a council in regard to it. All came to the conclusion to make peace with you, providing you make peace with the Kioways, Comanches, Arapahoes, Apaches * and Sioux.

We are going to send a message to the Kioways and to the other nations about our going to make peace with you.

We heard that you have some Indian prisoners in Denver. We have seven prisoners of yours which we are willing to give up, providing you give up yours. . . . We want true news from you in return.

On receiving the letter, Major Wynkoop took 130 men and a battery of artillery and went to the Cheyenne village at Bend of Timber, 80 miles northeast of Fort Lyon. As usual, the young braves were set to make a fight of it, but the chiefs kept them under control and turned over four white children, promising to give up three more as soon as they could be brought in from other villages.

Major Edward W. Wynkoop was something of an anomaly among the Colorado military leaders. Instead of having a fixation about killing the natives, he recognized a chance to promote peace and seized it. He did not have the authority to make peace, he told the chiefs, but he would accompany a delegation of them to the big white chief, Governor Evans, to make sure that they were not harmed on the way. The chiefs, accepting his sincerity, agreed, and on September 28 a group of them, both Cheyenne and Arapaho, arrived at Camp Weld on the edge of Denver with an escort of Wynkoop's soldiers. Black Kettle, leading Cheyenne chief, was spokesman for the group.

* The Apaches referred to are not the Southwestern tribe of such fearsome reputation for ambush and homicide, but a separate people, the Kiowa Apaches, who were closely confederated with the Kiowas even though they spoke completely different languages. Like the real Apaches, they were members of the great Athabascan linguistic family; the two had probably come down out of the north at somewhat near the same time because their languages were still quite similar. There resemblances ceased; the Kiowa Apaches were so closely attached to the Kiowas as to be considered another band in the tribal circle while the Southwest Apaches were traditional enemies of the Kiowas.

Proofs of their sincerity, said Black Kettle opening the council, were their delivery of the prisoners and the very fact that they were there. "We have come with our eyes shut, following his handful of men, like coming through the fire," Black Kettle said, referring to the trip to Denver under Wynkoop's escort. "All we ask is that we may have peace with the whites. We want to hold you by the hand. You are our father. We have been traveling through a cloud. The sky has been dark since the war began. These braves who are with me are all willing to do what I say. We want to take good tidings home to our people, that they may sleep in peace. I want you to give all these chiefs of the soldiers here to understand that we are for peace, and that we have made peace, that we may not be mistaken by them for enemies."

Black Kettle's proffer of the peace pipe got a chilly reception. For all his screaming to Washington about the terrible threat that hung over Denver and the surrounding region, Evans was strangely reluctant when the opportunity came to remove the danger. The Governor told the chiefs it had taken them a long time to get around to talking about peace instead of coming to the forts when he had told them to; he asked them searching questions about the early incidents in the troubles without conceding that his own boys might have been at least partly at fault.

"I have learned that you understand that as the whites are at war among themselves," the Governor went on, "you think you can now drive the whites from this country; but this reliance is false. The Great Father at Washington has men enough to drive all the Indians off the plains, and whip the rebels at the same time. Now the war with the whites is nearly through, and the Great Father will not know what to do with all his soldiers, except to send them after the Indians on the plains. My proposition to the friendly Indians has gone out; I shall be glad to have them all come in under it. I have no new proposition to make."

Evans said he had no power to make a treaty now that war had begun; the chiefs would have to deal with Major General S. R. Curtis, commanding the Department of Kansas (which also included eastern Colorado), whose headquarters were in Fort Leavenworth. Evans probably did not give a great deal of thought to how a band of tepee-dwelling Indians was to get in touch with the General.

Colonel Chivington spoke last. His speech was short and simple, in a style he evidently felt befitted a blunt fighting man. Most of it, and all its meaning, was contained in a couple of sentences: "I am not a big war chief, but all the soldiers in this country are at my command. My rule' of fighting white men or Indians is to fight them until they lay down their arms and submit."

The chiefs left; their interpreter afterward said that they were "perfectly contented, deeming that the matter was settled," and that their peaceful overtures had been accepted. Many young men were still out on the warpath, but there was a sharp autumn chill in the night air of the high plains that would bring them in soon. Winter was never a war season for the Plains Indians; their grass-fed ponies could run rings around the heavier grain-fed cavalry horses during the spring and summer when the grass was green and thick but they could not extract enough nourishment from frost-killed grass to carry an Indian on the strenuous riding of the warpath.

However, the authorities in Colorado had no wish to call an end to the fighting, whatever impression the chiefs may have received. They were bolstered in their decision by a telegram from General Curtis in Fort Leavenworth, which arrived shortly after the chiefs had left; "I want no peace till the Indians suffer more. . . . I fear Agent of the Interior Department will be ready to make presents too soon. . . . No peace must be made without my directions."

As a matter of fact, Governor Evans had been so interested in proceeding with the war against the Indians that the arrival of Wynkoop with the peace-minded chiefs had been a severe embarrassment. He had pleaded with Washington for help against the murdering redskins; he had depicted a scene of suffering and terror and bleeding bodies, almost with orchestral background, and now that the War Department had given permission for the raising of hundred-day troops against the Indians, he was suddenly and desperately faced with the possibility that the Indians would turn docile and eager to be friendly. It would, to put it in the most simple terms, leave him looking like a fool. He did not want to have to report back to Washington that he had let his fears run away with him and that the hundred-day soldiers, the 3rd Colorado Volunteers, had not been necessary at all. At the close of the council he had expressed his displeasure with Major Wynkoop for bringing the chiefs to Denver: "What shall I do with the third regiment if I make peace?" he asked. They were, he said, "raised to kill Indians and they must kill Indians."

Returned to his post at Fort Lyon, Wynkoop gave the Cheyennes permission to bring their camp in close to the fort, which they did. There, he said, they would be under the protection of the government and completely safe. But they were not completely safe. Governor Evans, rankling over the young major who embarrassed him by bringing the chiefs to Denver, had Wynkoop replaced by Major Scott J. Anthony, whose principles swung like an unlatched gate in the plains wind.

Anthony, in a change-of-command conference with Wynkoop and the chiefs, agreed to continue Wynkoop's permission for the Indians to camp under the protection of the fort. Then, after Wynkoop departed on November 26, the new commander became worried that he might be overstepping his authority and ordered the Indians away from Fort Lyon. They packed up their camp and moved forty miles away to set up a new camp on Sand Creek. There were no complaints; Anthony appears to have handled things in an amicable manner and, as a matter of fact, made Black Kettle a gift out of his own pocket.

3. "ALL ACQUITTED THEMSELVES WELL"

Now Colonel Chivington entered the arena, meaning to get some service out of the 3rd Regiment before its hundred-day period of enlistment drew to a close. There were still a good number of warriors out on the plains, enough to occupy this quondam man of God who had told the chiefs in Denver that his rule of war was simply to fight until his enemies laid down their arms and submitted. He chose, instead, to make his war on Indians who had already submitted.

Along with the 3rd Volunteers, Chivington also had a part of the 1st Volunteers, making a total force of perhaps 750 men. He arrived at Fort Lyon with this force on November 28, after traveling over ground covered with snow, and immediately threw pickets around the fort to prevent any news of his coming or his purpose from getting out. He conferred regarding the situation with Major Anthony, who swung with the winds of opportunity. He heartily hoped the Colonel would attack the Indians, Anthony said, and he would have done it himself if he had had troops enough.

But others at the post were not completely willing to sell principle to curry the colonel's favor. Second Lieutenant Joseph Cramer argued with Chivington that Wynkoop had promised to protect the Indians, and he felt that he and all other post officers who were serving under Wynkoop at the time were indirectly bound by the same promise. Chivington was scornful and abusive, and said, as Cramer later testified, that "he believed it to be right and honorable to use any means under God's heaven to kill Indians that would kill women and children and 'damn any man that was in sympathy with Indians,' and such men as Major Wynkoop and myself had better get out of the U. S. service."

The force was on its way again at nine o'clock that night, and rode until morning. Robert Bent, one of the half-breed sons of William Bent, was forced to go along as guide. George and Charles Bent, and Julia Bent Guerrier were all living in the camp on Sand Creek as Cheyennes. Only one of Bent's children, his oldest daughter, Mary, would miss the tragedy that was almost at hand.

Chivington's instructions to his boys were simple: "Kill and scalp all, big and little; nits make lice." Two of his officers later claimed he made a further inspirational exhortation just before the battle: "Now boys, I shan't say who you shall kill, but remember our murdered women and children."

Dawn comes late at the end of November. The first light was in the sky when the soldiers saw the Indians' pony herd, about five hundred animals, still half-shadows on the frosted grass meadow. Then the conical lodges showed up, in the creek bottom below a low bluff. The cannon were swung around and aimed while a detachment ran off the ponies to deprive the Indians of any chance of fleeing or fighting on horseback.

A woman coming out of a tepee saw the soldiers on the bluff and shouted an alarm. Black Kettle ran from his lodge shouting reassurance, and raised an American flag and a white flag on a pole. Then, in a withering blast, cannon and rifle fire swept through the camp. Few of the Cheyennes had arms or any opportunity to obtain them because the first overwhelming charges drove them away from their lodges. White Antelope, an old chief of seventy, refused to retreat, saying that it was the fault of himself and other chiefs that this was happening. He folded his arms and sang his death song, "Nothing lives long, except the earth and the mountains." Then a bullet took his life.

Here and there, braves with weapons attempted to make stands in hollows or pits in the creek bank to protect women and children. In one such defense, George Bent had his hip broken by a bullet. Black Kettle attempted to make a death stand as White Antelope had done, but his young men almost carried him from the field. His wife, however, was shot down, and passing soldiers, in a spirit of thoroughness that would have been commendable in any other cause, put seven more bullets into her. She lived, though, and recovered.

The bravery of the Cheyennes in their hopeless situation won the admiration even of their enemies. The changeable Major Anthony, who presumably was on the side of God and Elder Chivington at the moment, described it later: "I never saw more bravery displayed by any set of people on the face of the earth than by these Indians. They would charge on the whole company singly, determined to kill someone before being killed themselves."

Most of Chivington's boys, though, were too busy with homicide to pay tribute to desperate valor. At times, soldiers were firing from opposite sides of the camp so heavily as to seriously endanger each other; it is highly probable this is the way some of their casualties occurred. At least one man, however, was having no part in the fighting. Captain Silas S. Soule had remonstrated bitterly with Chivington against the attack; he made his own private protest at the camp by refusing to give his men the order to fire. It had not prevented them from going ahead on their own, but it kept a burden off Soule's conscience. The captain strode up and down amid the drifting powder smoke, an anguished witness to the massacre he refused to join.

The Colonel had told his boys to kill and scalp all, big and little. They did more than that. Some of them went into an orgy of butchery and sadism that shrunk any imagined gap between the savage redskin and the civilized white man to nothing. Read, with a bit of nausea, Robert Bent's taut description of some of the things he witnessed when he accompanied Chivington onto the field as his unwilling guide:

> I saw five squaws under a bank. When troops came up to them they ran out and showed their persons to let the soldiers know they were squaws and begged for mercy but the soldiers shot them all. I saw one squaw lying on a bank whose leg had been broken by a shell. A soldier came up to her with drawn saber. She raised her arm to protect herself when he struck, breaking her arm; she rolled over and raised her other arm when he struck, breaking it; then he left without killing her. . . . Some thirty or forty squaws, collected in a hole for protection . . . sent out a little girl about six years old with a white flag on a stick. She was shot and killed. . . . I saw one squaw cut open with an unborn child lying by her side. I saw the body of White Antelope with the privates

cut off, and I heard a soldier say he was going to make a tobacco pouch out of them. I saw one squaw whose privates had been cut out. . . . I saw a little girl who had been hid in the sand. Two soldiers drew their pistols and shot her, and then pulled her out of the sand by the arm. I saw quite a number of infants in arms killed by their mothers. . . .

Young Bent's vignettes of horror should not be discounted on the grounds that he was half-Cheyenne and hence probably biased. On the contrary, his account is restrained in contrast to those given later by some of Chivington's own boys.

The slaughter went on into the afternoon; by that time the Indians had been pursued several miles. After making a halfhearted search for the main camp of Arapahoes along the Arkansas so he could treat them as he had the Cheyennes, Colonel Chivington led his victory-flushed heroes back to Denver. He had sent a conqueror's exultant report on ahead, direct from the smoking field of battle: "I at daylight this morning attacked a Cheyenne village of . . . from nine hundred to a thousand warriors. We killed . . . between four and five hundred. All did nobly." The Colonel's figures were blown full of air. There were not nine hundred to a thousand warriors in the camp; there were not that many persons all told; best estimates seem to be about seven hundred in the camp, of whom about two hundred were men. No one knows how many were killed. Estimates range from 150 to 500. George Bent, who lay in the camp with a broken hip and was the only one who stayed around long enough to make a thorough count, said that 163 were slain, of whom 110 were women and children. The boys also took 2 men, 3 women, and 4 children captive, but one of the men was shot later.

Chivington and the boys were received in Denver as heroes and saviors of the frontier. ("All acquitted themselves well," said the Denver *News*. "Colorado soldiers have again covered themselves with glory.") They appeared between acts of a performance at the theater, receiving great applause as they exhibited dozens of Indian scalps, with running commentary. The captured children were exhibited like monkeys in a zoo for a time until the government obtained their release.

The Sand Creek massacre brought a bloody reaction from the infuriated Indians, who, except for a few holdouts, had given up the warpath at the time Chivington went out after his cheap glory. During the summer, the older chiefs of the tribe had tried to restore peace even after the shooting had begun. It was mainly the young braves, hot of blood, short on judgment, and eager for a reputation, who did most of the raiding. But after the massacre, things were different. Everyone, old chiefs, young braves, squaws, were united in a single wish for revenge.

As usual, the wrong people suffered. Wagon trains along the Platte and Smoky Hill trails were attacked again, and whatever settlers had been missed during the summer were burned out and slain. Julesburg on the South Platte had not been touched during the summer raids; now it was twice attacked and pillaged. The Sioux were riding with the Cheyenne in the north; in the south the Comanche and Kiowa were striking into Texas again, farther and bolder than before, even to the vicinity of Austin and San Antonio, desolating the northern Texas settlements, with victims left unburied and nothing but chimneys to mark where farms had been.

The worst fury of the Indian attacks was abated by the fact that they came in winter. The dry grass did not give the Indian ponies the stamina needed for sustained action. Nor were there emigrant trains on the trails at that time of year; the only thing that jolted over the frozen ruts were wagon supply trains and stagecoaches. On the other hand, it was extremely unusual for Plains Indians to make war at all in winter; that they did is a measure of their bitter hate after Sand Creek.

After troops had tried fruitlessly to run the war parties down, it was decided to starve the Indians out by burning off all grazing for their horses and driving out the game in the region. Fires were started at intervals in the dry grass along many miles of the south bank of the Platte River. Swept south by the wind, the individual fires spread, joined, moved on in a solid wall of flame. Wherever a river barred the way, sparks blew across in a hundred places to start new blazes that joined again to make a solid front of destroying prairie fire. Not until they reached the northern Panhandle of Texas did the last flames flicker out. It must have killed a frightful number of wild animals and birds, but it did not bother the Indians because they had already felt the pinch of hunger and had gone north, across the Platte River up into the Powder River country. It was a country teeming with game— the Sioux would soon be fighting to keep Americans out of it—and a hospitable refuge for the war-weary Cheyennes.

Brigadier General Patrick E. Connor, a man with a great reputation because of a victory over Bannocks and Shoshones in 1863, was sent up after them when summer came to teach them a lesson. Commanding 800 soldiers and 100 Pawnee scouts, Connor made great preparations for wiping out all resistance. After organizing his expedition into three columns to squeeze the Cheyennes and their allies between them, he issued orders as explicit as those of Chivington: "You will not receive overtures of peace or submission from Indians, but will attack and kill every male Indian over twelve years of age."

There was a to-do back East when General Connor's order became known among Indian sympathizers, and the Army was not happy about it, but there had been no need to worry unduly. Two of the Indian-killing columns went badly astray and lost most of their horses to Indian attacks; they ran out of rations, and finally wandered in on foot, hungry and lucky to have made it at all. The third column, personally led by Connor, fared better; it destroyed an Arapaho camp, but it was a very small result for a large effort. General Connor was sacked at the close of the campaign.

Colonel Chivington did not take part in the campaigns against the Indians after the Sand Creek massacre. Denver had treated him as a hero, but Denver was a frontier town; elsewhere, and particularly in the East, there was revulsion at the great and glorious victory on Sand Creek. Chivington soon resigned his commission to avoid a court-martial.

A military commission investigated. Of the 33 witnesses who testified, 14 supported Chivington, 17 condemned him. Most of those who spoke had been present at the massacre; a majority of those who spoke against him had been his own boys. The Colonel and the Colorado authorities took the position that the Indians at Sand Creek were still at war, no matter what Major Wynkoop might have told them, and the expedition against them was a punitive one to teach them a lesson. If they were peaceful, asked someone, why did they have those pits under the creek banks into which some of them crawled when the soldiers started shooting at them?

But the voices which damned Chivington and gave evidence of the peaceable actions of the Indians were more numerous and convincing. Even Major Colley spoke out. Colley had given no evidence of great intellectuality, but it took no genius to understand the situation in the terms he reduced it to: peace was when you have no war. And from the time Major Wynkoop had first gone out to talk to the Cheyennes and recover the white captives from them until the time Colonel Chivington had arrived at Fort Lyon there had not been any Indian depredation of any kind within two hundred miles of the post. To Colley, that had not looked like Indians very actively at war. Everyone at the fort, he testified, civilians and officers alike, had pleaded with the Colonel not to go out and stir things up and start the war all over. But the hundred-day Indian-fighting regiment had to be justified —and Chivington had to brighten his own reputation in preparation for his coming political career.

The great amount of testimony was concerned with the manner in which Indians died. The statement of Robert Bent has already been quoted; it is not necessary to add a mass of testimony in the same vein. One of the most bitter witnesses against the Colonel was Captain Silas Soule, he who had refused to order his men to fire on Black Kettle's camp. Feeling ran high; Soule was several times shot at from ambush in Denver. He ignored these omens of a short life and was married on April 1. On the twenty-third he was called down in the street in Western frontier fashion; both men fired; both were hit. Soule died, but the other man was only wounded and skipped the country. Picked up soon after in New Mexico and brought back, he was found dead of poisoning while waiting a hearing, presumably a suicide. though there is no good explanation why.

The nation-wide uproar led Congress to have its own look at the massacre and its causes. An investigating committee of three came to Fort Lyon in August, 1865 and plowed somewhat different ground than had been turned up by the military hearing. Kit Carson, as famous and as fair an Indian-fighter as the country had, was called as an expert witness. He was asked what he thought of Chivington's campaign. He replied succinctly that the Colonel and his boys were cowards and dogs.

Congress made reparations to the widows and orphans of those killed at Sand Creek (a not too meaningful recompense since most of the dead were women and children). But these small steps could not undo the harm. The Commissioner of Indian Affairs, having worked with the magnificent leisureliness of all government bodies, published its own report on Chivington's victory four years later, and concluded that it had been an expensive adventure:

No one will be astonished that a war ensued which cost the government $30,000,000 and carried conflagration and death to the border settlements. During the summer of 1865 no less than 8,000 troops were withdrawn from the effective force engaged in suppressing the rebellion to meet this Indian war. The result of the year's campaign . . . was useless and expensive. Fifteen or twenty Indians had been killed at an expense of more than a million dollars apiece, while hundreds of our soldiers had lost their lives. Many of our border settlers had been butchered and much property destroyed.

Major Colley had given his opinion when the congressional committee had come to Fort Lyon, and it had been both sententious and banal. "My opinion," said he, "is that white men and wild Indians cannot live in the same country at peace." Colley, in his attempt to be trenchant, had said a great deal, much more than he meant. Either the government had to give the Indians a place where they could live as "wild" Indians, keeping their own customs and ways, apart from all white men, or else the Indians had to begin to adapt themselves to the white man's way of living. The first way had failed tragically. William Bent and Kit Carson were eloquent advocates of the second course when they served on the commission which attempted to work out another treaty with the Cheyennes and Arapahoes in October of 1865. The war had simply burned itself out. The southern divisions of the two tribes had drifted back from the Powder River country; there had been a few minor raids, but it was like a wet firecracker fizzling out. The tribes wanted an end to fighting.

The council was held near the present site of Wichita. Both Bent and Carson talked in terms of supplying the Indians with farming implements, seed, training in agriculture, schools. Some of the more far-seeing Cheyenne chiefs had discussed the possibility of becoming a farming tribe again, as their tradition told them they had been in the past. It was obvious to them, as it was to Bent and Carson, that nothing but hunger could lie ahead for a buffalo-hunting people in a land where the buffalo were disappearing.

But the government commissioners, after agreeing in principle with Bent and Carson, provided no implements, no seeds, no schools. The Cheyennes and Arapahoes were forced to give up even their barren Sand Creek reservation; they, as well as the Kiowa and Comanche agreed to move south of the Arkansas. But the new reservations were drawn so clumsily, part of the Kiowa and Comanche reserve even on Texas land which the government had no legal right to use for reservations, that the Senate refused to ratify the agreements. As a result, the tribes roamed the southern plains for two years without a square inch of land they could call their own.

William Bent's two sons who had been Cheyenne warriors during the raiding and fighting continued to live as tribesmen. Both had been in Black Kettle's camp at the time of the massacre, when George had had his hip broken by a soldier's bullet. But it was Charles who reverted completely to his Cheyenne blood, and even beyond, demonstrating a savagery that the Dog Soldiers he led could not match. No cruelty against whites was too much for him; in a raid on a station on the Smoky Hill road, he and his fellow warriors captured two of the men there by drawing them out of their defenses by guile and false promises; then, in full sight of the remaining beleaguered station workers, he fed the flames of his measureless hate by staking one of the prisoners out on the ground, cutting out his tongue, building a fire on his stomach, and performing other abominations. His savageries became so inhuman that his father disowned him, a compliment that was returned with interest; once he came back to the ranch to shoot his father from ambush but luckily chose a time when the elder Bent was away. He was one of the worst the plains had known; it was good riddance for all when he was badly hurt in a fight with Pawnees in 1868, caught malaria when in a weakened condition, and died.

George Bent, the second brother, also continued to live as a Cheyenne. He had as much reason to go savage as Charles, but, although he went on the warpath with the Cheyennes after the massacre, the same fierce hate was not there. He continued to ride to the ranch occasionally to see his father, his brother Robert, and sister Mary, and when the tribes were called together in 1867 for the Treaty of Medicine Lodge, George was one of those who helped bring them in.

And John Chivington—what became of him? The ex-colonel found his reputation as an Indian-killing hero not completely an asset, even in tough, frontier Colorado. His political enemies accused him of deliberately stirring up trouble in order to make a name for himself; there were some citizens, even on the frontier, who remembered the blood-drenched camp on Sand Creek and agreed with Kit Carson that a man who would serve even an Indian like that was a dog and a coward. Chivington finally went back to his native Ohio where he did enter politics at last, running for minor offices with less than spectacular success.

IV

Give Me Eighty Men

1. JOHN BOZEMAN'S ROAD

WHEN the Civil War ended, Major General William Tecumseh Sherman, hero of Atlanta and the Great March, stood only a step below Ulysses S. Grant in the estimation of a jubilant Union. He was in the fortunate position of being pretty much able to pick his next duty assignment, and, having no stomach for policing the beaten South, he asked for, and in September, 1865, was given command of the Military Division of the Mississippi.

The Division of the Mississippi included the territory from Canada to Texas and from the Mississippi River to the Rockies, plus the Department of the Ohio which was composed of the states north of the Ohio River. Within a year, however, the states north of the Ohio would be detached to make it an entirely trans-Mississippi command, its name would be changed to the Division of the Missouri, and with few changes thereafter, it would administer the Army's complex affairs over the vast plains, involving thousands of men in isolated wind-swept and sun-baked posts spread thinly over endless miles of grasslands, until the Indians were finally beaten to their knees.

The face Sherman turned to the world was not a warm one. It was gnarled as a chunk of applewood, and somehow suggestive, with beard and hair awry, of an indignant rooster that had been tumbled about by a Kansas windstorm. He was a man without the faintest germinal stirrings of tact. When he stopped at Colorado Springs during his first inspection tour of his command and the citizens of the town asked for protection against the Indians, he replied, with full sarcasm, that he was sure it would be a good thing if there were an Army post in the vicinity to provide a market at high prices for farmers' grain, hay, and other products. During the same tour, a petition was handed him at Pueblo, Colorado, likewise begging protection from murdering red-skins. Sherman scanned it briefly, then remarked that more men had signed the petition than he had as garrisons at most of the Army posts in the area.

On the other hand, very many Westerners were opposed to the return of the Army and the replacement of local volunteers by regulars. Some of the more bloodthirsty among them were calling for a bounty on Indian scalps—$100 was a popular figure—which, they said, would be incentive enough for the local boys to go out and exterminate the Indians without any help from the Army. The Regular Army, in the days ahead, would commit savagely brutal acts against Indians—and not all of them because it was carrying out orders and helpless to do otherwise—but, by and large, it fought as part of a job that had to be done and not from hate.

Sherman replaced volunteers with regulars as rapidly as possible, and thereafter refused to authorize any territorial government to form its own volunteer units except under strict control by the United States Army, which would mean Army pay, food, and allowances. The West-erners did not want to play soldier that badly; they complained bit-terly, but volunteer units were formed in only one or two special instances.

For some time, Sherman's main concern was going to be the pro-tection of communications lines, a task that promised to be a large one with the means at hand and the tribes in an ugly temper. There were the three transplains roads to be kept open at all costs: the Santa Fe Trail, the Oregon Trail, and the Smoky Hill Trail. There was the Missouri River which provided access by steamboat—still mainly for traders—into the northern plains and foothills; it was not yet a major concern. There was the military telegraph crossing the plains along the line of the Platte River to Fort Laramie with various branches (for some reason, the Indians did not bother the telegraph line as much as they might have; either they did not realize how much trouble they could cause with almost no effort or, as some theories had it, they held the message-carrying wire in superstitious awe).

Sherman would, in a very short time, have to be providing protection for railroad construction crews. The Union Pacific had pushed ten or twelve miles west from Omaha in the fall of 1865 when Sherman took over his western command, its destination an eventual meeting with the Central Pacific working east from California. Across the plains the Union Pacific would follow the north side of the Platte, the opposite side from the Oregon Trail, which would then soon pass into oblivion. That same fall, the Kansas Pacific had also laid down its first dozen miles of track westward from Kansas City, on a route that would follow the general line of the Smoky Hill Trail to Denver. The Army would have a heavy responsibility during the building if the Indians continued hostile; once they were completed, the railroads would make it possible to shift troops rapidly over long distances and would hasten the pacification of the Plains tribes.

One other major road lay in Indian country and under the probable danger of Indian attack: the Bozeman Trail. It was a new road, cutting off from the Oregon Trail west of Fort Laramie and running north and west into Montana Territory; its importance resulted entirely from the accident that intrepid prospectors, risking lives and scalps, had found gold in the Rocky Mountains in Montana.

The Bozeman Trail was not only particularly vulnerable to Indian attack, it was an invitation to trouble because it ran through the choicest of all the hunting lands of the Sioux nation, and the Sioux resented its existence. For that reason, forts were being established along the road during 1866, and General Sherman himself made the trip in May out to old Fort Kearney in Nebraska Territory on the Oregon Trail to wish Godspeed to an expedition just setting out to establish Army authority.

General Sherman had been working for several months to acquaint himself with the problems of his sprawling command. There must have been some things he missed, or else he would not have permitted this expedition to take wives and children. Not only permitted, but assured the colonel in command that he saw no prospect of danger to the women and children. Whatever his sources of intelligence, they were badly misinformed about conditions on the Bozeman Trail.

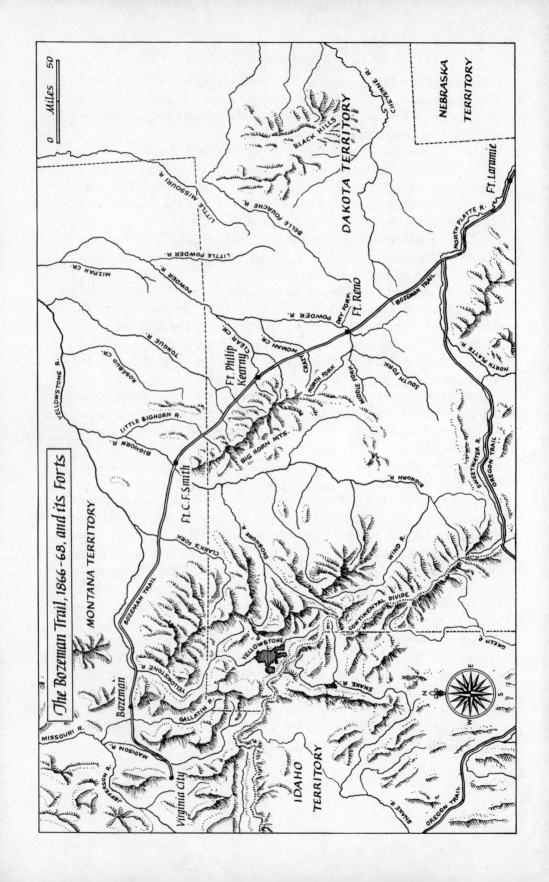

The Bozeman Trail, 1866-68, and its Forts

Colonel Henry B. Carrington was in command of the expedition, which was composed of the 2nd Battalion of the 18th U. S. Infantry, about 700 men. The battalion was driving a herd of a thousand cattle, and had a train of 226 mule-drawn wagons with baggage and stores, as well as a number of Army ambulances carrying a couple of dozen women and children (the ambulance was a high-wheeled, covered wagon; it became a popular vehicle for personal transportation on the plains because it was the only wagon with springs that were at all effective). Several officers with families brought a cow, chickens, and similar impedimenta indicating they had every hope of living a reasonably well-ordered home life in the wildnerness. The expedition even included a twenty-five piece regimental band, which tootled as the long column left the sagging old fort behind.

The Bozeman Trail, whither Colonel Carrington and his expedition were heading, was the creature of one John M. Bozeman, who came from Colorado to the new gold fields centering around Virginia City in Montana in 1862. The fields had been reached either from Fort Hall in Idaho on the Oregon Trail, or from Fort Benton, the ordinary head of navigation on the Missouri. Either way was difficult, hazardous, and roundabout. Bozeman set himself the task of finding a route that would connect directly with the Oregon Trail and would be suitable for freighting in supplies to the gold fields by wagon.

He and a companion named Jacobs found the answer to the problem when they discovered a pass that took them from Virginia City and the mining country into the valley of the east-flowing Yellowstone. Their trail then continued east till it cleared the north spur of the Big Horn Mountains, when it turned southeasterly to skirt the east flank of the mountains. It struck the North Platte and the Oregon Trail at a point about seventy miles west of Fort Laramie. The Sioux caught them before they had quite finished their free-lance survey, and took their weapons, horses, and even clothes. With fine forebearance, the Indians refrained from physically harming the two men—although turning them loose on the high plains naked with winter coming on was not precisely an act of mercy. Nevertheless, they made it safely through to settlements on the Platte River.

The next spring, Bozeman undertook to lead freighters with a pack train back along his new trail to the Montana camps. Sioux warriors met them before they had made a good beginning; placed themselves athwart their path, and motioned them to go back. They had no choice, but once out of sight of the Sioux, they doubled back, and made it through to the mining country by traveling during the night and hiding by day. The road was so practicable and so profitable for men willing to put up with hardships and risk life and scalp that wagon and pack trains were soon traveling over it, making up in sufficient strength to discourage Indian attacks, though never enough to guarantee safety.

Inevitably, an anguished cry for government protection echoed back across the plains into the halls of Congress; as a result an act was passed to create certain federal roads in several parts of the western territories, one of these being the Bozeman Trail. The act put the Army squarely into the business of protecting the Bozeman Trail (it was often called the Powder River Trail because it cut across the upper waters of that river).

So far, the Army had not been able to do much. When Brigadier General Patrick Connor made his ill-fated expedition into the Powder River country in pursuit of the Cheyennes and their allies to punish them for their depredations following the Sand Creek massacre, one thing he accomplished was to build a fort where the Bozeman Trail crossed the main branch of the Powder River. It was called Fort Connor at first—until the War Department put an end to the practice, commanding officers showed a shameless lack of modesty by naming forts and posts after themselves—but it was changed to Fort Reno the next year, 1866. Establishing the fort was a small accomplishment; the section of the Trail north of Fort Reno was the part the Sioux were most concerned about, and they were beginning to make travel on that section hazardous indeed.

The Sioux—particularly the Oglala and Miniconjou bands—had dug in their heels and were prepared to make a last-ditch fight for their hunting grounds in the Powder River region through which the road passed. Here the Great Plains become broken and uneven and finally splinter against the Big Horn Mountains. It was a beautiful land, with slope after slope covered with meadows of excellent grass. Trout-filled streams of clear snow-water flowed out of the mountains, through valleys wooded with aspen, willow, cottonwood and chokecherry. Raspberries, cherries, strawberries, currants, and plums grew in meadow and underbrush. Nearer the flanks of the mountains were forests of pine, fir, and spruce.

Buffalo, elk, and antelope grazed on the open grasslands, deer abounded in the breaks, and there was an abundance of bear, sage hens, rabbits, and lesser game. The animals were so abundant and so well-fed that hunting was easy, and the Sioux, understandably, did not want it despoiled as they had seen other hunting grounds ruined when white men had driven their roads through them.

Having arrogantly moved to take control of the road at the time of General Connor's expedition and been badly set back, the government now attempted a belated diplomatic approach to the matter. Chiefs of the western bands of the Sioux were called to a council at Fort Laramie in June, to meet with a commission sent by the Indian Bureau. The government showed rare timing in its council; the negotiations had no more than got a good start when Colonel Carrington and his column arrived at Laramie with a rattling and creaking of wagons, the bawling of their beef herd, and making no secret that they were on their way to establish forts to keep the Bozeman Trail open.

There was an angry outcry from the assembled chiefs, who very understandably considered it bad faith that the government had sent a powerful force of soldiers to take possession of the trail at the same time it was negotiating with the Indians for permission to use it. "Great Father sends us presents and wants new road," Chief Red Cloud of the Oglala Sioux said during the stormy council that followed Carrington's arrival, "but White Chief goes with soldiers to steal road before Indian says yes or no."

Most of the chiefs stalked out. Red Cloud was adamantly opposed to the Bozeman Trail, so was Young-Man-Afraid-of-His-Horses, another Oglala chief. Spotted Tail of the Brule argued for a peaceful settlement, as he had on every question since he had gone to prison at Fort Leavenworth as a belated victim of the affair of the Mormon's cow. During his prison year, Spotted Tail had become convinced that the number and strength of the Americans was endless; it had taken the heart out of him so that ever since, he had felt it was folly to oppose an irresistible force. Red Cloud and Young-Man-Afraid-of-His-Horses disappeared from Fort Laramie with the Oglalas; Spotted Tail and a few of the old chiefs remained to sign a treaty which meant very little as far as guaranteeing the security of the Bozeman Trail was concerned.

Colonel Carrington pressed on, still following the Platte and the Oregon Trail. Jim Bridger, one of the great mountain men but growing creaky now, was guide for the expedition. He was beginning to warn of the need for caution, although not suggesting that any special danger existed. About seventy miles west of Fort Laramie, the column abandoned the Oregon Trail and struck off northward, for here the Bozeman Trail began. For the 2nd Battalion of the 18th Infantry, the road was going to lead straight to tragedy.

2. FORT PHILIP KEARNY

Five days of hard travel brought the column to Fort Reno. The post was located where the Bozeman Trail crossed the Powder River, a few buildings of logs with roofs of dirt. Two companies of low-morale volunteer troops garrisoned the place, wondering, until Carrington's arrival, whether they were ever going to be relieved.

No Indians had been seen between the Platte River and Fort Reno although Jim Bridger had insisted that they were watching the column. He was proved right the evening of the day of arrival at Fort Reno when braves swooped down and ran off horses of the post sutler who had grown complacent and kept a very loose watch on his animals. There had been no Indians attacks on the post before, he said plaintively.

The volunteers were relieved and sent back toward civilization, Carrington left one of his eight companies to garrison and rebuild the post, and the column headed up the trail again on July 9 after a two-week stay. Five days and sixty-five miles later Carrington selected a site for a second fort, where the road crossed a tributary of the Powder River named Big Piney Fork. The location was a level, grassy shelf of land in the fork of Big Piney Creek and a branch called Little Piney. Tents were pitched and the force lived under canvas for the time being. Five or six miles up Big Piney, one of the most crucial of the expedition's operations got under way as quickly as possible: sawing lumber for the buildings of the new post.

Establishing a self-contained fort on virgin land involved more than putting up a barracks with a stockade around it. There were perhaps two dozen buildings, such diverse structures as officers' quarters, hospital, workshops for blacksmiths, carpenters, and other mechanics, guardhouse, and bakery. Carrington did not forget a bandstand, out there in hostile Indian country. These structures were surrounded by a palisade of posts, eight feet high and sharpened at the top, enclosing a space 400 by 400 feet. Stables and certain other less important buildings, as well as haystacks and woodpiles, lay in an area outside the stockade; an extension of the stockade was later built to enclose them but it was not a part of the fort to be defended to the last ditch.

The post was named Fort Philip Kearny, in honor of Major General Philip Kearny of the Union Army who was killed in action in Virginia in 1862.* Only two days after it was laid out, the Sioux made their first attack, stampeding and making off with 175 horses and mules, and killing two soldiers and wounding three in the chase that followed. Almost at the same time, Indians attacked parties of emigrants and soldiers between Forts Reno and Kearny, making travel between the two strongholds extremely risky. From that time on, Fort Phil Kearny could look for an attack of some kind at almost any time: a foray against the stock, an attack on the wagon trains bringing timber from the woods, occasionally a solitary exploit as when a brave under a wolf skin crawled near enough at night to shoot a sentry. The Indians made raids, attacks or threats near the fort fifty-one times in five months; they undoubtedly had the post under constant watch.

On August 3, Captain Nathaniel C. Kenney with two companies of infantry was sent to establish a third fort where the road crossed the Bighorn River, about ninety miles to the northwest. The new post, which would be named Fort C. F. Smith, was placed just about at the point where the Bozeman Trail cleared the northern spurs of the Big Horns and swung almost due west. It was in Montana Territory; Forts Reno and Kearny were in present Wyoming, though then in Dakota Territory. Approximately 280 miles still lay between Fort Smith and Virginia City but it was mainly through the lands of the Crow Indians who had elected friendship with the Americans long before and had never seriously departed from their resolve. Even so, there were still dangers; the next year, 1867, John Bozeman was killed on his own trail while on his way from Virginia City to Fort Smith, not by Sioux or Crows, but by a band of marauding Blackfeet.

All the lush and beautiful hunting grounds east of the Big Horns

---

* The post, except in official correspondence, was usually called Fort Phil Kearny. There was, for some reason, an irresistible compulsion to insert an additional "e" in the name and make it "Kearney." That had happened to Fort Kearney on the Oregon Trail in Nebraska, named after Stephen Watts Kearny, Mexican War commander and uncle of Philip Kearny. Even officers stationed at Fort Kearney insisted on putting the unnecessary "e" in the name until at last the War Department surrendered and made it Fort Kearney. Officers at Fort Phil Kearny more often than not did the same thing and wrote it "Fort Philip Kearney" in official correspondence.

that Red Cloud and his Sioux were so vehemently determined to keep free of white men had been dominated by the Crows not long before. Then for several years the Crows had been outclassed in the endless wars of raid and counterraid that went on between them and the Sioux, and had been pushed out of most of the prized Powder River country. In 1866, however, Red Cloud had been careful to protect his flank by arranging a truce with the Crows so that the full Sioux strength could be turned against the Americans.

Operations went on at a feverish pace at all three forts to get them in shape before winter. Besides constructing buildings, the garrisons had to pile up mountains of cordwood for fuel against a winter when the land would be locked by deep snow and cold far below zero; tremendous amounts of hay for horses and cattle had to be put up. The Sioux made regular attacks on the wood-cutting and haying details, especially at Fort Kearny, where several men were killed. Indians had run off a large part of the Kearny horses and mules, which had been in short supply even at the beginning, while by the end of September only one hundred of the seven hundred beef cattle brought with the column remained.

Despite Sioux activity, emigrant trains continued to pass at intervals over the Bozeman Trail. Carrington was shocked by the lackadaisical way in which travelers took heed of warnings of the Indian threat and by their slipshod precautions against surprise attack. However, he was not able to wet-nurse them, and went no further than setting up the rule that travelers would not be permitted to proceed on the road unless they had at least forty able-bodied men in their company. Now and then there were desertions from the fort, enlisted men either bored by the tedium of post life or lured by gold in Montana to the point that the desire to get out was stronger than the remembrance of the smell of blood on the bodies of comrades they had seen brought in, mutilated and scalped, after an Indian attack. It was very seldom that anyone knew whether they made it through to the mining camps or not.

For the women and children, life in Kearny had been circumscribed by the walls of the stockade since very soon after arrival. Margaret Carrington had taken seriously General Sherman's advice at Fort Kearney on the Platte that the women of the expedition should keep diaries. At first her entries had been expansive with descriptions of the sun on the Big Horns, of the immensity of a sky full of stars in the clear mountain air. Very shortly she was writing more like a prisoner;

there were twelve women and eleven children at the fort, and with Indian attack always imminent, they seldom saw the world except over the top of an eight-foot palisade.

Early in November, a company of cavalry, long overdue, arrived at Fort Kearny. Colonel Carrington had been badly hampered in his pursuit of Indian raiders because he had had to depend on mounted infantry, men not trained to fight from the back of a horse. The company comprised sixty-three men under Lieutenant Horatio S. Bingham. Traveling with the company were Captain James Powell and Captain William J. Fetterman, both of whom were destined to command in important battles against the Indians.

Captain Fetterman was no stranger to the 2nd Battalion of the 18th Regiment, for he had fought with it through the war where he had achieved a splendid combat record, winning the brevet rank of lieutenant colonel for battlefield valor. He was a type that occurred frequently in the Indian-fighting Army—and often did not last very long at the trade. It was a type that was arrogant, contemptuous of Indians and their fighting ability, usually excessively brave, a braggart, and loud talker. Lieutenant Grattan, he whose Indian-fighting career had begun and ended at the Battle of the Mormon's Cow near Fort Laramie in 1854, was one such. George Armstrong Custer, whose story is yet to be told, was another, albeit a more complex character. And Captain Fetterman fell into the classic pattern.

He immediately became a divisive influence. Carrington had operated cautiously, letting the Indians come to him and fighting only a defensive war. It was a strategy forced on him. Until Bingham arrived with his company, there had been no cavalry, and even the use of mounted infantry had been hampered because horses and mules were in poor condition since there were too few and they were being worked too hard. Many rifles were in bad condition; ammunition was in short supply. Moreover, he had had to use his men for building the fort and getting ready for winter because cold weather, if they were not prepared, would be more deadly than Indians.

Fetterman, however, was not interested in practical considerations. He was a fire-eater who talked always of attacking; he belittled Carrington for treating the fighting abilities of the Indians with so much respect. Inevitably, the officers and many of the enlisted men drew up sides.

Henry Carrington had recruited and organized the 18th Regiment in Ohio early in the war and became its Colonel. It was only a nominal command, for he was kept in the North against his will all during the war doing various administrative work while the regiment was fighting. Now that the war was over, he was at a distinct disadvantage in the unhealthy rivalry with Fetterman for influence; the captain had served in the war with several of the other officers of the 2nd Battalion and could pluck the chords of comradeship and shared perils.

"Give me eighty men and I would ride through the whole Sioux nation," was one of Fetterman's boasts. Possibly if he had been able to travel forty or fifty miles north he might have changed his mind. Crow Indians reported that the hostile camps were lined for forty miles along the Tongue River. Other bands had rallied to the Oglalas and Miniconjous who had been the original opposition: Hunkpapas, many young Brules from the band of the peaceable Spotted Tail, and Santees exiled from Minnesota, as well as northern Cheyennes and Arapahoes. When the battalion had first arrived, the Cheyennes had professed neutrality, but the taunts of the Sioux, along with the disinclination of soldiers to draw any distinction between friendly and unfriendly Indians, swung them into the hostile alliance. According to the Crows, there were perhaps four thousand warriors in the enemy camp as mid-December neared.

3. "UNDER NO CIRCUMSTANCES PURSUE OVER LODGE TRAIL RIDGE"

The Bozeman Trail ran in a northwesterly direction past Fort Phil Kearny. It crossed Little Piney Creek, passed on the northeastern side of the fort, forded Big Piney Creek, and then disappeared from sight of the post behind a long hill known as Lodge Trail Ridge. Behind the far end of Lodge Trail Ridge a spur ridge extended from it; the road ran along this spur somewhat below its crest for more than a mile until the spur ridge ended and the road dropped down to cross a small stream then known as Peno Creek.

The road passed on the north side of Lodge Trail Ridge; Big Piney Creek lay on the south side of the ridge. South of the creek again was another ridge, which Carrington had named Sullivant Hills in honor of his wife's maiden name, and south once more of Sullivant Hills was the wood road from the fort to the "pineries" of timber about six miles away. The wood road, Sullivant Hills, Big Piney Creek, Lodge Trail Ridge, and the section of the Bozeman Trail on the opposite side of the ridge were all very nearly parallel; it was the habit of the Indians to come over the ridge, cross the creek and, passing over the Sullivant Hills, swoop down on the wood trains, attempting to take them by surprise.

Colonel Carrington had devised tactics for meeting such threats. On a high point near the fort, Pilot Hill, a lookout station was manned whenever wood trains were out; from it the wood road could be kept under observation and the fort informed, by a system of flag signals, of the number and direction of approaching Indians and of actual attack on the wood trains. Frequent drill had reduced the time needed to get a relief force on its way from the fort to a wagon train under attack. Finally, a discipline was worked out for the wood trains themselves that made them invulnerable except to a very large force: they traveled in large trains of about thirty or forty wagons with well-armed escorts, moving along in double lines in such a way that they could form a defensive corral almost on the instant. Lives hung on the perfection of such specialized skills.

On December 6, a party of Sioux made one of their many attacks on a wood train. Colonel Carrington ordered Captain Fetterman to take a cavalry company and a force of mounted infantry down the wood road to relieve the besieged wood train while he took another force and came up behind the Sullivant Hills in an attempt to cut off the warriors. But everything went wrong. The Colonel had taken along one squad of cavalry; its young lieutenant, George Grummond, dashed ahead against orders in his excitement and escaped being cut to pieces in an ambush only by the speed of his horse and some lucky strokes of his saber. Not so fortunate was Lieutenant Bingham who had commanded the cavalry under Captain Fetterman; when the Sioux had broken off their attack on the wagon train he had led a pursuit over the Sullivant Hills, across Big Piney Creek and up Lodge Trail Ridge where he had also spurred ahead of his men and into an ambush. His body, when found, had more than fifty arrows in it. An enlisted man had died in the same ambush; several men had been wounded during the fighting.

Nothing of what had happened during the brief engagement had escaped the Indians. Again and again during the summer they had noted each change in the habits and routine of the post, each bit of careless procedure, and wherever possible they had taken advantage of it. The growing number of graves in the cemetery above the fort was an indicator of their skill in utilizing each lapse in the defense's vigilance.

And now Red Cloud and other leading chiefs were convinced, from the lack of skill, discipline—and even common sense—with which the soldiers had fought that day that they had found a way to defeat them. The whites had been led into ambushes so easily—why not a great ambush into which a considerable part of the fort's strength could be drawn and cut to bits?

A plan was carefully worked out to decoy troops into ambush by an attack on the wood train, and was even rehearsed so that excitable young warriors would not spring the trap prematurely if only a handful of soldiers came into the ambush instead of the large force for which it was being baited. Ten warriors—two Cheyennes, two Arapahoes, six Sioux—were carefully selected for the honor of acting as the main decoys. The place selected for the ambush was the section of the Bozeman Trail that ran along the spur ridge behind Lodge Trail Ridge. Here the warriors picked out their places of concealment among boulders and in high grass on both sides of the road.

On December 19 the Indians attacked. Colonel Carrington sent Captain James W. Powell out to relieve the wagon train, giving him explicit orders not to pursue across Lodge Trail Ridge. Powell, the most cautious of Carrington's officers, refused to let any of his men be drawn out of formation by the decoys, and turned back as ordered when he reached the top of the ridge. The Indians' ruse had failed, but they would try again.

However, the next day the wood train went unmolested to the pineries and returned without an Indian being seen. During the night a snow had fallen; the impossibility of putting fifteen hundred or two thousand warriors into hiding without leaving a web of tracks that would have blared the secret to the world undoubtedly explained why the Indians remained in camp.

In the meantime, Captain Fetterman had made up his mind to settle the whole Indian business, once and for all. That evening he came to Colonel Carrington, and in all seriousness asked to be permitted to put into action his frequent boast that he could ride through the entire Sioux nation, except that now he was proposing to do it with a hundred men instead of eighty. He was accompanied by Captain Frederick H.

Brown, regimental quartermaster, who agreed completely with Fetterman that the only way to whip Indians was to go out after them, and damn the odds, because everyone knew a good white man could whip a room full of Indians. Brown was being detached from Fort Kearny and wanted a last chance at the Indians.

What the two officers proposed was an attack on the camp on Tongue River. Fifty civilian employees at the fort, they said, had agreed to join fifty mounted soldiers in an expedition to wipe out the Sioux villages. The request was so preposterous it had the ring of lunacy. The tepees lay for perhaps as much as forty miles along the Tongue River; merely to ride through them would take hours. And if there were four thousand warriors there, as Crow Indians had reported to old Jim Bridger, then the odds would be forty to one.

Carrington possibly may have wished he could have sent Fetterman against the Indian camps and so have gotten rid of him for good. Instead, he denied permission for the mad scheme, pleading that the fort had neither the men nor the horses to spare from its regular duties and commitments.

On the twenty-first, the Indians tried again. And now events were beginning to move forward, with the inexorable purpose of a Greek tragedy, to give Captain Fetterman his eighty men and his chance to ride against the Sioux. The snow had melted off during the day the Indians waited; if they had delayed one more day their chance would have been gone for the year because the load of logs to be brought back on the twenty-first was to be the last of the season. Carrington had provided a strong guard for this last logging party; escort, woodcutters, and teamsters together formed an armed force of more than eighty men. It left the fort a short time after ten o'clock; about eleven the lookout on Pilot Hill signaled that the train was under attack.

Bugles sounded and men assembled on the parade in quick time. Captain Powell was given command of the relief column by Colonel Carrington who had been pleased with the way Powell had handled the situation two days before. But Captain Fetterman, reporting with his company, came over to Carrington and demanded that he be given command of the entire force since he outranked Powell. The Army being what it is, the Colonel had no choice but to acquiesce, although he admitted later that he had not been happy about the change.

In Fetterman's infantry company were forty-eight enlisted men. Second Lieutenant George W. Grummond commanded the cavalry

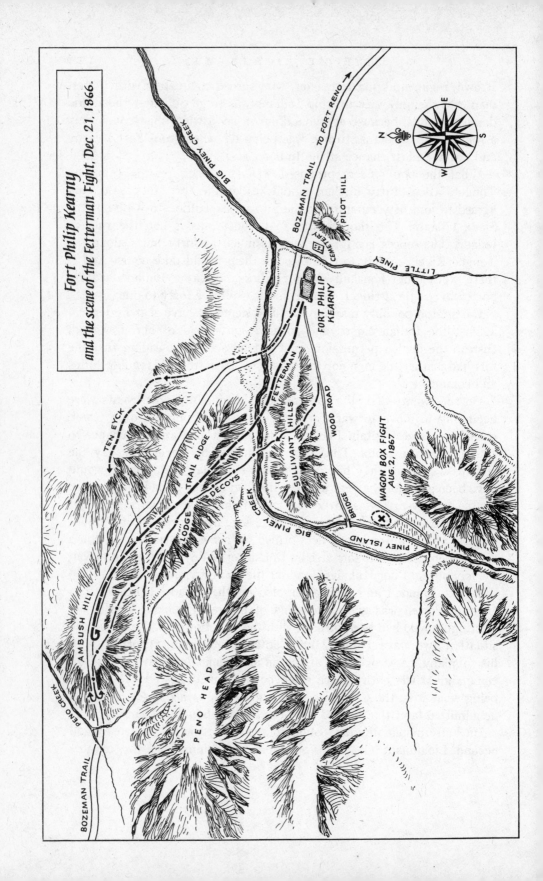

Fort Philip Kearny
and the scene of the Fetterman Fight, Dec. 21, 1866.

company; he and his twenty-seven men increased to a grand total of seventy-six the men under Fetterman's command. One almost hesitates to continue the enumeration; it seems too contrived, too much like bad melodrama. But Captain Brown rode up on a borrowed horse, seizing his last possible opportunity to kill another Indian before leaving Fort Kearny—and Fetterman had seventy-seven.

While last-minute inspections of arms and equipment were being made, Private Maddeon, armorer for the regiment, repairer of small arms, appeared with a rifle in hand and asked Colonel Carrington for permission to join the relief force. Maddeon, as an artificer who spent all his time within the fort with the garrison, probably had his own private dreams of glory; he wanted to be able to write the folks back home at least once that he had shot at an Indian. Carrington granted permission, and Fetterman now had seventy-eight men.

Now, also asking for permission to accompany the force, came two civilian employees at the fort, James Wheatley and Isaac Fisher, and permission was granted. The two would not be excess baggage or mere sight-seers; both were Civil War veterans and both carried sixteen-shot Henry rifles, whereas the infantrymen still were armed with single-shot muzzle-loaders.

Fetterman now had his eighty men, and on the other side of Lodge Trail Ridge lay, not the entire Sioux nation, but enough of it for a substantial beginning.

Colonel Carrington's orders to Fetterman were explicit: "Support the wood train. Relieve it and report to me. Do not engage or pursue Indians at its expense. Under no circumstances pursue over Lodge Trail Ridge."

Fetterman moved out with his company, but Carrington sent his adjutant across the parade to stop him at the gate to repeat the Colonel's orders. Carrington had his misgivings about the young fire-eater with his contempt of Indians; he wanted to leave no room for misunderstanding.

After the infantry had departed, a roll call and inspection showed the cavalry company ready in all respects—carbines in good condition, each man with full ammunition box—and after Lieutenant Grummond had been ordered to report to Captain Fetterman, the company set out after the slower-moving infantry. Colonel Carrington was not quite finished; he stopped Grummond at the gate, and once again repeated his admonition: under no circumstances was he to cross Lodge Trail

Ridge. It is hard to see how he could have made it any more emphatic.

The first part of Fetterman's progress could be watched from the fort. Instead of following the wagon road, which ran along the south side of Sullivant Hills, directly to the wood train, he took his force around on the north side of the hills, apparently meaning to cut off the retreat of the Indians attacking the train and to catch them from the rear. It was perfectly sound strategy, and was no cause for worry as long as Captain Fetterman obeyed his basic orders.

Colonel Carrington had his attention diverted from the relief force by four or five Indians who came out of the brush on the far side of Big Piney near the Bozeman Trail ford. The Colonel ordered a couple of canister shot from one of the howitzers fired at them; one warrior was knocked off his horse and the hail of balls brought about thirty more boiling out of the woods and sent them away up the road at full gallop.

When Carrington turned back toward the relief force, Fetterman's command had disappeared from sight behind the Sullivant Hills. It occurred to the Colonel that the party had no surgeon, and he sent the assistant post surgeon, C. M. Hines, with an escort of four men, to join up with Fetterman. Hines left; soon after, the lookout on Pilot Hill reported that the Indians had broken off the attack and the wood train was proceeding on its way.

It was then about 11:30 A.M. Surgeon Hines came galloping back about noon, and reported to the commanding officer that he had not seen a sign of Fetterman's command, and that he had not been able to look further because Lodge Trail Ridge and the valley of Big Piney below was alive with hundreds of Indians. While Carrington was trying to digest this news, the sound of rifle fire was plainly heard at the fort; it came from the northwest, the direction of Peno Creek, which flowed near, then crossed, the Bozeman Trail.

Carrington recognized from the intensity of the firing that something important was afoot. He immediately ordered Captain Tenedor Ten Eyck to take a force to the relief of Fetterman, and had a column of fifty-four officers and men, with an ambulance and wagons, on its way in little more than fifteen minutes. Ten Eyck took his force down the road at double time while the Colonel immediately set about putting a column of reinforcements together, and soon sent forty more men, with extra ammunition, to follow and join Captain Ten Eyck.

Captain Ten Eyck did not go straight down the road. He followed it over the Big Piney ford and for a short distance thereafter, then bore off to the right onto a ridge that paralleled the road and over-looked it. He reached the high point of the ridge just about the time the last sounds of gunfire died out, at about 12:45 P.M. The shooting had lasted approximately forty-five minutes.

There was no possibility whatever at that moment that Captain Ten Eyck could have led his command down from the ridge toward the road and Peno Creek to learn what might have happened to Fetter-man. There were hundreds of Indians on the road below him; as soon as his force appeared many of them moved to the base of the ridge and began hurling taunts, calling on the soldiers to come down and fight. Despite their enormous superiority in numbers, they made no move to attack—this is one of the mysteries of the Indian character, why, when they held an overwhelming advantage, they did not make the most of it. They apparently had to celebrate and digest one triumph before moving on to another. Beyond the warriors below the ridge were others moving off up the valley; the soldiers on the ridge gasped at the num-ber of them, more Indians than they had ever seen before, two thou-sand, they guessed.

But the mass of Indians was thinning out as they streamed west on their ponies, and those immediately below the ridge gradually left off their demonstrations and joined in the withdrawal. Captain Ten Eyck and the men in his detachment had been straining their eyes for some sign of Captain Fetterman's force. Now, as the Indians below joined the great throng riding away through the valley, it became easier to make out objects on the road; a private was the first to sight the bodies of soldiers, and all dead.

Dark comes early on December 21, the time of the shortest day of the year, and it was dusk as Captain Ten Eyck led his force cautiously down from the ridge onto the road, where the shape of disaster became very clear. The bodies that had been sighted from the ridge lay near a scattering of great boulders. Most were stripped naked, scalped, and mutilated. Among them were the bodies of Captains Fetterman and Brown, bullet wounds with powder burns on temples; every indica-tion was that they had shot each other to prevent being captured.

Ten Eyck had the dead loaded into his wagons and ambulances; the bodies were beginning to freeze and retained the same attitudes in the wagons they had had on the ground, resulting in horrible grotes-queries. Forty-nine were piled aboard the vehicles "like you see hogs brought to market," the surgeon afterward recalled. There was no time to search for more; it was growing dark—and besides, nerves were probably overwrought more than anyone cared to admit.

In the meantime, Colonel Carrington had felt the great hand of doom closing in on the fort during the afternoon. Captain Ten Eyck had taken a mounted courier with him when he left; as soon as he reached the crest of the ridge and found an estimated two thousand warriors in the valley below, he sent word back to the fort, with the ominous detail that Fetterman's force was nowhere in sight.

Colonel Carrington had been alerted for bad news since the rifle firing at noon; the message sent back by Ten Eyck left little doubt that something very serious had happened to Captain Fetterman. And if there were as many Indians as Captain Ten Eyck reported, or even a half or a quarter as many, they might well ride in and take the fort without serious trouble, because it was an empty shell at the moment. Captain Fetterman had taken eighty men; some fifty soldiers, as well as thirty civilians, were with the wood train; ninety-four soldiers were out with Ten Eyck. Only about one hundred and twenty remained in the fort.

Carrington released all men under arrest, armed civilian employees, and manned the stockade to repel attack. A courier was sent to recall the logging party at once; on its arrival at the fort the force manning the stockade was strengthened. And so apprehension and fear were at their height and everyone on the post rushed out on hearing the sound of the wagons, Ten Eyck's returning force. The gates swung open. The early winter darkness was deep enough to hide some details as the wagons with their gruesome freight swung across the parade like a line of butcher's carts, but not nearly dark enough to blot out all the horrid truth of heaped-up bodies, bloody and maimed, with arms and legs reaching out in grotesque postures.

That night Fort Philip Kearny slept on its arms, when it slept at all.

How had this situation come about? What had happened to Captain Fetterman and his eighty, from the time they disappeared behind Sullivant Hills until, only about two hours later, their mutilated bodies were first sighted beside the Bozeman Trail, far across Lodge Trail Ridge?

The story of Captain Fetterman's defeat can never be known in all its details, but deduction and the stories told, usually many years later, by warriors who had taken part have left little mystery about the battle. After the relief force had come around Sullivant Hills, the decoys had broken off their attack on the wagon train and rode across the hills to intercept Fetterman and draw him up Lodge Trail Ridge. They retreated slowly, taunting, yelping, making obscene gestures, dashing away when the infantry raised rifles on the order to fire.

The decoys reached the crest of the ridge and continued down the other side, but Fetterman stopped when he reached the top. His orders had been unequivocal: "Under no circumstances pursue over Lodge Trail Ridge." He despised Carrington's caution, and he probably cursed him as he sat looking down the slope where the decoys were jeering and waving blankets to try to frighten the cavalrymen's horses. It must have been particularly galling for the captain, who held the fighting qualities of Indians in low esteem.

On their part, the Indians became fearful as the soldiers paused that the plan would fail, as it had two days before when the careful Captain Powell had turned back after reaching the top of the ridge. They redoubled their efforts; one of the Cheyenne decoys drove his horse in so close to the troops that, to the Indians hidden along the road below, he seemed to be actually among the troops. At just about this time, the small party of Indians which had just been fired on by a howitzer from the fort came riding down the Bozeman Trail and joined the decoys. The taunts of the decoys, the arrival of more Indians to kill— it was a combination Fetterman was unable to resist. He gave the order, and the force moved over the crest and down onto the Bozeman Trail in pursuit.

Lieutenant Grummond had almost lost his life two weeks earlier in an ambush when he had dashed heedlessly ahead of the rest of his force. This day he was doing the same thing, probably whooping just as joyfully, as his cavalry pulled ahead of the infantry, while both cavalry and infantry began to string out. The force was losing some of the characteristics of a disciplined military unit and was starting to act a little like a crew of schoolboys racing to see who would be first in the water.

Very soon the strung-out force was on the stretch of road atop the spur ridge, completely within the ambush area, while the decoys had reached the end of the ridge and had clattered on down the road, across Peno Creek. There half of them swung off the road to the left, half to the right, and circled in returning arcs back to the road again. The maneuver was the signal for the springing of the trap. On the instant, hundreds of Indians sprang out of high grass and from behind rocks; other hundreds spurred on horseback from concealment behind rock ledges at the side of the ridge. Only a small portion of the warriors carried guns, but the lack placed them at little disadvantage under the conditions of the fighting. The main superiority of the Springfield muzzle-loaders of the infantry over Indian bows and arrows was in range—and range was of no importance here where the enemy was usually less than a stone's throw away. Arrows were as accurate as the muzzle-loaders, as deadly, and could be fired many times as rapidly.

Lieutenant Grummond, in the van with his cavalry, held most of his men together for a period and made a courageous fight, apparently trying to cut their way back to rejoin the infantry. Grummond was killed in the attempt; his body was found on the road. Indian accounts say that the pony soldiers became panicky when their chief fell, and retreated in confusion to higher ground at the west side of the road. The road ran somewhat below the high point of the backbone of the ridge at this point, and it was up toward the imagined greater security of the higher land at the peak of the ridge that the cavalrymen worked their way after Lieutenant Grummond was killed.

In the meantime, the two civilians, Wheatley and Fisher, were causing more trouble for the Indians than any other two men in the force. Both were war veterans of considerable combat experience, not the type to panic in a tight spot, and each carried a nice, deadly sixteen-shot Henry rifle. It was, as a matter of fact, mainly to try out their new rifles that they had come along this day—and the guns were getting a real test. The pair found shelter behind some large boulders and were joined by several of the more experienced of Fetterman's infantrymen, also veterans. The latter were armed with Springfield muzzle-loaders, but the Civil War had shown that muzzle-loaders, handled by men to whom the complicated sequence of loading, ramming home, aiming, firing, and all the rest had become second nature, could be a deadly weapon.

Now, as the Indians came in yelling, Wheatley and Fisher coolly knocked them off—twenty, thirty, no one knows how many were piled in the circle around them—with the infantrymen's steady shooting adding to the total. Eventually, of course, it had to end. Ammunition ran short; the warriors finally overwhelmed them as the whites died defending themselves with clubbed rifles and knives.

The main body of the infantry had been rallied by Captain Fetter-

Fort Kearney, Nebraska, in 1860. This major Army post was built in 1848 to protect travelers on the Oregon Trail. Its buildings were not so trim as this contemporary sketch makes them appear; with lumber scarce and expensive, many structures were made largely of cottonwood logs and sod, and soon sagged into a dilapidated condition. (Courtesy of The Bettmann Archive)

William Bent, "trader, good friend to the Cheyennes; . . . their blood was in his wife and his five children." No one worked harder to prevent the Cheyenne War of 1864, but it was not a propitious season for a man of good will. (Courtesy of the Library of the State Historical Society of Colorado)

Colonel John M. Chivington, commander of Colorado militia and perpetrator of one of the most infamous massacres of Indians by whites in frontier history. "My rule of fighting white men or Indians is to fight them until they lay down their arms and submit," he told a group of chiefs— then fell on them after they had submitted completely. (Courtesy of the Library of the State Historical Society of Colorado)

James W. Lynd, clerk at a trader's store and probably the first victim of the Minnesota Sioux uprising. "Lynd was a former state representative, but the Sioux knew him better as a man who had fathered children by several of their daughters." (Courtesy of Whitney's Gallery, St. Paul, Minn.)

Little Crow, or the Hawk That Hunts Walking, chief leader of the massacre of whites in Minnesota in 1862. "When he found the Sioux meant to fight regardless of his warnings, he decided that it was better to lead a lost cause than become a nobody." (Courtesy of the Bureau of American Ethnology, Smithsonian Institution)

Lieutenant Colonel George A. Custer, his Indian scouts, and a mere two of the forty hounds he brought to the Northern Pacific surveying expedition on the Yellowstone in 1873. The Indian pointing to the map is the Arikara Bloody Knife, Custer's favorite, who was killed beside Major Reno at the Little Bighorn. (Courtesy of The Bettmann Archive)

Henry H. Sibley, in charge of all military operations against the Sioux during the uprising in Minnesota. He was a former governor; he had been a fur trader for years; he was well acquainted with the Sioux and their ways. "But, as far as fighting Indians was concerned, he was completely without experience." (Courtesy of the Minnesota Historical Society)

Lieutenant Timothy Sheehan was in command of Fort Ridgely during the early days of the Minnesota uprising, and led the spirited defense that stopped the Sioux advance. "The soldiers fought so bravely we thought there were more of them than there were," a Sioux warrior said. (Courtesy of the Minnesota Historical Society)

General Alfred Sully's force at Fort Berthold, Dakota Territory, in 1864. The long (1863–65) and fumbling campaign to punish the Santee Sioux for the Minnesota uprising also succeeded in upsetting the western Sioux. (Courtesy of the Minnesota Historical Society)

efugees from the Sioux in Minne-
ota. "Twenty-three counties were
evastated and left almost com-
letely without humans, a region 50
y 200 miles." (Courtesy of the Min-
esota Historical Society)

Two Moons, Cheyenne chief. Friendly up to the time his camp was attacked without provocation, he thereafter became an implacable foe of the Army, and led his people against Custer at the Little Bighorn. (Courtesy of the Museum of the American Indian, Heye Foundation)

man—under difficulties without doubt, because it must have been almost impossible to make his orders heard amid the high-pitched yelping of the Indians—who tried to move his men forward to join up with the cavalry to close the fatal gap which had developed during the pursuit. Then (and the reader recognizes that this account of the sequence of events is laced with surmise, albeit surmise based on historical evidence) Grummond died and the cavalry took its own course toward higher ground, while Fetterman led his men off the road to a group of large boulders that offered good cover.

There, among the rocks, they held out for a while, perhaps ten or fifteen minutes, while they mechanically dropped cartridges in muzzles, rammed them home, and fired, again and again. Not all among the constant flights of arrows splintered on the rocks; some found flesh and defenders died or dropped mortally wounded, although probably more than one soldier, hurt and hampered by the feathered shaft that had suddenly appeared in his body, broke off the projecting portion and so was able to continue fighting a short while longer.

But the tide of Indians clamoring to get at the knot of soldiers was impossible to resist. The streams of arrows were so heavy and continuous they endangered the warriors who came between and over the boulders, performing feats of reckless bravery; many died, but they quickly overwhelmed the defenders in a melee of hand-to-hand fighting of clubs, hatchets, and lances against clubbed rifles and bayonets.

Captain Fetterman died there among the boulders, and with him his good friend Captain Frederick Brown who had got exactly what he was hoping for: one last chance at the Indians before he was transferred out of Fort Phil Kearny. With the Indians closing in, and facing the possibility of capture and torture, they had saved the traditional last bullet for themselves. Then they probably put their pistols at each other's temples, and counting in unison, "One! Two! THREE!" their fingers tightened on the triggers at the same instant. Their bodies were found together; there were smoke burns around the bullet holes in the temples.

A few of the surviving infantrymen had escaped from the tightening ring of warriors and had run up the ridge to where the cavalrymen still held out, the only survivors now, although it is doubtful whether more than fifteen or twenty minutes had passed since the force had had its first horrified shock on seeing grass and rocks come alive with yelling Indians beyond counting. The cavalrymen owed their longer survival simply to the circumstance that the Indians had not given them their full attention yet—few carbine shells and no bodies marked their first position part way up the slope. They had then climbed higher, at last reaching the top of the ridge, where they took up a position among rocks. They were there when the full fury of the attack struck them.

The soldiers had an advantage of higher position; they had good cover among the boulders and their carbines gave them heavy fire-power, and for a while they held the oncoming warriors to a standstill. Then Indian lookouts reported more soldiers coming from the fort—it was Ten Eyck's column—and the attack was redoubled. Indians swarmed among the rocks faster than they could be killed, shooting arrows, clubbing, thrusting lances. One of those who died here was Adolph Metzger, bugler, an old cavalryman since long before the Civil War. It was appropriate that his only weapon at the last should have been his bugle; with everything else gone he used it as a club until it was beaten completely out of shape. One of the men who later helped bring in the dead said that Metzger's body alone was not mutilated in any way, but had been covered with a buffalo robe. (A number had crosses slashed on breast or back, the Indian mark of recognition of a brave man. They did not sell their lives cheaply.)

After Captain Ten Eyck had come back with his wagonloads of dead, Carrington was certain a massive assault was about to break on the fort. Such was his mood of pessimism now that he not only strengthened the defenses of the fort in every way possible but made preparations for catastrophe. He had a barricade of upturned wagons placed around the underground powder magazine which was located in one corner of the parade. The women and children of the post were to enter the magazine in case of attack; if driven from the stockade, the defenders would retire within the barricade for a desperate final defense; if the fight were being lost at the barricade, Colonel Carrington would touch off a powder train leading to the ammunition storage and women, children, soldiers, and a great many exulting Indians would go to Glory together.

That same black evening he wrote out his report of the battle, with a plea for reinforcements and handed it to a civilian employee of the post, John (Portugee) Phillips, who had volunteered to try to take it through to Fort Laramie, 236 miles away. The weather was bitter, there was every sign that a blizzard was about to break over the Big

Horns. Between Indians and weather, Phillips appeared to have only the slightest chance of getting through. But, mounted on a thoroughbred belonging to Colonel Carrington, the best mount in the fort, he set out after dark.

The snow came, pushed by high winds; the temperature fell far below zero. Phillips reached Horseshoe Station, the end of the military telegraph forty miles west of Fort Laramie, at ten o'clock on Christmas morning. Then, having had the operator send his messages, he refused to take any chances that they might not get through, and rode on the remaining forty miles to deliver them in person. It was well he did; the message from Horseshoe Station had been badly garbled and the post commandant at Fort Laramie refused to credit them. Phillips arrived at eleven o'clock at night just four days after leaving Fort Kearny; the post was holding its Christmas ball when, garbed in buffalo-skin clothing from hat to boots, caked with ice, and plastered with snow, almost too exhausted to walk, he stalked like some monstrous specter through the holiday crowd. He was a long time recovering from exhaustion and frostbite, while Carrington's thoroughbred had run its heart out on the long trip and died soon after.

At Fort Philip Kearny, Carrington had turned his attention to the immediate problems of defense as soon as he heard the hootbeats of Portugee Phillips's horse receding down the trail. He got no sleep that night, and early the next day set out with eighty men to recover the bodies of the remaining thirty-two victims. The most elaborate precautions were taken to guard against another surprise attack, but, although Carrington did not know it, the Indians had departed, leaving only a few scouts who lingered on for a few days more to report on activities around the fort.

Most of the remaining bodies were found at the top of the ridge where the cavalrymen had died. Lieutenant Grummond's body was found by the road; so were those of Wheatley, Fisher, and the few veteran infantrymen who had made a stand with them. The Henry repeating rifles of Wheatley and Fisher had plainly done great slaughter; Colonel Carrington counted sixty-five pools of frozen blood surrounding their position, marking spots where dead or badly injured Indians had lain. The warriors, in retaliation, had shot arrows into Fisher after they had stripped off his clothes; 105 of them bristled from his corpse. (The Indians had treated a number of bodies in this manner; perhaps they had been men in whom some breath of life still flickered after they had been stripped and scalped.) There were no warrior dead; the Indians had followed their usual custom of taking their slain with them.

Threatening skies were bringing dusk on even earlier than it otherwise would have been at this time of short days, and it was long after dark before the grisly search was concluded and the wagons had returned to the fort. That same night a blizzard struck, driving the temperature to twenty degrees below zero, and piling in great quantities of snow.

The next five days were spent in preparing the bodies for burial, building coffins, and in digging graves in the frozen ground of the snow-swept cemetery. Although a large crew of men aided the medical officers, they needed two days to get the bodies ready. The official report prepared by Carrington two weeks after the disaster explains why this grim task was so difficult: "I give you some of the facts as to my men, whose bodies I found just at dark, . . . Eyes torn out and laid on rocks; noses cut off; ears cut off; chins hewn off; teeth chopped out; joints of fingers, brains taken out and placed on rocks with other members of the body; entrails taken out and exposed; hands cut off; feet cut off; arms taken out from sockets; . . ." (The gruesome catalogue continues to a length it is not necessary to pursue.) *

The burial took place on the day after Christmas. Red Cloud had done quite well in his war to keep the Americans from taking over the Big Horn country. Since Colonel Carrington had come out with such bright hopes to build his fort by Big Piney Creek, 154 soldiers and civilians had been killed on the Bozeman Trail. More than half had died in a single action, the one that within days would begin to be called the "Fetterman Massacre." It was no massacre, it was a battle in which the military had been outwitted and hopelessly outnumbered, and one of the two battles in American history in which there was not a single American survivor (or one of three, if you choose to think of

---

* Such mutilations, barbaric and horrible as they are, were not inspired by savage blood lust but had their basis in Indian religious beliefs. Men enter the afterworld, the Plains Indians believed, in the same form they held immediately after death. It was only common sense, then, to make sure that an enemy should be sightless in the hereafter, or without hands to hold a warclub, or perhaps with teeth knocked out so that he could not enjoy roast buffalo and the other good things of the shadow world.

The other side of the coin was the supreme risks warriors would take to recover the body of one of their own dead; they were thereby saving a comrade from the mutilations by the enemy which would have crippled him in the spirit world.

the defenders of the Alamo as Americans. The other no-survivor battle was nine years in the future but only about seventy miles distant; many of the same warriors who ambushed Fetterman's command would be present at the Little Bighorn).

It is not known whether Red Cloud himself was even present at the greatest triumph of his nation's arms. In later years he claimed that he personally led the fight, but others who fought there say the chief was elsewhere that day. However, the great Oglala chief, Hump, was present and very probably was the leading chief. As for Indian casualties, the accounts given by the natives varied so widely as to be meaningless. One set the figure at only fourteen dead, another made it fifty or sixty, others agreed that about sixty were killed and at least a hundred of the wounded were so badly hurt that they died later.

When word of the disaster reached Colonel Carrington's immediate superior, Brigadier General Philip St. George Cooke, commanding the Department of the Platte (Iowa, Nebraska, and most of Wyoming), that crusty old Indian campaigner at once ordered reinforcements sent from Fort Laramie; Lieutenant Colonel (Brevet Brigadier General) Henry W. Wessells who had been post commander at Fort Reno since November was ordered to assume command of the reinforcements on their arrival at Fort Reno and bring them on to Fort Kearny where he would relieve his commanding officer, Colonel Carrington, assuming command of all three forts.

As a matter of fact, the move was more complex than that. The Army was increasing its forces on the frontier, and the 2nd Battalion of the 18th Infantry was being expanded into a new regiment, the 27th Infantry. Carrington was still Colonel of the 18th Regiment whose 1st and 3rd Battalions had been serving elsewhere on the frontier while he was at Kearny, and a new 2nd Battalion was to be organized, but he deeply resented the way Cooke had ordered his relief, before getting his full report, as though to place the onus of Fetterman's defeat on him. However, it was a game others could play; Sherman had not been happy with Cooke as one of his departmental commanders; he considered the general, whose Indian-fighting career went back to the Black Hawk War of 1832, to be too old and inflexible. Soon after Cooke relieved Carrington, Sherman removed Cooke.

Carrington left Fort Philip Kearny on January 23 with an escort of sixty men, taking with him all women and children. The snow was deep, the temperature got as low as forty below zero, and by the time the sixty-five miles to Fort Reno had been traversed, two of the cavalry escorts had frozen their legs so badly they had to be amputated. Women and children rode in covered wagons made as cold-proof as possible and provided with small stoves; even so, the temperature within the wagons often stood well below zero. The trip in the jolting wagon was a special torture to the widow of Lieutenant Grummond whose pregnancy was far along. One wagon carried the pine coffin with her husband's body; she had prevailed on the Colonel to let her take it back for burial in Tennessee.

4. A STATE OF SIEGE

Sherman (now Lieutenant General Sherman) had undoubtedly learned a great deal about the Plains tribes and their temper since the May day when he had said, at old Fort Kearney, that he did not see any danger ahead for the women and children accompanying Colonel Carrington to the Bozeman Trail. But he still had not learned enough to prepare him for the news he had received just after Christmas. "I do not understand how the massacre of Colonel Fetterman's party could have been so complete. . . . We must act with vindictive earnestness against the Sioux, even to their extermination, men, women and children. Nothing else will reach the root of this case."

One of the most frequently used words in Sherman's vocabulary would be "extermination." For the world of William Tecumseh Sherman was black and white. It was a world in which orders were given and obeyed—and in the West it was for the Army to command and the red man to do the obeying. Sherman was fairly representative of the military attitude—and an excellent argument against returning the Indian Service to the military, as the Army had been demanding ever since 1849 when it had been given to the Interior Department.

However, that is not the same as saying that the Interior Department was doing an ideal job with the Indian Service—far from it. The Fetterman disaster brought the old controversy between the two services to a high pitch again. The arrangement between the two was custom-built for trouble: the civilian Bureau of Indian Affairs handled all relations with the natives until trouble broke out and it became necessary to apply force; then it called on the Army to take over. The Army claimed that the Bureau mishandled affairs until events got out of hand and then had to call in the military to put its mistakes right, a chore that cost human lives.

Another favorite Army charge was that the Indian Service supplied the warriors with guns and ammunition (or, what amounted to the same thing, permitted traders to supply firearms), often more modern than the Army issue, which were then turned against Army troops; the Bureau replied that whatever guns the Indians got they desperately needed for hunting game which was getting scarcer all the time. (The truth lay somewhere between. The number of firearms furnished to Indians, and their superiority over those used by the Army has been grossly exaggerated; the legend of heroic soldiers with muzzle-loaders fighting off superbly armed Indians was developed mainly on the verandas of Old Soldiers' Homes. Throughout the plains wars the bow and arrow remained the predominant Indian weapon—at the Fetterman fight, which set off the squabble, there were very few Indian guns of any kind.)

The Bureau had its own list of complaints against the Army; its outstanding one was, in blunt terms, that the Army was brutal in its treatment of Indians. However, while the Bureau talked about its own humanitarian objectives, the tribes had not exactly thrived under the guardianship of a long series of corrupt, indifferent or stupid officials, from Commissioner on down to agent.

The nation, though, was wearied for the moment of the endless wrangling between Army and Indian Bureau. Rather strangely, the news from Fort Kearny had not given rise to a call for revenge, but instead had sent the country into one of its rare moods of introspection and soul-searching about its treatment of its Indians. An investigation was made of the entire Indian policy and the obvious was discovered: a great deal of trouble was caused by the split authority between Interior Department and War Department. Even more at fault, said the report, was the constant violation by white men of rights which the government had solemnly guaranteed to the Indians, very often with the Army protecting the whites while they did the violating.

As a result, Congress passed a bill in March, 1867, to establish peace with the tribes, and to settle the Indian problem with justice and without interference by the War Department. However, in spite of all good intentions about preventing War Department interference, military influence was going to make itself felt, for of the seven Peace

Commissioners to be appointed to talk with the Indians, three were to be generals. One of them would be Sherman.

Sherman had spent a frustrating winter. First had come the unnerving news of the catastrophe on the Bozeman Trail. Then, in January, he received reports that Indians in Kansas and Colorado were getting guns and ammunition from traders, although he had issued an order in June which permitted only authorized persons to sell arms to the natives. He hit the ceiling when he discovered that the Indian Bureau had, on its own, given such authorization to all traders, and ordered General Winfield Hancock to put a stop to the trade.

But the most irritating of all to him was a persistent rumor that Fort C. F. Smith, most remote of the three on the Bozeman Trail, had been taken by the Indians and destroyed, with its entire garrison killed or tortured to death. Like all rumors, it sifted through his fingers when he tried to get hold of it; one person responsible for disseminating it, he did learn through devious channels, was the wife of some officer in his own Omaha headquarters. If that were true, it was fortunate for the lady that the commanding general could not pinpoint the source—by discovering her identity.

While the rumors spread hundreds of miles away, things were not going well on the Bozeman Trail itself. Lieutenant Colonel Wessells had stepped into a post where food supplies were limited, during an exceptionally cold winter that exhausted firewood supplies long before spring came. Hay and other feed for horses and mules ran out and the starving beasts were fed cottonwood branches. Clothing was inadequate; scurvy from improper food became prevalent; morale dropped low, and as soon as the snow went, the Sioux were back. Communications were maintained during the winter, though with great difficulty, from the outside world with Fort Reno and Fort Kearny, but Fort C. F. Smith to the north had dropped from the earth since before Fetterman and his force were wiped out. When a detail finally got through from Fort Kearny in March, 1867, half-expecting to find everyone dead, they discovered that Fort Smith had actually come through the winter in better shape than they had, without scurvy, thanks to the antiscorbutic properties of a good supply of potatoes and cabbage which had been purchased from the Montana mining towns in the fall.

The return of spring brought no lessening of the isolation of the three forts because the returning Indians held the road in as tight a grip as the winter ever had. During the next months the three posts lived in a virtual state of siege; only well-armed Army supply convoys traveled the road between them, and that only rarely. Attacks were frequent, especially on Kearny, which, in the center of the Sioux hunting lands, was the main focus of their hate. Then, at the beginning of August, the Indians struck in heavy force at Forts Smith and Kearny.

On August 1, Red Cloud sent something over five hundred warriors, mostly Cheyennes, against Fort Smith. There they found and attacked a haymaking detail at work in a meadow of tall grass about three miles northeast of the fort where a stream called Warrior Creek emptied into the Big Horn River. There were six civilians in the haymaking crew, guarded by nineteen soldiers. The detail did not ordinarily return to the fort at night but kept its mules and made its own camp within a corral of logs. The corral was hardly a fort but it gave good protection because the lowest log rested directly on the ground, a good gun rest for a prone man and a stopper for arrows and bullets.

Small bands of Indians had made hit-and-run raids from time to time and had been fought off from the corral, but the haymakers lashing their mowing machine teams to a gallop to reach cover in the corral this morning had never seen anything like the hundreds of warriors who suddenly appeared. All took cover behind the bottom log and began firing—all, that is, except Second Lieutenant Sigmund Sternberg who commanded the guard. He said he believed a soldier should fight standing up. It was a noble-sounding idea but it had one weakness; he was killed very soon by a bullet through the head.

The natives were unable to pierce the defenses in several hours of fighting. Twice they tried to overwhelm the defenders by their traditional tactic of riding back and forth close to the corral, clinging to the off-side of their ponies by a leg hooked over the back, and shooting under the neck. Several attempts were made to set fire to dry grass near the corral and to hay inside it, and a final charge was made by warriors on foot but was driven off. After this last repulse, the Indians withdrew, except for a few snipers who lingered for a time.

Three of the defenders were killed, three injured. The success of the small force in the corral against such heavy odds was almost entirely a matter of firepower. Only a week earlier, Springfield rifles modified to make them breech-loaders had arrived at the fort. They were a much faster weapon than the old muzzle-loaders; although still single-shot weapons, the empty cartridge could be ejected and a new one slapped in the breech in a moment—and almost without taking the sights off a target, something decidedly not possible with a muzzle-loader.

Although the fort was the primary objective of the attack, the Indians never got close to it. Nor, as a matter of fact, did the commanding officer show any eagerness to get close to the Indians. As soon as he was informed that an attack was under way, he closed the gates and confined all hands to the fort, and refused permission to an officer who wanted to take a relief column to the beleaguered corral. The commander, Lieutenant Colonel L. P. Bradley, appears to have been haunted by the fear of another Fetterman episode. Only after a messenger from the corral informed him that the war party had gone did he send help.

The day after the fight at Fort Smith—which, not too surprisingly, has become known as the Hayfield Fight—Chief Red Cloud himself appeared near Fort Philip Kearny with an estimated 1,500 or more warriors. Woodcutting operations were going on at the pineries just as they had been the year before when Captain Fetterman was decoyed to his death. However, this year the woodcutting crews and their guards, like the haymakers at Fort Smith, camped near their work in order to save time getting started in the morning.

The woodcutters' camp was located about six miles from the fort and a very short distance from the scene of logging operations, on an area of open, grassy land. An oval enclosure had been laid out with fourteen wagon boxes set on the ground; the wheels and bases were being used to haul wood. Ordinarily, the enclosure was a corral for horses and mules at night. But ready boxes of ammunition were provided at intervals inside the enclosure, and miscellaneous objects, as ox-yokes, logs, sacks of grain, bags of the ever-present Army beans, and the like were at hand, ready to come to the defense of white civilization if needed. They would be needed this second of August, 1867.

About seven o'clock in the morning, hundreds of Indians appeared over the hills north of the wagon box corral. By that time, a wagon train of cordwood was heading for the fort and a string of empty wagons from the fort was nearing the pineries. There was confusion and bravery and lost opportunity before affairs took definite shape. A party of warriors ran off the mule herd of the woodcutters, isolated pickets and mule herders fought their way to the corral and had a dozen hairbreadth escapes. The wagon train from the fort was unable to reach the corral and battled its way all the way back to the fort, bearing the alarm.

There were thirty-two men in the enclosure, four of them civilians. In command was Captain James W. Powell, an old Fort Kearny hand, who had arrived on the same day Captain Fetterman had. It was Powell, careful and given to exemplary obedience of orders, who had been ordered to relieve the wood train on the day when Fetterman had pulled his rank and taken command—with results the whole country knew.

In the situation in which he now found himself, all Powell could do was look around the enclosure, make sure his men were all posted where they could hurt the enemy without exposing themselves too much, and let it go at that. Powell, apparently, was not given to inspirational exhortations; he is reported to have sent his men into battle with a simple, "Men, here they come! Take your places and shoot to kill."

The wagon boxes with their thin sides were no protection against bullets but they did hide the man inside from view; they were possibly not even much protection against arrows since Indians sometimes had the disconcerting habit of getting behind a defense by arcing their arrows into the air in a high, plunging fire which came down almost vertically. The boxes were very like the familiar old covered-wagon type but no canvas was drawn over the wooden roof bows. Loopholes had been bored in the outer sides of the boxes for just such a situation as this, and the piles of oxen yokes, sacks of corn, a barrel of salt, and similar breastworks between the wagon boxes provided good firing positions.

The attacking Sioux—there seems to have been few or no Cheyennes and Arapahoes in this war party—were also provided with shelter on one side because the level, grassy shelf on which the wagon-box corral stood ended about a hundred yards away where it dropped away to the valley of Big Piney Creek. The drop-off gave cover to Sioux snipers.

The first attack was made by a large group of mounted warriors (five hundred, Captain Powell estimated) riding hidden behind their ponies and coming close to the corral. The Sioux tactics were spectacular, with the pounding of hundreds of hoofs, the shrill yelling of warriors, the surge of galloping ponies only half-seen through a pall of dust, and all too often the headlong dive and rolling somersault of a badly hit horse and rider.

However, the warriors had not planned to ride back and forth indefinitely, like ducks in a shooting gallery. They knew from experience that after the first blast of fire from the corral there should be a pause while the defenders reloaded; they were ready to thunder in and overwhelm the men inside the ring of wagon boxes the instant the fire diminished. But the pause never came; the cracking of rifles went on at a tempo far greater than the number of beleaguered whites warranted, while the number of dead and wounded Indians and horses on the grassy plain mounted into the dozens. At last the bewildered Sioux ended their assault.

The Indians' perplexity at the heavy rifle fire was understandable. Fort Kearny, like Fort Smith, had very recently received modified breech-loading Springfields to replace the old muzzle-loaders. The mounted warriors had planned to make their final assault while the defenders' rifles were empty after the first volley and the soldiers were going through the complicated loading procedure with the ramrods. But there had been no break in the murderous fire.

With several other chiefs, Red Cloud sat on his horse on a rise of ground, making no move to interfere or direct the attack until it ground to a halt. Then a council of war was held, in which an attack on foot was decided on, to come from the north, where the sharp slope down to the creek valley would provide cover for such an assault. Indians with guns—probably most of them the firearms gathered up after the Fetterman battle—had been stationed behind the rim of this drop-off during the fight, keeping the corral under fire. Their aim had been effective; they had killed an officer and two enlisted men, all three shot through the head. From the same protected position, flights of fire arrows had arced into the corral, starting hay to blazing and setting smoldering fires among accumulated dry horse and mule dung which sent up choking clouds of smoke. The fires did no damage but they were an acute discomfort.

Now, behind the same rim the attack on foot was organized. There was a small ravine in the plain; hundreds of warriors, almost naked, moved from behind the drop-off up this ravine, taking advantage of the cover it gave till they were forced to cross the open plain toward the corral. They came on in a compact wedge while the defenders fired rapidly and accurately, but with mounting panic as the seemingly irresistible tide moved down on them. But, at the last moment, the Sioux broke and ran, leaving a few of their dead within five feet of the wagon boxes.

It was, at the same time, a telling demonstration of one of the weaknesses of the Plains Indian as a military man. He seldom had the ability to improvise tactics, especially consecutive tactics. When the foot attack was so near to succeeding, a small amount of support would probably have carried it through. The defense had concentrated almost all its strength against the courageous men attacking over the open plain; the south side of the corral was almost unprotected and could have been carried by a sudden and determined assault. Yet hundreds of mounted braves remained aloof, merely interested spectators. Nor apparently did Red Cloud make any attempt to intervene.

With the smashing of the foot attack, the heart went out of the Sioux. Sniping continued from behind the rim of the drop-off, but the Indians gave most of their attention to rescuing their wounded and recovering the bodies of their dead, something in which they often took risks greater than in the battle itself.

Shortly after noon a relief party armed with a howitzer arrived from the fort and the Indians withdrew far enough to be out of range of the big gun. The corral was evacuated at once and the return to the fort made with no attempt at harassment by the Sioux. The siege had lasted probably five hours but only three of the defenders were killed and two wounded, resisting possibly fifteen hundred Indians (Captain Powell estimated three thousand, but this figure is hard to swallow). How many men the Sioux lost is a matter of guesswork for the estimates run all the way from six killed to more than a thousand. Both extremes are completely ridiculous. Captain Powell estimated sixty killed and a hundred and twenty badly wounded, a figure probably bearing some approximate relation to the truth. Years later Red Cloud said he lost the flower of his men in the fighting.

The two defeats suffered by the Indians on the Bozeman Trail had not affected the resolves made earlier in the year in the East to work out a solution to the Indian problem which would recognize and honor the just claims of the tribes. The seven-member Peace Commission to treat with the Indians was appointed in August, not long after the Hayfield and Wagon-Box Fights. General Sherman was one of the three military men. (Another was General Harney, who had attacked an innocent Brule village long ago as retribution for the Mormon's cow affair and so became one of the first Indian fighters on the plains.) N. G. Taylor, Commissioner of Indian Affairs was a member, so was Senator John B. Henderson of Missouri, Chairman of the Senate Committee on Indian Affairs, and two prominent private citizens completed the group.

After a 1,300-mile steamboat trip to talk to tribes on the Missouri River, the Commission next went by train to North Platte, Nebraska, in mid-September for a meeting with a delegation of Oglala and Brule Sioux. At the council, the Indians complained about the way the whites were ruining the hunting along the Smoky Hill Road in Kansas and Colorado and along the Bozeman Trail; the whites, they said, would have to get out of those regions. Sherman answered that both roads were necessary to the white man and would have to stay. Then he went on to describe how well tribes like the Cherokees and Potawatomies had done farming their own lands, and suggested that the Sioux pick themselves a nice reservation before the good land was all gone. Having left these thoughts, and promising to be back in November, the Commission moved on to negotiate with the Southern tribes.

On November 6 they were back at North Platte, but only a single chief, Swift Bear of the Brule Sioux, was there of a dozen or more important leaders who had been present in September. Even Spotted Tail, the great lover of peace, did not show up the second time.

They moved on to Fort Laramie. Messengers had been sent up into the Powder River country asking Red Cloud and other chiefs to meet them at the fort for a council, but on their arrival they found no one. The chiefs had had the delicate courtesy to send a message saying they were too busy to appear just then. General Harney and another two of the commissioners considered this a piece of insolence which a white man should not have to take from one with red skin, and they asked Sherman how many troops would be required to whip the Powder River Sioux thoroughly.

However, there was no talk in the Bozeman Trail forts about thrashing the Sioux. The men there could see the snow whitening the Big Horns, and they damned the portent of the skin of ice that edged the streams in the morning. Those who had spent the previous frigid and hunger-stalked winter in the forts did not welcome another season there. But, though they would stay on, the jig was up with the forts. The day Sherman was asked how many soldiers it would take to whip the Powder River Sioux, he knew, no matter what answer he gave to the question, that the Sioux had won and that peace overtures had been approved.

For already in October, the quartermaster at Fort Kearny, Captain

Dandy, had met with Sioux, Cheyenne, and Arapaho chiefs on a meadow about a quarter mile from the fort for the first talks between the government and the Indians on the matter of abandoning the Bozeman Trail and the three forts. Red Cloud was not present.

The next spring the Peace Commissioners returned to Fort Laramie and on April 29, 1868, signed a treaty with leaders of the Brule, Oglala, Miniconjou, and Yanktonais bands of the Sioux and of the northern Arapaho. The tribes agreed to accept reservations, and all of the present state of South Dakota west of the Missouri River was set aside as Indian reservation land. The tribes also insisted on their right to hunt buffalo on lands north of the North Platte and on the Republican River, and the treaty guaranteed them this right "so long as buffalo may range there in numbers sufficient to justify the chase."

Sherman was not present at the signing, but he objected to the buffalo clause and later wrote to General Philip Sheridan that the best thing that could be done would be to invite all the sportsmen of England and America to a great buffalo shoot. For, he said, until the Indians were out from between the great transplains roads the danger of collisions would remain.

Red Cloud did not appear for the signing and would not accept the treaty—or any treaty—as long as the Bozeman Trail and the forts remained. And even though Oglala and Miniconjou chiefs had touched the pen at Fort Laramie, probably the greater part of the two bands were still sitting it out with Red Cloud.

Sherman had already made up his mind that the road would be given up. (The advance of the railroad made it possible to use a road into Montana farther west, he said, a statement that seems to have a little of the flavor of sour grapes.) The actual order for abandonment was given on May 19 by Major General Christopher C. Augur, commanding the Department of the Platte, and in August the soldiers marched out and left what had not been consumed or hauled away during the summer. Fort C. F. Smith was first, then Fort Philip Kearny, and finally Fort Reno. Before August was over there was nothing left except the dead in the post cemeteries (a numerous company), they and some heaps of ashes because the jubilant Indians had burned each fort almost before the departing rearguard of the garrison had disappeared over the first ridge.

At last, on November 6, Red Cloud came to Fort Laramie to sign a treaty. He was the first and only Indian leader in the West to win a war with the United States. He had fought for two years to preserve the beautiful hunting lands of the Sioux and now the soldiers were gone. The Bozeman Trail was empty. The forts were destroyed. And in the treaty, the government agreed that the Big Horn country would be considered as unceded Indian territory, forbidden to whites, where the Sioux and their Cheyenne and Arapaho allies were to have full and unrestricted rights to hunt.

Red Cloud promised not to make war again, and he kept his promise, through a period of great turbulence for the Sioux nation. Some among his people questioned his motives and many were deeply puzzled by his decision to walk a road of peace, but no one accused him of being a coward because Red Cloud had counted eighty coups, that is, he had performed eighty feats of valor meriting special recognition. Have nothing to do with white men, he told his people, and added cynical advice on how to become wealthy like the white men: "You must begin anew and put away the wisdom of your fathers. You must lay up food and forget the hungry. When your house is built, your store-room filled, then look around for a neighbor whom you can take advantage of and seize all he has."

Red Cloud could afford the luxury of being cynical. He had done about as well as any Indian ever had.

V

The Great Road

1. GENERAL HANCOCK'S WAR

IN his annual report to the Secretary of War early in November, 1866, General Sherman had stated that the Sioux would have to be kept north of the Platte River, west of the Missouri, and east of the Bozeman Trail (here Sherman proposed but Red Cloud disposed), while the Arapaho, Cheyenne, Comanche, and Kiowa should be kept south of the Arkansas River and east of Fort Union, New Mexico. "This," he wrote, "would leave for our people exclusively the use of the wide belt, east and west, between the Platte and the Arkansas, in which lie the two great railroads, and over which pass the bulk of travel to the mountain territories."

There is in Sherman's report a quaint echo of the Great American Desert, a survival of the idea that the plains were only an expanse to be crossed in moving from East to West. Actually, settlers were becoming interested in them. The Homestead Act of 1862 offered land to men and women for no other coin than the courage to farm it, and pioneers were already seeking their dream in a sod shanty and a horizon over which nothing much appeared but clouds. (Sherman, who thought in military terms, was not in sympathy with these early settlers; he

135

believed it would be better if they abandoned their exposed positions and gave the Army a more compact perimeter to defend.)

Settlement was bringing a profound change to the plains but it tended to be a gradual one; a few sod-busters today, a couple tomorrow and half a dozen the next day, and almost without anyone quite realizing it was going on, a dozen townships had been settled. On the other hand, there was nothing gradual about the changes being wrought by the railroads. To the Army, they meant a change in both logistics and tactics. They were making it possible to abandon many small Army posts and garrisons scattered throughout Indian country. Sherman pointed out that it would be far easier to bring detachments out onto the plains by railroad in the spring and let the soldiers live under canvas during the summer and fall than to try to maintain them on the plains the year around.

Indian war parties very seldom operated in winter, anyway, while for the soldiers, there was something less than complete comfort in spending the cold months on the plains in buildings of sod or cottonwood logs, most of them none too airtight and miserably uncomfortable when the wind blew across the plains and the thermometer registered far below zero.

The two railroads left much of the plains unaffected, and garrisons in scores of posts were still condemned to frostbite, boredom, and other hazards of winter station on the frontier, but where the lines reached, winter soldiering was changed drastically and made a less irksome occupation. By the end of the summer of 1866, the Union Pacific had built some 200 miles west of Omaha; the Kansas Pacific was about 125 miles west of Kansas City.

To the military, to promoters, to settlers, to land speculators, to the great heterogeneous collection of humans that makes up an advancing frontier, the railroads were the ultimate herald of advancing civilization. To the Indians, the building of the iron road was little less than catastrophic. Great crews of white men came to lay the rails, and soldiers protected the builders. Noisy locomotives and trains frightened the game. Professional hunters shot thousands of buffalo to keep the cook cars supplied with the mountains of meat needed to feed an army of railroad builders. It was not a good year for Indians on the middle plains.

There was no warfare, but there was no peace, either. Red Cloud was fighting to close the Bozeman Trail and the Sioux were edgy as a result; the Cheyennes were still smoldering over the Sand Creek Massacre. It was not surprising that Indian resentment broke out now and again in the killing of a surveying party, or a sudden attack on a grading or track-laying crew. All that was needed to break a good number of eggs was for some clumsy-footed fool to walk through the scene at this point. And just such a person was on hand: Major General Winfield Scott Hancock, commander of the Department of the Missouri.*

General Hancock was one of those men who capped grandeur with anticlimax. He had been one of the greatest of the great during the war, a general with a record surpassed by very few. A Beau Brummel among officers, the rare type who was cheered by the ranks when he rode by, he fought with distinction all through the war with the Army of the Potomac, but the moment when the rays of true glory shone down came on the third day at Gettysburg. He commanded the II Corps on Cemetery Ridge; he exposed himself to the enemy's fire to inspire his men, and went down at the last, grievously wounded after repulsing the supreme Confederate effort known ever after as Pickett's Charge.

Things were different out on the plains. It was hot, dusty, and barren, or else cold and windy—no place for a Beau Brummel to appear at his best. However, a man of action could operate in this kind of country—even if he did not know exactly what he was doing—and Hancock decided on a great spring campaign against the Arapahoes and Cheyennes. It was about as ill-conceived an idea as one can look for. The Indians in his department were not at war. A campaign could only antagonize them. All indications are that he merely meant to go out and swagger around a bit, daring the natives to fight.

Or, as he put it in a letter to the Indian agent at Fort Larned, his campaign was only to awe the Indians and to impress them with the might of the white man. He was not looking for war, he said, but added rather ominously that he would not avoid it. The agent had begged him not to send a military expedition into the plains because the memory of Sand Creek was still fresh in the minds of the Cheyennes, even in this spring of 1867, and they would be certain that armed forces would

---

* Not to be confused with the Division of the Missouri, of which it was a part. The Department of the Missouri included Kansas, Missouri, eastern Colorado, and northeastern New Mexico. The Division of the Missouri, Sherman's over-all command, was divided into five departments at that time, although there were adjustments in later years.

be approaching only for another massacre attempt. Sherman, of course, had approved the campaign and so deserves part of the blame, but it is doubtful that he anticipated Hancock's arrogance and ineptitude in carrying out his plans.

"No insolence will be tolerated from any bands of Indians whom we may encounter," Hancock wrote. "We wish to show them that the government is ready and able to punish them if they are hostile, although it may not be disposed to invite war." The general sounded like a man determined to start trouble through sheer stupidity.

The Indian agent at Fort Larned was Colonel Edward W. Wynkoop, the same who, then a major, had been commanding officer of Fort Lyon, and after bringing the Cheyenne chiefs to Denver to see the governor and Colonel Chivington, had promised them security if they camped near the fort. Perhaps he carried a sense of guilt over his unwitting part in leading Black Kettle's Cheyennes into a slaughter trap and felt he could atone for it by serving them; whatever the reason, he was now agent for the Southern Cheyennes and Arapahoes. He had been patiently working to regain their confidence and to get them to congregate closer to Fort Larned. Now Hancock was about to upset the entire applecart.

General Hancock set out from Fort Leavenworth late in March loaded for bear, with a column that included six companies of infantry, a battery of light artillery and—how to state the incredible as simple fact?—a train whose freight included pontoons for bridging the ankle-deep rivers of western Kansas. At Fort Riley, Fort Harker, and Fort Larned the column was joined by companies of the 7th Cavalry until at last the expedition was 1,400 strong. The colonel designated to lead the newly-formed 7th Cavalry not having arrived, its acting commander was George Armstrong Custer, who held a brevet rank of major general but at the moment was only a lieutenant colonel in the Regular Army.

At Larned, Colonel Wynkoop once more tried to make Hancock see sense. There was a camp of Cheyennes with some Sioux on the Pawnee River about forty miles west of the fort. They would become frightened and take it as a warlike move if the soldiers moved on them, warned Wynkoop. They would run away, he said, but they would retaliate on the first stage station they came to. Hancock complied with Wynkoop's warnings to the degree that he remained at Fort Larned and summoned the chiefs to a council. Then, after the chiefs had shown up, and Hancock had falsely accused them of having white prisoners, he marched anyway.

A delegation of chiefs and warriors met the advancing column and asked Hancock not to bring his soldiers near the camp because the women and children were frightened. He would have to bring his soldiers closer, the general insisted, but he would see that none of them approached the lodges. There is no way of knowing whether it was complete pigheadedness that drove this man on, or whether he had some obscure end in mind, possibly to force the Indians into an overt hostile move.

The state of mind of the natives by this time must have bordered on panic. At midnight, Hancock ordered Custer to surround the camp —for what reason, it is again difficult to guess. However, it is not difficult to imagine what would have happened had the cavalry surrounded the camp before the Indians discovered it. The Cheyennes, on finding themselves encircled, would beyond a doubt have decided on the instant that they were about to be killed as they had been at Sand Creek. They would have tried to fight their way out without stopping to make inquiries, and then there would have been a massacre. It is difficult to believe Hancock could have been so obtuse as to have thought anything else could have happened. On the other hand, it is not easy to understand many things Hancock did during the entire misbegotten campaign.

In any event, the tragedy never occurred. The nervous Indians had quietly abandoned their camp as soon as darkness fell; Custer's men carefully surrounded a camp which the gray morning light revealed to be absolutely deserted. General Hancock was enraged at this perfidy and ordered the cavalry out in pursuit. It was a hopeless quest. Even under the best of conditions, cavalry stood little chance of catching the Indians during the summer months when the light ponies of the warriors could run rings around the heavier government horses. And Custer was not operating under the best of conditions. He knew next to nothing about fighting Indians at that stage in his career, while the 7th Cavalry was a new regiment whose men, for the most part, were not much past the stage of raw recruits. Whenever Custer came on a good, strong trail, it had a maddening way of dividing and dividing again, until soon he found himself following the tracks of only three or four horses.

In the meantime, the angry Cheyennes, convinced that they had barely escaped another massacre, had attacked and burned several stage stations, just as Colonel Wynkoop had warned they would. Hancock thereupon set fire to the deserted Cheyenne village—it was about the only thing he could do in his frustration—and took most of his infantry and his pontoons and headed back toward Fort Leavenworth by easy stages, leaving Custer and the 7th to carry on. The government shortly thereafter declared the Cheyennes, Arapahoes, and the Sioux south of the Platte to be at war with the United States, all in all a very good showing for Hancock's little expedition to awe the Indians and impress them with the white man's might.

As for Custer, while he was accomplishing little, he was trying hard. He was pushing his men beyond the point of endurance for many of them; had they been old campaigners it would have been a rigorous and exhausting period of soldiering, but his men were far from seasoned. As a result, many had deserted, most were exhausted and saddle-sore. George Custer was not a man who wearied like ordinary mortals; he had no understanding of physical frailties or any sympathy for them. A strict disciplinarian (for everyone but himself), his answer when his men began to complain was to give them a stronger dose of the same medicine.

The matter came to a small climax one midday early in June when the regiment had halted for a rest. Twelve men—seven mounted, five on foot—decided during the stop to desert, and, with no show of stealth, simply left camp, their destination the Platte River not many miles away. It was one thing to desert, it was quite another to walk out in broad daylight in such a manner that it was tantamount to thumbing noses at the commanding officer. Colonel Custer, losing both his temper and his head, shrilled an order to the officer of the day to go after the deserters and to "bring none in alive." Two officers took up the chase. The mounted men escaped easily, but three of those on foot were shot, of whom one died several weeks later. Two avoided injury by pretending to be dead.

This was the great General George Armstrong Custer, the man turned legend, who in popular fancy stands with the great ones—Lewis and Clark, Kit Carson, the Pony Express Riders, Buffalo Bill, Wyatt Earp—as openers of the West. But an order, in rage, to shoot a dozen soldiers was not the act of a great man, nor even that of an officer of average competence and self-control. Did the god have feet of clay? Does the legend, after all, mask a man who was no more than other men?

It is difficult to find a starting place for describing Custer. Those who have already formed opinions about the man have done so with such vehemence that it is hard to believe that the two sides are talking about the same person. To one group, he remains the brave and gallant soldier and peerless Indian fighter who died heroically and gloriously battling against hopeless odds; to the other he was a big-mouthed braggart and incompetent who blundered away the lives of more than two hundred men by rushing joyfully into a deadly situation without taking the simplest precautions demanded by military prudence. On one point all agree: Custer was a man of supreme physical courage who apparently did not know what it was to feel fear. Beyond that, there is agreement on very little.

Custer graduated at the bottom of his class at West Point, in large part for demerits received for what his admirers like to describe as "boyish pranks and escapades," although a good part of his bad record was the result of slovenly habits. This last was highly ironic because no officer would demand more later from his men in the way of snap and polish and taut discipline than he. He received his commission just in time to get into the First Battle of Bull Run.

He had a dash about him and a vivaciousness, to say nothing of his courage, which could not help but attract the attention of his superiors, and he received choice assignments for such a very young officer. He had a superb confidence that fortune was always working for him; "Custer's luck," he called this continual smile of the gods, and for a number of years it appeared that he was right and that it actually existed. As it turned out, "Custer's luck" was not an inexhaustible commodity.

Some points in his career remain hazy. He was, for instance, jumped all the way from first lieutenant to brigadier general after having played only minor parts in engagements where he performed in no manner worthy of such recognition. Even Custer's luck could not explain such a promotion; it seems possible that political influence was also involved. In any event, at twenty-three, he was (and still is) the youngest man ever to have held the rank of brigadier general in the United States Army; two years later he was breveted major general and so became the youngest ever in that rank—with the single exception of the Marquis de Lafayette during the Revolution.

He was a flamboyant leader. He designed his own uniform which consisted of a wide-brimmed hat, trousers with a double stripe running down the seam, a sailor's wide-collared shirt, a red cravat, and on the sleeves of his jacket an intricate arabesque of interlacing loops of gold braid. Add to this the golden hair grown long and lying in ringlets on his shoulders and the man becomes rather overpowering in his gaudiness and glitter.

However, these were personal things; the important thing in a soldier is whether he can fight. General Custer could fight all right, but there was a great deal of question about his competence as a commander. During the war, he two or three times showed a disconcerting habit of forgetting his main responsibility to go whooping off after some side issue that was more exciting—as the time he entered a Virginia town and spied a Confederate locomotive and cars about to make their escape; he left his command to take care of itself and made a wild dash to capture the train. Such actions can turn disastrous, and it was perhaps only Custer's luck that saved him each time.

Because of his impulsiveness, he was not a good tactician. His joy was leading a cavalry charge, saber swinging, yellow hair streaming in the wind, the field behind him thundering with hundreds of men and horses answering to his command. He had not enough patience for the careful reconnoitering, the consideration of alternatives, the working out of plans that make a good commanding officer.

Custer had been a teetotaler since the day when, a young and arrogant lieutenant home on furlough, he had been staggering under more than he could carry and had met Elizabeth Bacon. Miss Bacon, the future Mrs. Custer, was not amused; young Custer took the pledge and never drank again. He appeared not to know the meaning of weariness; he could spend a day campaigning on the plains that exhausted the men with him, and then come back to his tent and spend most of the night writing a long letter to Mrs. Custer. On occasion, if no operations were scheduled for the next day, he would be up early and out on an all-day hunt after getting only one or two hours of sleep. He seemed completely unable to understand that his men could not do likewise; the result was over-strict discipline—and a "bring-none-back alive" incident. Add miscellany on Custer: he carried hound dogs with him, sometimes as many as two or three dozen, and let them share his tent and—within capacity—his bed.

The preceding, and all other facts about Custer, add up to a man of supreme courage and boundless energy who had retained the enthusiasm of a youth at the cost of never quite attaining the judgment of a man. His inability to accept the harsh restraints of discipline had shown itself on occasion during the war; now it came to the surface once again when he received orders from General Hancock to move farther west and make his base at Fort Wallace.

Fort Wallace was on the Smoky Hill River in western Kansas, almost at the Colorado border; Custer arrived there on July 14. His orders directed that "The cavalry will be kept constantly engaged." He had also been ordered to leave wives of officers behind—the danger from Indians was too great. So, while Custer was now at Fort Wallace, Elizabeth Custer languished at Fort Riley far to the east. However, Custer also languished. It is difficult to say whether he felt an overpowering love for his wife, or whether he needed her to feed his ego; he showed her the gallantries of true love but at the same time ruthlessly and selfishly demanded that she devote all her time, attention, and solicitude to him.

There was cholera, always a dreaded disease, at Fort Wallace, although apparently nowhere near epidemic proportions. There was also word that the disease had struck Fort Hays to the east—and furthermore, that it had hit Fort Riley, way back where Elizabeth Custer was. There was no telegraph to Fort Wallace, no way for Custer to pin down the rumors. He took the direct method, exactly what he had ordered twelve men shot for doing a little more than a month earlier. He deserted his command. On the fifteenth, the day after he arrived at Fort Wallace, he left the post.

However, a commanding officer has ways of doing such things so that, if black cannot be made to appear white, it can usually be given a gray tinge. Custer selected the seventy-five horses of his command that looked the least exhausted, took men to mount them as an escort, selected three officers, including his brother Tom (General Custer was a strong believer in nepotism; the 7th Cavalry would collect several family members as time passed), and set out along the Smoky Hill Trail headed east.

An explanation was needed for such an unusual procedure; Custer's was that he was going to Fort Hays to pick up a load of important supplies. It was a weak explanation; a commanding officer of a regiment leaves the procurement of supplies to his quartermaster and busies himself with other matters. On the other hand, it was about as good a reason as Custer could have come up with; there are not many ways a commanding officer can justify leaving his post.

Near Downers Station, an important stage stop garrisoned by troops, the rear of the detachment was hit by Indians and two soldiers killed. Custer had been pursuing Indians for weeks, and pushing his men beyond their endurance in doing so; now, with a fresh trail and real reason to seek revenge, he merely gave the command to march on. He made no attempt to pursue the Indians, or even to bury the dead; he ordered the captain in command of the infantry detachment at Downers Station to take care of that small chore.

The detachment reached Fort Hays, 150 miles from Fort Wallace, in fifty-five hours. Only six of those fifty-five had been wasted on rest. His escort had almost given out by now, so he left it, and rode on with brother Tom, another officer, and two orderlies. The ride had been costly, if he had been interested: twenty of his escort had had their bellies full of that particular kind of soldiering and deserted on the way.

Custer, the obsessed, pushed on, covering the next sixty miles to Fort Harker in less than twelve hours. Fort Harker was the end of the rails for the Kansas Pacific Railroad just then; Custer took the train on to Fort Riley for a reunion with his wife which lasted one night. The next morning he received peremptory orders to return at once to his command. About a week later he was placed under arrest and, beginning in mid-September, he went on trial before a court-martial at Fort Leavenworth on seven charges, among them deserting his command, having ordered the shooting of deserting men, damaging horses belonging to the government during his dash to his wife's arms, failing to pursue Indians who attacked his escort, and not recovering the bodies of his men who were killed by Indians.

Custer's luck ran thin; he was found guilty on all charges and was suspended from his rank and his command for one year. Or possibly Custer's luck ran strong; a string of charges like that would have gotten many men cashiered from the service permanently.

General Hancock also disappeared from the plains. Sherman brought Major General Philip Sheridan up from Texas where his over-harsh handling of the occupation had created angry protest and sullen resistance, and put him in command of the Department of the Platte. General Hancock, in return, was made military governor of Texas and Louisiana but was not much of a success because he did not have the heart for the stern measures sometimes required of him in dealing with the beaten South. Hancock, it would seem, found it easier to be stern with red men.

2. "WE ARE BEYOND ALL HUMAN AID"

The year previous to Hancock's war, the government had prepared the way for the concentration of Indians on (supposedly) worthless reservations by a completely shameless swindle. After their removal from the southeastern states along the Trail of Tears, the Five Civilized Tribes had started anew in the territory given them, the present state of Oklahoma, and had once again established their separate nations. When the war came, they were caught in a cruel dilemma. They were occupied by the Confederacy; many of their citizens owned slaves. However, most of the Indians tried to remain neutral, and many actually fled north where some of the men joined the Union forces.

Nevertheless, it was a golden opportunity, not the kind to pass up lightly, so the government charged the Five Tribes with treason for aiding and abetting the Southern cause and forced them to give up half their territory. How little the government was really concerned about treason, and how much about the land, may be detected in the fact that the lighest punishment fell on the Choctaws and Chickasaws who had contributed most to the Southern fight. The tribes received compensation of a sort for part of the land; the most unconscionable robbery was that of the Seminoles who were given fifteen cents an acre for their lands and then forced to buy a smaller reservation at fifty cents an acre. The Indians were forced, in almost all cases, to leave their farms, mills, roads, and other improvements to start over again. By the end of 1866 the job was completed and the western half of their former lands was empty. The entire Oklahoma area was named Indian Territory; it was firmly believed that this was land that would be worthless to white men and could be held by the Indians forever. O! oft-heard words!

The next year, agents of the Indian Bureau began another round of uprooting tribes. The Osage, Oto, and Kansa nations, once-proud peoples of the prairie lands, were moved onto small reservations in Indian Territory, and so were the sad remnants of the eastern tribes, so often moved by now that most of their members had lost all tribal traditions. Then, in October came the Peace Commissioners, except for General Sherman who had been called to Washington, to meet with the

Comanches, Kiowas, and Southern Cheyennes and Arapahoes on Medicine Lodge Creek in Kansas. This, it should be remembered, was the year when American consciences had begun to bother, and Congress had ordered that peace with justice should be made with the Indian tribes.

It is interesting that the Commissioners had had no trouble making contact with the tribes during the summer in preparation for the council, even though they were at war, particularly the Cheyennes. The Indian concept of war was more flexible than that of his white antagonist. Now, as the council opened, there were between two and three thousand Indians from the four tribes present. The horse herds grazed over hundreds of acres; the conical lodges ranged on and on; the camp was noisy and busy, and from its activities rose a thin haze of dust that blended with the autumn haze hanging over the prairies. And, as the council drew on day after day, the typical odorousness of an Indian camp ripened and grew stronger.

Applying the new concepts of understanding between the two races and justice toward the Indian, the Commissioners used a combination of bribes and threats, cajolery and coercion to get the tribes to accept reservations in Indian Territory. The great and tempestuous Satanta, he who formerly announced dinner with a French horn, wanted no part of settling down and acting like poor imitations of white men: "I love the land and the buffalo and will not part with it," he said. "I want the children raised as I was. I don't want to settle. I love to roam over the prairies. A long time ago this land belonged to our fathers, but when I go up the river I see the camps of the soldiers on its banks. These soldiers cut down my timber; they kill my buffalo; and when I see that it feels as if my heart would burst with sorrow."

Although Satanta was opposed to the treaty, he nevertheless signed, and promised to abide by it. The Comanches and Kiowas signed a treaty on October 21, the Cheyennes and Arapahoes approved theirs a week later, October 28. The Comanches and Kiowas were given a reservation in western Indian Territory between the Red and Washita rivers; the Cheyennes and Arapahoes accepted one of about three million acres just to the north of them, a tract so arid that the streams dried in the summer. The treaties also included promises of food, clothing, and other supplies (a promise which would be kept only sporadically), and of seeds, farming implements, and instruction in agriculture, something the tribes wanted no part of yet. The council ended with the opening of a mountain of boxes filled with gifts: blankets, clothing, food, guns, ammunition, hunting knives.

The Commissioners moved on to treat with other tribes. The Crows agreed to a reservation on the upper Yellowstone, the Colorado Utes accepted a large reservation in the western part of the state, the Shoshone and Bannock gave up their lands in Wyoming and Idaho except for two reservations in those states. The Commissioners split into two groups to talk to the Navajos, the Snakes, the Southern Shoshones and various other tribes. And, as already related, they got the Sioux and northern Cheyennes to accept reservations in western South Dakota. Only Red Cloud and the Powder River Sioux still had not signed a treaty, but it was by then certain they would, for the Bozeman Trail forts were being abandoned. Sherman therefore issued an order on August 10, 1868, to his departmental commanders to bring the Indians in to their assigned reservations. Avoid force, Sherman directed; use only persuasion.

Sherman was concerned almost entirely with the Sioux and with the four Southern tribes; they had been involved in most of the fighting and presented the only potential source of future fighting on the plains. Unfortunately, many Indians were not in a mood to be persuaded to move onto the reservations. A good number, like the redoubtable Satanta, had not approved them from the beginning. Others, during the long winter months in the tepees, had decided that the treaties had been sold to them by misrepresentation.

For the Southern tribes, one of the main causes of growing Indian resentment was the continued wanton slaughter of buffalo. Hunters who took only the tongue and left the rest to rot had been bad enough, but there were many soldiers among them who killed for no other reason than to watch the shaggy beasts go down. Passengers on the Kansas Pacific Railroad kept their guns with them, and when the train ran through a herd of buffalo—a frequent occurrence—everyone grabbed his rifle and banged away rapidly and at random, shooting into the herd with no concern that many more animals were crippled than were killed. The dead buffalo were left where they fell until there were thousands of carcasses along the right of way in all stages of putrefaction, creating a stench that was carried for miles by the prairie wind. In 1868 the Kansas Pacific began boosting its revenue by selling round-trip tickets to sportsmen from Leavenworth to the shooting grounds where the hunters could kill their animals with a little more finesse—

though not much more—than shooting them from a moving railroad coach.

The accumulated resentments of the natives broke out into open warfare in the middle of August, just a few days after Sherman had issued his orders for Indians to be brought onto the reservations. Cheyenne and Arapaho war parties rode north and began attacking settlers between the Solomon and Saline rivers in northwestern Kansas, killing 117, taking seven women captive, burning buildings. Sheridan reported that the Indians were committing acts more bloody even than the newspapers reported; the order came back from Omaha to herd the Indians south of the Kansas line into Indian Territory at once, killing all who resisted.

But Sheridan was in no shape to do much herding. He had about 2,600 men under his command, about evenly divided between cavalry and infantry. However, most of these were committed as garrisons at military posts, for escort duties, as railroad guards, and for other irreducible chores. As a result, he could send only about eight hundred men into the field, and he estimated that the two tribes had six thousand warriors against him, each supplied with two to ten extra horses. It was a gross over-estimate—there were probably nearer two thousand warriors—but the difference was only one of degree for he was outnumbered either way.

To compensate for his shortage of troops, Sheridan attempted the expedient of using civilians. Late in August of 1868, he ordered Major George A. Forsyth of the 9th U. S. Cavalry, his war-time aide-de-camp, to hire "fifty first-class hardy frontiersmen, to be used as scouts against the hostile Indians, to be commanded by yourself." The theory was fine, but even in those days the West had already developed its legends, and one of them was that it was peopled with hardy frontiersmen, dead shots and skilled in fighting Indians, waiting for a call to action. There was that kind of man, but he was not usually unemployed. What Forsyth got in his recruiting among the civilian hangers-on around Forts Harker and Hays were a lot of young drifters who would turn their hand to anything, including stage-coach robbery, that meant a meal and a dollar. The surprising thing was that he got so many good men.

First Lieutenant Frederick H. Beecher of the 3rd U. S. Infantry was made second in command; he had served long enough on the plains to understand the special problems of soldiering on the great empty grasslands. A Dr. John Mooers had signed on as surgeon, and Abner Grover, an Indian scout of considerable reputation, was guide.

Major Forsyth led his command westward from Fort Hays, scouting without success for signs of Indians, and a week later brought his men into Fort Wallace. There he got a fresh report: a Cheyenne war party had attacked a wagon train a few miles to the east, near Sheridan, the boom town and work camp, long since disappeared, which marked the temporary end of the tracks of the Kansas Pacific. He set out at once, picked up the trail, and refused to be discouraged when it thinned out as the Indians followed their usual tactic of splitting up to throw off any pursuit. The Major had never fought Indians but he was a good officer who had learned all he could by listening to experienced Indian fighters; as a result, he was traveling light, with only a week's rations, no tents, and a train of four mules that carried little in their packs besides extra ammunition.

Gradually the trail grew stronger and included the drag marks of many travois poles, proof positive that they were following not merely a party of raiding warriors but a large camp on the move. Some of Forsyth's hardy frontiersmen were all for calling an end to the whole thing and finding a party of Indians more manageable in size. Forsyth refused such counsel; their assignment was to find and fight Indians, he said, and that was what they were about to do. It was strange how men new to Indian fighting could approach the subject from completely different directions and end up in much the same place. Captain Fetterman, arrogant and contemptuous of the fighting ability of Indians, had been certain that he could ride through the Sioux nation with eighty men. Major Forsyth, who had carefully learned all he could about Indian-fighting by talking to old hands, was nevertheless going ahead as though fifty-one men could whip any number of warriors. Either way there were possibilities for trouble.

The command had followed the trail of the Indians along the upper Republican River and then up one of its tributaries, the Arickaree River, into northwestern Kansas and just across the border into Colorado. There, on the evening of September 16, the force made camp on the Arickaree where it flowed through a shallow basin with good grass for the horses. The stream itself had only a few inches of water running in its bed; the only feature of the site worth noting at the moment was a low island about 20 yards wide and perhaps 100 long in the center of the creek opposite the camp, a place only a little higher than the

creek bed (on these plains, nothing was very much higher than anything else), covered with brush, and dignified by a lone cottonwood
tree at its lower end. Grover, the party's Indian scout, marked the island
as the one place suitable for a stand in case of attack, not because he
especially anticipated an attack, but because such things were his
business.

Forsyth had come closer to the Indians than he realized; he had
camped ten or twelve miles downstream from a very large village of
Sioux and northern Cheyennes with a few northern Arapahoes (the
tribes north of the Platte had not been able to resist the opportunity to
get in their licks against the whites). Indian scouts had sighted his
force, lost it, and then found it again in time to bring a dawn attack
screaming up the sandy bed of the creek.

Forsyth was up and awake and talking to his sentry when the first
Indians appeared, whooping and yelping. There was no total surprise
in this attack. Forsyth and the sentry yelled an alarm; thanks to their
good field of view they saw the enemy coming far enough away so that
Forsyth had time to get his men and their horses onto the island. Then
the yelling, pounding tide swept by, throwing up a cloud of mud, gravel
and spray from the shallow stream, and the battle was joined.

Forsyth's command was well armed, with seven-shot Spencer carbines as well as Army revolvers, and they met the onrushing Indians
with a very considerable amount of metal, working their weapons as
fast as they could fire. The island was so low that the red horsemen
could have ridden over it without difficulty, and they apparently
planned to do so, but the heavy fire discouraged all but a few so that
they split and thundered by on both sides. Two or three did gallop
straight down the length of the island, through the scrub brush and
among the scouts.

The Indians made two or three of their typical horseback attacks,
riding past the island hidden behind the off-side of their horses. More
damage, however, was done by natives who took up positions on the
banks of the creek behind bushes and tall grass and shot arrows or
guns from there. Forsyth ordered his men to dig pits for protection; in
the soft sand they were able to scoop out shallow entrenchments with
knives, cups, metal plates, or anything else at hand. It was during the
first part of the attack, before they had dug in, that the scouts suffered
most of their casualties. Major Forsyth was hit in his upper right leg
by a bullet; a few minutes later a bullet broke his other leg. A third

bullet grazed his skull, producing a slight depressed fracture that caused him terrible pain but did not quite put him out of action. Dr. Mooers, the surgeon, was hit in the head and from that time on was unconscious, although it was four long days before he drew his last breath. Lieutenant Beecher, the second in command, was mortally wounded. One man recalled—it was years later when memories sometimes play tricks—that Forsyth, after his skull had been broken, had cried out, "We are beyond all human aid, and if God does not help us, there is none for us."

All the horses were killed within the first hour. When night fell, the scouts counted three dead, two mortally wounded, another seventeen wounded in various degrees. The Indians appear to have had rather few losses, considering that there were probably somewhere between seven hundred and a thousand of them involved, and that they exposed themselves in several charges to the rapid-firing carbines of the scouts. They suffered one grievous loss in the death of their leader, Roman Nose. The great Cheyenne leader—no chief, but the bravest of the brave in war—was helped along in his valor, as so many Indians were, by the knowledge that great magic protected him from harm as he performed incredible feats of daring in battle.

Such magic was a powerful, but also a fragile thing, and Roman Nose's special medicine was rendered impotent if his food touched iron after being cooked. Visiting at the lodge of a Sioux chief just before the battle, he was served food which his host's wife had lifted from the cooking pot with an iron fork. He had eaten before he discovered the lapse; there was no time to go through the elaborate ceremony of purification necessary to renew his power.

Roman Nose remained out of the battle at the outset, but eventually he gave in to the entreaties of his men who were certain they could prevail if only he would lead them. The Cheyenne leader, knowing he was a doomed man, took his men on the next thundering charge and —just as any writer of melodrama would have had it—he was hit and fell from his horse, dead.

Superstitions of this sort made the Indian an erratic fighting man. He lived surrounded by strange powers to help or harm, and if his magic were vitiated, he might as well go home—and usually did— giving up the battle or the war. On the other hand, when the omens were right, he was prone to take unnecessary risks in the assurance that he was invulnerable.

However, at this moment it did not appear that the Indians would have to take many risks. If they were willing to wait a short while they could take the island with very little cost to themselves. When night came, Major Forsyth, still in command although in agonizing pain from his three wounds, told his men that their one chance of coming out alive lay in getting aid, and asked for volunteers to try to get through to Fort Wallace, 125 miles away. Pierre Trudeau, a man on the distant side of middle age, and Jack Stilwell, a nineteen-year-old, but both skilled scouts, agreed to try, and slipped away in the middle of the night.

The detachment deepened its defense works, collected a supply of meat from the dead horses, and dug a well so they could have water without having to expose themselves by crawling down to the shallow flow in the creek. When morning came, the Indians made a few horse-back charges, but without any great enthusiasm because the scouts were putting up a great volume of fire from their defenses. Thereupon the Sioux and Cheyennes dug their own rifle pits on the banks and settled down to a siege.

Firing went on into the third day, but now both sides were too well protected for any decision to be reached in that manner. Only one scout was wounded, but otherwise the plight of the defenders was turning desperate. The dead horses were beginning to stink, and the meat salvaged from them had likewise gone rotten. Some of the wounded were in extreme pain. That night, two more volunteers were sent to try to make it to Fort Wallace, for there was no way of knowing whether Trudeau and Stilwell had succeeded.

The Indians did not fire at the island on the fourth day. Once again they were demonstrating the inability of the Plains Indian to carry on a prolonged siege. Their tradition of battle was a tradition of action. The coming of the horse had not only turned the Plains Indians into buffalo-hunting nomads, it had also given them the instrument and the leisure to turn war into a great game—which is exactly what it was, a dangerous game, but still a game, with very formalized rules. For example, under those rules, no special honor accrued to the warrior who killed an enemy, but a man was acclaimed for "counting coup" on a dead enemy, that is, being the first to touch his body after he was slain, or for touching a live enemy. There were, of course, also wars fought with deadly purpose—to defend a hunting range from encroachment or the current conflicts to preserve something from the rapacious white men—but even then the Plains Indian could not bring the deadly implacability of purpose to his fighting that the Americans did. To him, battle was motion and excitement, the thunder of hoofs over the grass. There was no prestige, no glory, no coups to be counted in defeating a foe by starving him.

So, on the fourth day, the Sioux and Cheyenne warriors began moving away. On the island, Dr. Mooers, unconscious since he was shot in the head early on the first day, at last quietly died. Forsyth, suffering agonies from one of his legs, took his razor and cut out the bullet himself. All food was gone; a coyote that ventured too close and some wild plums did not go far among forty-six men. The stench from the putrefying horses had become almost unbearable.

An occasional Indian was seen on the fifth day, but there were none at all after that. However, the detachment could not move out of its defenses, because there was no way of knowing whether the enemy lingered nearby; and even if the enemy was gone, they could get nowhere without food, without horses, and burdened with injured men.

On the morning of the ninth day, help at last arrived, the 10th U. S. Cavalry, a Negro regiment.* Trudeau and Stilwell had made it through to Fort Wallace. The first night they had walked backward in their stocking feet so that if Indians saw their tracks they would think they were made by moccasin feet going in the opposite direction. Thereafter they were unable to wear their boots because their feet were in such bad condition from cactus spines, so they wound strips of blanket around their feet and kept going. On the evening of the third day they reached a station called Cheyenne Wells on the stage road and waited for the stage coach which took them the rest of the way in comparative comfort; they arrived at Fort Wallace the next night.

The 10th Cavalry had been sent to the rescue at once; on the way it met the other two scouts who had also made it safely through the Indian lines. Five scouts were dead, including one who died of an emergency amputation of his leg, performed immediately on the arrival of the rescue force. Eighteen lay wounded amid the maggot-swarming

---

* There were two such mounted regiments, recruited when the Regular Army was increased in size in 1866: the 9th Cavalry, Major Forsyth's regiment from which he was on detached duty at the time of the fight, and the 10th Cavalry. They were officered by whites but all enlisted men were Negroes; the 9th, especially, was a crack outfit, although both had excellent records. The colored troopers were called "buffalo soldiers" by the Indians from a fancied resemblance of their hair to that on the head of a buffalo.

carcasses of half a hundred dead horses. All were suffering from extreme exhaustion.

Forsyth survived his wounds, although there were two years of pain before his legs were whole again. The head wound caused him head-aches the rest of his life but he remained in the Army—he was breveted brigadier general for bravery in the battle—and would command in another famous engagement, though not so creditably, many years later.

The fight on the Arickaree River was called the Battle of Beecher Island (so named from the young lieutenant who, with the other four dead, was buried there), and the site is still known as Beecher Island.

Buried just as surely as the dead from the battle were Sheridan's plans to use "first-class, hardy frontiersmen" to fight Indians. After Forsyth's last-ditch stand, no more was heard about the scheme.

3. CUSTER'S FIRST STAND

Sherman took a simple and direct view of the situation on the plains. "We have now selected and provided reservations for all, off the great road," he said in September of 1868. "All who cling to their old hunting grounds are hostile and will remain so till killed off."

In a letter to his brother John, a United States Senator from Ohio, he was even more blunt, and would have had the Indian sympathizers of the East screaming for his hide if they had read it: "The more we can kill this year, the less will have to be killed the next war, for the more I see of these Indians the more convinced I am that all have to be killed or maintained as a species of pauper. Their attempts at civilization are simply ridiculous."

When the Peace Commission met in Chicago to tie up loose ends after finishing their year of treaty-making, five of the seven members agreed with Sherman that now the Indians should be given the stark choice of going on reservations or being killed. As Sherman argued, the natives had been given liberal treaties and large reservations in per-petuity, and still they were fighting. What more did they want? There is something almost quaint in the hurt indignation of the Commission-ers over the refusal of the Indians to accept the latest treaties gratefully and at face value. The Plains tribes had signed other treaties and had been given other lands in perpetuity—for as long as waters run and the grass shall grow. Every other promise had been cynically broken. It occurred to many other officers fighting the Indians, but apparently never to William Tecumseh Sherman, that there came a time when Indians decided that the only way to keep anything was to fight for it.

It was a fight in which they could look for very little sympathy or understanding where it would do any good. General Grant was in Chicago and backed Sherman completely. It was absolutely necessary to protect emigrants on the plains, he said, "even if the extermination of every Indian tribe was necessary to secure such a result." Grant, as commanding general of the Army, was Sherman's superior; he was also Republican candidate for the Presidency and there seemed little doubt he would be successful in the election less than a month ahead.

With a clear go-ahead from above, Sheridan planned a campaign to drive the four warring Southern tribes back onto their Indian Territory reservations. He was outnumbered and he could not hope to match the warriors on the plains where their fast, light ponies could hit and run and be miles away before his cavalry could reach the scene. It was getting late in the season, however, and he decided on a winter campaign, a completely unorthodox kind of Indian fighting.

Jim Bridger, erstwhile mountain man, guide to emigrant trains, and lately scout at unhappy Fort Phil Kearny, was asked for expert advice and threw cold water on the scheme. So did other men who knew the plains and the Indians. But Sheridan's arguments made sense. In winter the Indians went into permanent camps; they could not flee very far nor fight very effectively with no feed for their ponies except the withered remnants of plains grass. Their villages could be destroyed and they could be beaten or starved into submission. It was a concept very familiar to the general who had gone through the Shenandoah Valley in 1864, turning it into a burned-out desert "so that crows flying over it . . . have to carry their provender with them." The phrase had been Grant's but Sheridan had done the work. Now he was going to try it out in Indian fighting.

The winter camps of the four tribes were believed to be concentrated just west of the Texas Panhandle, and probably along the Washita River. General Sheridan's strategy was one of which he was fond: three converging columns to sweep up and crush between them any Indians who might be out in the field. One was to come down from Fort Lyon in southeastern Colorado and march toward the Antelope Hills in northwestern Indian Territory. A second was to originate at Fort

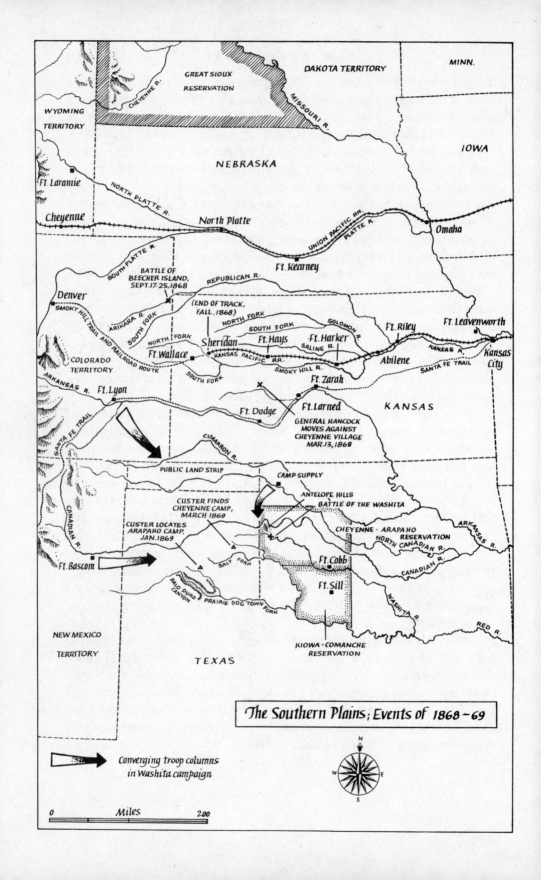

The Southern Plains; Events of 1868-69

Converging troop columns
in the Washita campaign

0   Miles   200

Bascom in New Mexico and follow the Canadian River across the Texas Panhandle. The third and main column was to operate from a base established north of the Antelope Hills by an advance element. The base was named Camp Supply; its location is well commemorated today by the community of Fort Supply, Oklahoma. The main force operating out of Camp Supply was to consist of the 7th Cavalry with eleven companies, five companies of infantry, a train of 450 wagons, and the 19th Kansas Volunteer Cavalry, commanded by Colonel S. J. Crawford, such a fire-snorting believer in the benefits to be gained by killing Indians that he had resigned as Governor of Kansas to head the regiment. The Kansas regiment was one of the few formed after Sherman had laid down his firm rule that any volunteer units would serve under firm Army control, with Army pay and allowances. Sherman authorized the unit because of the frequent Indian attacks on railroad construction crews in Kansas.

Sheridan may have been a bit nervous about his decision to conduct the first winter campaign against Plains Indians. "I deemed it best to go in person, as the campaign was an experimental one—campaigns at such a season having been deemed impracticable and reckless by old and experienced frontiersmen," he wrote, "and I did not like to expose the troops to great hazards without being present myself to judge of their hardships and privations." He took the Kansas Pacific as far as Fort Hays in central Kansas, then, with an escort, traveled south for six days to Camp Supply. During the first two days, the weather was mixed rain and snow, so wet and windy it was impossible to make a fire, but nothing other than personal discomfort marred the trip.

Even in Indian country, the Army remained the Army; officers observed protocol and made their courtesy calls on their newly-arrived commanding officer. There was even a concert by the 7th Cavalry band, blaring away in the snow that had begun falling just after Sheridan's arrival.

Back in command of the 7th Cavalry was Lieutenant Colonel George Armstrong Custer (but still entitled to be addressed as "General" by virtue of his brevet rank). Custer would never achieve full command of the 7th but it made little difference, for the colonel of the regiment, for various shadowy reasons, never appeared on the scene. Custer had returned after completing his year of penance, more like a hero than a man who had been punished. General Sheridan sent a telegram to Custer at his home in Michigan:

Fort Hays, Kansas, September 24, 1868

General G. A. Custer, Monroe, Michigan

Generals Sherman, Sully, and myself, and nearly all the officers of your regiment, have asked for you, and I hope the applications will be successful. Can you come at once? Eleven companies of your regiment will move about the first of October against the hostile Indians, from Medicine Lodge Creek toward the Wichita Mountains.

P. H. Sheridan, Major General Commanding

Custer arrived six days later, to be told by Sheridan that the General relied completely on him and would allow him to act on his own judgment on the coming campaign. It was more an expression of Sheridan's confidence in Custer than the carte blanche it appeared, but it was still a hearty welcome home. Custer had served under Sheridan in the Shenandoah Valley, and in the fighting from Petersburg to Appomattox when his division had played a large part in blocking the retreat of the Confederate Army. His dashing type of leadership had appealed to Sheridan—at least the part visible to him—because he had been that kind of commander himself: everywhere on a foam-flecked horse, urging on the faltering, shoring up a threatened breach in the lines, riding from Winchester twenty miles away.

Custer immediately took up the work of fashioning the 7th into a unit. It had never fought together as a regiment before; now he worked to give it that all-important element called *esprit*. One of his devices was to "color the horses," a cavalry term meaning to give each company horses of the same color. Another was to reward the forty best marksmen of the regiment by making them an elite unit which rode separate from the rest of the regiment and was excused from guard and picket duty. Of such details are military morale built. It is worth noting that the officer who had driven men to desertion a year earlier was now giving them pride of company and regiment.

Sheridan waited two days for the Kansas Volunteers; when they failed to arrive he decided to go ahead without them. On the morning of November 23, the 7th rose to a cold three o'clock reveille, with the snow a foot deep and still falling. Three hours later the column set out, its band playing the 7th's regimental song, "Garry Owen," a tune that sounds vaguely as though it would be more at home on bagpipes, and with words about carousing through the streets of Limerick, breaking down doors, beating up the bailiff, and other delinquencies.

Custer's orders from Sheridan were to go south to the low range called Antelope Hills, then head toward the Washita River. Any warriors not killed in battle were to be hanged; all women and children were to be taken prisoner; all villages destroyed, and all ponies killed. These were brutally explicit orders. Sherman could lose his temper and talk about extermination; Sheridan could coldly put extermination into effect.

General Sherman's own policy was rather high-handed; he had personally declared that the portion of the Medicine Lodge Treaty which permitted the Indians to hunt buffalo anywhere south of the Arkansas River was abrogated; he had ordered all four tribes to concentrate around Fort Cobb on the Washita River, and had declared that any bands which did not comply would be considered outlaws. Thus, Sheridan's orders to kill and hang were not directed against tribes which had made war the past summer, but against any which Custer happened to find camping off the reservation. The Comanches and Kiowas had had almost nothing to do with the fighting in Kansas (though they had raided south in their continuing war with Texas), and a number of Cheyenne and Arapaho bands had remained aloof from the fighting. However, the Army subscribed to the genial theory that one Indian was as good as another for purposes of punishment, and neither Sherman nor Sheridan was going to change the system.

On the twenty-eighth, Major Joel Elliott, who had commanded the 7th during Custer's year of suspension, found the trail of a large band of Indians while scouting along the Canadian River near where it crossed the Texas border. When Custer was informed, he sent word back to Elliott to keep on the trail, detailed about eighty men to guard the wagon train, made each man leave his overcoat with the wagons and take on a small pack of hard biscuit and coffee for himself and grain for his horse, and set out with the main part of the regiment to catch up with Major Elliott.

It was long after dark before they came up with Elliott, who had stopped because his Osage Indian trailers were certain an Indian village was only a short distance ahead. The advance was resumed, very cautiously, with the Osages well in advance till about 1:30 A.M., when the trailers reported a village among the trees lining the Washita River. Custer turned the regiment about, eight hundred men moving as quietly as possible and trying to muffle the creaking of saddles and gear, and withdrew to a safer distance, where he divided the command into four columns which circled to take up positions at separate points around the village. After a long wait through the bitter night, during which the men were forbidden even to stamp their feet, the trumpet sounded the charge at dawn, the band swung into "Garry Owen," and the regiment closed in, cheering and shooting, from four sides.

The village was that of the Cheyenne chief, Black Kettle, who must have sprung awake to the sound of the attack convinced that a nightmare was repeating itself; it was his band that had been camped at Sand Creek. This time Black Kettle had come to the end of his trail and died trying to defend his camp. Although caught completely off-guard, the Cheyennes recovered quickly and began a spirited return fire. Many of them jumped into the icy, waist-deep waters of the Washita and used the banks as breastworks. Others took advantage of trees, hollows, and other protection. Captain Louis Hamilton was killed at the beginning of the action; Lieutenant Tom Custer, who suffered a minor wound, was one of two officers and a dozen enlisted men hurt during the fight.

Women and young boys took part in the desperate fighting, but the odds were too great and the surprise too overwhelming for the Cheyennes ever to have had a chance. Even so, Indian resistance continued on the edge of the camp through mid-morning. Major Joel Elliott took a detachment of nineteen men in pursuit of a group of Indians and disappeared behind a rise of ground; gunfire was heard indicating that he had caught up with his quarry. There were a white woman and boy in the camp as captives; they were slain by Indian women to prevent their rescue.

As soon as resistance had been beaten down, the regiment set about the methodical destruction of the camp—there were forty-seven Cheyenne lodges, two Arapaho and two Sioux. Custer, in his report made out later, gives a very complete inventory of all that was destroyed, so precise, in fact, that one wonders how the regiment found time to count everything in the confusion and excitement. Some of the items he listed were: 1,100 buffalo robes, 4,000 arrows, 500 pounds of powder, 1,000 pounds of lead, tons of dried meat, 875 ponies. The lodges and the combustible materials were put to the torch; the rest was thrown into the river.

The work of destruction went on now at an increasingly frantic pace. The number of Indians on higher ground overlooking the village had been steadily increasing, and Custer learned the reason from cap-

tive squaws: Black Kettle's village was only the first in a series of
Cheyenne, Arapaho, Comanche, and Kiowa winter camps along the
Washita. Little fault can be found with the way Colonel Custer organized and carried out the attack on Black Kettle's village. However, as
a regimental commander, he had other responsibilities besides yip-
yipping at the head of a charge, and one was to reconnoiter his ground.
For several hours during the night he had kept his command, including
white and Indian scouts, standing around idle waiting for dawn, when
a short scout up and down the river, no more than a mile, would have
revealed the situation. Custer was prone to overlook the duller details
of command. The lapse was not a costly one this time, however, for
the Indians were still overawed and outnumbered and made no real
effort to attack.

Over a considerable period of time, shots were heard in the distance,
plainly from the guns of Major Elliott and his detachment who were
somewhere engaged with Indians. The fact was duly reported to the
commanding officer several times, but Custer made no move either to
send a strong detachment out, or to move to the rescue with the entire
regiment. He later explained that, among other reasons that would have
made it dangerous to have gone in search of Elliott was a shortage of
ammunition—yet at the time his men were engaged in shooting 875
captured Indian ponies. No one ever accused Custer of cowardice;
the abandonment of Elliott and his men remains unexplained. But from
that day on, there were officers and men in the 7th Cavalry who no
longer trusted their commanding officer completely, or felt that they
could depend on him in time of real trouble.

It was getting late in the afternoon; the men were feeling the cold
without their overcoats, and the Indians from other camps were still
gathering. To disengage himself, Custer marched the regiment, band
playing (sometimes it seems that the real heroes of the 7th were its
band), straight down the valley toward the other camps. The surprised
warriors withdrew before the advance; then Custer countermarched
back through the destroyed village, leaving the Indian warriors well
behind him. At two o'clock in the morning he deemed it safe to make
camp for a few hours, then continued on to join up with the wagon
train.

Custer sent scouts ahead to announce the victory to General Sheridan, and to say that he would like to pass in review before the commanding general when the 7th arrived at Camp Supply. With his flair

for the flamboyant gesture, he turned the review into a small Roman triumph. The Osage guides, in bright clothing and paint, carrying fresh scalps on lances and firing their rifles into the air, led off the procession. The white scouts came next, followed by the band playing the inevitable "Garry Owen," then Colonel Custer and his staff, next the captured women and children, then the sharpshooters' corps, and finally the regiment, company by company. Sheridan was well-pleased both with the review and the results of the campaign.

Colonel Custer's official report claimed 103 warriors killed, a figure considered completely ridiculous by many plainsmen for a camp of fifty-one lodges, for it was ordinarily reckoned as a rule of thumb that there were two warriors to a lodge, and there was not any doubt that a great many warriors escaped. On the other hand, his report said nothing at all about women and young boys being slain, although an unknown number were—in some cases, at least, in pure self-defense by soldiers who were being fired on by women or boys. The 7th lost two officers and nineteen men killed, three officers and eleven men wounded.

There had never been any real doubt about the fate of Major Elliott and his detachment, but any small uncertainty was removed when Sheridan moved on farther into Indian Territory on December 11, nine days after Custer's triumphal return to Camp Supply, and passed within eight miles of the devastated village. With Custer and an escort, he visited the site. It was a shambles in the literal meaning of the word. The smell of smoke and death hung over everything. Thirty bodies still lay amid the charred debris, and the frozen carcasses of almost a thousand horses lay over a large area. Some distance away the bodies of Elliott and his command were found, stripped naked and mutilated.

The punitive force continued on toward Fort Cobb, in the northern part of the Comanche and Kiowa reservation. The Comanches were now assumed to be at peace again, but the Kiowas were fleeing in panic before the avenging columns of Sheridan and his long-haired cavalryman. General W. B. Hazen, commanding at Fort Cobb, finally halted the nemesis with a dispatch to Sheridan. All Kiowas south of the point the expedition had reached were friendly, wrote General Hazen, and had not been on the warpath that season.

Sheridan and Custer were not happy at being stopped, but Hazen spoke in a loud voice that could not be ignored: he was Sherman's own appointee, and he was not a typical Indian agent of the kind the military scorned so much, but an Army man who was performing this duty while he recovered from a wound—a wound received fighting Indians.

A number of Kiowa chiefs, including Satanta and Lone Wolf, the head chief, accompanied the courier who brought General Hazen's message, and the disgruntled Sheridan made one belligerent gesture still possible: he had the two chiefs seized and brought in to Fort Cobb as prisoners. There was, apparently, a bitter quarrel between Sheridan and Custer on the one hand, who claimed at first that Satanta and Lone Wolf had been at the Washita fight, and General Hazen, on the other, who quickly set them straight by informing them that the two chiefs had slept in his tent during the night that had ended in the massacre, well over a hundred miles away. But if Sheridan could not hang the Kiowa chiefs for being present at the Washita, he could use them as hostages; he announced that he would hang them unless all Kiowas still at large came to Fort Cobb within two days. Runners were sent out to find and inform the scattered bands of the danger to the chiefs; all hurried to the fort within the time specified, and Satanta and Lone Wolf were set free.

The Cheyennes and Arapahoes had also fled, but they had no one to stand up to General Sheridan and insist on fair treatment for them. Their agent was a mere colonel, and he had resigned—and well he might, for he had proven to be extremely bad luck for his charges. He was the unhappy Colonel E. W. Wynkoop. Through no fault of his own he had played a part in the massacre of Black Kettle's band at Sand Creek; three years later, in spite of all he could do, he had been involved in General Hancock's clumsy blundering which had destroyed a Cheyenne camp and started a war. Once again he had tried, only to have his work shattered again in the moment when the 7th Cavalry swept down on a sleeping Cheyenne camp to the unearthly blare of "Garry Owen."

Wynkoop had resigned because his life, he said, would no longer be worth anything among the Cheyennes; after the three episodes they would be convinced he had been deliberately betraying them and would kill him for revenge at the first opportunity. He insisted that Black Kettle, despite all his reasons to be bitter, had not joined in the summer's hostilities, but had continued to work for peace.

On the other hand, defenders of the night attack pointed to the captive white woman and boy in the camp who were ruthlessly murdered when the soldiers attacked, as well as to scalps of whites and to various other proofs of depredations. There is no way of knowing where the truth lies. It was perfectly possible, in a society as individualistic as that of the Plains tribes, that Black Kettle's village contained several young braves just back from a summer on the warpath even though the leading chief of the band deplored war and had kept most of his men at peace.

General Sherman completely backed up his two officers in the field. He wrote to Sheridan on December 23, saying that the captives, stolen horses, and other trophies found in the village proved it to be a war camp: "I am well satisfied with Custer's attack, and would not have wept if he had served Satanta and Bull Bear's band in the same style. I want you to go ahead; kill and punish the hostile, rescue the captive white women and children, capture and destroy the ponies, lances, carbines &c &c of the Cheyennes, Arapahoes and Kiowas; mark out the spots where they must stay, and then systematize the whole (friendly and hostile) into camps with a view to economical support until we can try to get them to be self-supporting like the Cherokees and Choctaws."

At the same time, there was a roar of criticism in the East when the news of the attack became known there. The so-called humanitarians were soon referring to the Washita attack as another Sand Creek Massacre. Possibly some echo of this criticism came back to Sheridan and Custer, or perhaps it was the result of their confrontation with General Hazen, but the two men ignored Sherman's sanguinary exhortation to go out and kill more Indians. They also lost their own former fervor to do the same thing, decided the tribes had learned their lesson, and set about bringing the Arapahoes and Cheyennes onto the reservation. Custer, against Sheridan's better judgment, went out in mid-January with his forty sharpshooters, a few scouts, and a pack train of mules with supplies. His object was to talk rather than bludgeon the tribes into submission.

It was a new role for the cavalry commander. So far his concept of dealing with Indians had been to kill them; now he was going to be forced to rely on diplomacy. From warrior he had become peacemaker. And he carried out this difficult assignment in a manner greatly to his credit.

The fleeing tribes had gone west, toward the upper Red River. The camp of the Arapahoes was located first, on Mulberry Creek in the Texas Panhandle. Custer went through the long business of sitting with the chiefs in council and convincing them they should go onto the reservations. Patience won out; they gave their promise that they would go back, following their leading chief, Little Raven.

The small detachment went on. Their mounts gave out; they ate horse meat and continued on foot but still no sign of Cheyennes. At last Custer gave the order to return to Fort Sill, a new post which the expedition had built during January and February to replace Fort Cobb; it was south of Cobb and just about in the center of the Kiowa-Comanche reservation. After Custer's return, Sheridan at last headed back toward Fort Hays, turning operations over to Custer.

The cavalry commander went out into the field again, but this time with the entire 7th Cavalry and the 19th Kansas Volunteer Cavalry. The Kansas regiment, however, was mounted on shank's mare. It had finally turned up at Camp Supply, a week too late to take part in the Washita raid because it had become lost in the snow that was falling at the time; it had wandered around for days and had lost 700 horses from exhaustion and exposure. The event gave considerable satisfaction to Sherman who considered that it vindicated him in his continuing opposition to those who argued that state militia could do as good a job of policing the frontier as the Regular Army. As the force moved out on March 2, the Kansans were getting a taste of soldiering at its toughest.

At last, after many days of searching, the column's Osage trackers found a trail where two or three Cheyennes had traveled, then one where twenty or thirty had passed with lodges and families, but the scratch marks of the travois poles had grown faint because the winter wind had sifted dust into them for two weeks. By that time a third of the 7th had lost its horses and the men were trudging along on foot like the Kansans. Custer stayed doggedly with the old trail; at last it brought them to the Cheyenne camp.

Because he was riding well ahead of his command, and because he was George Armstrong Custer, he rode with a single orderly down into the broad valley, making the sign of friendship. The Colonel began a long council with his unhappy hosts, while the soldiers on the edge of the village and the Cheyennes quietly jockeyed for position. Custer had three warriors seized as hostages to force the Indians to give up two white women captives believed to be hidden somewhere in the camp; he threatened a hanging the next sunset unless the women were produced. The bluff worked and the captives were released, whereupon

Custer did a double cross and announced that he was still keeping his three hostages and would not turn them loose until all Indians were back on the reservation.

There was no way the Indians could be made to go in then, late in March, with the grass still sere and useless to feed their ponies. Custer accepted the pledge of the Cheyennes that they would come in as soon as the grass turned green enough for traveling—always remembering that he held three of their leading warriors, Dull Knife, Big Head, and Fat Bear, to make sure they complied. The force started toward home; both Arapahoes and Cheyennes did come to the reservation later by themselves. Custer had accomplished his difficult task without firing a shot.

The 7th and the Kansas Volunteers moved north across the plains where the iron-hard grip of winter had been broken and the buffalo wallows were filled with wind-rippled water left by melting snow. They reached Fort Hays on April 7, but Custer's great and good sponsor was not there to welcome him. On his way back from Fort Sill to Fort Hays, General Sheridan had been met by a courier bringing him the message that he had been promoted to the command of the Division of the Missouri. Grant had just been inaugurated President; Sherman had succeeded to the post of commanding general of the Army vacated by Grant; Sheridan had moved up into Sherman's former command.

They were not changes that promised much comfort to the Indians.

VI

Ten Million
Dead Buffalo

1. PHILANTHROPISTS AND WARRIORS

THE Indian Service had, almost from its beginning, been notorious for inefficiency and corruption. From time to time, attempts had been made at reform, but they had always foundered on the inertia of established bureaucracy and the opposition of too many men reluctant to give up a lovely opportunity to put some of the public money into their own pockets.

On his inauguration in 1869, Ulysses S. Grant became the latest person to attempt some reform of the Indian Service. His program was a simple one; it aimed only to improve the caliber of the men serving as Indian agents. The means which were to be used to accomplish this laudable and long-overdue reform appear quaintly naïve to a more skeptical generation; religious denominations were to be asked to submit lists of nominees, and from these lists Indian agents were to be appointed. The plan soon became known as the "Quaker Policy" because the Society of Friends took over responsibility for the first two agencies; surprisingly, it worked well enough to produce a definite improvement over several years in the general quality of men serving as agents, although it was not able to produce miracles.

An honest man who became an Indian agent could expect little more than that virtue would be its own reward, for the pay was pitifully meager, and living conditions could seldom be called luxurious. Political patronage-seekers clamored after agency posts only because there were so many attractive ways of diverting a steady stream of Indian Bureau money into their own pockets, but an honest man who planned to live on his salary would not eat very high on the hog.

To the extent that the Quaker Policy replaced corrupt and indifferent agents with honest men honestly concerned for the welfare of the Indians under their charge, it was a success. However, corruption in the Indian Service was not limited to the agencies. At times it reached the Commissioner of Indian Affairs in Washington himself, and extended on down to agents and sub-agents in the most remote posts.

Frauds were perpetrated and funds misappropriated, often with complete indifference to public opinion. In 1867, Congress made an investigation of Indian policy and a subsequent report was prepared by the Commissioner of Indian Affairs. The following excerpt describes the activities, not of a mere agent, but of the superintendent for the entire Territory of Idaho:

> The credit of the Indian Department is utterly destroyed, and the tribe is greatly disaffected toward the government, . . . Mr. O'Neill, who is the only Indian agent within the territory, is utterly powerless to remedy the evils. The regulations of the department require him to conduct his correspondence through the Superintendent of Indian Affairs for his district. "Caleb Lyon of Lyondale," who is governor and ex-officio superintendent of Indian Affairs, has not been heard of in Idaho since last spring.
>
> His absence from his post, however, seems to entail no embarrassment on the management of Indian affairs. When present, he conducted them with an ignorance unparalleled, and a disregard of the rights and wants of the Indians, and of the laws regulating intercourse with them, deserving of the severest rebuke. . . .
>
> I have examined invoices and purchases made by the department or its agents in eastern cities, where the prices charged were from fifty to one hundred percent above the market value of good articles. Upon examination of the goods, I have found them, as a general thing, worthless and deficient in quality. "Steel spades" made of sheet iron; "chopping axes" which were purely cast iron; "best brogans" with paper soles;

"blankets" made of shoddy and glue which came to shreds the first time they were wet. . . . Many articles were purchased which would be utterly worthless to the Indian . . . ; in one case forty dozen pairs of elastic garters were sent to a tribe in which there was not a single pair of stockings.

There is no record that "Caleb Lyon of Lyondale" suffered even a mild chastisement for his gross abuse of his office. But the corrosion had eaten into much higher places. It was somewhat ironic that Grant, who was going to clean up the Indian Service by starting at the ground floor and getting honest agents, should before his term ended have both his Secretary of the Interior and Secretary of War forced out of office because of corruption in connection with Indian affairs.

Along with his Quaker Policy, Grant turned a hospitable ear to those who advocated a peaceful approach to relations with the Indians. A special committee of philanthropists (the word "philanthropist" acquired a special connotation during this era and came to mean a person interested in the welfare of the Indians) had been appointed to advise the government on Indian policy; this Board of Peace Commissioners had prominent supporters who could marshal powerful political forces if necessary, and was able to make its weight felt in Indian matters. But the great, onrushing current of events was too powerful for such a group to stem or divert.

For, when it came down to it, no Board of Peace Commissioners or any other organization of Eastern philanthropists, no Quaker Policy or other reform on the agencies was going to save the Indian as long as he stood in the way of Western pioneers. Indian sympathizers might improve his condition while he was on a reservation, but nothing was going to protect him when settlers decided they wanted the reservation itself.

To Westerners, of course, any hint of softness in Indian policy was idiocy. Strong voices among them were still insisting that the best way to solve the whole Indian problem would be to put an attractive bounty on scalps. Far too many rapacious, land-hungry whites considered Indians little more than annoying vermin, to be got rid of without inhibitions as to methods. When the Nez Percés demanded that treaty terms be enforced to evict whites who were squatting on their reservation lands, a Boise, Idaho, editor wrote indignantly against such presumption, and proposed that a shipment of blankets infected with smallpox be obtained. The good citizens of Idaho would see, he said, that they were distributed among the Nez Percés where they would do the most good.

A fight occurred between Indians and frontiersmen at a Montana trading post shortly after Grant's pro-Indian policy became known and cursed in the West. Several warrior dead were left behind, and the victorious defenders demonstrated their sentiments, if not their superiority to the barbaric red man, by cutting off the heads of the slain enemy, pickling the ears in whiskey (for reasons not made clear), and boiling the flesh from the skulls. The bleached skulls were then inscribed with what the Montanans considered apt, and probably hilarious, sentiments: "I am on the Reservation at Last," "Let Harper's Tell of My Virtues," and "Horace Greeley Knows I'm Out." (*Harper's* Magazine and Greeley's New York *Tribune* gave sympathetic treatment to the Indian and his problems.) There was also a more cryptic legend; "A good-looking half-breed, the son of a very distinguished Peace Commissioner," which appears to be a sly reference to some imagined miscegenation.

So much for philanthropy and understanding as far as the West was concerned, and so much for the Peace Commission. All the humanitarians back East would do the Indian very little good because the Westerners were going to continue to play the tune he would have to dance to.

While Sherman was disgruntled with the administration's Indian policy, he soon had worse worries. Grant's first Secretary of War remained in office only a few months, and was succeeded by William W. Belknap, who very shortly began to operate as though William Tecumseh Sherman, commander of the Army, did not exist. Belknap had served in the Western armies during the war, much of the time under Sherman's command. He had been an excellent officer and had been promoted to brigadier general by war's end. Hence, frustration during his military career could not have moved him to act as he did.

Whatever the cause, he not only acted as War Secretary but also as commanding general, handling even such minor details as the appointment of commanders of minor Western posts. Sherman tried to get Grant to intercede and straighten out the lines of authority but his old commanding officer was much surrounded now by prosperous-appearing men with diamond stickpins. He was always glad to reminisce with Sherman about old times at Shiloh or in front of Vicksburg, but on the Belknap matter he said he was sure things would work out but that it wouldn't be right for him to go over his Secretary's head. Sherman, a mere figurehead, was reduced to useless shuffling of papers on his desk, and finally moved his headquarters from Washington to St. Louis.

The beginning of Grant's term was a time of comparative peace on the plains, a lull of two or three years before the final series of wars. There was no complete tranquillity. Skirmishes occurred here and there; settlers were occasionally killed; cavalry patrols traded long-distance shots with bands of Indians. One small campaign was carried out, beginning late in 1869, when the 2nd Cavalry, commanded by Colonel E. M. Baker, took out after the Piegans, one of the three bands of Blackfeet, in Montana. Miners and settlers had been complaining; General Sheridan decided that a winter campaign was the best way to teach the natives to behave.

Baker and his cavalry found and struck a Piegan camp in January, killing 173, burning forty-one lodges. Almost immediately, curiously conflicting stories of the attack—it was not a battle; only one soldier was killed—began to be heard. The Peace Commission sent a man to investigate; he was told by an agent for the Blackfeet that 140 of the dead had been women and children; 18 were old men, and only 15 were men of fighting age. The agent, a Lieutenant Pease, was an Army man and hardly a hostile witness.

Colonel Baker denied that it was so; 120 of the 173 had been vigorous warriors. He deeply regretted that 53 women and children had died; every effort had been made to spare them during the battle but it was not always possible due to the fierceness of the fighting (witness that one dead cavalryman). General Sherman came to the support of Baker: "Did we cease to throw shells into Vicksburg or Atlanta because women or children were there?"

One additional but very important fact came to light. The Army refused ever to admit its truth, but it explains why the cavalry was able to take an Indian camp so completely by surprise that only one soldier was killed. It turned out that this was a friendly camp whose people had no idea they were to be attacked until it was too late to defend themselves.

On the southern plains, Sheridan's and Custer's campaign had driven the Southern tribes onto their reservations, but the Indians were showing no real inclination to settle down and become farmers. For one thing, the people themselves were not yet ready to give up their free ways; farming was women's work, hunting was for men. For another, the government was not doing much to help them make the transition. Agents more often than not promoted their own welfare more vigorously than they did the good of the Indians. Instruction in the crafts of civilization was lacking; much of the land was unfit for farming; and annuities were so often late in arriving or insufficient in amount that the tribes were forced to continue their buffalo-hunting ways in order to keep from going hungry.

The Kiowa and Comanche were the most intractable of the four tribes, at least at the outset. They continued to raid into Texas, killing people, running off stock, destroying property. The Kiowas committed acts of calculated insolence. Once they even attacked the Kiowa-Comanche agency at Fort Sill, drove off the agency cattle, killed and wounded several employees, and then challenged the soldiers at the adjacent Army post to come out and fight. In these displays of high spirits the two tribes were egged on by the Kwahadi Comanche, the fiercest band of the Comanches, who had never signed a treaty, and who roamed the Staked Plain of northwestern Texas and eastern New Mexico, the inhospitable high plains rising toward the Rockies. The taunts of the Kwahadi helped to keep their already high-strung reservation brothers stirred up, and the result was constant trouble. The situation became so bad that in 1870 (only a year after Custer and Sheridan had supposedly beaten and cowed the Southern tribes!) the Indian Commissioner proposed that a line of military reservations be established along the southern border of the Kiowa-Comanche reservation as a barrier to raiding into Texas, and that the two tribes be placed under military control until they had learned how to behave.

In May, 1871, General Sherman went to have a personal look at the situation—and narrowly missed becoming a casualty himself in another instance of Kiowa truculence and insolence. A band of 100 to 150 Kiowas, led by Chiefs Satanta, Satank, Big Tree and Eagle Heart, attacked a train of ten wagons of grain, about seventeen miles from Fort Richardson in north-central Texas and headed for the fort. If they had happened along about three hours earlier, they would have caught much bigger game: Sherman with a small escort had passed down the same trail on his way to Fort Richardson. As it was, the marauding warriors killed the wagonmaster and five teamsters; five teamsters escaped to the fort where Sherman heard the story and reacted in a characteristic way. He ordered the colonel in command to take 150

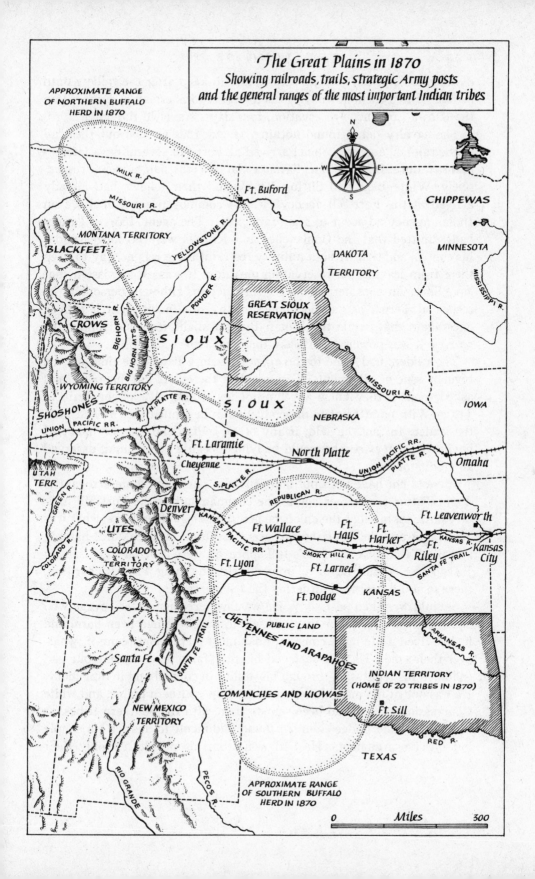

The Great Plains in 1870
Showing railroads, trails, strategic Army posts
and the general ranges of the most important Indian tribes

APPROXIMATE RANGE
OF NORTHERN BUFFALO
HERD IN 1870

MILK R.

MISSOURI R.

Ft. Buford

CHIPPEWAS

MONTANA TERRITORY

MINNESOTA

BLACKFEET

YELLOWSTONE R.

DAKOTA
TERRITORY

CROWS

POWDER R.

GREAT SIOUX
RESERVATION

BIGHORN R.

BIG HORN MTS.

S I O U X

WYOMING TERRITORY

MISSISSIPPI R.

SHOSHONES

N. PLATTE R.

S I O U X

MISSOURI R.

IOWA

UTAH
TERR.

UNION PACIFIC RR.

Ft. Laramie

NEBRASKA

North Platte

UNION PACIFIC RR.

PLATTE R.

Omaha

GREEN R.

Cheyenne

S. PLATTE R.

REPUBLICAN R.

Ft. Leavenworth

COLORADO R.

Denver

KANSAS PACIFIC RR.

Ft. Wallace

Ft.
Hays

Ft.
Harker

KANSAS R.

Kansas
City

UTES

COLORADO
TERRITORY

SMOKY HILL R.

Ft.
Riley

SANTA FE TRAIL

Ft. Lyon

Ft. Larned

Ft. Dodge

KANSAS

CHEYENNES AND ARAPAHOES

PUBLIC LAND

ARKANSAS R.

Santa Fe

SANTA FE TRAIL

COMANCHES AND KIOWAS

INDIAN TERRITORY
(HOME OF 20 TRIBES IN 1870)

NEW MEXICO
TERRITORY

Ft. Sill

RIO GRANDE

PECOS R.

RED R.

TEXAS

APPROXIMATE RANGE
OF SOUTHERN BUFFALO
HERD IN 1870

0   Miles   300

cavalrymen and thirty days' rations and to keep after the raiders until
he had hunted them down. He was to report to Sherman at Fort Sill on
the Kiowa-Comanche reservation, four days' travel to the north.

The cavalry detail found nothing. Heavy rain washed out the trail
of the raiders, and the colonel arrived at Fort Sill several days later to
report failure. By that time, Satanta, Satank (the names mean, respectively, White Bear and Sitting Bear), and their fellows had already
arrived at the Fort Sill agency (it was common practice to have an
Indian agency adjacent to a military post). The agent, Lawrie Tatum,
had admitted that the Comanches and Kiowas were no longer under
his control and that without military restraint there was no way to keep
them from leaving the reservation on raids. It was an admission that
gave Sherman considerable secret satisfaction, although personally he
respected Tatum as "a good honest man," for in his sight it proved
once again that, while the Indian Bureau might feed and supply the
natives, it was powerless to make them behave.

The raiders had come to the agency because it was the time for the
regular issue of allotments. Tatum called the chiefs into his office and
asked them if they knew anything of an attack on a wagon train in
Texas. With no attempt to dissemble, Satanta replied that he had been
the leader. In fact, he said, if any other Indian claimed the honor of
having led that party, he would be lying, because he, Satanta, deserved
all credit for it.

It could not have been put more plainly, nor much more arrogantly.
Agent Tatum sent a message to the commandant of the Fort Sill military post, asking that the chiefs be arrested. Eagle Heart saw what was
happening and fled, but the rest were captured, and Satanta, Satank,
and Big Tree, with Sherman's full approval, were ordered to be sent to
Jacksboro, Texas, the town immediately adjoining Fort Richardson,
there to stand trial for murdering the teamsters.

Satanta was then past sixty. He was an unreconstructed savage who
had remained true to the way of life into which he had been born, and
he had lived a life more complete than most men even dream of, whatever their color. He had achieved his first fame as a warrior but had
solidified his reputation through his ability in council and in diplomacy.
He was one of the most skilled orators of the southern plains, and white
Commissioners who had been sent to treat with the Southern tribes, as
at the Medicine Lodge Council, found it difficult to answer his simple
but incisive arguments. He had won from his people not only their

respect but also a certain affection, and had been leading chief of the Kiowas for several years.

Satank, on the other hand, was quite generally feared and disliked in the tribe, because he was believed to possess magical powers and because of a vindictive nature. He was chief of the Kaitsenko, a Kiowa military society, and somewhat of a distinctive figure because, unlike most Indians, he cultivated a mustache and beard—a bit scraggly, perhaps, but very definite. A year before his arrest, his son, also named Satank, had been killed in a raid into Texas. Old Satank, with friends, went down and recovered the bones, which he wrapped in several fine blankets and put on the back of a led horse. After the old chief returned home, he had a tepee set up with a raised platform inside, on which he placed the blanket-wrapped bones that had been his son. Then he went out through the camp issuing an invitation to a feast, "My son calls you to eat." Thereafter, the bundle of bones was always on a platform in camp and on a led horse when the chief moved. He acted always as though his son were only sleeping.

For the trip to Jacksboro, Satanta and Big Tree were carried in one wagon, and Satank in another. A guard rode in the wagon with Satank, others were with the other two chiefs, and a squadron of cavalry and several Tonkawa Indian scouts rode beside the wagons. The small procession had not passed much beyond the gates of Fort Sill before Satank called to the other two Kiowas that he was a chief and warrior and too old to be treated as a child. Pointing to a tree where the road dipped to cross a small stream about a mile south of the fort, he announced, "I shall never go beyond that tree."

Although he spoke loudly, no one but the other two chiefs understood him; the post commander, in his wisdom, had neglected to send along an interpreter with three such important prisoners. He sang the death song of the Kaitsenko:

> O Sun, you remain forever, but we Kaitsenko must die.
> O Earth, you remain forever, but we Kaitsenko must die.

When the song was ended, he removed his manacles by wringing them off over his hands, at the cost of considerable skin and flesh and a great deal of pain. Then, suddenly producing a butcher knife which he had somehow secreted about his person, he attacked the soldier guard in his wagon, severely wounding that worthy. (Many Kiowas, who had long been convinced that Satank had occult powers, were ever after certain that he had swallowed the knife and disgorged it when it was needed.) He was struggling to get a shell into the chamber of the guard's rifle—not with any thought of escaping but only hoping to kill another American before he died—when the cavalry guard around the wagon recovered from its surprise and knocked him down with several shots. He lived for twenty minutes or so, in great agony, but without a groan or complaint.

Satanta and Big Tree made no move to court death or seek freedom, and arrived in chains, in due time, in Jacksboro. They were found guilty—a verdict it is hard to quarrel with—after a surprisingly fair trial, and were sentenced to die by hanging. There was an immediate and loud outcry among the pro-Indian groups in the East who considered the sentence too harsh and an incitement to Kiowa reprisals. Texans demanded that the sentence be carried out, but the philanthropists brought their influence to bear on the President, and Grant, who had seldom been able to resist pressure applied by prominent men, interceded strongly with Governor Davis of Texas. That bedeviled gentleman, pulled from several directions, succumbed to the political leverage applied by the President. Satanta and Big Tree were sent to the Texas State Prison for life.

Only it was not for life, or anything near it. The two chiefs had hardly been well established in prison before the philanthropists— "Lo! the Poor Indian advocates" they were often called in derision by Westerners—were calling for their release. Their continued imprisonment would only make the wild tribes more excited and unruly, it was claimed. Secretary of the Interior Columbus Delano appealed to Governor Davis to pardon the chiefs. Texans brought their own alarmed pressure to bear on the unhappy governor, and the state's legislature passed a joint resolution, without a single no-vote, asking Davis not to release the pair from prison.

Satanta and Big Tree were not important enough, in themselves, to cause such a ruction across the country. They merely provided a focus about which opposing forces could polarize: the philanthropists of the East, whose grandfathers had taken the land from the Indians so long ago that now they could afford the luxury of consciences; and the settlers of the West, who were still grabbing and finding the Indian a dangerous nuisance. But because the chiefs were such a focus, the big guns on both sides continued to roar. And once again, Governor Davis gave way to the Easterners rather than his own people, and freed the two. Whereupon William Tecumseh Sherman, who could become more indignant than anyone else, sat down and, pen jabbing the paper, shot off a short but hot letter to the Texas governor:

> I believe in making a tour of your frontier, with a small escort, I ran the risk of my life, and I said to the military commander what I now say to you, that I will not again voluntarily assume that risk in the interest of your frontier, that I believe Satanta and Big Tree will have their revenge, if they have not already had it, and that if they are to have scalps, that yours is the first that should be taken.

The two chiefs were released in October, 1873. Almost immediately Texas newspapers were trumpeting loudly that they were leading raids again. A Quaker, Thomas Battey, who spent eight months or so among the Kiowa as a schoolteacher without accomplishing a thing except to establish very friendly relations with the Indians, wrote, "To my certain knowledge the latter [Big Tree] was at home, sick in his lodge, and the former [Satanta] enjoying, after two years' confinement in prison, the pleasures of the buffalo chase, on territory assigned for the purpose." Innocent or guilty, the two were going to be blamed for anything that happened from then on.

As a matter of fact, there was a sharp increase in the amount of raiding and the depredations not only by the Kiowas but by other Indians, particularly the Comanches, whose hate for Texas had not cooled with passing years. Some of it may have resulted from exuberance over release of the chiefs, who very possibly took part in it after Big Tree recovered his health and Satanta had had his fill of hunting buffalo. But the trouble on the southern plains had larger dimensions than the influence of a pair of impetuous chiefs on a tribe with a flair for homicide. The Indians were increasingly restive and resentful for a number of reasons, large among them the old matter of broken promises in regard to annuities, because food and goods arrived late, or in insufficient quantities, or sometimes not at all.

These things were serious enough, but they were not the main cause of the deep anger that was beginning to burn in the Southern tribes in 1873. White hunters were carrying out an unceasing mass slaughter of the buffalo herds; the plains people saw their way of living threatened as nothing that had happened so far had threatened it.

2. THE TIME OF THE HIDE HUNTERS

By the Medicine Lodge Treaty of 1867, the Cheyennes, Arapahoes, Comanches, and Kiowas, "as well as such other bands as might be located there," i.e., in Indian Territory, had been granted the right to hunt not only in the Territory, but also north into Kansas as far as the Arkansas River "so long as the buffalo may range thereon, in such numbers as to justify the chase." There, and out west of their reservations into the empty Texas Panhandle they continued to hunt, and there were buffalo in plenty for them. Now, only five years or so after the treaty, all that was coming to an end.

For years, the buffalo herds had been under heavy pressure, and had been decreasing in numbers. Many men had a part in their dwindling: meat-suppliers for railroad work gangs, so-called sportsmen, killers for commercial butcher firms, wanton killers who shot into herds for no reason other than the momentary excitement of seeing one of the great beasts stagger and drop. The Indians did their part; they were not the great conservationists they are made out to have been, and did a great deal of wasteful killing. Many early travelers tell of Indians killing buffalo for nothing but the tongue, and the maneuver of stampeding a buffalo herd over a cliff, when one was handy, killing far more animals than could possibly be used, was standard practice. A band of Western Cree in Canada so thoroughly wiped out the buffalo in their area by driving them over cliffs that they were forced to move to new hunting grounds; they chose the buffalo range of the Blackfeet who were thereafter their bitter enemies.

A special condition that did not help the survival of the herds in the slightest was the highly superior meat of the cows. Hunters who took the animals for food and not for sport killed the females almost exclusively until some herds that had been heavily hunted had three or four times as many bulls as cows.*

* Elizabeth Bacon Custer survived her husband by almost fifty-seven years, and spent every one of them glorifying his memory. Among other things, she wrote three books which, while giving valuable insights into Colonel Custer's character through her ingenuous revelations of his foibles, at the same time offer some of the purest moonshine in attempting to prove that the heroically dead love of her life was all that was brave, gentle, and noble. Witness this passage from *Following the Guidon*, relative to hunting buffalo:

. . . I hardly need say how careful the officers were not to shoot the cows. The reverence for motherhood is an instinct that is seldom absent from edu-

For these several reasons, the great buffalo herds were doomed to be eventually wiped out. Indeed, it was almost necessary that they should be, because great buffalo herds were not compatible with cities, farms, and railroads.

But there was still plenty of time, and plenty of land that no one would want for two or three generations, where small buffalo herds could graze and grow fat. Then, in 1871, a small technological development wrote the death sentence to the millions of bison still roaming the plains. A method of tanning buffalo hide to produce excellent leather was developed.

Until that time, buffalo skins had been used almost entirely with hair on, as sleigh and carriage robes, overcoats, cold-weather gauntlets, and the like. The tanning process was a painstaking one that had been left entirely to Indian women, and inroads on the herds for robes had not been catastrophically heavy. A small amount of leather had been made from hides but it was too soft for other than a few limited uses, as in belt drives for machinery. Then, in 1871, a young Vermonter named John Mooar, who had a wood-cutting contract at Fort Hays, became interested in buffalo hides. A friend, who hunted buffalo to supply meat for the post commissary, threw away the skins, and probably young Mooar's frugal New England soul was repelled by the waste. He and the hunter, James White, put together a bale of about fifty skins which they sent to Mooar's brother Wright in New York; Wright sold them to a tannery willing to experiment, and out of the tanning vats came a superior leather, suitable for shoes, saddles, upholstery, harness, or anything else cowhide had been used for until then. An order for three thousand buffalo hides at $3.50 each went to John Mooar and James White, and the rush for buffalo hides was on.

Dodge City, Kansas, became the outfitting point and market center for hide hunters by the pure coincidence that the rails of the Atchison, Topeka & Santa Fe had reached that point when the great new bonanza developed. The first passenger train rolled into Dodge City in 1872; it was held up several miles outside the raw new settlement by a buffalo herd said to be three miles long and two miles wide. The men in the train spent the waiting period happily shooting into the massed beasts, killing some, wounding and crippling many more, and starting small

---

cated men. Besides, I know too many instances in proof of the poet's words, "the bravest are the tenderest." Our officers taught the coarsest soldier, in time, to regard maternity as something sacred.

stampedes in which the herd trampled the injured members. When the track was finally cleared and the train puffed on, about 500 buffalo were left behind, thoroughly and uselessly dead.

It was not for long that trains were so inconvenienced, or passengers given a chance to enjoy such artlessly cruel slaughter. For when that first train arrived in Dodge City in 1872, the booming of the hide-hunters' guns was just getting under way in earnest—and very soon there were not enough buffalo along the rails to hold up a train. In the spring of 1872, a good bull hide was bringing $3.50 in Dodge City. It was a magnet too strong to resist. Every sod-shanty settler who had not made a crop, every drifter between jobs, every man looking for the pot of gold at the end of the Western rainbow, got himself a Sharps 50-caliber rifle, a supply of ammunition, a wagon and mule team or ox-haul to take out the hides he expected to get, and then set out to make his stake, sometimes alone, more often with a partner or two. The next year, 1873, was a panic year, and the stream of hopeful hide-men became a flood, each man expecting to recoup his blasted personal fortunes with a few loads of buffalo hides.

The inevitable happened. By September, 1873, the buyers in Dodge City were picking and choosing, and hides were worth only 80¢ to $1.50. A few months later, during the winter of 1874, bull hides were bringing only one dollar, cows sixty cents, a calf hide but forty cents.

There is something terribly wrong in the spectacle of a magnificent brute of a buffalo, which had withstood blizzards and bitter cold, drought and dust, heat and windstorm, at last sinking to earth to give up a hide worth a mere dollar—and a dollar which the hide-man as like as not spent on cheap whiskey or the charms of a dance-hall girl reduced to accepting the buffalo skinner trade. The picture is even more depressing when it is considered that during the first year or two only about one out of three or ·four buffaloes killed supplied a usable hide. So many inept amateurs were in the field that the majority of hides were lost by being ruined through clumsy skinning, or by spoilage through poor drying or by failure to protect against insect damage.

The hide hunter played his part in the opening of the West, just as definitely as did the mountain man, the sod-buster, and the cowtown marshal. But he was perhaps the most unattractive harbinger of civilization the frontier has known—and the frontier has not been famous for men and women sleeked down and smelling of cologne. "The great American buffalo hunters, fearless as a Bayard, unsavory as a skunk!"

Colonel Richard I. Dodge, commandant at Fort Dodge, saluted them. Over weeks and months of skinning buffalo, a hide man's clothing became impregnated with grease and tallow and liberally encrusted with blood. Since neither facilities nor his inclinations were conducive to frequent baths or laundry, he quickly became very gamey, not a good man to share a warm room with.

Hide outfits ranged in size from the loner, who preferred to do his own shooting and skinning, to large outfits which would establish a camp on the plains and then fan out for the day's shooting in units of a killer and three or four skinners. Once it was systematized, the killing of buffalo for hides was a pathetically businesslike operation in which the beast had not the slightest chance. The killer, having located a small herd, crept as close as possible on the leeward side of them, usually managing to get within about 300 to 400 yards before the sentinels became uneasy. Then the hunter settled down on the ground with his canteen, a supply of cartridges, and often an extra rifle, for a gun became overheated with continuous shooting.

By always selecting as his target the most uneasy buffalo, or the one that was starting to lead the herd away, the hunter could keep the stupid beasts completely bewildered while one after another of them staggered and went down. A skilled shooter, wise to the ways of buffalo, could often get nearly a hundred animals from a single stand without moving, and on several occasions hunters brought down more than a hundred. One man got 204 from a single stand, but this seems clearly a prodigy in a class by itself—although the same hunter, a Frank Nixon, also claimed to have killed 120 buffalo in forty minutes on one occasion, one every twenty seconds! Otherwise, the highest claim seems to be 121 from a stand, a very impressive bit of murder. Another mighty slayer of buffalo, one Orlando A. Bond, averaged 97 a day during two months in the fall of 1876 (no time off for Sunday devotions), a total of 5,855 animals. Bond kept five skinners busy at their greasy and bloody trade during this time; he suffered a just retribution by going deaf from the constant roar of his own rifle.

There was nowhere for the buffalo to go. An English sportsman, William Blackmore, traveled thirty to forty miles along the north bank of the Arkansas River east of Fort Dodge in the fall of 1873; he wrote: "There was a continual line of putrescent carcasses so that the air was rendered pestilential and offensive to the last degree. The hunters had formed a line of camps along the banks of the river and had shot down the buffaloes, night and morning, as they came to drink. I counted sixty-seven carcasses in one spot covering four acres."

The Indians came to bear the hide men a bitter hate which led to attacks on the hide camps and on skinners at work on the plains. The attacks became more frequent as the buffalo killers worked their way nearer to Indian Territory and to the Texas Panhandle. It did not take them long to get there. A number of outfits were on the Cimarron River at the southern edge of Kansas in 1873, and there was talk of pushing south to the Canadian River. The rights of the tribes to hunt in Kansas south of the Arkansas were just about a thing of the past, because in another year, at the most, the buffalo would not "range thereon, in such numbers as to justify the chase." What was of more concern to the Indians was the southwestward drive of the hide men. The remaining hunting ground of the tribes was in the Texas Panhandle, and the hunters were coming dangerously close.

Hide men were a tough lot. Some of them had already slipped across into the Texas Panhandle to look at the situation, and had come back with wildly enthusiastic reports of the great herds of buffalo roaming there. Parts of Kansas that had been carpeted with grazing buffalo a season ago were now great expanses of bones.* When a drought hit eastern Kansas very hard in 1873, the government sent soldiers to the rich bison grounds of the Republican River valley in western Kansas to shoot buffalo and ship back the meat for the relief of the striken settlers; the Army hunters found only a few forlorn buffalo amid uncountable stinking carcasses and half-bared bones left by the hide men.

With such a situation, the hide hunters were becoming worried, and the Texas reports had the same effect on them that news of a new gold strike would have on a prospector working a failing vein. However, the Panhandle was dominated by Indians, and white hunters were forbidden to enter it. Wright Mooar and another leading hide man, John Webb, went to Fort Dodge to talk to the commandant there, Colonel Richard Irving Dodge, to try to sound him out on what the Army's attitude

---

* For many settlers on land where the hide men had been active, buffalo bones were their first "cash crop," the one thing that carried them through the first lean years. They gathered the bones and sold them at the nearest railroad station, whence they were shipped to fertilizer plants for phosphates and to sugar refineries for carbon. Huge ricks of bones were piled along railroad sidings (one 12 ft. high, almost 12 ft. wide at the base, and ½ mile long was reported at Granada, Colorado), entire freight trains sometimes carried nothing but bones, and the Santa Fe alone hauled seven million lbs. of them in 1874, one year in a sad commerce that continued for many seasons.

Red Cloud, chief of the Oglala Sioux. "He was the first and only Indian leader in the West to win a war with the United States." (Courtesy of the Museum of the American Indian, Heye Foundation)

Little Wolf (standing) and Dull Knife, Cheyenne chiefs. Renowned warriors, their greatest exploit was leading a homesick band of their people over hundreds of miles of plains through troops alerted to capture or kill. (Courtesy of the Bureau of American Ethnology, Smithsonian Institution)

Satanta, tempestuous Kiowa chief who took his own life to escape a white man's prison. "I don't want to settle. I love to roam over the prairie. . . . These soldiers cut down my timber, they kill my buffalo, and when I see that it feels as if my heart would burst with sorrow." (Courtesy of the Bureau of American Ethnology, Smithsonian Institution)

Scarface Charlie, Modoc warrior. Although Charlie wanted to bring the Modoc War to an end, it was he who led the deadliest ambush of the entire conflict. (Courtesy of the Bureau of American Ethnology, Smithsonian Institution)

Sitting Bull, perhaps not the greatest, but certainly the most famous Sioux leader during a tragic period. The photo shows him in 1885 when he was just past fifty years of age; he was an embittered man, a prophet whose visions had been replaced by memories of past glories. (Courtesy of the Smithsonian Institution)

Chief Joseph, Nez Percé leader, won the deep respect of everyone but the bureaucrats. Said an officer who had once fought him, "I think that in his long career, Joseph cannot accuse the Government of the United States of one single act of justice." (Courtesy of the Bureau of American Ethnology, Smithsonian Institution)

Quanah Parker, Comanche warrior, was given his un-Indian last name because his mother had been a white captive. From chief of the most untamed Comanche band, he changed to become a leader in walking the white man's road when he realized the old days were forever gone. (Courtesy of the Bureau of American Ethnology, Smithsonian Institution)

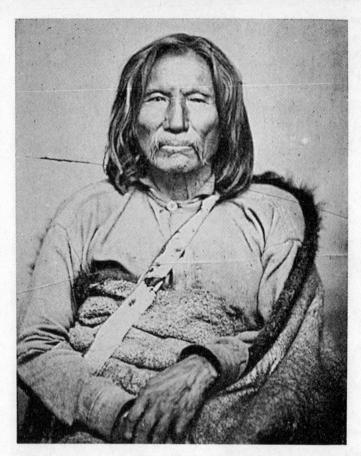

Satank, a noted Kiowa warrior and chief—and one of the few Indians who cultivated a mustache. His own people feared and disliked him; he was believed to possess magical powers which he used for vengeful purposes. (Courtesy of the Bureau of American Ethnology, Smithsonian Institution)

Captain Jack, leader of the Modoc Indians in their long resistance to outnumbering Army forces. He asked for a reservation only six miles square; he got a noose and six feet of ground. (Courtesy of the Bureau of American Ethnology, Smithsonian Institution)

Gall, famed Hunkpapa Sioux warrior. His greatest hour came on the Little Bighorn when he was leading chief of the force that wiped out Custer's battalion. (Courtesy of the Bureau of American Ethnology, Smithsonian Institution)

Looking Glass, considered by some to be the greatest of all Nez Percé chiefs. He fought through the long retreat only to die by a chance bullet in the closing moments before the surrender. (Courtesy of the Bureau of American Ethnology, Smithsonian Institution)

Issuing rations to Sitting Bull's band at Fort Randall, Dakota Territory, in 1882. The band had returned from Canada the year before, and its members were still being treated as prisoners. The man in the foreground is apparently merely curious about the photographer. (Courtesy of the Bureau of American Ethnology, Smithsonian Institution)

Wood gatherers, women of Sitting Bull's band in 1882. The tepees indicate the destitute condition of the band on its return from Canada; all are of government canvas rather than the Indians' own buffalo hide. (Courtesy of the Bureau of American Ethnology, Smithsonian Institution)

Unconscious—an episode in the Ghost Dance. "As they danced to bring the new day nearer, the excess of their emotions sent many of them into trances in which they saw visions. . . ." (Courtesy of the Bureau of American Ethnology, Smithsonian Institution)

Aftermath of a massacre: collecting the Indian dead at Wounded Knee on New Year's Day, 1891. "A blizzard had swept over the Dakotas after the massacre, and the bodies were found partially covered with snow and frozen into the attitudes of violent death." (Courtesy of the Bureau of American Ethnology, Smithsonian Institution)

Gathering up the Dead on the Battle Field at Wounded Knee S.D. Copyrighted by the North Western Photo Co. Jan 17 1891 Chadron Neb

The slain Sioux Chief Big Foot lies at Wounded Knee like a man still struggling to rise. The "battlefield" was plainly tidied up before this picture was taken, for most of his band died with Big Foot under the rifles and cannon of the 7th Cavalry, and the area of greatest slaughter was immediately around where the sick chief was killed. (Courtesy of the Bureau of American Ethnology, Smithsonian Institution)

might be if they hunted into northern Texas. They found Dodge affable and full of questions about their business and its problems, but he volunteered no answer to their oblique questions. At last they were forced to ask him point-blank what the government might do if they crossed into Texas.

"Boys," said the Colonel, "if I were a buffalo hunter, I would hunt where the buffalo are."

So much for the protection the Indians could expect in preserving their hunting grounds. Dodge's slightly veiled proposal to the hide men to move across into the Panhandle was a deliberate invitation to trouble with the Indians, and he was not so naïve as not to have known it. However, he was not speaking carelessly and expressing only his own views; Sherman, Sheridan, and other (but not all) Army officers had taken the position that the quickest way to tame the roving Indians and keep them on the reservations would be to hurry up the extermination of the buffalo.

Mooar and a number of like-minded hide men did not care whose policy it was; it was sufficient that the Army would not cause trouble. When the plains dried out sufficiently the next spring—1874—to take the weight of the big hide wagons, the hunters left Dodge City and splashed across the Arkansas, heading south for Texas. The caravan, however, was not composed entirely of hide men. During the winter it had occurred to a trader named A. C. Myers that the Panhandle is a long way from Dodge City, and that a man on the grounds with guns, ammunition, and a hundred other things to sell would have the perfect market with no competition. Moreover, he would be able to buy the choice hides before the Dodge City traders ever saw them. Myers laid in a stock of goods and made ready. A blacksmith, Tom O'Keefe, was won over by the same logic of big demand and no competition and put his tools and forge in a wagon. A gentleman named Jim Hanrahan decided to operate a saloon at the post. Some time after the first contingent had left, another trader and hide buyer, Charles Rath, followed with a large stock of goods, and William Olds and his wife came to open a restaurant.

The post was built on the Canadian River in what is now Hutchinson County, Texas. Although it consisted of several structures of sod and small logs with a horse corral, it became known as Adobe Walls because it was located only about a mile from the remnants of an old adobe trading post built by the Bents in the long ago and soon abandoned, possibly in 1844. (There had been a battle at Adobe Walls in 1864 when Kit Carson had destroyed a Kiowa camp, and then had been lucky to escape with almost a full skin when the Indians had recovered from their surprise and had driven him into retreat.) A log-and-sod shanty is no palace but, compared to what the hide men were used to, it was high living—and at how many other camps was there a saloon at the end of the hard day?

The hunters and skinners fanned out from the post in the morning and came back at night if at all possible because these plains were not friendly. Indians hung around out of sight, waiting a chance to steal in, and two or three isolated parties lost lives and scalps. An attack on the post itself was inevitable, but when it did come, it had something of the accidental about it. In May, 1874, the Comanches were in a high state of excitement, not only because of the buffalo hunters and lagging annuity payments, but because they had come off second best in fighting with a small tribe called the Tonkawas during recent raids into Texas and had lost several men. The Tonkawas were the remnants of a tribe that had once been of much more consequence, but they had not lost their fighting spirit, as the Comanches had discovered. They were thoroughly hated by other tribes. For one thing, they had sold out completely to the white man, and served him as scouts on campaigns against any and all other Indians. Worse yet, they were, or had been, cannibals.

In the Comanche lodges, wives, sisters, and mothers of warriors slain by the despised Tonkawas wailed, blackened their faces, tore their flesh and otherwise mourned after their fashion, and called for revenge. And, contrary to the popular misconception of the Indian woman as a creature completely subservient to her man, she could bring to bear taunts and pleadings to which he was no more resistant than any tamed and civilized male today.

While the tribe was in a state of excitement and indecision over both the Tonkawas and the post at Adobe Walls, a young man named Isatai came forth from the untamed Kwahadi Comanche proclaiming himself a great medicine man. He could bring the dead back to life, said Isatai, and cure all diseases. He had been taken into the spirit world many times by the Father of all Indians, who had given him control over wind and rain, thunder and lightning, heat and drought, and other meteorological phenomena, which he could send down on the world as he pleased. He could protect his friends against the guns of the whites so that enemy bullets would fall harmless at point-blank range, and he could supply them with all the ammunition they needed by producing it in unlimited quantities from his stomach.

Now, they were rather strong claims which, if he could support them, would make Isatai a valuable man to have about. It would seem that someone of a skeptical turn of mind would have called on him for a demonstration, perhaps to reanimate a dead person, or bring on a rain out of a clear sky. Such are the capabilities of humans to delude themselves that the medicine man did not even have to face challenges. Many members of the tribe stepped forward to testify that they had personally witnessed these marvels; some had seen him rise into the sky to talk with the Spirit and later descend again; there were others who had watched in wonder as he produced almost a wagon load of cartridges from his stomach. After such testimonials, no Comanche dared question further, and many of the Cheyennes and Kiowas were convinced.

With the supernatural powers of Isatai on its side, the tribe began seriously to plan an expedition to take revenge on the Tonkawas. In May, the young medicine man called a meeting of the entire tribe where Elk Creek joins the Red River. So great was his reputation by then that all bands of the Comanche nation showed up, the first time in the memory of the oldest men that the entire tribe had met in council. Moreover, most of the Cheyennes were present, and part of the Kiowas. The Arapahoes, though, had had an end of fighting; they were doing their best to follow the white man's road.

Isatai told them that he had had another meeting with the Great Father, who had sent down orders with him that they should exact vengeance for their fellow warriors who had been killed by the Tonkawas. But there had been too much talking beforehand; word of the threat against the Tonkawas had reached the commanding officer of Fort Griffin (not far north of today's Abilene, Texas) near where the Tonkawas lived, and he had gathered the threatened tribe in under the fort's protection. The news reached back to the war party on Elk Creek before it had started out, but with war spirit at a high pitch, it was easy to change plans to an attack on the hide hunters at Adobe Walls instead.

However, enthusiasm for fighting white men was not what it had been a few years before, in spite of the bitterness the Indians felt. More and more, the thoughtful among them were coming to see that they never won, no matter how much right was on their side; in the end the soldiers always came to punish them. A number of the Comanche, including one entire band, the Penateka, were unhappy with the decision to attack Adobe Walls. Tonkawa scouts and cannibals were one thing; white men were something completely different.

The war leaders had anticipated that there might be some faint hearts, and had announced that they would prevent anyone from leaving before the attack was over, even if they had to kill all their horses to do so. They were determined this attack was not going to be ruined, as the one on the Tonkawas had been, by word getting out to the prospective victims. Nevertheless, many Comanches did manage to slip away, although the Cheyennes present remained resolute, and so, apparently, did the small group of Kiowa who were there.

As the planners had feared, the secret did get out. Traders were told of the council, apparently by Comanches who had stolen away from it, and they carried the word to Adobe Walls. But at that outpost of trade and meager comfort, the news was kept within a very elite circle: the Mooar brothers, the two traders, Myers and Rath, and saloonkeeper Hanrahan. These gentlemen considered the possibility that word of the impending attack might send all the hide men running back to Dodge City, leaving the post undefended, then decided to keep quiet. After all, they had a big investment to think about.

The warning of the approaching attack had come on June 18, and it had even had a date on it: June 27 appeared, from all signs, to be the most likely day. Indian raids increased. A pair of hunters were killed, then two more, and one day a raiding party followed the Mooars to the trading post from the prairie. The Mooars' nerve broke a couple of days before the day predicted for the attack. They loaded the big hide wagons, and in the morning headed the six-horse teams north toward Kansas and safety. They had been on the trail only a few hours when Myers and Rath, on horseback, caught up with them; the traders had succumbed to their own cases of cold feet.

Only saloonkeeper Jim Hanrahan was left of those who knew the secret—for some reason blacksmith O'Keefe, though also a founder of the trading post, had never been told of the warning. Even when the evening of the twenty-sixth came, he was reluctant to tell the men; if they waited up in the middle of the night for an Indian assault that never came (first morning gray was a favorite time for Indian attacks), he would be the butt of their heavy-handed humor. After all, the attack might not come on the twenty-seventh—or on any other day. On the other hand, he could not leave them—and himself—to be killed in their beds if it did come. Hanrahan's way out of the dilemma was ingenious. In the middle of the night he fired a pistol into the air, shouting that the ridgepole was breaking. Three or four men were sleeping in the saloon under the heavy sod roof supported by the threatened ridgepole; they were out in a hurry, and other men awakened by the commotion also appeared. It was warm weather and men were sleeping outdoors as well as in the buildings. No one questioned that the sharp report that had wakened them was the sound of wood cracking.

Someone found a pole suitable for propping the ridgepole even though it showed no signs of sagging or cracking, and Hanrahan served up free drinks to everyone to keep them awake. Several men decided that, since they were up, they might as well get an early start. It must then have been about three o'clock and the first hint of gray showing in the eastern sky, as two hunters walked out of the saloon, one to get things ready in the wagon, the other to bring the horses from the corral.

The two men saw the long line of Indians thundering out of the darkness at almost the same instant. Billy Dixon, at the wagon, had his buffalo gun with him, and got off one shot before he took to his heels and ran to the saloon. Billy Ogg, at the corral, had no weapon; when he saw the mass of Indians riding straight for him he did what any rational person would do and ran at top speed, also to the saloon. Then the roar and thunder of hoofs was around the buildings of the post, mounted Indians pounded on doors and windows, and the fight was on.

The supreme leader of the war party was the leading chief of the Kwahadi Comanche, a man named Quanah whom the whites, however, always called Quanah Parker because his mother had been a white woman, Cynthia Ann Parker, who had been captured by the Comanche when a young girl. Isatai had worked his medicine beforehand to assure success in the fight: all warriors had been bullet-proofed, and incantations had been performed so that the men at the post would be deep in sleep and all doors open. Isatai rode stark naked except for a little cap of sagebrush stems; it was all an essential part of his medicine. The picture is ludicrous; it is also pathetic, for by such forlorn and futile means the Plains people hoped to overcome the men who were ravaging the last of their buffalo country.

Two brothers, Ike and Shorty Shadler, haulers of freight, achieved their small immortality in Western history by being killed in the first charge, probably without quite realizing what was happening. They had arrived from Dodge City with a load of supplies only the day before, and had immediately reloaded with hides and were sleeping in their wagons, ready to start back as soon as daylight came. It never dawned for them; the wave of Indians engulfed their wagons and the brothers were killed and scalped.

There were left twenty-seven defenders, one a woman, forted up in three buildings, against an unknown number of Indians, probably somewhere between five and seven hundred. The first charge carried the warriors right up to the buildings, where they battered away at doors and windows, getting one partially open before being driven away. The defenders, as they overcame their first surprise and became organized, finally forced the Indians to retreat.

That was the only dangerous assault. There were some weaker charges later in the day, but the warriors seemed more interested in trying to recover some of their dead than in anything else. The heart had gone out of them with the discovery that Isatai was a false prophet, one more disappointment on a long trail of broken hopes. Isatai himself sat on his horse apart and did not enter the battle in spite of taunts which rose to loud jeers when his horse, in spite of a complete covering of bullet-proofing paint, was shot from under him.

A third white man was killed early in the day when the warriors were still dashing in close, but they soon stopping taking chances. The defenders were well protected and a number of them were equipped with rifles of tremendous power and range and were dead shots at long range. The warriors established a siege but it was not a very tight one, for hunters who had been out on the plains made their way in to the post, and a messenger was sent for help to Dodge City. Rescue forces, one of buffalo men from Dodge City, the other a cavalry detachment, set out for Adobe Walls. The Indians, as always, soon wearied of siege and drifted away. On or about the first of July, one warrior appeared about a mile away. Billy Dixon, who had sighted the first morning charge of the Indians, carefully rested his Sharps 50-caliber on a support, allowed for windage and extreme range, and pressed off his shot. The Indian brave tumbled from his horse. It was a shot that awed even the buffalo men, who always referred to it as

Dixon's mile shot, although measurement showed it to be 1,538 yards, a stone's throw scant of a mile, close enough for all but quibblers.

The defenders suffered their fourth and final casualty on July 2 when a party of Indians was reported on the plains and William Olds, the man who, with his wife, had come to Adobe Walls to start a restaurant, started up a ladder to the lookout post that had been established on the roof of one of the buildings. He was careless; the trigger of his rifle caught in something, and the gun went off. The charge caught him in the head and he tumbled down at the feet of his wife.

Soon after, the decision was made to abandon the post and leave the country. The hunters with their hides, O'Keefe with his blacksmith tools, Hanrahan with his liquor and his dreams of a nice profit, all went back to Dodge City. Behind them, drying on the pickets of the corral, they left the heads of twelve warriors, dead Indians the war party had not been able to recover. In August, almost two months later, Colonel Nelson Miles passed that way with troops and found the heads still on the posts, looking across the plains with hollow-socketed, lipless grins.

3. THE RED RIVER WAR—1874–75

The anger of the Indians following the Adobe Walls attack had spread to encompass all whites. More and more warriors were riding off the reservation, once again filled with the old dreams and illusions that the warpath was a road filled with glory. Raiding parties struck far from home, into Kansas, Colorado, New Mexico, as well as Texas, killing perhaps eighty persons. Most of the attacks were cruel and senseless ones, on white men who had nothing to do with killing the buffalo or with repressing the Indians, chance-met men whose only fault was that they were white. For instance, there was Patrick Hennessey who, with three other men, was taking a small wagon train of supplies from Wichita, Kansas, to the Wichita agency at Anadarko in Indian Territory when they were attacked by Cheyennes at a spot now commemorated by the town of Hennessey, Oklahoma. They were not enemies of the Indians; in fact, at that moment they were hauling food meant for red men, but they were nevertheless killed and scalped. Hennessey suffered death by torture on a pile of burning grain taken from the wagons, but it was not the Cheyennes who did the torturing. Several Osages, members of a tribe that had been walking the white man's road for years, came along during the attack. They took charge of poor Hennessey, and put him to death with savage cruelty. There were, apparently, deep resentments even in tribes which had been assumed to be completely tamed.

There was no unanimity in this last journey down the warpath. Whirlwind, an important chief of the Cheyennes, came in to the Cheyenne-Arapaho agency at Darlington with his followers and settled down, refusing to have anything to do with the conflict that was breeding, and two or three other bands of Cheyennes joined them, although in general the Cheyennes were to be the staunchest fighters in the days ahead. The Arapahoes, after fighting white men for many years as loyal allies of the Cheyennes, at last decided that they had had enough of being whipped and bloodied. They remained completely friendly, and moved in to the Darlington agency where they furnished a police force that stood guard every night till all danger was past.

Neither did the other two tribes show any singleness of purpose about making war. Probably as many as three-quarters of the Kiowas (including the entire Kiowa Apache band which refused to join in any more fighting) declared themselves friendly. Early in July, after the tribe's annual religious convocation, the Sun Dance, most of the Kiowa, except for a minority under Chiefs Lone Wolf and Swan, had come in to their agency at Fort Sill to declare themselves for peace, and had been duly enrolled as friendly and directed to camp near the fort. A large number of Comanches had also come in and been enrolled, and were also told to set up their tepees in the friendly camp. Any Indian who came in later would not only have to give up his arms but would have to convince the agent that he had not committed any warlike acts.

On July 21, the order came from Sheridan's headquarters to carry out active military operations to punish the hostiles, even to pursuing them onto the reservations. General Pope, in command of the department, at once began organizing troops for a vigorous campaign.

Every Indian conflict seems to have some blunder or stupidity that makes it worse than it need be, and this was no exception. In late August, before there had been any important contact between warriors and soldiers, a number of Comanches of the Nokoni band came in to the Wichita agency at Anadarko to surrender. The agency served the Wichitas, Caddoes, Delawares and Pawnees, and on this day, because it was ration day, a large number of Comanches and Kiowas were also present. So, too, was the commanding officer and a detachment of troops from Fort Sill, some thirty miles to the south, come to keep order during the distribution of rations.

The agent explained to the surrendering Nokoni Comanches that they would have to give up their weapons, and this they readily agreed to. A number of guns had been given up when the question arose as to whether bows and arrows would have to be surrendered too. Apparently there was no rancor in the dispute, and a messenger was sent to the commanding officer to obtain his interpretation. While his return was awaited, the Nokoni chief—his name was Red Food—gave a whoop. Afterward, the Comanches insisted the chief was merely calling to another chief; the military insisted it was a warwhoop and a signal for an attack, something that seems unlikely because Red Food would hardly have waited until many of his men had given up their guns before calling for action. No one ever learned from Red Food what he meant for the result of his whoop was disastrous to him; he was immediately shot down by soldiers.

Infuriated Indians began shooting at soldiers. The fighting spread, although it was only Kiowas and Comanches who became involved; the other tribes had lost their taste for combat long since. Warriors burned the agency school and several houses belonging to friendly Indians, looted a store, killed four civilians and wounded several soldiers. Not all took part in the fighting; many fled, but others continued the attack the next day before finally giving up the attempt to capture the agency. Some of those who had run from the fighting returned to Fort Sill where they had been enrolled as friendlies before going to Anadarko without permission; they had been innocent bystanders and were permitted to return without reprisals. But most of those who had been present, even though they had been friendly and had avoided the fighting, kept going right out into the Panhandle to join the hostiles already there. The quickness of the military to shoot first and ask later was going to cost a number of lives.

Satanta and Big Tree, a year out of prison now, were caught up in the separation of the sheep from the goats, the friendlies from the hostiles. They, with their followers, had enrolled as friendlies at Fort Sill but the monotony of sitting in a camp while things were happening was too much for them. They left without permission and rode out along the upper Washita before eventually returning, not to Fort Sill but to the Cheyenne agency at Darlington. They did not like their own agency, they explained. There was no proof that they had taken part in hostilities while away, but with their reputations, and the truculent history of the tribe, it was assumed that they must have. They were treated as surrendered prisoners of war, their horses and weapons taken from them, and the entire band sent back to Fort Sill. Satanta, whom the military looked on as a hostage for the good behavior of all Kiowas, was sent back to prison in Texas for breaking his parole.

In the meantime, military operations were underway against the Indians on the Texas plains. Five columns, some three thousand troops in all, converged on the plains of the Panhandle, from Fort Griffin and Fort Concho to the south in Texas, from Fort Supply to the northeast and Fort Sill to the east, both in Indian Territory, and from Fort Union in New Mexico. The five columns operated more or less independently, with the sole mission of pursuing Indians, but Colonel Nelson A. Miles (brevet brigadier general) was in overall command. Miles personally commanded the force coming from Fort Supply, and had one of the first brushes with the Indians when he encountered them near the head of the Washita and drove them west in a running battle. A few days later, a strong hostile force attacked his wagon train. The wagons immediately went into corral and fought off the Indians—one of those scenes so dear to early motion picture makers, wagons drawn up in an oval with defenders firing through wheel spokes at circling warriors—until relief came after several days. The force moving from Fort Union also had a hard fight with Indians before finally defeating them.

But these Indians were not out on the plains for the purpose of fighting soldiers. Most of them wanted only to get away from them, the farther the better, and to return to an old way of life. Most of the places where they had roamed so freely within the memory of men still young and vigorous were shut out to them. The empty grasslands that had once seemed to go on forever, beyond where the sky bent down to meet the horizon, were no longer empty. Settlers and ranchers had moved into the most attractive stream valleys, and plumes of smoke and crawling strings of railroad cars moved across the once magnificently empty horizon. Even the buffalo were gone from the old places, slain by men who did nothing else but kill them from morning till night. But out on the Panhandle the old way remained, where there was still space and buffalo—if only white men could be kept out.

This northwest corner of Texas is more than an expanse of flat grassland; it has complexities that made the war against the Indians more than a series of chases over open country. An escarpment runs in an irregular line north and south through the southern Panhandle along about the 101st meridian. Here the land abruptly rises from the rolling plains on the east side of the escarpment to the high plains on the west, a difference in height in places of as much as 1,000 feet. The high plains extend on to the west, rising gradually all the while, till they finally merge into the foothills of the Rockies well into New Mexico. The expanse of high plains is called the Staked Plain; it was so named by early Spanish explorers, Llano Estacado, for reasons not known for certain although it was probably because one of the early Spanish expeditions drove stakes at intervals to guide it on its return over the flat, monotonous region which had no more landmarks than the middle of the ocean. It was on the Staked Plain that the Kwahadi Comanches had been able to maintain their freedom when all other bands of the tribe had been forced to sign treaties.

However, it was not to the bleak and austere security of the immense spaces of the Staked Plain that most of the hostile bands went to make their winter camps. There are various canyons and gorges extending from the escarpment back into the higher Staked Plain, eroded by streams through geological eras. The most notable of these is Palo Duro Canyon, the work of the Prairie Dog Town Fork of the Red River, a great slash through the plain perhaps forty miles long in its main portion, eight hundred or more feet deep, and averaging perhaps half a dozen miles wide. The floor of Palo Duro Canyon held pastures of grass and clumps of cottonwood and cedar.

Deep in the canyon, Cheyennes, Comanches, and Kiowas had set up their camps, not as warriors but as families, provided with fuel and water, and grass for their ponies, and out of reach of any brutal storms that might roar across the plains above. In fact, they were already there when an especially early harbinger of winter whistled across the Staked Plain on September 24, a raw, cold north wind with driving rain. They had apparently forgotten the lesson of the Washita and the months following, that the Army did not stop making war, as Indians did, when the grass turned dry.

It was the 4th Cavalry, a veteran outfit about 450 strong, out of Fort Concho in Texas and commanded by Colonel Ranald Mackenzie, that first found the Indians at the bottom of the canyon. When Mackenzie arrived at the lip of Palo Duro Canyon at dawn on September 28, he looked down into the deeper gloom in the shadows of the can-

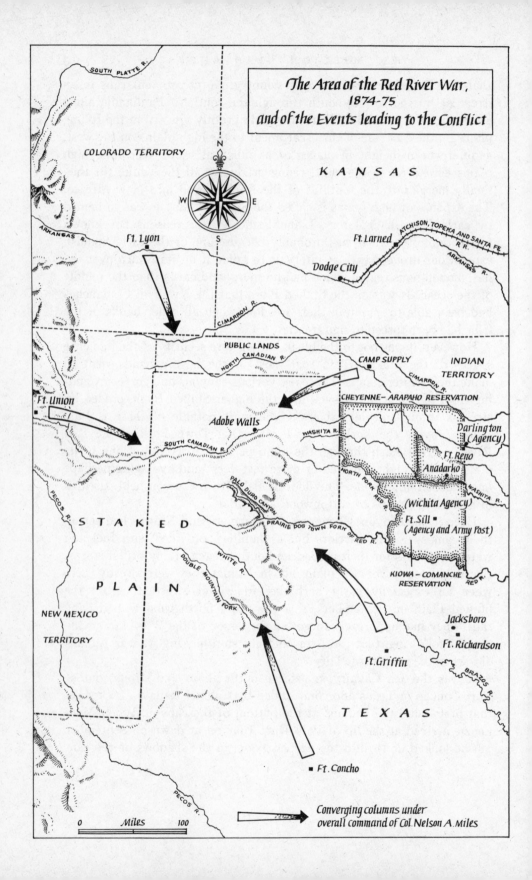

The Area of the Red River War, 1874-75 and of the Events leading to the Conflict

SOUTH PLATTE R.

COLORADO TERRITORY

KANSAS

N
W · E
S

ARKANSAS R.

Ft. Lyon

Ft. Larned

ATCHISON, TOPEKA AND SANTA FE R. R.

ARKANSAS R.

Dodge City

CIMARRON R.

PUBLIC LANDS

NORTH CANADIAN R.

CAMP SUPPLY

CIMARRON R.

INDIAN TERRITORY

CHEYENNE – ARAPAHO RESERVATION

Ft. Union

Adobe Walls

SOUTH CANADIAN R.

WASHITA R.

Darlington (Agency)

Ft. Reno

Anadarko

PECOS R.

S T A K E D

PALO DURO CANYON

NORTH FORK RED R.

PRAIRIE DOG TOWN FORK OF RED R.

WASHITA R.

(Wichita Agency)

Ft. Sill
(Agency and Army Post)

P L A I N

WHITE R.

DOUBLE MOUNTAIN FORK

KIOWA – COMANCHE RESERVATION

RED R.

NEW MEXICO

TERRITORY

Jacksboro

Ft. Richardson

Ft. Griffin

BRAZOS R.

T E X A S

Ft. Concho

PECOS R.

0   Miles   100

Converging columns under overall command of Col. Nelson A. Miles yon bottom below on an Indian camp that was asleep and unsuspecting. The regiment located a narrow trail and was already halfway to the bottom before a brave sighted it and gave the alarm.

To the Indians in Palo Duro Canyon, the coming of the cavalry should not have been less of a surprise if it had been announced by trumpets. A small party of warriors from the camp had discovered Mackenzie's cavalry two days earlier and had tried to run off his horses; they had, beyond all doubt, reported the presence of soldiers in the area to the canyon camp. The most elementary prudence should have demanded that a guard be set on the plains above—but the individualistic Plains Indian was as temperamentally unfitted for guard duty as he was to carry out a siege. As a result, the Indians had not even known the soldiers were approaching until they were halfway down the canyon—and then, instead of hurrying to attack when the cavalry was strung out along a narrow bluff-side trail and unable to maneuver, they fled in panic down the canyon, abandoning everything they owned, including most of their horses.

When it was too late to go any good, the warriors began rallying and shooting back, but by then the troops were in possession of all the Indian camps which extended for about two miles. While part of the regiment held the warriors back with long-distance carbine fire, the rest of the soldiers methodically went about destroying everything in the camps. Tepees, robes, tanned hides, arrows, dried meat, everything that would burn or be ruined by heat or smoke went into the great bonfires. Holes were knocked in the bottoms of cooking kettles, nothing usable was spared. While the great coils of greasy smoke rose far above over the canyon's rim, the horse herds were rounded up.

When the work of destruction was complete, the regiment, driving the captured ponies, made its way up the trail to the canyon rim again. The ponies were destroyed soon after on Mackenzie's orders, after first allowing the Tonkawa scouts to take their pick of the animals. More than 1,400 horses and mules were killed. As far as the actual clash of fighting men and loss of life was concerned, the battle in the canyon had not amounted to a great deal. But the Army had learned that the best way to fight Indians was to go after them, coldly and ruthlessly, with the main purpose of wiping out everything they possessed.

With their tepees burned, their buffalo robes destroyed, most of their weapons gone, and their ponies captured, the peoples of the plains faced a degree of destitution that anyone born to four walls and a brick chimney can approximate in his imagination only by supposing his own house to be destroyed and himself thrown, without shelter or food, into a harsh and bitterly cold world where there are no friendly neighbors, no kindly welfare people to open doors to him. Even the most simple-appearing matters became major problems to an Indian band left destitute in this way. The replacement of the cone of poles that supported the hide covering of the lodges might mean a trip of two or three hundred miles to the foothills where the nearest tall, straight, sky-reaching saplings grew. And this was a minor problem, compared with killing buffalo and tanning its skin to cover the lodge and to provide clothing and robes. A band of hardy braves might survive, even young men with tough and resolute young wives. But for an ordinary band, with aged men and women, and especially children and infants, the thing was almost impossible. It was a matter of surrender or starve.

As early as the first part of October, a band of Comanches sent word to Fort Sill that they wanted to give themselves up. They were met by a detachment of troops which led them in to the fort; more came a few days later, totaling about four hundred with some two thousand horses (these were not completely whipped Indians; as long as they had that many horses, they were far from destitute). Disheartened hostiles straggled in all during October in small parties, Kiowas and Comanches, many of them in acute distress and privation as a result of the fight in Palo Duro Canyon. All were put under guard as fast as they came in and their horses and weapons taken away.

All the while the Army continued its relentless pressure. The 11th Infantry attacked and completely dispersed a large camp of Kiowas on the Salt Fork of the Red River on October 9, and on the seventeenth, the 6th Cavalry caught another camp of Kiowas so completely by surprise that they fled without attempting any defense, leaving their lodges and belongings behind. From the beginning of this, which came to be known as the Red River War, the Army never gave the Indians a chance to rest themselves or their scrawny ponies, never allowed them a chance to hunt and prepare a supply of dried meat and pemmican, never permitted them to repair tattered clothing or rips in tepees.

The Army lists fourteen pitched battles during the war, but it was not so much the battles as the constant pursuit and the attrition on their equipment and their nerves that wore the Indians down. The pressure was maintained so unrelentingly, as a matter of fact, that by mid-November a message to "ease down on the parties hostile at present," came from none other than William Tecumseh Sherman, that apostle of the heavy hand and spokesman for extermination.

An unusual engagement took place early in November when Lieutenant Frank Baldwin of the 5th Infantry was convoying a train of twenty-three empty wagons drawn by six-mule teams from the Red River to a supply camp on the Washita. He had with him a company of cavalry, one of infantry, and a howitzer, a force strong enough for protection against most attacks that might be expected. When the detachment reached a stream named McClellan Creek, it was met by its scouts who had come hurrying back with the information that the camp of Cheyenne chief Grey Beard was just ahead.

Lieutenant Baldwin was too near the camp to turn around and retreat, because if he were discovered and attacked while withdrawing he would be caught at an absolute disadvantage. On the other hand, even if he could commit every soldier to battle, his small detachment would still be greatly outnumbered by the Cheyenne warriors—and it would be impossible to send his entire force into action because it was necessary to leave a substantial detail at the rear to guard the wagons. Tossed between the horns of this dilemma, Baldwin found a third way out. He put his twenty-three wagons and his howitzer into line abreast, loaded the infantry into the wagons, and put the cavalry on the two flanks. Then, with the trumpet sounding the charge, the whole fantastic line of battle swept over a rise in ground and bore down into sight of the startled Cheyennes in their camp, with teamsters and infantrymen yelling, and cavalrymen whooping and shooting as soon as they got within range.

Audacity paid off. The terrified Indians did not stop to assess the force bearing down on them, but turned and ran, abandoning the camp and everything in it to Baldwin's onrushing line of battle. The Cheyenne warriors paused only once to give battle, and then just long enough to hold the Army forces while women, children, and old people got away. At last, after a pursuit of a dozen miles or so, the last Indian warriors faded away into the plains.

In the abandoned camp, Lieutenant Baldwin found two very small white captives, Adelaide and Julia German. The German family homestead on Smoky Hill River in Kansas had been attacked in September by a wide-ranging band of Cheyennes who had killed parents, a son and one daughter, and had taken four other daughters captive.

The two small girls had been separated from their older sisters at the time of their capture and had not seen them since.

The war went on through the winter, until the last important group of reservation Indians still at large were Cheyennes. Their breaking point under the constant harrying and driving came in March, when their leading chief, Stone Calf, came in with the entire part of the tribe still at large. In surrendering, they gave up the two older German girls, aged fifteen and seventeen, who, for half a year had, as the journals of the period would put it, "suffered all the unspeakable horrors of Indian captivity." Those horrors were very real. A woman could usually expect to find herself traded from brave to brave, and her lot was not at all mitigated by the jealousy of wives whose beds she temporarily usurped and who took every opportunity to cuff the captive about and load her down with onerous tasks. In his treatment of women captives, the best that could be said of the Plains Indian is that he was not a whit worse than his white brother.

Colonel Nelson Miles later became guardian of the four German girls. They were installed in a comfortable home at Fort Leavenworth, and to assure their support, Congress authorized that an amount sufficient to take care of them be withheld from the annuities of the Cheyennes.

As the Cheyennes came into their agency at Darlington after their surrender, they were disarmed and their horses were taken from them. But they gave up mostly bows and arrows; there was enough guile left in them that they had hidden most of their firearms before they came in to the agency. Physically, they had resisted until they had nothing left to fight with. Their agent wrote:

> A more wretched and poverty-stricken community than these people presented after they were placed in the prison camp it would be difficult to imagine. Bereft of lodges and the most ordinary cooking apparatus; with no ponies nor other means of transportation for food or water; half starved and with scarcely anything that could be called clothing, they were truly objects of pity; and for the first time the Cheyenne seemed to realize the power of the government and their own inability to cope successfully therewith.

However, events soon proved that there was still fire in the Cheyennes. In its constant and usually clumsy and heavy-handed attempts to devise ways to keep the tribes under control, the military had come up with a new dodge at the close of this, the Red River War. It had been decided that the best way to render the tribes incapable of making war again would be to strip them of their leadership, to select the men most responsible for the war, and send them into exile. The Cheyennes were required to provide thirty-three; two more came from the Arapaho, but for other crimes since that tribe had remained aloof from the conflict.

The selection of the Cheyenne prisoners to be exiled was done at Darlington agency on April 6, with the two older German girls present to help in picking out culprits who should be sent away. But by the end of the day the task was still far from complete; only fourteen men had been selected, and one woman, whom the German girls had spotted in the crowd of onlooking women and children and recognized as having taken part in the murder of their family. But the officer in command, Lieutenant Colonel Thomas H. Neill, decided to call a halt to the chore for the time being, and, in order that no unfinished business would appear on the record, he ordered that eighteen men be arbitrarily taken from the line to complete the required quota of thirty-three. Naming the men to be exiled, he said, would be continued later; then the unhappy eighteen would be replaced by men identified as deserving punishment.

Colonel Neill, what with this and that, did not get around to resuming the selection; other matters kept coming up, until finally he decided one Indian was as good as another and concluded to let things stand. On April 9, the thirty-three prisoners, including the unlucky eighteen, were brought out to have balls and chains fastened on their legs. As the warriors were led, one by one, to the blacksmith to have shackles riveted on, Cheyenne women taunted their men for submitting tamely to being fettered like animals. One young warrior, the possessor of many coups, Black Horse by name, was stung by the scorn of the women enough to knock the blacksmith aside and attempt to get away. A volley from the soldier guards caught him, but their aim was not the best; Black Horse was seriously but far from fatally injured. The Cheyennes began an attack on the guard with bows and arrows, and even with a few guns that had somehow appeared from concealment, and then, while military reinforcements were being sent for from Fort Reno (built the previous year, 1874) only two miles away, the Indians hurriedly fled to sandhills on the opposite side of the North Canadian River where they had hidden most of their firearms when they had come in to the agency and surrendered.

There was a sharp fight, with several killed on each side. The Army forces brought up Gatling guns; the Indians, already destitute after their long resistance on the Texas plains, fought off the troops till dark when they fled—men, women, and children—once again. Colonel Neill reported that about 250 warriors, with their families, left the agency. Many of them soon surrendered again but a small band headed for Dakota country. Traveling across the plains was not what it had been a few years ago—or for that matter, even a year ago, things changed that fast. The buffalo were virtually gone in Kansas—wiped out by the hide hunters; there were ranchers and farmers to avoid; telegraphs reported the movement of a band of Indians far ahead of them.

Lieutenant Austin Henley with a detachment of the 6th Cavalry and about twenty-five buffalo hunters attacked the fugitive Indians while they were camped on the Sappa River in northwestern Kansas. There, in a murderous onslaught with annihilation as its purpose, the soldiers and hunters disregarded Indian attempts to surrender, shot down every person capable of defending himself, and then dragged wounded women and infants from pits under the river bank and clubbed them to death. Some escaped, and with others who had not been at the Sappa camp, eventually found haven with their brothers, the Northern Cheyennes.

The Sappa River afterwards was a bitter name to the Cheyennes, a Sand Creek on a smaller scale. The Army never boasted about it either. Lieutenant Henley's official report said that nineteen men and eight women and children had been killed, but only after the Indians had refused to surrender. Two soldiers were killed in the line of duty. There was no mention of buffalo hunters. However, it was impossible to keep rumor down, and some of the buffalo men claimed that the number of dead Indians was around a hundred—some said more, some less—and that most of them were women and children. It was not an engagement the Army was especially proud of.

The naming of the thirty-three most guilty Cheyenne leaders for exile never was resumed. Those already selected (except for Black Horse who had broken away and precipitated the entire flight), together with the eighteen poor devils who had been grabbed at random to fill out the quota, were sent to ancient Fort Marion in Florida.

There were still a number of Comanches out, most of them Kwahadis who had never submitted to the government and had never been on a reservation. Although the band had taken a leading part in the attack on the trading post at Adobe Walls, it had spent most of its time during the war far out on the Staked Plain. It was a vast country and a miserable one for an army to operate in. At one time, Colonel Miles' command became so tortured by thirst while operating on these plains that men opened their own veins to get blood to relieve their thirst. This was the home of the Kwahadi Comanches, men made lean and tough from living on the stark, high plains. The Army was never able to bring them to bay; the best it could do was to keep them on the move so constantly that they had difficulty hunting, and wore out or lost much of their camp equipment.

Colonel Miles at last gained by diplomacy what he was not able to get by force of arms, sending scouts out to treat with the Comanches and argue the case of peace on the reservation as against war and privation for themselves and their families. In April, almost two hundred came in and gave themselves up. Another message sent out with an experienced plainsman reached Quanah Parker, leading chief of the Kwahadis, who was himself becoming convinced that remaining at war was slow suicide. He led his band in to Fort Sill, arriving there on June 2. They turned over their weapons and 1,500 horses and mules, an indication that they were not destitute. Actually, while their equipment was shabby, they had lost very few men in fighting, and only about twenty had been captured; all the rest had surrendered voluntarily.

With the Comanches—and the Kiowas—a surrender was a surrender; there was no burying of weapons to be used in another outbreak. Both tribes were required to send their leaders responsible for the outbreak off to exile as the Cheyennes had, and nine Comanches and twenty-six Kiowas were selected. The list of Kiowas selected to go was a joke to almost everyone except those whose names were on the list. The chore of making the selection was turned over to Chief Kicking Bird, who had long been the leader of the peace faction among the Kiowas. He picked half a dozen chiefs who had been notorious in the fighting, but for the rest he shielded his friends by naming men of no importance, many of them Mexicans who had been captured and made members of the tribe.

The prisoners joined the Cheyennes in Florida at Fort Marion. Their captivity was not onerous. There was no close confinement; the prisoners were merely kept under a general surveillance. They were released in May, 1878, after three years. Even so, it had not been an easy exile. The strange climate and separation from friends and families caused many to sicken and die.

Eastern philanthropists took a great deal of interest in the prisoners while they were there, and tried to give them a smattering of white man's civilization and a large dollop of Christianity, it being considered a truism that no Indian could accomplish anything worthwhile without first becoming a Christian. Some of the younger men were persuaded to remain on when the rest were permitted to return, some in private homes, some in the Normal Institute at Hampton, Virginia, a Negro school which became an Indian school as more young tribesmen were brought in. The experiment was considered so successful that a year later, in 1879, the famous Indian school at Carlisle, Pennsylvania, was started to carry on the work permanently.

And what of the one other warrior who was put in prison during those times? Satanta remained in the Texas penitentiary; no one came this time with an offer of amnesty. His first imprisonment of two years he had borne with equanimity, but after he was sent back in 1874, he was an embittered old man who argued that many others were much more guilty than he, and that he had, in fact, kept his parole and had not turned his weapons against the white man again. In 1878, finding imprisonment too much to bear after a lifetime of roaming the plains, he leapt to his death from an unbarred upper window.

Oddly, it was Quanah Parker, chief of the Kwahadi Comanche, the most completely untamed of all Indian bands until the Red River War, who was one of those best able to adjust to changing times. Once he became convinced that it was hopeless for Indians to attempt any longer to resist the advance of the white man's civilization, he became a progressive, counseling his people always to walk in the white man's road. It was popular to explain Quanah's progressiveness in terms of his "superior" white blood. This was poppycock. His mother may have been white but Quanah was pure Indian in culture, and he thought as an Indian.

There were, alas, limits to Quanah Parker's ability to abandon the comfortable old ways. He had, because of his prominence, been appointed a judge on a Court of Indian Offenses, one of the bodies set up at agencies to help the agents administer their Indian charges. The courts heard complaints against Indians who the agents felt were not making proper speed toward civilization—and many agents, with a

Caucasian myopia, considered the persistence of tribal dances, the activities of medicine men, even some Indian ways of dressing and wearing the hair, as prima facie evidence of savagery still unshed. Bigamy, of course, was a sure sign of a savage. Eventually the agent got around to inquiring into Quanah Parker's own household arrangements. He discovered five wives, living contentedly but unprogressively together.

This is ahead of the story, however. The trouble had started because the Indians had tried to protect their buffalo from the hide hunters, and in the end the buffalo were killed anyway. With the Indians driven back onto the reservations, and the Army completely happy to have the buffalo wiped out, the hide hunters had nothing to fear. Charles Rath, who had helped to set up the trading post at Adobe Walls, and Bob Wright, of a large and prosperous hide-buying outfit, established a post in the Panhandle on Sweetwater Creek. The enterprise prospered; a mushroom settlement grew up that not only supplied the necessary supplies to hunters but had three saloons and a dance hall that catered to the redolent skinners' primitive vices while two restaurants took care of their more conventional appetites.

The great Texas herd began to melt away under the deep booming of the Sharps Fifties. It did not take long; in the spring of 1878 the hide hunters looked about, incredulous, to discover that there was not going to be any buffalo hunting on the southern plains that year. Six years it had taken to wipe out the millions of bison that had ranged from northern Kansas southward into Texas and New Mexico. The mighty brown sea had turned into a nightmare of rotting, putrid carcasses, and at last into a vista of white bones. A few buffalo survived here and there in the isolation of the Staked Plain after the hunters had gone away to wipe out the northern herd. But these few were fair game to every roving cowboy and homesteader; what was apparently the last band, fifty-two in number, was killed by a hunting party in 1887.

So, from the close of the Red River War in 1875, no free Indians roamed anywhere on the southern plains. The magnificent horse-and-buffalo days were over forever south of the Platte River, in the land that had once seemed so measureless. And that same year when the end of freedom came for the Southern tribes, events were closing in on the Northern peoples to deprive them of what remained of the old ways.

VII

Diversion in the
Far West

1. HOW TO START A SMALL WAR

WHILE events were leading toward war on the southern plains, the Army found itself involved in another Indian war in a very unexpected quarter, a flare-up of fire in old ashes far from the Great Plains. It should have been the most inconsequential of skirmishes, the United States against half a hundred warriors on the California-Oregon border. Instead, it turned into the most costly Indian war the Army had ever fought, considering the number involved. It was also, beyond doubt, one of the most humiliating.

As a general thing, the Indians of the Far West had not put up a very effective resistance to the settlers and prospectors who shoved them aside (there were notable exceptions), and the Indians of California were among the most vulnerable of all. It was their misfortune that they belonged to a hodge-podge of tribes, were poor, lacked the social organization to combine for defense, and were low in warlike spirit to begin with. It was their calamitous misfortune that they stood in the path of the gold rush, and that the gold-hunters included a high proportion of "hard cases": thieves, jailbirds, cutthroats, and assorted gallows bait.

In no other part of the United States were the Indians so barbarously treated and so wantonly murdered. There were an estimated 100,000 of them in California in 1848, the year it was annexed and gold was discovered. By 1859, there were only 30,000 left, a considerable accomplishment in only eleven years, and by the end of the century a scant 15,000. Indians were ruthlessly driven from their tribal grounds—and when they did attempt to resist by attacking isolated miners, the prospectors hunted down all natives in the area in the same joyous fashion they would have gone after jackrabbits. Women were brutalized by gang rapes; men were captured like animals and forced to do field labor, kidnaped children were treated as slaves.

Thus did the gentle and enlightening hand of white civilization touch and raise up the Indians of California. But not quite all the natives were so docile and easily victimized, and among the exceptions were the Modocs. The tribe lived in the area close around Tule Lake, a large shallow, reedy body of water astride the California-Oregon border (today most of it is drained) in a region whose terrain varied widely within short distances: lakes, small mountain peaks, areas of grassland, and, bordering the south shore of the lake, an area of strange and fantastic ancient lava outflows which today is set aside as Lava Beds National Monument. From the Tule Lake center the Modocs ranged over a radius of fifty miles or so in all directions in their hunting, and were not noticeably hospitable to white men who trespassed on their preserve. The South Emigrant Road, an alternate route for the western end of the Oregon Trail, skirted the eastern shore of Tule Lake, and the Modocs frequently hid among the jumbled boulders at the spot and ambushed wagon trains.

When prospectors made their way up the wild valleys of the Northern California rivers, the Modocs attacked them just as they had the emigrants, but the miners fought back a great deal more roughly. By fortunate happenstance, no gold was found near the heart of the Modoc range, or the tribe might have suffered near-annihilation like so many others. Instead, a mutual accommodation developed between miners and Indians. The Modocs became frequent and welcome visitors in Yreka, about sixty miles from Tule Lake; they liked the excitement of the busy, noisy mining camp, and in return they peddled their women to the miners, who provided an active market for such rental merchandise.

This last was one of the less endearing traits of the Modocs. When they began trading with other tribes early in the century, they made themselves brokers in female flesh because they had nothing to offer in the way of handiwork, pelts, feathers, or the other ordinary commodities. They brought girls and young women to the annual trade meetings, where the Northern tribes eagerly purchased the unhappy slaves for concubines. So, when they turned their women over to the miners, it was sanctioned by old custom and was not a depravity forced on them by white men.

While the miners and the Modocs worked out a fairly amicable relationship, the same was not so true of ranchers who began settling around Tule Lake, particularly to the north of it in Oregon. There, on a stream called Lost River which flowed into the lake, the villages of the Modocs were centered, close by lands the settlers were finding desirable. In such situations, the Indian was always the one who had to move out of the way, so in 1864 a treaty was negotiated whereby the Modocs moved to a large reservation whose nearest boundary lay about twenty-five miles to the north. The Klamaths, who outnumbered the Modocs about two to one, shared the reservation. The two tribes were much alike in language and customs, but that was the only way in which there was any closeness between them. The Klamaths were well pleased with the reservation since it was part of their original tribal range; the Modocs, to whom it was alien ground, were said to have signed the treaty very reluctantly.

Things did not go well for the Modocs on the reservation. This was partly due to an overbearing and bullying attitude of the Klamaths, partly to a struggle for leadership between two Modoc chiefs, Old Schonchin and one whose Indian name was Kientpoos but who was never called anything other than Captain Jack by the whites. Schonchin was more amenable to the direction of the agency officials and received their support; Captain Jack, nobody's man but his own, got fed up with things after a year and led his followers back to Lost River, declaring that his signature on the treaty had not meant a thing.

During the year the Modocs had been gone, more settlers had moved onto their old lands near Lost River and Tule Lake, and the return of Captain Jack and his band, about 175, caused a small panic. An appeal to the government to force the Indians back on their reservation got nowhere. The Army was busy with other concerns, and the Indian Bureau was pretty much indifferent. In four years, only twice did any Indian Bureau officials come to try to talk Captain Jack into returning; after a year, a subagent managed to make the fifty-mile trip from the agency, and after still another year, the Indian Superintendent for Oregon got around to calling. Jack was polite but adamant. In fact, he was so opposed to having anything to do with the reservation that when the first annuities came in 1867, he refused to accept them if it meant coming to the agency to collect them.

Four years after Captain Jack and his band had bolted the reservation, things were no more settled than the day they had left. His band lived in their villages near the mouth of Lost River, they hunted, the young men and women went in to Yreka for excitement, and they caused little or no trouble. But their presence was becoming intolerable to the ranchers in the vicinity, and it was unfinished business to the Indian Office. Then, in 1869, Grant became President and appointed a man named Alfred B. Meacham Indian Superintendent for Oregon. Meacham's immediate qualification was that he was a Republican faithful who had worked hard for Grant's election, but he had more pertinent qualities which showed up after he had been appointed. When he was young he had helped in the unhappy removal of the Sauk and Fox tribe from Iowa, but his real knowledge of Indians came from carefully observing them in the West and from a sincere interest.

Meacham was appalled at the conditions he found on the Klamath reservation, and set about putting them right. Gambling, polygamy, and all forms of slave-holding were forbidden, and he directed that any white man living on a reservation with an Indian woman should either marry her or give her up, a directive aimed not only at occasional traders but at widespread concubinage practiced by Army officers who purchased Indian girls to relieve some of the tedium of frontier duty.

Meacham also began a campaign against the ancient shamanistic or witch doctor practices of the Indians. This was not a bit of smug Christian superiority; shamanism had caused all manner of trouble and mischief and had frequently led to ritualistic murders. The campaign was quickly successful; when Indian agents ignored witchcraft countermeasures by the shamans and nothing happened to them, the prestige of the medicine men quickly declined.

After getting affairs in order around the state, Meacham at last went to see Captain Jack in December of 1869. He had asked the chief for a meeting and Jack had agreed, on the condition that the Superintendent would come to him. When he arrived, Meacham was accompanied not only by the agent from the reservation, but also by Old Schonchin, a small detachment of soldiers, and various auxiliaries.

The talks at Captain Jack's camp went on for two days. At the end of that time, Jack had agreed to try reservation life again, provided he could select the section on which his band would be settled. Actually, the decision was not all that simple. Curly Headed Doctor, the shaman with Jack's band, had spoken up to damn all white men and vehemently oppose any return. The Doctor, of course, had a big personal stake in the matter; he was a man of importance and influence at Lost River but he would not stand so tall on the reservation where Meacham's campaign against the shamans had had considerable success. At one point, Curly Headed Doctor made such inflammatory remarks that it appeared as though the Modocs were about to kill the white negotiators; at the critical moment, the detachment of soldiers which had been camped outside the village suddenly appeared and scattered the threatening Indians.

Jack brought his band back to the reservation, and Meacham did his best to see that things worked out this time. He arranged a ceremony of reconciliation between Jack and the Klamath chief, and tried to fill it with symbolisms of a new beginning between the two tribes. Jack appears to have tried sincerely to get along, but the Klamaths again took advantage of their superiority in numbers and their proprietary feelings about the reservation. They demanded that the Modocs turn over to them, as tribute, part of the wood they cut for their wickiups or shelters; they beat and taunted the women when they went to gather wild grain at the lake, and harassed the men when they went fishing.

Meacham had tried, but he was Superintendent for the entire state and could not remain to oversee events on one reservation. That was the responsibility of the agent, but that gentleman's attitude toward his job was that the less he had to do with Indians, the better. When Captain Jack went to complain about the way his people were being treated, he got neither help nor sympathy. Not only that, the agent cut off all rations to the tribe in April of 1870; the Modocs, he said, could go out and find their own food.

Whereupon, that same month, Captain Jack led his band back to Lost River again, loudly swearing for a second time not to have anything to do with the reservation. This time not only his own band went with him, but so many of Old Schonchin's band that the latter had to follow along or be a chief without anyone to lead. After a short time, though, the old chief and some of his people returned, and most of his band gradually trickled back to join him. Then, and only then, a solution to the problem came to the obtuse and slow-moving minds of the Indian Office bureaucracy. Schonchin and his people were given their own agency at Yainax, about thirty-five miles from the one the Modocs had formerly shared with the troublesome Klamaths. The answer was so simple, so effective—and it had taken so long to occur to anyone. A little sooner, and it would have prevented Captain Jack from going back to Lost River—and made the coming war unnecessary.

The reception of Captain Jack's band at Lost River was somewhat less than overwhelmingly cordial. More white settlers had come into the Tule Lake country, certain that the Modocs, at last, were gone for good. But Jack's band settled down again on Lost River, and there, overlooking the reedy waters of the shallow lake to the south, they built once again their lodges of earth and timber, odd, rounded structures entered by ladders through holes in the roofs.

The Lost River Modocs got along in relative peace with the ranchers, but the ranchers were not happy with the relationship. Indians often walked into ranchers' homes without warning and demanded to be fed; they flopped down on beds, or otherwise made nuisances of themselves, and frightened settlers' wives. They turned their horses loose into pastures, until some ranchers paid an annual tribute as the simplest way to be rid of this kind of harassment.

Jack refused to listen to further talk about returning to the reservation; twice was more than enough. His counterproposal was clear and uncomplicated. The Lost River country was the old land of his people, and he claimed he had never agreed to the 1864 treaty by which it had been given up. He was perfectly willing, however, to accept a reservation, provided it was on Lost River at the head of Tule Lake; he demanded a tract six miles square. Meacham supported it as a fair claim, even though there were several ranches on the proposed reserve. No one else, however, had a good word to say for the plan.

So once again time passed without decision, but a resolution of the problem could not be delayed much longer. The country was still sparsely settled, but there were by now enough ranchers to make themselves heard, and they were clamoring for protection. The military was not able to do much at the moment—far-Western posts had been stripped to send men to Arizona to fight Apaches—but the Army warned the Indian Bureau that something was going to have to be done, and soon, about Captain Jack's band. At last, in 1872, the Indian Bureau acted. A new superintendent, T. B. Odeneal, had replaced Meacham who had been sympathetic to Jack; in the summer he received orders to take Captain Jack's band to rejoin the rest of the Modocs at Yainax agency on the reservation, "peaceably if you can, forcibly if you must."

Odeneal sent one last mission to Captain Jack to ask him to come in to talk things over. His emissaries, a pioneer rancher named Ivan Applegate and another man, not only received a refusal from Jack but had the very harrowing experience of listening helplessly while the chief argued with firebrands who were all for killing the two whites and starting a war then and there.

When the pair returned to report their failure and the manner of it, Odeneal was highly upset by the talk of war by the Modocs, and went at once to Fort Klamath on the reservation to ask Major Green, the commanding officer, for troops to use against Jack's Indians. And for some unexplained reason, Green immediately complied with this request from a civilian, without first obtaining approval from his superiors (General E. R. S. Canby, commanding the Department of the Columbia, had specifically asked to be advised before soldiers were used against the Modocs). Major Green ordered Captain James Jackson to take Company B of the 1st Cavalry to Lost River, "to arrest Jack, Black Jim, and Scarfaced Charley by the next morning." (With few exceptions, the whites knew these Modocs only by nicknames they themselves had given them. A very few, like Old Schonchin, were known by transliterations of their Modoc names; none by translations of their Indian names into the Yellow Horses, Standing Bears, Great Hawks, and the like so familiar in other tribes.)

Within a short time, Captain Jackson was on his way with some forty officers and men, a small pack train, and five packers. On the way they were joined by about fifteen ranchers. It was November 28 —a freezing rain was falling that turned worse as gray day turned into night, until soon it was freezing on men and horses. Captain Jack's village was on the west side of Lost River almost at its mouth on Tule

Lake. Directly on the opposite bank was the village of Hooker Jim, a subchief of Jack's band.

Captain Jackson asked the ranchers to remain on the opposite bank near Hooker Jim's village in case there was trouble and they were needed in that quarter. Then he led his detachment into Captain Jack's village, at about seven in the morning. But there was no surprise. A man crossing the river in a canoe after a night of gambling in Hooker Jim's village saw the soldiers and gave the alarm, so that when the troopers rode up, Captain Jack and several other Indians were there to receive them. While Captain Jackson (those two names are confusing!) parleyed and tried to plan his next move, the Indians hurried into the wickiups to grab weapons. Jackson's planned arrest was turning into a very tense situation.

On the other side of the river, the ranchers, waiting outside Hooker Jim's village, could see nothing through the grayness and sleet, and assumed from the absence of gunfire that all had gone well. They therefore went on into the village, only to find it wide-awake and perfectly aware that something was happening across the river. Seventeen fully armed men faced them suspiciously as they rode in.

A small spark would have been enough to set off such an explosive situation, and the Indians provided a bonfire. Scarfaced Charley, one of the three who was to have been arrested, suddenly pointed his rifle at Lieutenant Boutelle, Jackson's second in command. Boutelle in quick self-defense took a snap shot with his pistol that missed Charley but threw his aim off enough that he only grazed the lieutenant's arm. The two shots set off a general fusillade of rifles and shooting of arrows among Indians on both sides of the river.

In Hooker Jim's camp, the ranchers ran ingloriously, although a few fired their weapons as they fled, and one of these wild shots, a blast from a double-barreled shotgun, wounded a woman and killed the baby in her arms. Two ranchers who ran in the wrong direction were killed. In Jack's camp, the soldiers did a great deal of shooting but their aim was far from spectacular, and casualties were about even: one killed on each side, seven soldiers wounded, and probably about the same number of Indians.

And so the Modoc war was on. The engagement lasted no more than five minutes at the most. The Indian warriors fled through the sagebrush, sending back a few shots at the soldiers who briefly attempted a pursuit. Captain Jackson ordered the village burned, and women and old men were told to leave the camp. They did so in canoes, taking the wounded with them and paddling across Tule Lake, more than ten miles, where they were almost swamped when the wind caught them on the shallow, choppy lake. All, however, made it safely to the south shore.

The warriors went on foot to join up with their families. Captain Jack and his men, on the west side of Lost River, had only to go down the west side of Tule Lake, through an uninhabited region. Hooker Jim and his men, on the other side of the stream, went around the lake in the opposite direction, not only a much longer trip but one that took them through a number of ranches on the north side of the lake. Thirteen unsuspecting men, most of them caught at work away from their homes, were killed, but no attempt was made to harm women. Scarfaced Charley, on the other hand, traveling separately with several other men, met several ranchers who did not know that trouble was afoot; he told each of them to get on home because he did not want his friends to be hurt.

One other small band of Modocs was caught, quite unhappily, by the course of events. About ten miles east of Tule Lake a small stream called Hot Creek flowed through sagebrush and rock outcrops to Lower Klamath Lake. In the vicinity of the creek lived a small body of Indians who had left the reservation with Captain Jack but had built their wickiups well apart, a good twenty miles from the rest of the band. They also had ranchers for neighbors, but these were California ranchers, who, at least in this particular instance, seemed to be a more easygoing lot than those on the Oregon side of the line.

When word of the fighting at Jack's village reached the Hot Creek Modocs, they wanted nothing at all to do with it. They went to a rancher in the area, John Fairchild, for help, and Fairchild suggested that the best thing for them to do would be to get back on the reservation as soon as possible. Not only that, he offered to escort them there, enlisted the help of another rancher, a man named Dorris, also trusted by the Indians, and the two started north with their charges.

The news of their coming preceded them and in Linkville (today's Klamath Falls, Oregon) the usual crowd of loud-talkers congregated, found courage in bottles, and agreed that "something ought to be done." A small group started out to take the Indians, but the two ranchers had been forewarned, and, with the help of three or four other ranchers with level heads, were able to talk the small mob out of its purpose. The brave Indian fighters were cooling off, anyhow, as the cheap courage they had taken aboard in a Linkville saloon wore off in the chilly night air, and they gave up their purpose rather meekly.

One fool, though, was not content to let it drop at that point. While the talking was going on, he sidled up to the Modocs, to assure them, in lurid detail, that many other whites were lying in ambush on the road ahead and that they were certain to be killed if they went any further. Fairchild and Dorris could not convince the terrified Indians that they had been lied to. They ran away, and hurried straightway to join forces with Captain Jack. There were about forty-five of them, of whom at least fourteen were warriors. This may not seem like a large number, but it becomes large when it is considered that the total number of Jack's warriors never was much higher than fifty. From that point on, the Hot Creekers formed an intensely prowar faction, absolutely opposed to all proposals to negotiate or surrender. The war would have been much shorter and less costly if they had been taken back to the reservation without interference.

2. "TREACHERY IS INHERENT IN THE INDIAN CHARACTER"

The problem had grown beyond Captain Jackson and his forty horsemen, nor was it any longer in the hands of Major Green, commanding at Fort Klamath, who had sent Jackson to arrest Captain Jack. Jurisdiction had moved to a higher military level, and Lieutenant Colonel Frank Wheaton, commanding the District of the Lakes, with headquarters at Camp Warner about one hundred miles east of Fort Klamath, assumed control.

From Camp Warner he sent two companies of the 1st Cavalry, commanded by Captains David Perry and R. F. Bernard, to join Captain Jackson's Company B of the same regiment, already on hand. Two companies of the 21st Infantry, under Major E. C. Mason, were sent from Vancouver by boat, railroad, and overland under their own footpower during a week of rain which turned the roads to mud of such depth and adhesiveness that wagons had almost to be lifted at times to move them forward.

Having obtained all the men immediately available, Colonel Wheaton then went to the scene of action to take personal command for a sharp and decisive campaign. However, he took his time preparing his forces so that when he did attack, his victory would be overwhelming. The Governor of Oregon issued a statewide call for volunteers to rein- force the Army, and sixty-five patriots hastened to defend the state against the Indian menace. An Oregon rancher did slightly better sticking to his own neighborhood; he signed up sixty-eight volunteers in the vicinity of Klamath Lake—but most of these were Klamath Indians from the reservation. California ranchers Fairchild and Dorris also raised a group of about thirty volunteers to act as scouts because no one else knew the California terrain in which the campaign was developing.

There would be no cavalry charges, or lines of men advancing with bayonets over grassy fields in this fighting. The region in which Cap- tain Jack and his followers were making their defense was—and is— called the Lava Beds. They began at the south shore of Tule Lake and extended about twelve miles southward, in a belt perhaps ten miles wide. The surface of this region is a weird jumble of cracks, chasms, caves, ridges, and pits, the result of a series of outpourings of lava in relatively recent geological times. More than one person, attempting to describe it, has summed it up by saying it looks like a sponge.

The Modocs were holed up in a small portion of the beds, an area which quickly came to be called the Stronghold; it fronted on the lake and was perhaps half a mile long and a third as wide. Large cracks in the lava rock up to ten feet or more deep provided perfect trenches. Where there were gaps, the defenders piled up rocks, leaving loopholes. The Indians lived quite comfortably, making their homes in the large pits common throughout the Lava Beds. These pits in places have overhanging walls, and under the overhangs the Indians found quite snug shelters, often hanging skins or blankets in front for added warmth and privacy. Within this fortress, Captain Jack had approxi- mately 165 people, of whom about fifty were fighting men.

Wheaton's job was to pry this small kernel of Indians out of an enormously tough shell. They could not be shot out because they could not be seen, and their protection against rifle fire and even artillery was almost perfect. They could not be starved out because there was plenty of game and water in the Lava Beds. The one remaining alternative was direct attack.

It was, however, the Modocs who drew first blood. The progress of a wagon train of rifle ammunition had been watched by the Indians as it came down the east side of the lake and approached the Army camp on December 21. When it was less than a mile from the camp, a raiding party dashed out of the protection of the lava outcrops and struck the train. So certain had the military been that the Indians would not venture beyond the safety of the lava flows that only five soldiers had been sent out to meet the train and escort it back. The surprise attack killed two of the escort and five horses; the remaining three soldiers and the teamsters fled. The ammunition was saved only by a quick-thinking lieutenant who charged out with half a dozen men whose horses happened to be saddled and drove off the raiders. This skirmish, the Battle of Land's Ranch, was the first of many incidents that soon filled the soldiers with an unreasoning fear of the Modocs.

Christmas, 1872, passed miserably, with the men cold, bored, and, worst of all, without their holiday whiskey. But Lieutenant Colonel Wheaton continued to ready his big offensive, which was at last set for January 17. He had three hundred men, and he confidently assured his superiors that it would soon be over.

His strategy was basically simple—at least, on paper. Two independent forces drawn up in line of battle were to attack the Stronghold from east and from west. Their northern flanks were to be on the lake; as the northern sections of the two lines of battle struck Indian resistance and slowed down, the unopposed southern sections would continue ahead, pivoting as they went, until east and west forces met and the Indians were completely enclosed, with troops on three sides and the lake on the north. Then the forces would drive north, pushing the Modocs toward the lake. In analogy, it was to be very much like a pair of outstretched arms enfolding, drawing in and crushing an object. There was the slight modification that the right arm was going to be considerably longer and stronger.

On the west side, where the advance was to begin, was a long north-and-south ridge, rising gently from the west, but falling in a steep bluff on the side facing the Lava Beds. Army forces moved onto the ridge on the afternoon of the sixteenth, advancing slowly through a heavy fog. There were a few Modocs around; the Indians were good soldiers and had sentries out on the ridge. They upset the advancing soldiers by pinging rifle bullets around them, but it was impossible to hit anything in the fog and they soon withdrew down the bluffs and took up positions nearer the Stronghold.

The handful of California volunteer scouts, twenty-four of them, held the extreme left flank, next to the lake. Next were two companies of the 21st Infantry, commanded by Major E. C. Mason, which were expected to provide the heavy muscle of the attack. To the right of the infantry were the Oregon volunteers, about seventy-five men, and after them, on the extreme right flank, was Captain David Perry's company of cavalry, dismounted, which was to take part in the great pivoting movement, like a huge gate swinging shut to trap the Modocs.

On the other side of the Lava Beds, the cavalry companies of Captain James Jackson and Captain C. F. Bernard, formed the eastern force, with the latter as force commander. On the sixteenth, Jackson took his men on a reconnaissance and got too near the Stronghold; four soldiers were wounded and the Modocs were alerted that the attack was going to come from the east as well as the west.

The infantry battalion built sagebrush fires atop the ridge to keep off some of the bitter chill during the long evening and short night. In the Stronghold, the Modocs were making their own preparations for the battle. A great burden of responsibility fell on the shaman, Curly Headed Doctor, who had given full assurances that his magic would provide complete protection against the white soldiers. He had spent days braiding tule rushes from the lake into a rope several thousand feet long which was laid around the entire perimeter of the Stronghold; it was impregnated with magic powers which made it impossible for any white soldier to cross it. Now, with battle imminent, the Doctor erected a medicine pole which was nothing more than a limb from a small tree hung with assorted bits of fur, feathers, and other materia medica of his calling. All night long the Indians danced around a fire, which did nothing to soothe the edgy nerves of the white soldiers who could hear snatches of the chanting of the warriors floating eerily through the black night.

Bugles sounded reveille at four o'clock, but few of the men had been sleeping because of the cold and nervousness. It was six o'clock before the ranks had gotten their blood circulating enough to scramble down the bluffs and form up. On the opposite side of the Lava Beds, in the east force, preparations were simpler because there were no bluffs to negotiate, but there was no noticeably higher degree of dash and élan.

Dawn still had not come when three howitzer shots signaled that the battle was on. On the command to advance, the troops moved ahead, banging away blindly and uselessly into the fog and dark as they went. It was typical of the lack of battle discipline which was to mark this undistinguished army. The Modocs were still a mile away; even in good visibility the chances of hitting any of them would have been almost precisely zero. The advance was never rapid, and it became even less so when the Indians began shooting back, so that the second mile required six hours to cover, even though no one had yet been hit.

The pivoting movement that was to swing Captain Perry's dismounted cavalry across the south of the Stronghold and drive the Indians into the lake never got started. The group of Oregon volunteers who held the position between the infantry and the cavalry lost interest in fighting Indians early in the day, although they had suffered nothing but fright. They simply turned around and got out of the engagement, and absolutely refused to go back. A large gap was left between the cavalry and the infantry; before it could be patched and the pivoting movement attempted, there were other things to worry about.

On the east side, the might of the United States Army was not being displayed any more shiningly. Bernard's forces moved forward slowly and carefully for a short distance until they reached a long but not too spectacular fissure; this, they decided, was impassable, and lay there all the rest of the day. A few of the more intrepid souls raised themselves at intervals to send a rifle bullet at random toward the west but most of these shots arced across and struck among the positions of the western force.

In the meantime, the artillerymen stood idle by their howitzers on the west bluffs. It was impossible to give any support; the fog hung on long after daylight came—and even with the best of visibility it would have been difficult to determine where the position of friend and where that of foe.

Colonel Wheaton made a late attempt to salvage something from the mess, which was growing worse by the moment, by massing the western force, dismounted cavalry and infantry, near the lake front and driving along the shore to join up with Captain Bernard's apathetic forces on the east. Major John Green (he who had triggered the war by sending out a force to arrest Captain Jack at Lost River), who was field commander for the west forces, won himself a Congressional Medal of Honor by jumping up on the rocks in full view of the Indians and loudly damning his men for arrant cowards while Modoc bullets pinged around him. It inspired some of the men, and they moved past the point of danger to effect a junction with Bernard's men, who, however, remained completely unstirred by the event.

The winter twilight was beginning to fall, and Wheaton decided it was time to call an end to the fighting before it turned into a complete debacle. He called for a general withdrawal—although most of the men had already anticipated him in that—and the hundred or so who could be considered still in action fell back. It was no army that retired, but a frightened, beaten mass of men who wanted no more of fighting these terrifying Indians (most of them had not seen a Modoc). Many had thrown away rifles and knapsacks in their hurry to escape.

But there was further panic and humiliation for them—for those, at least, of the west force. When they reached the bottom of the bluff, they were halted by the rumor that Modocs had somehow gained command of the top. And so they huddled in fear until around two in the morning when finally someone, brave or skeptical, climbed to the top and found no Indians, and the retreat was resumed.

To cap the tribulations of this inept force, no one had considered the possibility that there might be wounded, and so there were no stretchers. Those unfortunate enough to be hurt were carried in blankets, and were bumped against the ground and rocks in the dark. One man had been killed and five wounded among the west forces, while on the east side one had been killed and eight wounded.

In the Indian camp, Curly Headed Doctor could claim complete effectiveness for his medicine. Not one soldier had crossed the rope of braided tule rushes surrounding the Stronghold. Not one Modoc had been killed or injured in the fighting. The shaman had powerful magic, stronger than anything the white man could bring against him.

The Indians showed continuing audacity against a force that outnumbered them six to one. To the west, a good ten miles outside the security of the Stronghold, a small scouting party sent a few bullets down toward the Army camp from a peak overlooking it and caused a near-panic. On the opposite side of the Lava Beds, when Captain Bernard drew his forces back a few days later, Modocs attacked the wagons hauling his grain, driving off the escort and burning wagons and grain. And way around on the north side of Tule Lake, several doughty Oregon volunteers were attacked by a far-ranging band of Modocs. The volunteers, who had retreated and refused to fight in the attack on the Stronghold, now began to desert and go home.

A defeat so humiliating immediately became the concern of Colonel Wheaton's superior, who had given the colonel a free hand on Wheaton's assurance that his one offensive would crush Modoc resistance.

General E. R. S. Canby, commanding the Department of the Columbia, which included roughly what is now called the Pacific Northwest, was an able officer with a long and distinguished record. It is an interesting measure of the speed with which the West changed that the first duty assignment of Canby, a young lieutenant just out of West Point in 1839, had been to help in the removal of the Seminole Indians from Florida to the permanent Indian Country, the land that was to belong to the red men forever. Now, little more than thirty years later, the permanent Indian Country was long forgotten, and Canby, still only a vigorous fifty-five years old, was concerned with a war against an Indian band in a region that had not even been part of the country when he had taken his oath to defend the Constitution.

The first thing Canby did was to remove Lieutenant Colonel Wheaton from command and replace him with Colonel Alvin C. Gillem. It was hardly an inspired beginning because Gillem was thoroughly disliked and distrusted by other officers who knew him; they believed that he had received undeserved promotions through friendship with President Johnson. Canby also kept shipping more men to the scene of action, until there were almost seven hundred of them ready for action. And finally, he came to see for himself just what the situation was.

Gillem was in San Francisco; storms delayed him for some time from assuming his command, and by the time he did, the situation had been lifted out of the purely military realm. Alfred B. Meacham, the former Indian Superintendent for Oregon, was in Washington to take part in the quadrennial ritual known as casting the electoral vote, and one day was discussing the Modoc war with other Oregonians in the capital. Someone advanced the sound but usually ignored proposition that talking is better than fighting, and suggested that a peace conference would be worth trying. The idea grew, was approved by Secretary of the Interior Delano, and a Peace Commission was eventually appointed, headed by Meacham, who immediately threw some sand into the wheels of good will by objecting loudly to the other Commissioners. Changes were made; the final commission which satisfied Meacham consisted of himself, rancher Jesse Applegate from the Modoc country, and Samuel Case of the Indian Bureau.

War weariness was beginning to affect Captain Jack during this same period. He sent word to rancher John Fairchild that he would like to end the war, and he and Scarfaced Charley, who emerges as his chief supporter and right-hand man, started to leave the Stronghold

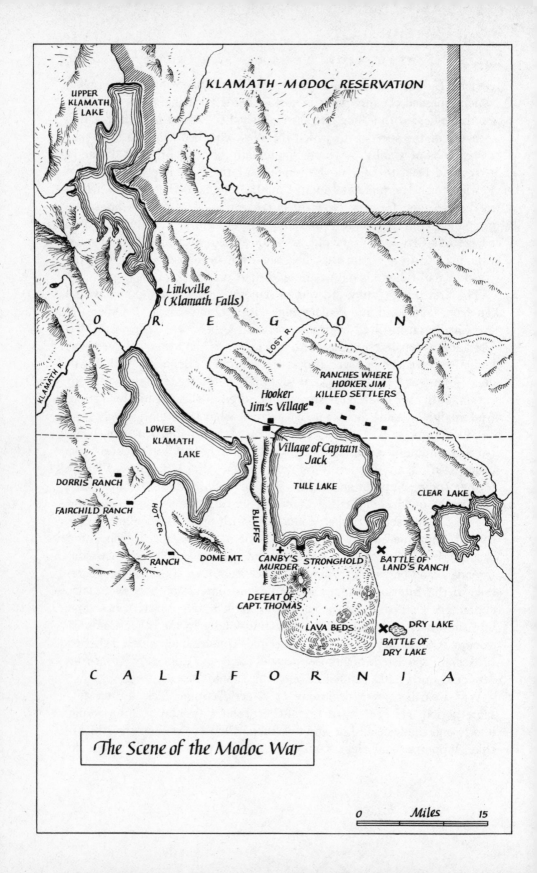

KLAMATH-MODOC RESERVATION

UPPER
KLAMATH
LAKE

O

R

E

G

O

N

Linkville
(Klamath Falls)

KLAMATH R.

LOST R.

RANCHES WHERE
HOOKER JIM
KILLED SETTLERS

Hooker
Jim's Village

LOWER
KLAMATH
LAKE

Village of Captain
Jack

TULE LAKE

DORRIS RANCH

CLEAR LAKE

FAIRCHILD RANCH

HOT CR.

BLUFFS

RANCH

DOME MT.

CANBY'S
MURDER

STRONGHOLD

BATTLE OF
LAND'S RANCH

DEFEAT OF
CAPT. THOMAS

LAVA BEDS

DRY LAKE

BATTLE OF
DRY LAKE

C   A   L   I   F   O   R   N   I   A

The Scene of the Modoc War

0   Miles   15

to confer with Fairchild. They were intercepted by Curly Headed Doctor and Shacknasty Jim, one of the Hot Creek band and now red-hot for continuing the war. There was a violent quarrel; Jack and Charley were told that if they left they must expect to be killed if they ever returned. They stayed, but the quarrel went on all night.

Beginning February 20, the Peace Commission conducted its tor-tuous and frustrating negotiations with the Indians. The initial contact was made by a couple of Modoc women, wives of white men. The Modocs wanted men; men were sent. Captain Jack announced that he was willing to negotiate but that he did not like anything about the present Peace Commission; two men he knew in the mining town of Yreka, one a judge of Superior Court, the other a lawyer, were ap-pointed to the Commission on his insistence.

As the negotiations went on, several of the Modoc warriors came into the Army camp two or three times (a strange Indian war, this one!) and vague suggestions of willingness to surrender were made by the Indians but faded away before they could be examined. The currents of optimism that floated periodically through the Peace Com-mission affected General Canby at one time so much that he sent a glowing telegram to General Sherman, saying that everything had been settled peaceably.

But nothing had been settled. One day Jack seemed eager for a settlement; the next he would be cooled off again. The state of Oregon was busily creating a major obstruction by insisting that the Modocs would have to stand trial for the murder of the ranchers by Hooker Jim's band at the beginning of the trouble, and since one of Jack's bedrock demands was a small reservation on Lost River in Oregon, a basic bargaining point was lost. The Army could only insist that the Modocs be sent to Indian Territory where they had no immediate enemies.

Captain Jack did not appear during any of the meetings, nor did any of the other Modoc leaders surrender. After almost two months even the sanguine General Canby decided that patience was ceasing to be a virtue. He directed Colonel Gillem to begin moving his forces closer to the Stronghold to put the Modocs under greater pressure. Although seven hundred soldiers were supposedly ringing them, the Indians had been undergoing the loosest of sieges. They had not only been moving through the Lava Beds outside the limits of the Stronghold, but on one occasion Hooker Jim and four companions had made a trip all the way to the reservation to visit friends and relatives there, and the Army command had known nothing of it until later.

At one time, this easy ability of the Modoc warriors to move about brought a face-to-face meeting between Captain Jack and Canby. While the troops were being shifted, the General and Colonel Gillem, with another officer, were riding along the top of the bluffs from which the abortive January offensive had been made when two Indians came to the foot of the bluff below them, and shouted that they did not want to fight any more. It turned out that one of the two was Scarfaced Charley, and that Captain Jack was back in the rocks with several other men, one of them John Schonchin, brother of the chief of the reservation Modocs and second in command to Jack. Charley proposed that the three officers come without their weapons and meet Jack, John Schonchin and a third Indian, also unarmed, and that the six should talk openly and unafraid.

Canby and Gillem agreed at once, but things did not come off quite as Scarfaced Charley had outlined. Instead of John Schonchin, Jack was accompanied by his nemesis, Curly Haired Doctor—and the Doctor carried weapons. Three other Indians appeared, all armed, to join the group. But no threatening moves were made, although the Modocs could easily have killed the three officers. Captain Jack repeated his demand for a reservation on Lost River, and Canby promised only that if the Modocs surrendered they would be given many gifts and would be treated fairly. It was about all he could offer; he had been given very little latitude for bargaining.

The Army squeezed a little closer to the Stronghold on the east side of the Lava Beds, and considerably nearer on the west side, where Colonel Gillem established his headquarters camp at the foot of the bluffs on April 1. The next day Jack sent word he was willing to meet the Peace Commissioners halfway between the Stronghold and Gillem's camp, and another series of inconclusive talks began.

The composition of the Peace Commission had changed. Three of the members had resigned in frustration over the vacillating actions of the Indians. Meacham alone remained, but his place as head of the group had been taken by General Canby. The other two new members were L. S. Dyar, subagent at the Klamath agency, and the Reverend Eleasar Thomas, a middle-aged Methodist minister from a small California town. Thomas' presence on the Commission was just one of the many improbabilities of this wholly improbable war; he was a completely unworldly gentleman and entirely incapable of comprehending what went on in the minds of the men he was dealing with. Two other members made up the Commission group: the interpreters, Frank Riddle and his Modoc wife, Winema, who was generally known as Tobey.

When the Army forces moved closer to the Stronghold, Jack became worried. He asked to see Canby again, but nothing came out of several new meetings. Jack repeated that he wanted his Lost River reservation; he wanted the soldiers to go home; he wanted a promise that there would be no punishment of Hooker Jim and his men for killing the ranchers. And Canby, with his limited bargaining power, could only offer the Modocs fair treatment by the Army if they surrendered.

As for that, Captain Jack's bargaining position was just about as circumscribed as Canby's. The war party was not only in the majority, its leader exerted the influence that goes with absolutely unspotted success. Curly Headed Doctor could point out that his medicine had kept the band off the reservation for several years, and now had enabled them to whip a much larger Army force without losing a man (the one killed in the fighting at the village on Lost River apparently did not count). Nothing succeeds like success, so when Tobey Riddle was sent to the Stronghold to say that anyone who wanted to surrender would be given protection against those who wished to remain, Captain Jack and eleven others were the only ones out of fifty-odd men who wanted to quit. The usual quarrel arose between Jack and Curly Headed Doctor, and their respective followers. Those who wanted to surrender were told bluntly that they would be killed if they tried to leave. When Tobey left this scene of discord, one of Jack's followers took her aside and warned her that she and the white Commissioners should not come to another meeting because plans for violence against the Commissioners were afoot.

On April 10, the Indians sent four men to Gillem's camp to say they would like another peace talk the next day, Good Friday. And that night, around the band's council fire deep in one of the pits in the lava rock, the leaders of the war party made ready either to force Jack out as chief or to make him take an unequivocal position in favor of continuing the war through to its end.

At the council, Jack presented his position: he was in favor of ending the war and going back to the reservation. The strength of the

Army would win in the end, Jack said, all the Doctor's magic notwithstanding. But the war party speakers argued that they could and should win the war in one stroke by killing the leaders of the whites, and especially the top Army leader, General Canby. The next day would be the best time.

At this, Captain Jack rose again. There would be no murders, he said. As chief, he absolutely forbade anything of the kind. The war party leaders were expecting this and were prepared for it. As Jack was warming to his theme, several men seized him and pinioned his arms while others put a woman's shawl and headcovering on him, jeering, "Woman! Coward!" and similar taunts.

What appears a malicious but puerile prank was deadly serious in purpose. If Jack could be made to look ridiculous before his entire band, the war party could oust him and put in one of their own men as chief. They did not get Jack out, but they did just as well. Jack pulled himself free, and shouted that if they wanted to murder the Commissioners that badly, he was the man to see that it was done. Moreover, he went on, he was demanding for himself the right to kill General Canby.

Plans were made. Two men, Barncho and Slolux, who otherwise would have gone through the war unnoted—so obscure the whites had not even hung nicknames on them—were to go to the rocks near the conference site (a tent had been set up by the military for use in bad weather) before daylight and hide with a supply of rifles ready for distribution at the critical moment. Each Modoc was assigned a Commissioner as his victim. It was agreed that Frank and Tobey Riddle were not to be harmed.

In the white camp, grapevine warnings had made a number of people very unhappy about the coming meeting. Meacham and Indian agent Dyar caught the pungent smell of danger so sharply that they slipped derringers into their pockets although weapons were forbidden at the peace talks. Tobey Riddle was ready for anything; she had been warned, and she was a Modoc, with a better understanding than anyone else of what was going on in the minds of the people in the Lava Beds. Her attempts to warn General Canby had fallen on unhearing ears; he seems to have approached the Good Friday meeting without hesitancy or even the slightest precaution, a strangely trusting attitude in a man who had dealt with many enemies, white and red. As for the Reverend Mr. Thomas, he lived in a world apart, and had greeted the news that the Modocs wanted another conference as a sign that they had seen the light of Christianity.

Two of the Modocs who had gone to Gillem's camp the day before to request the peace conference, Boston Charley and Bogus Charley, had spent the night there. Now they accompanied the Peace Commissioners as they rode to the meeting in no man's land, and both were carrying rifles, despite the prohibition. Canby appeared not to notice. At the tent they met Captain Jack, John Schonchin, Hooker Jim, Ellen's Man, whose short, fat figure belied his toughness, Black Jim, and Shacknasty Jim.

The conference started with a rehashing of the old proposals, but the only ones who were really interested were Canby and Thomas. Meacham had hung his jacket on his saddle horn; Hooker Jim walked over and put it on as though he were trying it for fit. "You think me look like old man Meacham?" he asked. Meacham, trying to make light of an incident which had ominous undertones, for he suspected that Jim very soon expected to be owning his jacket, held out his hat. "Better take my hat, too." "I will by and by," Hooker Jim said coolly. "Don't hurry, old man."

After some speech-making on both sides, Captain Jack suddenly dropped the play-acting and gave the signal that brought Barncho and Slolux out of their hiding place with guns for everyone. At the same time, Jack pulled out a pistol he had concealed under his coat and shot Canby under the eye at point-blank range. Although it was a mortal wound, some residue of strength in his dying body enabled the General to leap to his feet and run for more than a hundred feet before he fell to the ground, where Ellen's Man shot him again with a rifle and Jack came up and stabbed him.

Thomas was shot by Boston Charley. When the minister collapsed and begged the Modoc not to shoot again because he was going to die anyway, Charley sneered. "Why don't you turn the bullets?" he asked. "Isn't your magic strong enough?"

Meacham had been poised for trouble, and began running the instant things started happening, reaching for his derringer as he did so. John Schonchin had been assigned to kill him, but the sight of the little pistol made him pause and very probably saved Meacham's life by giving him a chance to get out of point-blank range. He stumbled, and bullets clipped off part of his ear and grazed his forehead, leaving him unconscious. Shacknasty Jim, coming up, assumed he was dead

and did not give the *coup de grâce,* but slashed at one side of his head
and was considering how best to take the scalp of a man nearly bald
when Tobey diverted him by shouting that the soldiers were coming.

Dyar, also, had been ready for trouble and ran, turning long enough
to wave his derringer at Hooker Jim who was pursuing. Jim turned
and fled, while Dyar kept running, unharmed. Frank Riddle also ran
toward the camp; Tobey threw herself on the ground to avoid bullets
and remained where she was.

While this was happening, three Indians—Miller's Charley, Curly
Headed Jack (not Doctor) and one other—approached the Army
camp on the opposite side of the Lava Beds and told the sentry they
wanted to talk to the top man in command. The sentry called the
Officer of the Day, Lieutenant William Sherwood, along with another
lieutenant who understood the lingua franca of the northwest tribes.
The three Modocs attempted to draw the officers away from the protection of the sentry, but when the officers became suspicious, the Indians dropped their pretense and started to shoot. Sherwood was hit so
badly he died three days later; the other man ducked and dodged with
bullets ricocheting off the rocks around him and escaped.

For all their elaborate preparations and their advantages in weapons
and surprise, the Modocs had done rather poorly: only three slain,
counting Lieutenant Sherwood. The body of Brigadier General E. R. S.
Canby, lying stripped of clothing (Captain Jack wore his uniform in
later fighting), however, represented an accomplishment unique in all
the long annals of Indian warfare: he was the only general ever killed
by Indians.

Tobey, going to Meacham after the Modocs had fled, saw or felt no
stirring and was certain that he, too, was dead. His face was covered
with blood from the gashes in his scalp and from his clipped ear, but a
party of soldiers soon came hurrying up and the surgeon with them
found life. Not only life but spirit. As the surgeon tried to force brandy
into the wounded man's mouth, Meacham clenched his teeth and
turned away his head, murmuring that he was a temperance man; he
had taken the pledge. Pledge or no, they got some brandy into him, and
carried him back to camp where he soon recovered.

The news of the murders reached the country almost immediately.
Newspaper correspondents, chronically bored because of the lack of
news while the inconclusive peace talks had dragged on, raced to be
the first to Yreka to get the story on the telegraph wires to their papers.

The news shocked the country; a great body of sympathy had developed for the Modocs in their stand of a few against so many, but now it was suddenly wiped out and the old cry of "murdering redskins" was heard again. President Grant demanded action, and Sherman sent a message with a familiar phrase to the Lava Beds, "You will be fully justified in their utter extermination." When asked whether this was not an act of treachery without equal, Sherman shook his head as he considered the unlimited capacity for perfidy of the American Indian. "No, sir. Treachery is inherent in the Indian character. I know of a case where the Indians murdered the man who not two hours before had given them food and clothing."

While the murders were acts of the most unjustifiable treachery, they were the result of a very definite if crude logic. The Modoc concept of social organization still had hardly risen beyond the tribe and the war party, and they naïvely believed that if they killed the leaders of the army besieging them, then the leaderless soldiers would lose heart and go home. They had not the slightest understanding that the United States could replace a dozen officers like General Canby and hardly notice the difference.

3. THE TIME OF RETRIBUTION

The great punishment to be meted out to the Modocs was delayed several days while a few details were cleaned up. Colonel Gillem retained immediate command of the forces on the scene, but General Canby had to be replaced. Sherman selected General Jefferson C. Davis, an officer with a fine record, who considered his name an undeserved slap by fortune at a man who had served the Union well and faithfully.

The advance started on Tuesday, April 15, five days after the murders. There was no bluff to climb down this time; the west force was camped in front of it and a great deal closer to the Stronghold than it had been in the January disaster. But it soon became clear that neither the long wait, nor a great increase in numbers, had instilled any new valor into these soldiers. The advance was so slow that it was almost two hours before the troops got close enough to the Stronghold for the Modocs to open fire on them, and then virtually all motion ceased. The strategy of this battle was to be almost exactly the same as that of the first encounter; the right wing of the western force was to pivot and swing like a gate, linking up with the east forces and then driving north either to wipe out the Indians or force them into the lake.

The army by now had five infantry companies, four companies of cavalry, four batteries of artillery, and seventy-two Indian scouts, a total of about a thousand men. There were about four hundred men in the right wing of the west force which was to accomplish the pivoting movement. From their own half hundred the Modocs sent eight snipers out to oppose and stop the maneuver. And stop it they did, completely and quickly; the first bullets that whined off the rocks sent all four hundred soldiers crouching low for protection. Officers tried to urge their men on; they would get a few crawling unhappily forward in one place but when they turned elsewhere to get a few more moving, the first ones would snuggle down into the protecting rocks again. At the end of six hours, the gallant four hundred had gone ahead approximately half a mile and had not even seen any of the eight Indians who were still sniping and keeping the fear of God and Modocs in them.

The attack on the east side, in the meantime, was doing even less to exact vengeance for Canby's murder. The artillery there had commenced the action with a bombardment of the Stronghold, but the howitzers had been located so far back that most of the shells did not even reach the Modoc positions. Captain Mason, commanding the east forces, directly disregarded orders by making almost no attempt to move his men up toward the Stronghold. It was almost certainly an act coolly calculated to embarrass Gillem. Mason, along with several other officers, disliked and resented Gillem intensely, but permitting personal feelings to guide decisions on the field of battle was so contrary to all military regulations as well as traditions that it is surprising Gillem did not call for a court-martial later.

Almost nothing had been accomplished by the attackers by nightfall. During the night, the howitzers lobbed shells from both sides into the Stronghold at intervals, and while the chance of any shell making a hit amid the labyrinth of fissures and pits was exceedingly slight, the explosions kept the Indians on edge. So they crept as close as possible to the Army lines where no shells were falling, and the opposing forces spent the night in a pastime of soldiers from time immemorial, shouting obscene insults back and forth.

The soldiers had lost three killed and half a dozen wounded for all their extreme caution. The Modocs, as usual, had not lost a man or had one hurt, and the magic tule rope around the Stronghold had not been crossed. Curly Headed Doctor's prestige was higher than ever—but its hours were numbered.

On the second day of fighting, April 16, the pivoting wing, the gate that was to swing around in the rear of the Modocs, showed even less spirit than it had the day before. Then, at least, the officers had tried to exhort their faint-hearted legions into advancing against the eight Modocs who opposed them. But this day even the officers showed no enthusiasm, and were willing to let a creeping advance lose its small momentum without making any attempt to keep it going; they reported back that the ground was impossible to move across, and soon ordered their men to retreat.

On the other hand, at the northern end of the lines the Army forces showed a surprising amount of spirit—reluctant and snail-like, perhaps, by most standards, but a display of something approaching fighting spirit for this sad army. From east and west the two forces advanced along the lake shore, and the remarkable thing is that they had been expressly ordered *not* to move forward across the lake front. Major Green from the west, and Captain Mason, immovable the day before, from the east, pushed their forces until they joined up, cutting the Modocs off from the lake.

The very opposite of the planned strategy had been accomplished. Instead of being hemmed in by a force to the south and driven toward the lake, the way south into the labyrinthine jumble of the rest of the Lava Beds stood open while a line of soldiers was cutting the Modocs off from the lake front and the water of Tule Lake. However, the action of Green and Mason had one unexpected result. In the movement of their men, the tule rope had been crossed. The Stronghold was not absolutely impregnable, then, as their shaman had assured the Modocs again and again.

That night, Indian morale suffered a second blow. A man had attempted to remove the fuse from a dud howitzer shell with his teeth; when the smoke cleared, his head was gone and so was the rest of Curly Headed Doctor's prestige. Within less than twenty-four hours, both the things he had repeatedly promised would never happen had occurred. The Stronghold had been violated, and a Modoc had been killed by a soldier's weapon. The Doctor's medicine was no good, after all.

Jack had regained complete leadership of his band again; it was a somewhat shaken group, although on the basis of past experience the Modocs were convinced they were more than a match for the Army, magic or no. With the water of the lake no longer available, Captain Jack ordered an immediate withdrawal from the Stronghold. A rear-guard kept up a busy sniping to give an appearance of normal activity; when it, too, withdrew to the south and things became unnaturally quiet, the troops cautiously moved in to investigate. They found one old, wounded man who was promptly killed and scalped; in the zeal for souvenirs his scalp was divided into half a dozen or more pieces and even his eyebrows taken.

The Modocs were now at large in the jumbled expanse of the Lava Beds where they had good prospects of playing hide-and-seek indefinitely with the Army. The beds extended for about a dozen miles south from the lake and were about ten miles wide. The terrain was far from being a uniform expanse of sharp, black volcanic clinkers. There were buttes where lava had thrust through breaks in the rock below and flowed upward to harden into rounded hills; there were long ridges; there were caves and mounds and depressions; there were loose rocks which had broken off larger lava masses. And between the lava out-croppings were expanses of ground almost level, where the stony earth supported sagebrush, mahogany bushes, and bunch grass. There was plenty of game to provision the Modocs, and there was water in a number of caves in the lava, either in pools or frozen into ice.

Gillem set about the tedious task of trying to locate and pin down the Modocs. Two or three times a few of them were sighted, but they disappeared and it was useless to attempt to follow them in the chaotic lava formations. It occurred to Gillem that the answer to his problem might be to establish himself boldly within the Lava Beds by emplac-ing artillery on commanding positions where it could control large areas in all directions and be always ready to fire on any Indians who showed themselves. To put the idea to the test, he sent Captain Evan Thomas, an artillery officer, with a strong sixty-four-man party com-posed of two artillery batteries and an infantry company to take a howitzer to the top of a lava butte about four miles south of head-quarters camp. Thomas and two or three of his officers had fine Civil War records but they were lacking in the much more pertinent experi-ence of Indian-fighting.

The march was made along the western edge of the Lava Beds, over fairly level ground. The force moved slowly; the men would have moved more slowly yet, or not at all, had they known that a band of Modoc warriors in the lava formations only about half a mile away was not only observing them but was traveling on a slowly converging course.

When it became obvious to the Indians that the column was headed for the butte, Scarfaced Charley, their leader, hurried his men on ahead to post them at the top of the butte and along both sides of the path the column would have to take to reach the top. It was a deadly ambush, and Captain Thomas was taking no precautions against being caught in such a trap. At first he had flankers out, and a skirmish line in front, but the nervous soldiers kept drawing in toward the column, and the inexperienced officers, not realizing the importance of such precautions in Indian country, soon gave up attempts to keep the men out.

When the column was on the butte and well within the trap, the Modocs opened fire. The soldiers responded as they always had to Indian bullets; they became panic-stricken and ran. Captain Thomas Wright, commanding the infantry company, attempted a charge with his men to allow the rest of the column to escape, but as soon as the infantrymen came under fire, they, too, turned tail and joined the general wild flight. Wright was killed, and the last semblance of organization among the infantry vanished; they fled in sheer animal terror, some of them making the four-mile trip over rocky ground back to headquarters camp in less than an hour.

A young lieutenant named Cranston had attempted to rally some of the men to make a stand; when he called for volunteers only five men stood by him—and when the gallant and forlorn six came out of the shelter of desert shrubs to try to help stem the rout, they were killed almost on the spot. Captain Thomas got a group of about twenty men into a rocky hollow but it was no shelter because Modocs on the ridge above were able to shoot down into them with the greatest ease. Thomas and most of the men with him were slain by midafternoon when the firing stopped unexpectedly and Scarfaced Charley called, "All you fellows that ain't dead had better go home. We don't want to kill you all in one day."

Back at headquarters, they were aware that Wright's column had had some sort of brush with the Modocs. A signal tower had been erected on high ground near the camp for communication with the east force; it also served as an excellent lookout, and from it the column was in sight of observers with glasses a good part of the time. When gunfire was heard and running men were seen, a watching officer interpreted it as a retreat in good order. Even when the first of the fleeing men reached camp early in the afternoon, still too incoherent from terror to explain what had happened, Gillem was not worried because he knew Captain Thomas would outnumber any band of Modocs that might oppose him, and he was sure Thomas could take care of himself (it is hard to say whence such confidence came, in view of the fighting record of men and officers to that time). Not till late afternoon did he order a relief column out, and for this delay he was relieved of his command almost immediately.

The relief column—and this could almost have been predicted in advance with this unhappy, maladroit army—got lost in the dark and had to make a bivouac of sorts for the night, and when it did reach the scene of the disaster in the morning, it was discovered that no one had thought of sending doctors along to care for the wounded. The relief force found a grim scene: twenty-three dead. Nineteen had been wounded; some had made it back to camp but many still lay on the battlefield. The Modocs, as usual, had not lost a man. And, as usual, the Indians had acquired stores of rifles, ammunition, and other supplies. They made no attempt to attack the rescue forces but perched on the ridges watching from a distance, making the soldiers very nervous.

Captain Jack, however, was having serious problems, and the most critical of them was the matter of water. The Lava Beds are dotted with caves into which water slowly percolates through the porous volcanic rock and collects, sometimes as pools of water but more often frozen into great ice masses which do not melt during the summer. The Modocs chopped out chunks of the ice and melted it for use, but there were about 165 of them, men, women, and children, and they could use all the ice in a cave in a short time. Then it was necessary to move on to another source of water. Since it took the caves months to replenish themselves by seepage, and most of that during the winter rainy months, the field of maneuver of the Modocs was being gradually compressed. But against the spiritless army they had been fighting, there was still plenty of water and game to enable them to hold out for a long time yet.

General Jefferson Davis had relieved Colonel Gillem and sent him back to San Francisco (this inconsequential war against half a hundred perverse Indians was costing military reputations as well as lives), and having personally assumed command, he pondered ways of putting some fighting spirit into this craven group that called itself an army. It was made up, much of it, of immigrants who had enlisted without the faintest stirring of patriotism but only because it offered three meals a day, a bed of sorts, and a few dollars to spend on pay day. It was a refuge, too, for ne'er-do-wells, who, in the Far West of 1873, hardly expected to be called on to fight Indians in dead earnest. And, without doubt, there were a good many young men who had enlisted with every expectation of being good soldiers but had been infected with the atmosphere of fear that had come to permeate an entire army of a thousand men that outnumbered its enemy twenty to one.

Davis's eye fell on Captain H. C. Hasbrouck and his company of cavalry, who had reported for duty after Thomas had been killed and his command cut to pieces; the smell of confidence was still strong about Hasbrouck and his men, and their morale was high. General Davis determined to make use of their rare quality before they, too, had been tainted by the unreasoning fear of the Modocs and the defeatism that obsessed everyone else in the camp. He sent Hasbrouck and his horsemen out after Modocs, giving him as support a battery of artillery and two companies of cavalry which had shown no talent for fighting in the past. A detachment of Indian scouts completed the column.

Hasbrouck's column went down the east side of the Lava Beds where the Modocs had last been reported as having been seen, and after an uneventful march, bivouacked by a body of mud called Dry Lake, while the artillery made its separate camp about a mile away. The Modocs, of course, had been observing every move and had decided that the Army forces were in an ideal spot for a surprise attack. By striking from the right direction they could stampede the soldiers —who had never yet failed to run when properly frightened—into a choice of running into the mud of the lake or toward the Modocs.

The attack came at daybreak. Its initial effect was just what the Modocs had anticipated. The soldiers were befuddled with sleep and unable at first to get their bearings and comprehend what was happening. Two were killed at once, and several wounded. There was a general flight from the attacking Indians which was halted, as the Modoc leaders had foreseen, by the mud of the lake, and there many of the soldiers huddled, numbed by fear and lack of direction. But

Captain Hasbrouck was a different kettle of fish; he at once began setting things to rights, bellowing commands and sorting order out of chaos. He sent one of his officers to the artillery camp a mile away for help, hurried others down to the lake shore to rally the men cowering there. The Modocs were pressing ahead, exploiting what they had come to expect as the typical panic of white soldiers caught unawares, when they, in their turn, were taken by surprise. The frightened soldiers on the lake front had rallied under their officers' exhortations, and were pushing ahead in a skirmish line, firing briskly as they came. The Indians were not prepared for such a turn of events, and in their turn began to retreat, a withdrawal that was greatly hastened when one warrior fell badly wounded and the Army's Indian scouts began firing on the Modocs from the rear.

The Modocs abandoned the field completely. On the face of it, they had not come out too badly. The Army had lost three soldiers and two Indian scouts killed and half a dozen soldiers and two scouts wounded while the Modoc losses had been only one man mortally wounded. But the Modocs had, for some curious reason, loaded their most important supplies on pack horses and had brought them close to the field of action. Twenty-four loaded pack horses were captured; they carried much of the Modocs' ammunition as well as other supplies. Previously, battlefields had been sources of supply to the Indians; now they suddenly found themselves facing scarcity.

The biggest failing of the Modoc band was that it could not stand adversity. There were too many factions and too much antagonism. The man wounded in the battle at Dry Lake was Ellen's Man who died a few hours later; he had been one of the murderers of General Canby, and he was one of the Hot Creek band who had been such vehement supporters of Curly Headed Doctor in the days when a tule rope promised perpetual security. Now that the war they had wanted so much was turning sour on them, the Hot Creek group tried to make Jack the scapegoat. Ellen's Man was dead, they charged, because Jack had deliberately put him in a dangerous position where he would be likely to be hit. There was a violent quarrel, and the Hot Creek band, along with Hooker Jim and Curly Headed Doctor—fourteen warriors and their families—departed the Lava Beds entirely, going about forty miles to the northwest.

The shape and tide of the war changed with surprising swiftness. The victory had performed the near-miracle of raising the morale of the spiritless troops who had been frightened for half a year by the mere mention of Modocs. Now the soldiers hunted for Indians as though they wanted to find them, and for ten days Captain Hasbrouck led a column of some three hundred men, trying to corner Captain Jack who now had only thirty-three warriors and was hampered by women and children.

But it was the Hot Creek band who surrendered first. They returned to the area, apparently out of pure curiosity to see what had been going on in their absence. Once there, however, they decided to give themselves up, and went to rancher Fairchild, the same man they had gone to for help when they had first tried to avoid the war. And having surrendered, they were eager to play the part of Judas. Four of them, Bogus Charley, Steamboat Frank, Hooker Jim, and Shacknasty Jim, offered to act as guides in helping the Army find Captain Jack. General Davis, quite certain the dispirited quartet would not betray his trust, sent them out to try to talk Jack into coming in. They found him well to the east of the Lava Beds and advised him to give himself up; after all, they said, they had been treated very well. Jack responded with justifiable anger; the men standing before him had opposed him several times when he had wanted to surrender; they had forced him to agree to the murder of the Peace Commissioners by the business of the women's clothes; three of them, in fact, had had a hand in the actual killing. Now they had earned forgiveness from the white men by offering to bring him in. Jack well knew that he could not, in his turn, buy his way out by offering to betray someone else. He told his erstwhile comrades-in-arms to go to hell.

But his followers gradually gave up as hunger, the fatigue of constant flight, and just plain hopelessness overcame them. Soldiers at last caught up with Jack himself. There was no drama; he was in a position where he could have slipped away and remained free for at least a while longer, or he could have put up a fight. He did neither, but capitulated, explaining matter-of-factly that his legs had given out. That day, June 1, 1873, the Modoc war came to an end, although a few other Indians came in later.

Four Modocs never did make it. They had given themselves up to that good friend of the Modocs, rancher Fairchild, who was bringing them in in a wagon when he was stopped by a band of Oregonians. Fairchild was forced to get down from the wagon; then the men fired into the four Indians from a few feet away, killing all four and wound-

ing a woman, although this last was apparently by mistake. The
Modocs were small fry; their names, Little John, Mooch, Pony, and
Tee-hee Jack, are not otherwise mentioned in accounts of the war. The
Oregonians who made this late contribution toward winning the war
were never known and General Davis made no effort to find out who
they were; very possibly some of them were among the heroes who
had deserted rather than face these same Modocs when they were
armed.

Davis believed, along with the rest of the Army, that hard and immediate punishment of the Modocs was necessary to deter other Indians
from flouting white authority, and he planned to hang a number of
the leaders as soon as preparations could be made. However, in this
case the matter was too important to be left to the discretion of a
commander in the field. The Modoc war had been thoroughly covered
by newspaper correspondents on the scene, and the public was well
acquainted with the situation and the principal figures involved. A
number of summary executions would raise a storm of protests among
the philanthropists and Indian sympathizers in the East.

So, while Davis fumed and the state of Oregon screamed for blood,
the War Department put its legal experts to work determining the
questions of law involved. Their findings were that since the Modocs
were not citizens of the United States they could not be punished for
violating the laws of either the nation or the state of Oregon. There
was something grotesquely comic in this solemn performance; for
almost a hundred years the United States and the several states had
been chastising Indians for all manner of crimes and misdemeanors,
including that of trying to protect rights that had been guaranteed to
them, and now it was ruling that they could not legally be punished.
However, having erected this wall which apparently protected the
Modocs against retribution, the devious legal mind then had to find a
way through it so that they could be punished, all orderly and according to law. While the Indians could not be brought to trial for anything
not considered a crime under their own law, the opinion continued,
treachery, by almost universal custom, was considered an act punish-
able by death. And so, very neatly, the way was left open to try the
Indians for the murder of the unsuspecting ranchers at the outset of
the conflict, but, more important, to exact retribution for the one dramatically barbaric episode of the war, the murder of the Peace Commissioners.

The Indians were taken north to Fort Klamath and put in a stockade which had been built to receive them. There were forty-four men and one hundred and eleven women and children; these and the half dozen men who had been lynched or otherwise killed were the mighty band that had stood off an army of the United States, numbering about one thousand men during the last half of the war, for half a year. Curly Headed Jack, one of the three who had killed Lieutenant Sherwood on the east side of the Lava Beds, grabbed the gun away from a guard and shot himself because he was certain that he would hang. Otherwise, all who had any connection with the murders were present when the trial began on July 1.

Hooker Jim, Shacknasty Jim, and Bogus Charley had hands as bloody as anyone, but the grateful Army granted them amnesty for betraying Captain Jack after they had surrendered. Hooker Jim's former band was put on trial for the murder of ranchers at the very outset of the war, but the only persons who had witnessed any of the killings were the wives of two of the victims, and on the stand they could not positively identify a single one of the murderers. The case was dropped.

That left six men who could not sidestep approaching doom. The names by which the white men called them were Captain Jack, Schonchin John, Boston Charley, Black Jim, Slolux, and Barncho, and the charge against them was murdering General Canby and the Reverend Eleasar Thomas. The entire trial lasted ten days, and was no more than an approximation of a trial under American law. The Indians had no defense counsel, and they did not understand enough English to know what was going on during most of the trial. Barncho was so indifferent that he slept on the floor under a table much of the time. At the same time, the court went out of its way to bring in any evidence that might have any bearing on the case, even when it meant departing from its own procedures to do so.

Even so, the results were foregone, and all six were sentenced to be hanged on October 3. But there was a wide demand that Slolux and Barncho be shown clemency; they were very young, said their pleaders, and were nothing but tools in the hands of the other men in the killings. The conduct of Barncho in the courtroom indicated that he did not understand or did not care that his life was at stake. In any event, President Grant did commute the sentences of the two to life imprisonment a month before the execution, but from an apparent belief that there was a redemptive power in looking close-on into the face of death, he specified that the two were not to know that they had been spared until they reached the foot of the gallows.

So, on the day of execution, the six men, sitting on four coffins, were driven to the gallows. It was not until the other four were led up the stairs to the nooses and they were left behind that Barncho and Slolux realized that they were being spared.

The rest of the band were put aboard train and taken to Indian Territory, to be settled before the end of November in the extreme northeastern corner of that dumping ground for unwanted Indians. Malaria got in its work, and the band dwindled to about one-third of its original number within the next thirty years. There was never any more sign of fight in them; they sent their children to school, did some farming, and adjusted well to a settled life.

In 1909, the government at last permitted any who wished to do so to go back to the reservation. As for Barncho and Slolux, the authorities had long since decided they were no longer menaces. They were sent to Alcatraz Island to serve life sentences, but were set free after only five years.

VIII

The Road to
the Little Bighorn

1. THE TECHNIQUES OF TREATY-BREAKING

THE Modoc War was fought in 1873, the Red River War in 1874–75. During all of those years, the government of the United States, to oblige various of its sovereign citizens, was moving with a sureness born of long practice down the path to another Indian war, another broken treaty, and still another land grab. The Sioux and their Northern Cheyenne allies were to be the victims and the battlefields would be on the northern plains and foothills.

At Fort Laramie in 1868, it will be recalled, most of the Sioux and Northern Cheyenne and Arapaho bands signed a treaty by which they accepted as a reservation that great segment of Dakota Territory which now comprises all of South Dakota west of the Missouri River. The Oglala chief, Red Cloud, refused to accept this Great Sioux Reservation, however, until he had forced the United States to abandon the Bozeman Trail and to agree that the game-rich Powder River country belonged to the Sioux, and was absolutely forbidden to white men. This has been related in detail earlier; now it becomes the beginning of a new episode.

After Red Cloud won his war with the United States, he promised never to fight again, settled down near an agency, and took up the responsibilities of a reservation chief. But when he moved with his band to the reservation, there were many who remained behind. It was not to become tame Indians in the end that they had closed the white man's Bozeman Trail and burned the forts, the recalcitrants said. They had fought to remain free—and remain free they would, living in the old way by hunting the buffalo, and not by waiting for Washington to send food in sacks and boxes.

Their victory over the United States had given these "wild" Indians delusions of invincibility; they were certain they could drive out any future force the Army might send against them. As for Red Cloud, he had lost their respect because of what they considered his surrender to the white man. The Indians who had refused to sign a treaty included notable men: Sitting Bull, medicine man and oracle, whose name is probably the best-remembered of any Indian who ever lived; Crazy Horse, a leader whose genius for handling even the individualistic red warriors earns him the right to be named among the great American cavalry leaders of whatever color; Gall, the serious-minded Hunkpapa who would be leading chief at the battle of the Little Bighorn; Two Moon of the Cheyennes, Crow King, Hump, Spotted Eagle, and others.

The nontreaty Indians remained in the Powder River country, which was "unceded Indian territory" according to the treaty. And there they were perfectly content to live, setting up their lodges in the valleys of the clear rivers, hunting the buffalo and lesser game, holding back the calendar and living in the past while everything in the outer world was changing. However, if that was what they wanted, they appeared to be perfectly within their rights in trying to protect here, in the shadow of the Big Horn Mountains, a last remnant of a way of life that had once been as normal on the western prairies and the Great Plains as the rise and fall of the grass before the wind.

But change was closing in on them. White civilization began moving with its heavy tread through the remaining untouched portion of the northern plains when the Northern Pacific Railroad, building west from Duluth toward the Pacific, sent its survey crews ahead across the plains. The portion of the route laid out through Dakota Territory did no violence to treaty agreements; it ran due west through present North Dakota, well north of the Great Sioux Reservation, and while news that a railroad was to come through the buffalo range caused some consternation to the reservation Indians, the white man was completely within his treaty rights in laying his tracks there. It was hardly possible to keep the entire northern plains an unspoiled buffalo range.

But quite another matter was the section of the railroad's line through Montana. The survey line, after crossing from Dakota into Montana, struck the Yellowstone River valley which it then followed as the only practical route toward a pass through the mountains. A preliminary survey had been made by Colonel D. S. Stanley in 1872, on the basis of which it had been decided that the tracks should be laid on the south side of the river—and the south side was Indian country.

Although the Fort Laramie treaty completely neglected to define the northern limit of the unceded land, there was not any doubt where it lay. The Sioux had taken the region as far as the Yellowstone River from the Crows by conquest more than a generation before, and had held it firmly ever since. They were completely in control of everything south of the river, so the government sent two Commissioners to negotiate with them for a right-of-way for the railroad. They were completely unsuccessful. The chiefs announced, without discussion, that they wanted no railroad or other work of the white man anywhere on their last hunting range.

The Commissioners returned and duly reported failure. They also suggested that the hostiles probably had neither sufficient ammunition nor other resources to prevent the building of the railroad. The Army moved fast. The two Commissioners had had their futile talks with the Sioux on May 9, 1873; on June 20 a military expedition, to act as escort for surveyors laying out the railroad line in the Yellowstone valley, set out from Fort Rice on the Missouri. There was more than one way to amend a treaty.

The column was a powerful one: 19 companies of infantry, 10 of cavalry, a couple of artillery pieces, and the inevitable wagon train and beef herd, in all more than 1,500 soldiers and some 350 teamsters, herders and other auxiliaries, and a couple of dozen Arikara scouts. Colonel (brevet Brigadier General) D. S. Stanley, wartime commander of cavalry in the Army of the Cumberland, was in command.

The ten cavalry companies with the expedition were the 7th Regiment, and commanding them again was Lieutenant Colonel (brevet Major General) George Armstrong Custer. Since 1870, the 7th had been split up and sent into the South, a company here, another there, to keep order during the lawless times of the Ku Klux Klan. In the

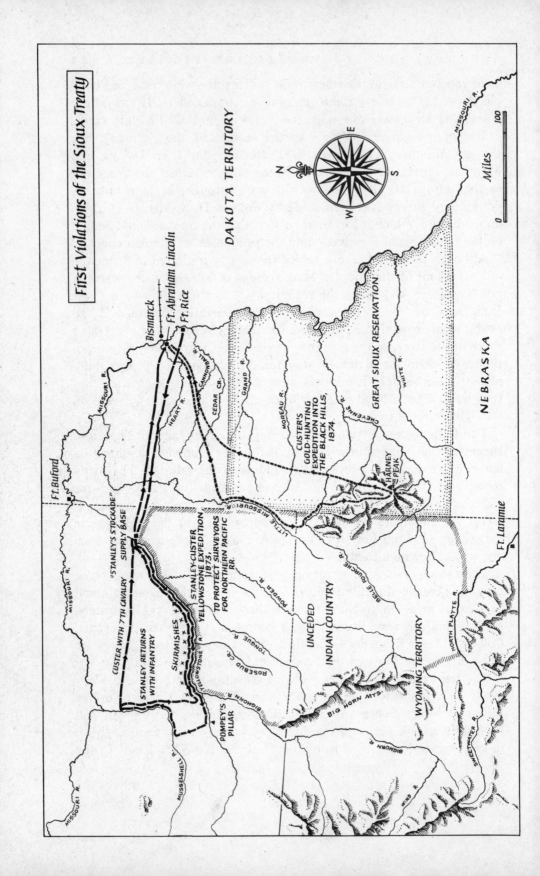

First Violations of the Sioux Treaty

spring of 1873 it was brought together again to serve on the plains. Custer had arrived at Yankton with his wife and his usual mountain of impedimenta, including his pack of hounds which on this trip had numbered forty dogs. His luck held; the colonel of the 7th was S. D. Sturgis, who had replaced the never-present Colonel A. J. Smith only shortly before the regiment had been broken up and sent south. Now, when it was together again and about to see action, Sturgis was detached and assigned to staff duty in St. Paul, leaving Custer once again in complete command. Ten companies were with the Yellowstone expedition; the remaining two, under Major Marcus Reno, had been detailed for duty as escorts to surveyors running the U. S.–Canadian boundary.

General Stanley was not favorably impressed with his young subordinate. In a letter to his wife he expressed his opinion that Custer was a "coldblooded, untruthful and unprincipled man. He is universally despised by all the officers of his regiment, excepting his relatives and one or two sycophants. He . . . carries an old negro woman and a cast-iron cooking stove and delays the march often by his extensive packing up in the morning. As I said, I will try but am not sure I can avoid trouble with him."

A few days later, Custer, trying how far he could take the bit in his own teeth, was brought up short. Stanley wrote to his wife:

> I had a little flurry with Custer as I told you I probably would. We were separate four miles and I intended him to assist in getting the train over the Muddy River. Without consulting me, he marched off 15 miles, coolly sending me a note to send him forage and rations. I sent after him, ordered him to halt where he was, to unload his wagons and send for his own rations and forage and never presume to make another movement without orders.
>
> I knew from the start it would have to be done. . . . He was just gradually assuming command and now he knows he has a commanding officer who will not tolerate his arrogance.

Colonel Stanley had no more trouble with Custer during the rest of the mission. The survey was carried out; there were several brisk clashes with the nontreaty Sioux and Cheyennes with dead and wounded on both sides, but considering the size of the forces on both sides that might have been involved, the campaign was completed with a rather small amount of fighting.

The crisis that actual construction of the railroad through the Yellowstone valley would have caused was averted when the Panic of 1873 stopped the rails on the east bank of the Missouri. The rough, raw frontier town of Bismarck grew up at the railhead; across the river and three or four miles down stream, the Army built a new post, Fort Abraham Lincoln; and there the 7th Cavalry was stationed, with its commanding officer also commandant of the fort.

Although the Northern Pacific had halted, it would not be forever, and General Sheridan, looking over his maps in his Chicago headquarters, contemplated the need for another fort to guard the line when building should begin again. Between Fort Abraham Lincoln and Fort Ellis far across Montana near Bozeman, there was nothing. It was a mighty big gap, and Sheridan decided that the Black Hills would be an ideal spot for his new fort: central location, lumber, water, firewood, all the other advantages.

There was only one thing wrong with the location: it was in the Great Sioux Reservation, Indian land, pure and simple. However, Sheridan cared less than a snap of his fingers for any rights of Indians, and he directed Colonel Custer to make a reconnaissance of the Black Hills to determine the best site for such a post. The move would be a brutal smashing of the Fort Laramie treaty—but then, General Philip Sheridan had often operated in a brutal manner.

The Black Hills were more than just a portion of the Sioux reservation. They were charged with a deep and mystical meaning for the Indians, for this was a sacred place, a spot where spirits dwelt. Here, in geological ages past, a section of the earth's crust, some 40 by 120 miles in extent, was lifted upward. It stands like an island amid the monotonous plains, a range of small mountains, split with shadowed canyons, dramatic with rock formations, cool with the shade of pine trees, watered with frequent streams. Even the climate is different in this place; the rains fall more abundantly while around the plains are dry and alkaline.

Custer led his exploration force out of Fort Lincoln on July 2, 1874. Besides ten companies of the 7th Cavalry (the remaining two were still guarding the surveyors marking out the U.S.–Canadian border), there were two companies of infantry, three Gatling guns, an artillery piece, Indian scouts, and the usual wagon train and complement of civilian auxiliaries. Lieutenant Colonel George A. Forsyth was on Custer's staff during the expedition, the same Forsyth who had been in command during the desperate fight at Beecher's Island six years earlier. Events would so order themselves that one day he would be Colonel of the 7th and would command it during its last and least praiseworthy action against Indians.

Besides exploring the area for possible sites for a fort, the expedition also included several scientists among whom geologists were prominent. There was no secret that the column also meant to look into the truth of persistent rumors that there was gold in the hills.

The expedition was out and back in somewhat less than two months, after a trip that often took on the aspects of a big picnic. There was no opposition from the Indians. Most of them did not even know what was happening until it was all over. By then their last hope of keeping the Black Hills was doomed, for the expedition had found gold. Not, it is true, gold in the quantities proclaimed by Custer, who announced that there were veins of gold-bearing quartz on the side of almost every hill, and that it had been found among the roots of the grass. He was so eager to trumpet these exaggerated accounts to the world without delay that he sent his scout, Lonesome Charley Reynolds, on a dangerous trip south across Indian country to Fort Laramie and the nearest telegraph. As a result, the country was burning with gold fever by the time the column returned, and no one listened to the protests of the expedition geologists that Custer's stories were extravagant and premature. As a matter of fact, prospectors were already entering the Black Hills before the column had reached Fort Abraham Lincoln. A few were killed by the angry Sioux, but many made it before winter closed down on the plains.

Having opened the door, the Army made ineffectual attempts to close it. Sherman announced that any white men who entered the reservation would be driven out at gunpoint, if necessary. It was all right for people on the frontier to complain about the Indians breaking the law, he observed, but they did not seem to see anything at all unjust about their going onto Indian land and grabbing it. He ordered officers in the area to arrest all civilians entering the reservation and to destroy their guns, transportation, and other property. (One almost has the feeling that Sherman would have liked to have threatened to exterminate them.) Not many officers carried out these stringent provisions; most were satisfied merely to escort prospectors off the reservation and there turn them over to the nearest civil authority—who, without exception, turned them loose for another try at slipping into the gold fields.

By the middle of 1875, there were hundreds of men panning for gold in the midst of the Black Hills.

The government could not keep its own citizens out of the Sioux lands, any more than it had been able to keep them out of any other Indian treaty land, in spite of solemn pledges, since the time when the land just across the Appalachians was the West. It was now up to the Indian Bureau to find some way to legalize this latest trespass. The government wanted the Black Hills and was willing to buy them—if the price was right, of course—and so it brought the leading treaty chiefs to Washington and there threatened and cajoled them. But the chiefs steadfastly refused to make a decision without talking things over with their people back home, and the frustrated government finally sent them home, promising it would take up the matter again very soon.

During that same summer, a geological party went into the Black Hills with an Army escort. Since the government was offering to buy the region from the Sioux, it wanted to see whether it really was worth anything, or whether the gold discoveries announced with such flourishes of trumpets by Custer were anything more than superficial indications which would soon be exhausted. The resulting report was more than satisfactory. In September, Commissioners arrived at the Red Cloud Agency to discuss revising the Fort Laramie treaty *—specifically, they wanted the Sioux to sell the Black Hills. Senator William Allison of Iowa was chairman; the Commission included other members of Congress and Major General Alfred Terry, commanding the Department of the Dakota. It was a distinguished group, but the Indians received it with no songs of welcome.

On the contrary, the Commissioners came close to being the central figures in a massacre during the first hours after their arrival. Bellicose Indians among the many hundreds present suddenly surrounded them with leveled guns; one of them, Little Big Man, called to his followers that this was as good a time as any to begin a war. Bloodshed was averted, but only narrowly, partly by the coolness of two cavalry offi-

---

* Actually, there was no writing of treaties with Indian tribes after 1871, when the entire ridiculous pretense that tribes were sovereignties was abolished. It would be pleasant to be able to report that the change was made because common sense prevailed, but such was not the case. The House of Representatives had long complained that the Senate had too big a hand in Indian affairs, for under the Constitution only the Senate approved treaties. So, in 1871 the treaty fiction was ended, and relations with tribes were conducted by "agreements" which required the approval of both Senate and House. The practical difference was small.

cers who formed their commands into line of battle with carbines at
the ready, and waited impassively and motionless, ready to charge
the instant a hostile move was made, partly by the imperturbability of
Spotted Tail, the Brule peace chief, who bluffed the war party by
offering them a fight then and there if that was what they wanted.

What composure remained to the Commissioners must have been
shaken when they sat in council later to discuss the purchase of the
Black Hills and heard Red Cloud calmly propose that $600,000,000
seemed like a fair price for a region that meant so much to the red
man, and appeared to mean even more to the white. When they had
recovered their decimal points, they suggested that $6,000,000 would
be a reasonable offer, and there the matter was left. The Commissioners
apparently had no heart for haggling after their chilling experience
and soon left. "The Commission were the gladdest people to get away
from that part of the country that had ever visited there," General
George Crook, who knew more about fighting than grammar, wrote.
"They didn't recover their courage until they got the Missouri River
between them."

Unfortunately for the Sioux, the discomfited Commissioners represented considerable influence in the government. They had been frightened and embarrassed, and their report reflected their resentment. It
was necessary to teach the Indians a lesson, they said, for the Sioux
had made no attempt to abide by the 1868 treaty—they had made no
move to learn farming, for instance—and all in all, these people on the
northern plains were never going to become civilized unless the government got very stern with them and taught them a lesson. The report
did not put it in exactly these words, but the tenor was unmistakable.

The government soon moved to bring the Indians to heel. In early
November, the Commissioner of Indian Affairs issued an ultimatum
that all Indians must come onto the reservation and report to their
agencies at once. The order was both impossible to comply with and a
flagrant violation of the Fort Laramie treaty. It was a violation because
the bands not on the Great Sioux Reservation were nevertheless on
Indian land when they were on the unceded territory, and nothing in
the Laramie agreement gave the government any right to restrict the
Indians' use of that territory. It was impossible to comply with because
agents were not able even to get word to all of their charges in the
winter-locked country by January 31, and it was even less possible
for the bands to make it back to the agencies. As for the nontreaty

bands of Crazy Horse, Sitting Bull, and Gall, it is doubtful if they even knew an order had been issued.

Winter is a gaunt and skeletal season on the northern plains. The cold is unbelievably brutal, especially when driven by the wind that blows unchecked over the flatlands. To the Plains Indians, it was a season for sitting around the fire in tight-laced tepees, in the shelter of stream valley bluffs. Even if an Indian band were foolhardy enough to expose children and infants to the hardships of a long trip during the dead of winter, its ponies would probably not be up to the task on the meager desiccated grass they could graze where the harsh wind had swept the ground free of snow.

The January 31 deadline came; one small band had come in and that was all. The Indian Bureau turned the matter over to the Army; the Indians still off the reservation were now assumed to be in a state of war against the government. General Sheridan made plans to smash the hostiles. The government had its war, one of the most cynically contrived in all the long history of Indian wars, for at no point had the Sioux or Cheyenne given the slightest provocation.

Sheridan, planning his strategy, decided to use one of his favorite concepts, three converging columns. Major General Alfred Terry, commanding the Department of Dakota with headquarters in St. Paul, was to lead one column of about 1,000 men west from Fort Abraham Lincoln to the Yellowstone. Brigadier General George Crook, commanding the Department of the Platte, was to move from the North Platte River northward through the Powder River country to the Yellowstone River. And finally, Colonel John Gibbon would command a third column of about 450, moving eastward along the Yellowstone from Fort Ellis in Montana Territory. The three would meet somewhere in the vicinity of the junction of the Bighorn and the Yellowstone Rivers, driving the hostiles into a surround until they had no choice but to surrender or be annihilated.

There were estimated to be about 1,000 warriors in the Powder River country—one or two officers thought there might even be as many as 1,500. When the true size of the Indian forces would be learned, it would be one of the rudest shocks ever suffered by American arms.

General Crook was the first to move when he marched up into the unceded Indian territory—the government had knocked that phrase to bits!—in March. Crook had been transferred the year before to command of the Department of the Platte from command of the Department of Arizona where he had succeeded in getting the Apaches under control without excessive cost in lives or loss of honor to either side. On graduating from West Point in 1852, Crook had been assigned to fighting Indians in California, and had spent his entire career since on the Indian frontier except for the Civil War interlude. General Sherman was to call him the greatest Indian fighter and manager the United States ever had. The Sioux, however, were not going to add greatly to the brightness of that reputation during the next few months.

George Crook was a man of somewhat startling personal appearance because his beard parted naturally and was forked; he braided the two sides to keep them under control during the rigors of a campaign. He was a rather prickly character; his standards of conduct, both for himself and for others, were high, so that his comments on many of the prominent personalities of his times were caustic, and his evaluations of them often more critical and severe than those since made by history. Sheridan, for one, he held in very low esteem; he believed that the General built his reputation largely by assuming credit for the accomplishments of others (including those of Crook).

Crook left Fort Fetterman on the North Platte on March 1, on what he planned should be mainly a scouting trip "to get some idea of the country and the difficulties to be overcome in a summer campaign." Fort Fetterman had been built in 1867 on the south side of the river at approximately the point where the old Bozeman Trail had cut north; now the column pushed up the abandoned trail. The force consisted of ten companies * of cavalry (five each from the 2nd and 3rd Regiments) and two companies of the 4th Infantry.

During the first days, the column marched in beautiful sunny weather; then, about 125 miles north of the fort it had just made camp at sunrise after an all-night march, when a blizzard struck, with snow and harsh winds so blinding it was impossible to see more than a few yards, and temperatures that dropped steadily. After waiting in vain a day for the weather to improve, the column pushed on. It had left its wagon train encamped a day's march behind, and the rations it now carried were too limited to permit it to wait longer for better weather. The march north was continued, to the Tongue River and down that

---

* "Company" was still used in 1876, and for some time after, as the name of the cavalry as well as the infantry unit of organization next smaller than a regiment. It was replaced by "troop" in cavalry parlance during the next decade or so.

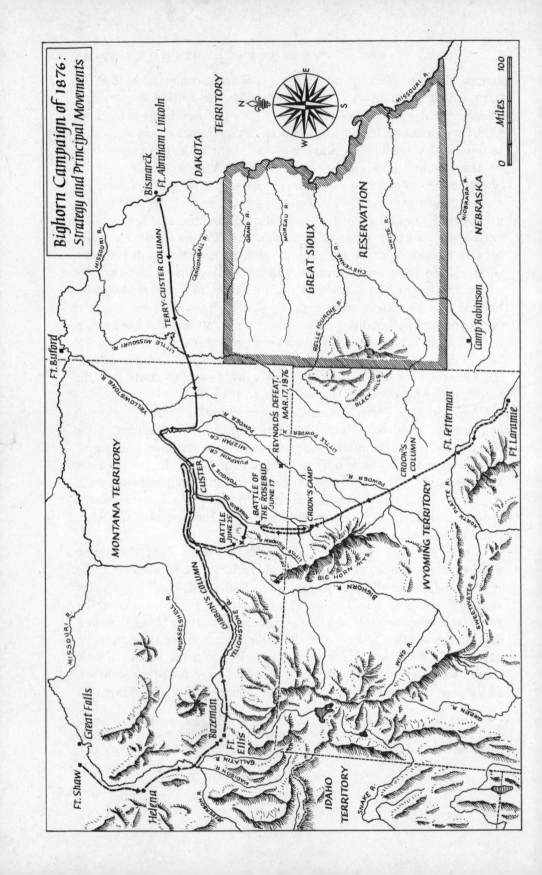

Bighorn Campaign of 1876:
Strategy and Principal Movements

stream to within less than a hundred miles of the Yellowstone; then, no signs of Indians having been found, the force cut east to the Powder River. For the first few days after the blizzard the cold was so intense that the thermometer often would not register—and mercury does not freeze until −38° F.

On the Powder, the tracks of two ponies were found and back-tracked to the village from which they had come. It was a camp set under a high bluff by the river. Colonel J. J. Reynolds, who with three companies of cavalry had followed the pony tracks, had come out on the bluffs almost immediately above the unsuspecting village just about at daybreak·on March 17. Reynolds gave the order to attack at once, and the horsemen scrambled down the steep slopes and fell on the sleep-befuddled Indians. What the Army did not know until afterward—and never was concerned about—was that this was a camp of friendly Northern Cheyennes of Chief Two Moon who had concluded, on learn-ing that soldiers were moving into the country, that it would be best to go back to the reservation. With the Cheyennes were some Sioux who had also decided to return to their agency.

"The army," Custer wrote in his book, *My Life on the Plains,* "is the Indian's best friend." The Indian could do without such friends. The Army on the Indian frontier could fight wars but—except under rare leaders—it had seldom shown much talent for preventing them. The tools of its trade were the sword and the cannon, and it instinctively fell back on them when confronted by a problem. Army officers com-plained that the civilian Indian Bureau, through ineptness and cor-ruption, created situations which the military had to put to rights, often at great cost and hardship. But, on a good many occasions, it had created its own situations of crisis, perhaps by retaliating against one band for depredations committed by another, perhaps, as here, by the stupidity of ruling that every Indian found in the region was, *ipso facto,* an enemy.

There was no doubt that Two Moon was friendly up to the time the yelling troopers fell on the camp that February morning. For that, we have the authority of young Lieutenant Sibley of Crook's staff who was a keen observer of all that occurred during the campaign. The chief and his Cheyennes would thereafter be implacable enemies of the Army, and four months later, on the heights above the Little Bighorn, would extract some small revenge for Reynolds' attack.

As a matter of fact, they did not wait that long. The cavalry swept through the camp, driving out the Indians and seizing many of their ponies as well as all their other belongings. But Cheyenne and Sioux warriors quickly rallied, and moved up to occupy the bluffs from which the soldiers had just attacked. There they held the advantage of position, and swooped down, putting up an intense rifle and arrow fire. Panic overtook the troops who retreated precipitously, leaving their dead behind, and there were dark whispers among the men that a wounded soldier had been abandoned. Even to leave dead was serious enough in view of the importance which the Indians place on the capture of bodies of enemies; to give up a wounded man was unthinkable.

The Indian pursuit of the cavalry continued until the next morning; the warriors recovered many of their ponies. General Crook himself retrieved something from the defeat by overtaking a party of Indians returning to camp and taking from them the ponies they were driving, but it was small consolation. The expedition returned to Fort Fetterman, where Crook brought charges against Colonel Reynolds and two captains as a result of the rout. The court-martial was an acrimonious one, with the three officers making counteraccusations, but all three were found guilty, two of them of neglect of duty, the third of the lesser charge of conduct to the prejudice of good order and military discipline. Colonel Reynolds, who received the sternest sentence, was suspended from command for one year.

It was not, from any point of view, a spectacular beginning to the great offensive against the so-called hostiles. Crook's setback had elated the tribesmen, and filled them with confidence. Agency Indians customarily moved out into the Powder River country in spring to hunt until cold weather drove them in again; this year the flow was greater than ever. A patriotic fervor was sweeping through the northern people moving them to cast their lot with Crazy Horse, Sitting Bull, and other nontreaty leaders who, after trying to avoid the white man, were now preparing to defend their land against him.

2 . WHOM THE GODS WOULD DESTROY

The three-pronged campaign had been planned for early spring, sometime in April, if possible, as soon as the ground had dried out enough to bear up under the sharp edges of iron wagon tires, and the buffalo grass had turned green and was tall enough to supply grazing for horses, mules, and beef herds. But April came and went, and the great expedition was still immobilized, for reasons rather complicated but ultimately amounting to nothing more obscure than the indiscretion of a single man. That man was George Armstrong Custer.

To begin with, Custer was to have led the eastern column from Fort Abraham Lincoln. General Terry, as commander of the entire Department of Dakota with both the Fort Lincoln force and Colonel Gibbon's column under his overall command, did not think it wise to tie himself too closely to either. Hence he had selected Custer, an officer experienced in Indian fighting, to command the column from the east.

However, as the time for taking the field arrived, the commanding officer of the 7th Cavalry and commander-designate of the Fort Lincoln column was in Washington, frantically trying to extricate himself from webs of his own weaving.

The previous fall, when cold winds had brought a season of routine campaigning on the plains to an end, the acting colonel of the 7th Cavalry and his lady had left the West behind for a three-month leave in New York. The couple had a pleasant and exciting time, and at the end of the three months, Custer requested, and was granted, an extension of two months. Then, the pleasures of the big city still not having palled as the extension drew to a close, he asked for still more time. By then he had had five months away from his post.

It was then getting near to March, and, one would think, time for Custer to be giving thought to returning to make plans for the summer campaign and to start honing a sharp edge on his command. But if he was willing to let his staff in Dakota handle all preparations until it was time for him to lead the column out onto the plains, Secretary of War Belknap had other ideas. The Secretary denied Custer's latest request for more leave.

If the refusal had come from any other man, the Colonel might have taken it philosophically and been thankful for the long vacation he had already had. But, since the rejection had come from Secretary Belknap, Custer did take it personally, very much so. He was a man who often lost his temper but he harbored almost no lasting animosities, so far as is known. Even within his own regiment he showed no special aptitude for holding grudges against the officers in the anti-Custer group. The one virulent hatred of his life was William Worth Belknap.

The feud, whose violence appears to have been almost entirely on Custer's side, seems to have arisen over the matter of the sutler at Fort

Abraham Lincoln. By way of explanation, a sutler was a civilian who was granted the concession to operate what in a later day would be called a post exchange; he sold shoelaces, canned oysters, needles and thread, licorice root, chewing tobacco, and the hundred other articles that soldiers far from the nearest town could not possibly get otherwise. It was, as might be expected, a lucrative business because there was no competition.

Formerly, post commandants had appointed and removed sutlers, but Belknap had transferred this power to the Secretary of War in 1870 on his assumption of one-man rule over the Army. When soldiers at Fort Abraham Lincoln complained about the high prices at the sutler's store, Custer could do nothing about the store itself. However, he did circumvent the sutler completely by having company officers go in to Bismarck, only three or four miles away, to make purchases for the enlisted men.

The idea was ingenious, but a lieutenant colonel should not have expected to win a battle with the Secretary of War. The sutler appealed to Belknap, who immediately ordered Custer to cease and desist in his attempts to interfere with the sutler's business. The rebuff came when Custer was already in short temper from having his active body and expansive spirit shut up within the limited confines of a northern plains post in winter. Perhaps at any other time, when he was busy, he would have forgotten it in a few days; now he had plenty of time to brood, and out of his dark musings grew a violent hate of Secretary Belknap.

A little later, Custer had an opportunity to show his contempt for the Secretary of War. Belknap, on an inspection trip through the West in the summer of 1875, had included Fort Abraham Lincoln on his itinerary. It was the most elementary military courtesy for the post commandant to meet the Secretary of War at the border of the reservation. Custer, with a fine instinct for self-destruction, waited in his headquarters for Belknap to come to him. When the sutler sent over a gift of champagne to be drunk at the meeting of the two men, Custer sent it back.

Thus, it may have been with a certain smug satisfaction that Belknap refused the leave extension—or very possibly, he thought nothing further than that it was time for Custer to get back to the duties the government was paying him to perform. All this has appeared to be far away, not only in distance but in relevance, from the Sioux and

Cheyenne Indians and the coming campaign. Custer, with some help from fate, would soon begin drawing the elements closer together.

Before the Custers had left New York to return to Dakota Territory, disaster struck Secretary Belknap. Grant's administration was collapsing under its dull weight of corruption as the extent of malfeasance, abuse of public trust, and stealing of public money began to come to light. Secretary of the Interior Delano had resigned some months earlier because of huge frauds in connection with Indian Bureau funds; now, on March 2, Belknap suddenly resigned when a House investigating committee discovered that he was involved in the selling of sutlers' concessions at Army posts and voted impeachment proceedings.

Custer, going ahead with his packing, seems to have heard of the fall of his enemy with satisfaction, but he could not resist a possible chance to kick Belknap when he was down. He sent off word to a Congressman acquaintance saying that he stood ready to tell all he knew about Belknap's part in many murky transactions involving Army posts on the frontier. Then, having set this time bomb which would hurt no one but himself, he and Elizabeth Custer ("Libbie," he called her) left on the steam cars for Bismarck.

The train stalled in deep drifts some forty or fifty miles short of Bismarck, but brother Tom came through from the fort in a bobsled, to rescue the Custers and three new hounds the Colonel had bought in the East. The homecoming was a brief one. They had been at Fort Lincoln only about a week when, on March 15, Custer received a summons to come to Washington and tell the House committee all about Belknap's questionable activities in the frontier posts, as he had offered to do.

Custer at first naïvely proposed to answer by mail a list of written questions sent him by the committee, but he quickly learned that Congress was not so easily put off. He went to Washington where, in the witness chair, he proved to know absolutely nothing. His every charge, every accusation was pure hearsay, rumor, gossip, a story heard at third-hand from dubious sources. Under the questioning of the committee members, all of his promised revelations turned out to have no more substance than an old woman's tittle-tattle. Custer became increasingly reckless as his stories of scandal in high places fizzled like wet squibs. His tactics in battle had always been to attack, and he could not suppress the instinct to do so now. In his wide and sweeping accusations, he included Orvil Grant, the President's brother, as one of those who had been involved in chicanery in the West, and he even hinted that the President himself had adjusted the boundary of the Great Sioux Reservation for the benefit of certain parties. His statements could not have been better calculated to put his neck in a noose.

Time was passing. General Terry had planned to start Custer and his column from Fort Lincoln about April 1; now April was almost over and Terry could not wait forever. Custer, in Washington, was becoming frantic with worry that he would miss the big show against the Sioux, and was sending plaintive telegrams from time to time asking advice and help of Terry and Sheridan. Then, on April 28, Sheridan telegraphed Terry that it was time to pick someone else to lead the column, and, after some discussion, it was decided that Terry himself would take command.

The decision to replace Custer did not spring from the brain of General Sheridan; it had originated as high in the chain of command as it was possible to go. Sheridan was merely forwarding orders he had received from Sherman (now reinstated in Washington that Belknap was gone), who in turn had received them from Secretary of War Alphonso Taft, who had had them from the President of the United States himself. Ordinarily, Grant would not have concerned himself with a relatively minor matter of who should command a force in a Western military department, but Custer had been more rash than he knew when he included the President's own family in his accusations.

Custer was at last released by the House committee, which told him he was free to go. However, Sherman advised him to see the President before he started for the West, so he presented himself at the White House on Monday morning, May 1, at ten o'clock, and sent in his card. He was still there at three in the afternoon when the President's secretary came out to tell him there was no point in waiting any longer because Grant would not see him. Custer then wrote a primly formal note saying he regretted any offense he might have given the President, but that it had been unintentional, etc., left the message, and departed. He appears to have blithely assumed that he had now completely taken care of Sherman's suggestion that he see the President. Military protocol required that he should call on Sherman himself before departing. He did call at the General's office once during the afternoon, and at his hotel twice during the early evening, but Sherman had not yet returned from a trip. And the cavalry officer, who should have known better, decided he had also discharged this obligation, and entrained for Dakota Territory.

At Chicago, Custer had changed trains and was waiting to start for St. Paul when an aide of General Sheridan located him. Sheridan had received a telegram from General Sherman, ". . . He was not justified in leaving without seeing the President and myself. Please intercept him and await further orders; meanwhile let the expedition proceed without him."

Custer sent a long and bewildered telegram back to Sherman, explaining about the hours spent waiting to see the President, and about his attempts to see Sherman. Perhaps this was all that was expected of him, that he abase himself. Sherman responded by directing that Custer be permitted to proceed to Terry's headquarters in St. Paul.

There is an element almost of Greek tragedy in the way this man, who had been a favored son of the gods, was being made their jest now. No matter how he tried to extricate himself from the trap he had built with his own indiscreetness, he only succeeded in embroiling himself still deeper. Nothing could have been more tragic for him, to whom campaigning on the Great Plains had become not only a professional assignment but a glorious and intoxicating way of life, than to be left behind by the greatest of all the expeditions against the Indians. Yet by this time Custer the confident, flamboyant egotist had been reduced to such a state of abject humbleness that he sent a telegram to Washington asking only that he be permitted to proceed on to Fort Abraham Lincoln, to join his wife rather than being required to remain in St. Paul during the campaign.

On May 5, General Terry received orders from Sherman: "Have just come from the President who orders that General Custer be allowed to rejoin his post, to remain there on duty, but not to accompany the expedition supposed to be on the point of starting against the hostile Indians under General Terry." During the war, the implacability of Grant had worn the Confederate armies down to bare bones; it now appeared that Custer was the hapless victim of that same stubborn character trait that refused to let an antagonist go until he had been crushed.

Missing the campaign would have been a personal tragedy to Custer, but one possible avenue of appeal still remained open to him, General Alfred Terry, his immediate superior. When his train reached St. Paul, he humiliated himself once more and begged Terry to be permitted to accompany his regiment on the campaign.

General Terry was no tough, hard-bitten officer, but a rather gentle man who looked as though he would be more at home in a scholar's study than at the head of troops. A lawyer at the outbreak of the Civil War, he had volunteered and quickly found himself in a colonel's uniform. In that day of regiments manned and officered entirely by volunteers, it was not at all unusual to find lawyers with no military training becoming colonels, especially if they had helped recruit the regiment. But Terry had had the feel of the business; he fought from First Bull Run to the storming of Fort Fisher on the North Carolina coast where, as a major general, he was in command. After the war, he decided to remain in the Army. His brilliant conduct of the Fort Fisher operation had caught the eye of Sherman so that, when the latter was organizing his Division of the Missouri after the war, he reached out without hesitation for Terry to command the Department of Dakota.

It would have been easy for many commanding officers to have turned Colonel Custer aside. After all, the President himself had ordered that the cavalry officer who talked too much about things of which he knew nothing should remain at Fort Abraham Lincoln. It was not that easy for the kindly Terry. As he explained long afterward to friends, "Custer, . . . with tears in his eyes, begged my aid. How could I resist it?"

The thing was done in formal military fashion. Custer, under Terry's eye, composed a letter to Grant, asking that he be permitted to serve with his regiment even though he was not to command the expedition. "I appeal to you as a soldier to spare me the humiliation of seeing my regiment march to meet the enemy and I not to share its dangers."

Terry added his endorsement in forwarding the letter: he had no desire to question the orders of the President, but if it were possible to modify those orders, Custer's services would be very valuable.

General Philip Sheridan was next in the chain of command. There had been another day when Custer had been under a cloud and suspended from duty, and Sheridan had intervened to bring him back to the plains. He had been Sheridan's protégé and darling then and for years was the cavalryman who struck some responsive chord in the General who saw only the dash and courage and never the shortcomings. But, at last, Sheridan was becoming bored with this perennial seeker after glory, now in his thirty-seventh year, whose ideas of leadership and responsibility were not much advanced from what they had been a dozen years earlier, and still found their highest expression in whooping at the head of a charge. Sheridan's thin endorsement did not advance Custer's cause:

I am sorry Lieutenant Colonel Custer did not manifest as much interest in staying at his post to organize and get ready his regiment and the expedition as he now does to accompany it. On a previous occasion in eighteen sixty-eight I asked executive clemency for Colonel Custer to enable him to accompany his regiment against the Indians, and I sincerely hope that if granted this time it may have sufficient effect to prevent him from again attempting to throw discredit upon his profession and his brother officers.

The next morning Terry got an answer from Sherman. No one knows what occurred, whether Grant decided that he had inflicted enough punishment on Custer, whether Sherman prevailed on the President to modify his stand, or whether Grant was influenced by the outcry in the Democratic newspapers that he was ruining Custer's career solely because of his petty vengefulness. Whatever the reason, the cigar-smoking man in the White House relented; Custer could go if Terry wanted him.

"Advise Custer to be prudent, not to take along any newspaper men, who always make mischief, and to abstain from personalities in the future," Sherman added soberly in his telegram sending along the good news for Custer. Sherman's advice was ignored by Custer. When the 7th Cavalry headed west, it was accompanied by newspaper correspondent Mark Kellogg who died at the Little Bighorn.

Custer was given the good news at Terry's headquarters. There is no record of his reactions, but certainly he must have profusely thanked Terry, who alone was making it possible for him to take part in the war against the Sioux. Yet, after leaving General Terry's headquarters to walk to his hotel he met an acquaintance, Colonel Ludlow, and informed him that he was now back in command of the 7th Cavalry. Custer, in obvious high spirits after the news he had just received, added that at the first opportunity during the campaign he was going to "cut loose from General Terry during the summer," that during operations two years earlier along the Yellowstone he had "got away with Stanley and would be able to swing clear of Terry." Aside from Custer's faulty memory of how he had been able to get away from Stanley in 1874, the episode indicates an ultimate in ingratitude, that within the hour after learning that his command had been restored, Custer should be openly planning to flaunt the authority of the one man responsible for getting it returned to him.

And so at last the campaign was underway, the greatest combination of forces ever sent out to do battle with Indians. General Terry's column was the first to march. It departed from Fort Abraham Lincoln on the morning of May 17. Reveille had been at three, and the column, 1,207 strong, swung out at Terry's signal at five o'clock, through wisps of cold fog which still clung to the ground. While the infantry and the train headed directly from the encampment area down the road that mounted the river bluff and headed west, Colonel Custer led the 7th Cavalry through the fort and across the parade so that wives and their men might see each other briefly once again. Then the regimental band tootled away at the inevitable "Garry Owen," and then the almost equally inevitable "The Girl I Left Behind Me." The last company passed out of the fort; the music dwindled in the distance, and the regiment passed over the edge of the bluff and was gone.

However, rank has its privileges, and Elizabeth Custer did not flutter her handkerchief in farewell that morning but rode along with her husband, to remain with him through the first night's bivouac and return the next morning with the regiment's paymaster. The presence of the paymaster on the first day's march had not caused any great rejoicing. Custer had arbitrarily held out the pay of the enlisted men even though it was overdue because, as self-appointed guardian of his men's morals, he had wanted to keep their pockets empty until they were a full day's march from the fleshpots of Bismarck. He undoubtedly prevented some morning-after headaches, but the episode did not increase his popularity. Later, some of the money was found blowing among the litter of the Little Bighorn battlefield.

The main strength of Terry's column was the 7th Cavalry. As late as the middle of February, the General had been pleading for the return of three companies that had been sent back to the South on duty; they had finally been transferred back and all twelve companies were now present. In addition to the cavalry, there were three companies of infantry, a special infantry detachment with a battery of three Gatling guns, forty-five Indian scouts, and 190 civilians: teamsters, guides, packers, herders, blacksmiths, interpreters, wheelwrights, and all the rest of the varied crew of craftsmen and specialized talents needed to keep an army operating on the frontier. Among these civilians was Boston, youngest of the Custer brothers, signed on as a forage master and hoping the dry plains air would help a bronchial condition, and nephew Armstrong ("Autie") Reed, seventeen, carried on the roster as a herder but really his uncle's guest on a glorious outing.

The column moved almost due westward, along the route followed by the Northern Pacific today, but then only a survey line, until it reached the Yellowstone River. It was to push up the Yellowstone until it met the column of Colonel John Gibbon moving downriver. The forces would be supplied by a Missouri River steamboat, the *Far West*.

Affairs went almost exactly as they had been outlined in the Plan of Operations, and the two forces met near the mouth of Rosebud Creek, whose waters flow into the Yellowstone from the Powder River country to the south. There was no sign or word of General Crook who was somewhere to the south, presumably driving the Indians toward the forces on the Yellowstone. As a matter of fact, Crook's course had brought him against the Indians, but he was doing very little driving.

3. "COME ON, DAKOTAS, IT'S A GOOD DAY TO DIE"

As he had in March, Crook moved north in May from Fort Fetterman, following the empty Bozeman Trail. At the site of Fort Reno, he found little to indicate that this had once been a busy Army outpost; in their eagerness to wipe out all vestiges of military occupation, the Indians had razed even the cemetery so that not a headboard remained standing. Fort Philip Kearny, which Colonel Carrington had built up from nothing, had returned to nothing, and those who had ridden out to die with Captain Fetterman lay in graves no longer marked.

Crook led a powerful force: five companies of the 2nd Cavalry, ten of the 3rd Cavalry, two of the 4th Infantry, and three companies of the 9th Infantry, totaling about 1,050 officers and men. There were also the usual civilian teamsters, packers, and other auxiliaries. Crow Indian scouts, 180 of them, arrived to join the force on June 14 when it was camped north of the site of Fort Kearny, at the junction of the two branches of Goose Creek. Two hours later, 86 Shoshones followed them. Crook drew up this troops in a regimental front on the flat now covered by the northern end of the city of Sheridan, Wyoming; holding his forces in formation he welcomed his red allies and then treated them to a feast.

Several streams flow northward to join the Yellowstone through the country where the nontreaty Indians ranged. The most important ones, from west to east, are Rosebud Creek, Tongue River, and Powder River. Of them all, the Powder River is the longest and has the most extensive set of tributaries, and for that reason gave its name to the entire region. Another stream to the west of these, the Bighorn River, had its own importance. Its upper waters lay west of the Big Horn Mountains, in Crow Indian territory, but its lower course to the Yellowstone was the boundary between the unceded Sioux territory and the Crow lands to the west. It had a tributary, the Little Bighorn, which came in through the unceded country from a southeasterly direction to join it. The Little Bighorn would acquire some considerable fame in the weeks immediately ahead.

Scouts brought in word that the Sioux were probably on Rosebud Creek to the north, and Crook at once began making ready. His wagon train was left behind with the civilians and a small infantry guard in camp; supplies were stripped to a minimum and put on pack mules. To make for greater speed, the infantrymen were also mounted on mules, although the gain was not as much as it might have been because many of the unhappy fellows knew almost nothing about riding. It would seem that it might have been advantageous to have given them some training before the eve of battle—but the Army has always been the Army. On the morning of June 16, almost 1,300 men, including the Indian scouts, rode out to meet the Sioux.

The hostile Indians were completely aware of what Crook was doing, for their scouts watched all his movements. They were optimistic about their prospects in battle, because only a week earlier they had held a Sun Dance in which Sitting Bull, after permitting fifty pieces of flesh to be cut from his arms and chest and undergoing other tests of fortitude, had had a vision of soldiers falling into the Indian camp. It was interpreted as a clear omen that the soldiers would be defeated, and the warriors consequently were eager for battle. So eager, in fact, that a large force of Sioux and Cheyennes traveled during the night of the sixteenth to come to grips with the Army forces. That same night, Crook's column had made its camp in a wide, grassy spot in the valley of the Rosebud in southern Montana, sleeping on the ground in the open

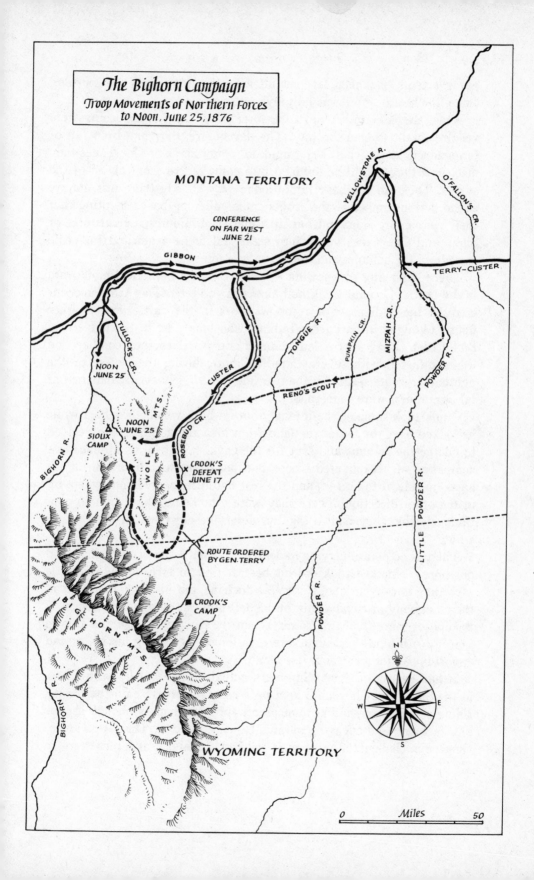

The Bighorn Campaign
Troop Movements of Northern Forces
to Noon, June 25, 1876

MONTANA TERRITORY

CONFERENCE ON FAR WEST JUNE 21

GIBBON

YELLOWSTONE R.

O'FALLON'S CR.

TERRY–CUSTER

TULLOCKS CR.

NOON JUNE 25

TONGUE R.

PUMPKIN CR.

MIZPAH CR.

POWDER R.

CUSTER

RENO'S SCOUT

BIGHORN R.

SIOUX CAMP

NOON JUNE 25

ROSEBUD CR.

WOLF MTS.

CROOK'S DEFEAT JUNE 17

LITTLE POWDER R.

ROUTE ORDERED BY GEN. TERRY

CROOK'S CAMP

POWDER R.

BIGHORN R.

BIGHORN MTS.

N
W E
S

WYOMING TERRITORY

0   Miles   50

because tents had been left behind with the wagons. When morning came, the hostile force was only five miles away.

When the column set out after breakfast, the Indian scouts were very reluctant to lead the way. The day before, they had been full of braggadocio about what they would do to any Sioux or Cheyennes they met; now they had to be prodded into going out to scout ahead of the troops. They did not have far to look; very shortly there was gunfire ahead and a number of the scouts came galloping back, shouting that there were many Sioux in front. In a matter of minutes, a great force of Sioux and Cheyennes swept into sight and made a spirited full-scale assault on the column, and the battle was joined.

There is no way of knowing exactly what the numerical odds were in the battle. General Cook had almost 1,300 men. The Army account credited the Indians with 1,500 warriors in the battle, and another figure, obtained in part from Indians who took part in the fight, says that Chief Crazy Horse led about 1,000 warriors into combat and was reinforced with several hundred more during the course of the fighting. It would seem that the two sides were fairly evenly matched as far as numbers were concerned.

Crook took some of the infantry onto a bluff which they held while he looked over the lay of the land from his vantage point. He decided to charge the Indians and sent for the cavalry, but in his absence two companies of his mounted troops had been sent to a high hill on the opposite side of the creek, and the rest had disappeared somewhere off in the other direction. There they were attacked so hard and so continuously that they had to take up defensive positions on the edge of a bluff.

There is no point in trying to describe the battle in terms of lines and positions. General Crook did his best at first to form a line of battle according to conventional Civil War doctrine, but his attempts to recall the main body of cavalry, out on his left and out of sight, produced no results for more than two hours. When the cavalry at last was able to join up with him, the Indians were no longer assaulting his front, and opportunities for an attack were gone.

It had been a mad, swirling fight, actually three battles within one, as the Sioux and Cheyennes kept up a constant pressure on the troops, riding among them, and at some points splitting them into small groups of a few men and engaging in hand-to-hand fighting. There was an incongruous element in the scene: wild plums and crabapples were in full bloom and their petals, shaken loose by the pounding passage of hundreds of horsemen, drifted constantly down, while their fragrance found its way even to men enveloped in dust and powder smoke.

Crazy Horse, the Oglala chief, was in the forefront of the fighting, exhorting his warriors to greater feats with his famous war-cry, "Come on, Dakotas,* it's a good day to die." At one point, when the Sioux started to fall back in the beginning of a retreat, Crazy Horse, with several other chiefs, rode among them, encouraging and heartening them, and they returned to the battle. Neither side would have to walk with heads bent in shame later, for bravery was in the air. At one point, the Crow and Shoshone scouts engaged in savage hand-to-hand combat with a group of Sioux while nearby soldiers had to hold their fire and watch because it was next to impossible to distinguish the copper skin of ally from that of foe in the whirling melee.

For the Army force, there would have been no chance to extricate itself, no opportunity to withdraw from the battle if it had so attempted. If the troops had panicked or broken anywhere along the line, the result would have been annihilation. The Sioux were carrying the fight to the soldiers in a very un-Indian manner; usually they were no desperate threat to resolute men who maintained a stout defense. But eventually the individualistic nature of the Sioux and Cheyenne warriors began to assert itself. Early in the afternoon they started to break off fighting and to drift away. It was not that they had at last become intimidated by the forces opposed to them; theirs was a simpler motive. One of the warriors explained it later, "They were tired and hungry, so they went home."

As the enemy began to withdraw, General Crook made a last attempt to achieve a decisive victory. His white scouts had told him that there was a large Sioux village about eight miles down the Rosebud. He had, in fact, been making ready to move on it in the morning when Crazy

* "Dakota," meaning "allies," is the Sioux's own name for themselves. The more common "Sioux" is an etymological monstrosity, the truncation of Nadouessioux, which in turn is a French form of the Chippewa Nadoue-is-iw, meaning little snake, and hence, enemy, the Chippewa appellation for their foes, the Dakotas (the Iroquois of the East were the big snakes). Although whites also used the word Dakota quite frequently, Sioux was by far the most common term, and for the sake of consistency has been used exclusively in this book.

The picture might be muddied by adding that Crazy Horse did not say "Dakota." The Sioux nation was a large one, and had three distinct dialects. The Santee Sioux of the eastern prairies, the Yanktons, and the western Teton Sioux, respectively called themselves Dakotas, Nakotas and Lakotas. So, Crazy Horse on the Rosebud: "Come on, Lakotas, it's a good day to die."

Horse caught him first and gave him something more substantial to cope with than a village whose inhabitants would have included a large proportion of women, children, and old men. Now, at midday, he sent Captain Anson Mills with eight companies of cavalry sweeping down the valley to overwhelm the village lying ahead.

But after the force was on its way, Crook looked more carefully at the valley of Rosebud Creek lying before him. It was narrow and quite steep and hemmed in, and everything considered, it would be an ideal place for an enemy force to ambush Mills's detachment. The General thereupon sent his aide with a single orderly dashing down the valley after Mills, who was finally overtaken after a chase of several miles. Mills sensibly led his command up out of the valley and back to the main force on higher ground. The move very possibly did save him from an ambush. At the same time, it enabled him to catch some of the Sioux from the rear as he circled behind them on his return. One thing it did not do was save a Sioux village from destruction, because Crook's scouts had been wrong and the village Mills had been hurrying to attack did not exist.

That night Crook camped where he had the night before, near the spot where the battle had begun. The dead were buried in the dark, and all traces of the graves obliterated. The next morning the bruised column retraced its way the forty miles to the camp on Goose Creek. Crook's official report claimed victory: "My troops beat these Indians on a field of their own choosing and drove them in utter rout from it, as far as the proper care of my wounded and prudence would justify." But Sheridan observed that if it was a victory, it was one without results since Crook had not followed it up. As a matter of fact, Crook in his own heart considered it a defeat, too, and it rankled all his life as the one real licking he had received at the hands of Indians. He insisted ever after that if the battle had gone as he had planned, if his orders had been obeyed and the cavalry had come up when he had summoned it, the Indians would have been defeated—and how many other commanders have made the same lament!

But there was more to it than that. The Army forces had fought well and there had been no serious mistakes in tactics. Crook failed to recognize that he had been up against something new in Indian warfare. These warriors had fought with a purpose and maintained a constant pressure completely different from their charge-and-run-away tactics of the past. It appeared that a new spirit was animating them, causing them to submerge, at last, their self-defeating individualism in common effort for the good of all. Unfortunately, the hour was very late and the red men had already lost too many wars.

While Crook lay glumly in camp awaiting reinforcements, the Sioux and Cheyennes filled the countryside about, harassing his force in every possible way. They set fire to the grass, tried to run off the horse and mule herds, shot at small details whose duties took them away from the camp, even came close enough to fire into the camp at long range. Crook's force remained completely immobilized for more than a month.

4. "NOW, CUSTER, DON'T BE GREEDY"

During the time General Crook had been moving toward his battle on the Rosebud, the combined forces of Terry and Gibbon were going ahead with operations. A supply base had been established on the Yellowstone at the mouth of the Powder River, and was provisioned by the Missouri River steamboat, *Far West*. It was the opinion of most officers that the hostiles would be found on either Rosebud Creek or the lower Bighorn River, and so it was decided that the logical first step in the campaign was to look into the possibility that they might instead be on either the Tongue or Powder River.

Major Marcus A. Reno, second in command of the 7th Cavalry, was sent with six companies of the regiment on an eight-day scout. His orders were to go up the Powder River to its head, cross over to the upper Tongue, and return down that stream to the Yellowstone. Major Reno for some reason chose to disobey his orders. Instead of returning down the Tongue River, he led his command across the valley of the Tongue and on to Rosebud Creek, which he reached on June 17, the same day Crook was being turned back by Crazy Horse forty miles to the south. However, Reno had no way of knowing of Crook's nearness, and turned north, following the Rosebud back to the Yellowstone. Terry had wanted to stay clear of the Rosebud for the time being for fear the Sioux might be alerted, but Reno saw no Indians. However, he did find the trail of many Indians, but he had not followed it to learn where it led.

General Terry was now almost certain that the Sioux had crossed over from the Rosebud to the stream known as the Little Bighorn, a tributary of the Bighorn River. His strategy, in that case, was obvi-

ous to him: he would send Gibbon up the Bighorn and the Little
Bighorn while Custer and the 7th Cavalry circled around and came
down the Little Bighorn from the south; the hostiles would be caught
between the two forces. Gibbon's column started on its way at midday
on June 21 from the camp opposite the mouth of the Rosebud, headed
up the Yellowstone for the mouth of the Bighorn River fifty miles away.
Colonel Gibbon and his cavalry commander, Major James Brisbin,
remained behind for a council of war; they, with General Terry, would
travel on the *Far West* to catch up with the column.

Terry outlined his strategy at a meeting with Custer, Gibbon, and
Brisbin on board the *Far West* on the evening of the twenty-first, as
the stern-wheeler lay tied up at the bank near the mouth of the Rosebud with the current of the Yellowstone gurgling past her hull. Custer
was to proceed up the Rosebud with his regiment till he found the
trail Reno had discovered a few days earlier. If he found that the trail
turned west and led across the divide toward the Little Bighorn, "as it
appears to be almost certain that it will be found," he was not to
follow it but to continue south up the Rosebud, even well beyond the
headwaters of that stream, before swinging west to the Little Bighorn
and down that stream toward the north again.

In his entire movement, Custer was to travel at a rate of speed
which would bring him, as nearly as he could estimate it, to the valley
of the Little Bighorn from the south at the same time Gibbon was
entering it from the north, so that any hostiles present would be
caught between the two columns and forced to surrender or be defeated in battle. General Terry laid off Custer's estimated daily
marches on the map with compasses to make sure the plan was feasible.

Custer was also ordered to scout the upper waters of a stream called
Tullock's Creek which flows from southeast to northwest into the
Bighorn; Gibbon's scouts would examine the lower part of the stream.
Crow Indian scouts had suggested that the hostile camp might possibly be on this stream. In order to learn the result of Custer's exam-
ination of Tullock's Creek as quickly as possible, General Terry sent
one of his own scouts, George Hernandeen, along with the 7th Cavalry;
he was to bring the news across country when the time came.

Custer had boasted long and often that the 7th Cavalry was capable
of whipping any and all Indians on the plains. The other officers at the
meeting were apparently not quite so sanguine about the invincibility
of the regiment and its leader. Terry suggested to Custer that it might

be wise to strengthen his column, at the expense of Gibbon's, by attaching Major Brisbin's cavalry to the 7th Regiment for the operation. Custer demurred; the 7th was such a closely knit outfit that reinforcements in the form of a strange unit would add nothing to its strength. It was then proposed that the 7th Cavalry be given more firepower by sending along with it the column's three Gatling guns. Again Custer objected. The guns would "embarrass" him; the regiment would be more than strong enough without them.

After the conference on the steamboat, Custer went ashore and called a meeting of his officers. The other officers remained aboard the *Far West*, which would soon be taking them upstream to rejoin Gibbon's column. Terry suggested to Brisbin, who was leaning over the rail and looking glumly into the river water coiling by, that he did not seem to have much faith in Colonel Custer. None at all, Brisbin replied, none at all.

The 7th left about noon on June 22. A review had been ordered by Custer, with General Terry, Colonel Gibbon, and Major Brisbin (Brisbin and Gibbon both held brevet ranks as generals) as reviewing officers, with Custer beside them, presenting his beloved regiment. Custer was on a sorrel horse named Vic; he wore a fringed buckskin suit in the best Western style with a double-breasted blouse with military buttons, and a light-gray, low-crowned hat with broad brim.

A shrill of the massed trumpets of the entire regiment announced the beginning of the review, with Major Reno leading the march-by. (The notes of "Garry Owen" were missing; the band as well as Custer's hounds were being left behind.) Custer sat proudly observing what he had wrought. However, his pleasure was diluted somewhat when the pack train went by. The regiment was leaving its wagons behind and it was rusty at the business of lashing on a pack saddle, consequently some of the results left a bit to be desired. Terry was a kindly man and his criticisms were gentle, but Custer flushed.

The last of the regiment passed, the dust settled, and Terry conferred briefly with Custer. Then the two shook hands, and Terry said, "God bless you." The colonel reined his horse around, ready to spur off and gallop to the head of the regiment. Colonel Gibbon called to him, "Now, Custer, don't be greedy. Wait for us." It was not a jocular remark; sharp-nosed, dour John Gibbon was not a man given to badinage, and certainly not at this moment when he was griped by an intestinal upset. Gibbon, who had been campaigning on the plains when Custer was still playing marbles, well knew the reputation of the cavalry leader for impetuousness and made his admonition, as he said afterward, in the hope that it might restrain the colonel of the 7th.

"Now, Custer, don't be greedy. Wait for us," Gibbon had called, and Custer turned in his saddle, waved gaily, and replied, "No, I won't." And with this cryptic reply, he galloped off.

The regiment continued its march through the twenty-third and twenty-fourth. It mustered about six hundred men, and had with it forty-four Crow and Arikara scouts, and twenty civilian guides, packers and interpreters. Boston Custer and nephew Autie Reed were present; Custer had had them transferred from the quartermaster department so they would not miss the fun. The trail that Reno had found was located and the regiment continued along it, passing through abandoned campsites that indicated a large number of hostiles had been there. The regiment traveled carefully, trying to raise as little dust as possible, with bugle calls forbidden. It had gone into camp on the evening of June 24 under a steep bluff when the scouts came back to report that the trail left the valley of the Rosebud just ahead and, as had been expected, went west across the divide into the valley of the Little Bighorn.

Custer supporters have defended their hero ever since 1876 against the charge that he willfully disobeyed orders. If he was not willful, he was decidedly contemptuous and highhanded in his disregard of the plan of operations that had been outlined on board the *Far West* and which, as written orders, he carried in his pocket.

Those orders, for one thing, directed him very explicitly to "thoroughly examine the upper part of Tullock's Creek" and to try to send a scout through to Gibbon's column with information on the result. He completely ignored Tullock's Creek; no orders were given to his chief of scouts to send men to look it over, and the white scout, George Hernandeen, whom Terry had sent with Custer specifically to carry word of the result to Gibbon's column, continued along with the regiment. That there were no Indians on Tullock's Creek is beside the point; it was a willful—call it a cavalier—disregard of orders. And it probably had its effect on events, because General Terry held Gibbon's column at the mouth of Tullock's Creek for more than a day, awaiting the arrival of the message from Custer which never came. If there had not been this delay, subsequent events might well have been somewhat different.

Now, after the scouts brought back word that the trail led over the divide into the valley of the Little Bighorn, Custer once again ignored his orders. Those orders were clear and unequivocal: "Should [the trail] be found, as it appears to be almost certain that it will be found, to turn toward the Little Big Horn he [General Terry] thinks that you should still proceed southward, perhaps as far as the headwaters of the Tongue, and then turn toward the Little Big Horn, . . ." Nothing could be clearer—and do not be misled by that "he thinks"; when a superior officer "thinks" or "suggests" or "believes," it is still an order. Nevertheless, Custer called his officers together in the dark and outlined a completely different plan of operation to them. During the night, they would follow the trail across the divide, a low range called the Wolf Mountains then and the Rosebud Mountains today. When daylight came, the regiment would remain concealed in the wooded and rocky high country, and would lie low all day (June 25) while the scouts located the hostile camp, and would then strike at dawn on the twenty-sixth.

The weary regiment was routed out, and the march resumed, with nothing but the stars for light, and they provided little illumination when the trail passed down deep ravines or under trees. Troopers gave their horses their heads and dozed intermittently at first, but confusion spread and soon there was no napping as the regiment, in single file, resorted to a clanking of tin cups to maintain contact through the complexity of ridges and ravines. Colonel Custer, the tireless, himself admitted the futility of the night march at last, and called an end to it about 2 A.M., when the regiment settled down for some rest.

The scouts had continued on ahead, and by daybreak had climbed to a high point on the divide between the Rosebud and the Little Bighorn known as the Crow's Nest. Lieutenant Charles A. Varnum, chief of scouts, had gone with the Crow scouts to the top of the peak, which overlooked the valley of the Little Bighorn for many miles. The Crows explained that their warriors used the high point when they were out to steal horses from the Sioux because from it the early daylight revealed the smoke of the morning cooking fires of any camp in the valley. This morning, as dawn spread over the valley, the Little Bighorn was so far away that it was revealed only by the trees and bushes along its banks outlining its course, merely a dark line meandering through the dusty wrinkled plain. But the sharp eyes of the Indians and of the two guides, Charley Reynolds and the half-breed Mitch

Bouyer, saw something in addition, the indefinable stirring of a dark spot by the river that their trained eyes told them was an immense herd of ponies, and along the river they were able to identify, even at that distance, a very large Indian camp.

They tried to point out the hostile camp to Lieutenant Varnum. "Look for worms," they told him, but strain his eyes as hard as he would, he could not make out any of the pulsing movement that marked the slow milling of the pony herd, much less the village itself. He had ridden for seventy hours without sleep, and, as Varnum admitted afterward, his eyes were sore and not much good for long distance. He wrote a message to the commanding officer, reporting what he had seen and been told; while he awaited for the dispatch to be taken back, he noted that the smoke rising from the regiment's campfires could be seen without trouble ten miles away. The Crow scouts were very angry that Custer would even have allowed fires at such a time and place.

The regiment concealed itself in a ravine about three miles short of the Crow's Nest while Custer rode on ahead to have a look for himself at the Sioux village. Although he climbed the Crow's Nest and used glasses, he was unable to make out any pony herd or village, for by that time the sun had come over the hills and cast an obscuring haze over the valley. He returned and told his officers he did not think there was any hostile camp there.

During the confused night march, one of the mule packs had become loose, and a sack and a box of hardtack had dropped off. As soon as the disappearance was discovered, a sergeant was sent back to recover the lost articles. He found them several miles back—but he also found several Sioux warriors sitting around, examining the contents of the sack. The Indians rode off when they saw the sergeant, but later, several more were observed watching the regiment. If surprise were planned, it was too late.

Custer decided to attack at once. The Army command was convinced that the Indians would attempt to run if confronted by a military force of any competence. In accord with this belief, Custer now made ready to pursue and bring the hostiles to battle before they could escape. However, by his self-willed action, he was going into action a day earlier than General Terry's plan called for—which meant he would fight without Gibbon's support. The cost of Custer's disregard of his orders was going to be high—very high—and the bill was coming due very soon.

Giving up all further attempts at concealment, Custer led the regiment from the ravine to the divide where the land sloped down into the valley of the Little Bighorn and there, a few minutes after noon, he halted and made his dispositions for action. The usual division of the regiment into battalions had been abolished during the march, and company commanders had answered directly to the commanding officer. Now Colonel Custer drew a short way apart with his adjutant, Lieutenant William W. Cooke, whose Canadian birth and imposing side whiskers had led Custer to dub him "The Queen's Own." With Cooke making notations in his memorandum book, Custer quickly divided the regiment into battalions.

One battalion, composed of Companies H, K, and D, was commanded by Captain Frederick Benteen, commander of H Company and senior captain of the regiment. A second battalion, also three companies strong—A, G, and M—was given to Major Reno, the only field officer, other than Custer, in the regiment. Five companies Custer retained under his personal command: Company C, his own brother, Captain Thomas Custer commanding; Company L of his brother-in-law, Lieutenant James Calhoun; and, to complete the list, for these units and their commanders would very soon achieve immortality, Companies E, F, and I, led by Lieutenant Algernon Smith, Captain George W. Yates, and Captain Miles W. Keogh. The one remaining unit, B Company, was detailed to guard the pack train, and each of the other companies was required to provide six privates and one noncom to lead the pack mules.

It took less than ten minutes to complete this task. The regiment stood at the small upper waters of a stream since named Reno Creek, which flows pretty much due west into the Little Bighorn about a dozen miles, as the crow flies, from where the regiment paused. The land between was furrowed and broken, cut by ravines and creeks, and wrinkled by hillocks and ridges, for this is country where the last fringes of the Great Plains are breaking against the mountains.

Colonel Custer ordered Captain Benteen with his three companies, about 125 men, to proceed to the southwest, angling away to the left from the line of march of the rest of the regiment which would follow the creek to the river. Benteen was to investigate some bluffs three or four miles away, then go on to the first valley beyond, attacking any Indians he might find, and report back to the commanding officer. Benteen signaled his command forward and almost immediately disappeared from sight because of the uneven ground. But in the next few minutes messengers were twice sent after him to amplify his orders: if he found no Indians in the first valley, he was to go on until he found a second one, and then a third.

Custer and Reno continued on their way toward the river, Reno and his battalion on the left or south bank of the creek, Custer and the other five companies on the opposite side, the pack train trailing behind. Their course was taking them, without their knowing it yet, almost directly toward the camp that had been sighted by the scouts from the Crow's Nest at daybreak; the creek emptied into the Little Bighorn only two or three miles below the lower end of the hostile camp. And the scouts had been right, it was a big camp.

It was, in fact, without doubt the largest Indian encampment that has ever assembled on the western plains. Plains Indians seldom gathered in great numbers because their huge pony herds quickly ate off the grass over a large area, while supplying game for the humans quickly hunted out the region for miles around the camp. But these were extraordinary times. Crazy Horse and his warriors had thrown Crook back only a few days earlier, and were still elated and ready to fight any other force the Army might send against them. Thousands of Indians had left the agencies, determined to fight after having seen their protests against the rape of the Black Hills ignored. All had joined together, ready for any soldiers who might come, and certain they could whip them. It was perhaps the last time in American history that a force of Indians stood ready to meet the United States Army with confidence of winning.

The camp lay on the west side of the river; from northernmost to southernmost tepee was probably three miles and in places it was half a mile wide. There were some 1,500 lodges, and many wickiups or temporary brush shelters. At the north lay the camp circle of the Cheyennes; the Hunkpapas of Gall, Crow King, and Sitting Bull had set up their tepees at the most southerly end of the great camp. Between the two were camp circles of other bands of the Sioux nation: Miniconjous under Chief Hump, Sans Arcs led by Chief Spotted Eagle, Oglallas under the great Crazy Horse and Low Dog and Big Road, and smaller contingents of Blackfeet Sioux, Two Kettles, Yanktons, Santees who had not forgotten their war in Minnesota, and even a few lodges of Arapahoes. There were, by the best later estimates, between twelve and fifteen thousand Indians in the encampment, of whom at least four and possibly five thousand were warriors.

As the regiment, less the three companies Benteen had led off into the broken badlands, and the lagging guard of the pack train, proceeded along the creek, it came to a solitary tepee, standing among circles of yellow grass left by the lodges of a village only recently moved. Inside, on a low scaffolding, was the body of a Sioux warrior, presumably one who had died in the battle with Crook—although Custer's force had no inkling of Crook's setback. The Arikara scouts set the tepee afire with considerable glee.

During this time, something else was discovered that interested Custer much more, a heavy cloud of dust about five miles away, on the other side of the Little Bighorn, and a short way downstream, the sign of a Sioux village with its pony herd, or possibly of fleeing Sioux. The general conviction that the Indians would flee when opposition appeared now seemed well-founded, for a civilian interpreter, Frank Girard, sitting his horse on a higher knoll apart from the regiment, called, "Here are your Indians—running like devils." Girard had sighted about forty warriors in the direction of the river and running away.

Custer at once ordered the Indian scouts in pursuit but they refused, even when the commander ordered them to turn in their horses and rifles in an effort to shame them. He then gave an order to Cooke which the adjutant rode over and transmitted to Reno, "General Custer directs that you take as fast a gait as you deem prudent, and charge afterward, and you will be supported by the whole outfit." A considerable number of men heard the order given, and although they disagreed afterward on whether Cooke had said "charge the village," or "charge the Indians," or "make for the dust," or some other wording, all were unanimous in agreeing that he had said that Reno's battalion would be "supported by the whole outfit." And with this attack order, the most famous Indian battle of the West was under way.

5. "FOR GOD'S SAKE, BENTEEN, HELP ME. I'VE LOST HALF MY MEN"

A brief look at Custer's troop dispositions may be helpful. The commander of the 7th Cavalry Regiment had not only put himself in a position where he would have to fight the hostiles alone (a situation he probably did not regret because there would be no sharing of glory for the victory he was certain he would win), but he was entering battle with a tactical ineptitude that would have been inexcusable in the most junior of his officers. He was completely aware that a very large hostile force was somewhere near at hand: his scouts had seen a large camp from the Crow's Nest and he himself had followed the trail beaten by many Indians across the divide into this valley. Yet, in the face of this evidence that he would soon be engaged in battle with a strong enemy, he had done what was almost militarily indefensible under all but exceptional circumstances: he had split his forces.

And he had split them not once, but into four parts. Under his own command, in five companies, he had about 225 men. Major Reno had 112 soldiers, augmented by about 25 Indian scouts, 3 white scouts, and a Negro interpreter. Benteen had about 125 men, and 130 soldiers— the escort company and men detailed from other companies to lead pack mules—were with the pack train. Moreover, not the slightest provision was made for coordination between these four elements. At the moment Reno was ordered into action, Benteen was ten or a dozen miles away to the southwest, and getting further away all the time on orders to scout one valley after another for Indians. The pack train, with most of the ammunition that would be needed in a heavy engagement, was several miles behind the rest of the force. No plan of battle existed to tie these scattered forces together, no instructions had been communicated by the commanding officer to the commanders of the several units except the vague one to Reno: ". . . charge afterward, and you will be supported by the whole outfit." Luck alone could prevent trouble if the regiment ran into determined resistance when it was in such poor disposition. But Custer had depended too much on luck, and the lady was not riding at his elbow this day.

Major Reno and his battalion had about three miles to go to the Little Bighorn; they reached and crossed it about 2:30 P.M. The ad-

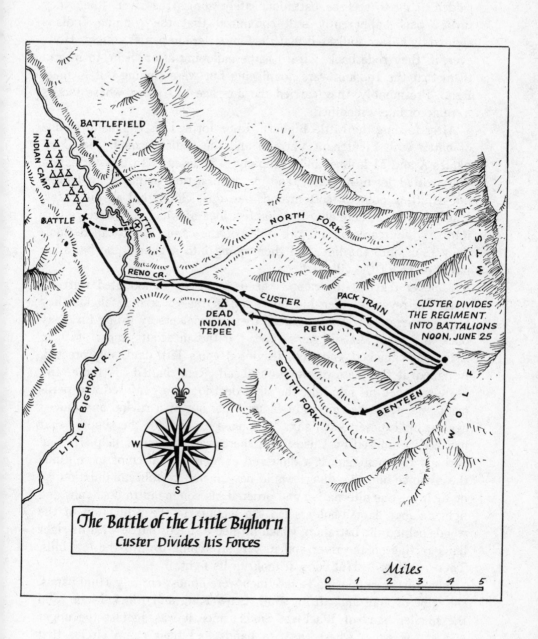

BATTLEFIELD
X

INDIAN CAMP

BATTLE X

BATTLE X

RENO CR.

NORTH FORK

MTS.

LITTLE BIGHORN R.

DEAD INDIAN TEPEE

CUSTER

RENO

PACK TRAIN

CUSTER DIVIDES
THE REGIMENT
INTO BATTALIONS
NOON, JUNE 25

SOUTH FORK

BENTEEN

WOLF

N
W   E
S

The Battle of the Little Bighorn
Custer Divides his Forces

Miles
0   1   2   3   4   5

jutant, Cooke, and Captain Keogh, Commander of I Company, had ridden along to see the battalion safely across the river; then they turned back, apparently still convinced that the running Indians sighted by Girard indicated that the Sioux were in panicky flight. However, as they rode back, Girard came galloping after them, to inform them that the Indians were not fleeing but were coming out to meet Reno. Presumably, they carried the message to Custer, whose tactics were accordingly modified.

After fording the Little Bighorn, Reno formed his command in line of battle with Lieutenant Varnum and the Indian scouts, and Companies A and M in line, and Company G in reserve. In this formation they trotted down the valley, and for the first time actually saw tepees, but a jutting point of cottonwoods and dust clouds hid all but a few lodges and gave them only the slightest idea of what they were getting into. As they came within two miles of the camp, Reno called Company G up into the line, and then, going into a gallop, the battalion swept on to hit the village.

It never reached the camp. Ahead, hundreds of mounted warriors were half-revealed, then hidden again, in the thick dust clouds they were deliberately raising to screen their movements by riding furiously back and forth. At the same time, the Indian scouts, most of them Arikaras, panicked and fled, leaving Reno's left flank unprotected. Appalled at the mass of warriors ahead, Reno halted his force, and as he searched his mind for the right decision in a confused and perilous moment, a large group of Sioux came out of a ravine and moved against his exposed left flank. He looked around for the support that had been promised by Custer, but there was no sign of help. He had perhaps 115 men against a thousand or more. To attempt to continue the advance into the village would have meant certain annihilation, so he took the one alternative and ordered his command to dismount and fight on foot. Horse-holders led the mounts to the protection of the woods behind the battalion, which formed a line of battle with its right flank resting on the river and its left stretching toward the low hills. There, against fearful odds, it took up its fight.

The warriors opposing Reno's men were almost entirely Hunkpapas, the tribe of Gall and Sitting Bull, Crow King and Black Moon, and the smaller band of Blackfeet Sioux, since it was against the upper end of the camp where the two bands had their camp circles that Reno's charge had been directed. Indians charged and darted away and drove in again, out of the obscuring cloud of dust, putting irresistible pressure against the thin line of troops. Sioux were working their way around the left flank of the dismounted line and appearing in its rear, and Reno, fearful that they would accomplish their favorite trick of stampeding his horses, sent Company G back to the timber to guard the mounts. The two companies remaining, A and M, had to spread out to fill the gap, but there just was not enough substance to take up the slack. The left flank was pushed back, and the Sioux galloped around in force to the battalion's rear.

Up to this point the battalion had lost no men, thanks to the common Indian failing of being more interested in shooting rapidly than accurately (two unhappy troopers were carried into the Sioux lines by their frantic and ungovernable horses on the first charge but miraculously escaped, though wounded). On the other hand, the soldiers were not inflicting much damage, either. The 7th Cavalry, despite its reputation as the *ne plus ultra* of Indian-fighting regiments, was not drawn to a sharp edge when it started the campaign. Its ranks were filled with recruits who were now in their first battle. For thirty to forty percent of the men in the companies, this was their first service. A sergeant in Company A of Reno's battalion later testified that about a third of his company, and about half of G Company, were recruits. "The new men had had very little training," he said; "they were very poor horsemen and would fire at random. They were brave enough, but they had not had the time nor opportunity to make soldiers. Some were not fit to take into action." But, fit or not, these men were courageously but futilely banging away, firing as fast as they could but with little attempt to aim while their limited supply of ammunition dwindled rapidly.

Major Reno recognized that his position was rapidly becoming impossible to hold. Behind him, in the timber where he had sent the horses, the terrain offered better possibilities for defense. He ordered a change of front and the battalion wheeled backward on its right flank as a hinge. Now the line stretched across the neck of a loop in the river, so that both flanks rested on the stream. The fight went on from the new position for another half hour or so, but the improvement was only temporary. Undergrowth was heavy, making it difficult to maintain contact between men. Sioux warriors were infiltrating the lines, and, like woodland Indians, were firing from behind trees and bushes from all sides and the rear. Both men and horses were now being struck by bullets. Reno saw that his position once again had become untenable, and gave the order to stand to horses.

The command was not given by trumpet, and in the noise and confusion, only those near heard the major. Although the order was passed on, it never reached some of the men. Those who had heard formed up in a clearing, and Reno gave the order to mount. Sioux were bursting through the woods into the clearing; at that instant, a bullet caught the scout, Bloody Knife. The Arikara, Custer's favorite scout, had stood firm when the rest of the Indian scouts with the battalion had melted away, and had continued to fight alongside Reno. The bullet that killed him hit him in the head, spattering blood and brains in the Major's face. At almost the same instant a soldier was hit and fell from the saddle with a loud cry. The events were momentarily too much for Reno, his mind stretched taut by the demands of leadership and decision-making in a situation that had worsened every moment since he had first led his command against the village. He barked out the order to dismount, recovered himself and gave the order to mount again, and led the column out into the open where it formed up hastily. Then, with Major Reno leading, the column forced its way through the mass of Indians and headed for the ford it had crossed an hour— and a lifetime—ago.

Losses had been heavy. Seventeen living were left behind when the battalion withdrew, besides several dead; two of the seventeen died very shortly as they tried to catch the fleeing column. Lieutenant Donald McIntosh, commander of G Company, had delayed to rally his men, many of whom had not heard the order to withdraw; consequently, he left the woods in the rear of the column and was surrounded and cut down. Guide Charley Reynolds also made a run to catch the battalion and fell from his horse with a bullet in his chest— Lonesome Charley Reynolds, the shy, soft-spoken scout who did the seemingly impossible so often that he had become almost a legendary figure even while still alive.

Lieutenant Varnum, lagging behind at the beginning, spurred his horse to the head of the column, shouting, "For God's sake, men, don't run; we've got to go back and save the wounded." The voice that replied beside him was that of Reno, "Sir, I am in command here."

The Sioux were pressing so hard the retreat was turning into a rout. Moreover, the hundreds of Sioux racing along beside the column were all on its right side, exerting pressure that was pushing it inexorably toward the river. It was impossible for the battalion to regain the ford by which it had crossed over, and so it made a crossing about a mile farther downstream. The bank at the point was about six feet high; most of the horses hesitated until forced over by the press of those coming behind. Then, as men and animals floundered in the water, Sioux on the banks fired down on them, not just from one side but from both. A number of good men died at the crossing, some helplessly, some bravely firing at the overwhelming mass of Indians.

The east bank which they had just gained rose to hills 200 to 300 feet above the river, and on a high point the survivors were organized by Reno, as best he could, for defense. About half the battalion were casualties, killed, wounded, or left behind in the woods. The men were confused, dispirited, their ammunition was almost gone, and they could undoubtedly have been overwhelmed by a determined assault. However, the Indian attack was unaccountably slackening off to almost nothing; all but a few of the enemy warriors had streamed away, their interest attracted by something else. What it was Reno's men could not see.

It was then about four o'clock in the afternoon. While Reno had been fighting his desperate battle, Captain Benteen had been carrying out his reconnaissance of the country south of the creek and the trail the rest of the regiment had followed. He had scouted the bluffs Custer had been interested in, sending an officer to their tops a number of times, and personally investigating them for several miles. His orders had called for him to go on to the first valley, then, if he found no Indians, to continue on to the second, and then the third valley. But after riding a dozen miles, he had not even found a first valley.

The terrain was a jumble of hills, ravines, gullies, bluffs, and badlands in general. Benteen was convinced that no Indians were going to be found in such country; he was equally convinced that a battle would take place and that he could be of use only by returning to the regiment. He directed a change in course, and the three companies angled back, striking the trail after having traveled fifteen miles on the fruitless scout. He was, Benteen admitted afterward, technically violating his orders, but he felt he might have gone on for twenty-five miles without ever finding any valley, and certainly no Indians.

The battalion stopped to water horses at a marshy place at the junction of Reno Creek and its south fork, and had just started on when the pack train, lagging far behind the main section of the regiment, came down the trail. The thirsty mules broke from control and, braying loudly, rushed into the morass where they immediately became mired. Benteen's column left them thus, with packers and troopers assigned to pack-train duty cursing and trying to get things straightened out again. Several miles on, the battalion passed the dead man's tepee which had been set afire earlier by the Indian scouts, and two miles beyond, Sergeant Daniel Kanipe of Captain Tom Custer's Company C galloped up. "We've got 'em, boys," he announced in high humor, and told Captain Benteen that he had been sent by Colonel Custer to direct that the ammunition packs be hurried as fast as possible because Custer was preparing to go into action against a large Indian village. Benteen sent him back to the pack train in the rear, and had proceeded another mile or so when a second messenger came up on a bleeding and exhausted horse.

Benteen knew him well; he was John Martin, trumpeter for his own Company H, who had been detailed that day for duty as Custer's orderly trumpeter. Martin had been Giovanni Martini when he had come to America only a year before; he had not been with the 7th Cavalry long and his English was poor, but he was excited and elated as he handed Captain Benteen a hastily scrawled message: "Benteen— Come on. Big village. Be quick. Bring packs. W. W. Cooke P.S. Bring pacs."

Custer had given the order which his adjutant, Cooke, had then written on a page of his notebook, Martin said. On his way back, Sioux had fired at him and had hit his horse which was bleeding badly, but Martin said that Custer was attacking the village and that on his dash he had seen Reno fighting down in the valley. There was no doubt about it, the happy trumpeter said, the Indians were "skedaddling."

Martin also offered the information that he had passed Boston Custer galloping to join the force Martin had just left. Boston had gone to the pack train for some reason and was hurrying to rejoin the fated battalion in order not to miss any of the excitement.

There was nothing more to be done about the ammunition packs; Sergeant Kanipe had already gone back with word to hurry them up as much as possible. Benteen moved forward faster now. The sound of guns reached him very plainly in a few minutes; very shortly he arrived on ground overlooking the river, just in time to see great numbers of mounted Sioux riding down and killing the last stragglers from

Reno's column, those unfortunates who had somehow become un-horsed and were making a forlorn and desperate attempt to fight through to the river. Appalled by the sight, the column moved forward cautiously until it met several of the regiment's Crow scouts who pointed out the hill where Reno was preparing to make a final stand.

Benteen led the command to the hill at a trot. Reno, a pistol in his hand, greatly agitated, greeted him. "For God's sake, Benteen, halt your command and help me. I've lost half my men." The command dismounted, and Captain Benteen immediately began disposing his men for a more effective defense.

Reno was badly unnerved, overwrought, and discouraged, as were most of his men at the moment. It would be unfair to judge Major Reno solely on his actions since the moment a Sioux bullet had split the skull of Bloody Knife and spattered him with its contents. The major had an excellent Civil War record and had been breveted for gallantry in action. But there was not much doubt about it, for the moment, Reno was only half a man. Captain Benteen took over the defense and, for all practical purposes, was in command during the next hours.

Benteen was a superb officer, brave, cool in action, with the natural instincts of leadership. His hair was pure white, and his pictures show a man with a rubicund and rather friendly face, giving him more than a little of the appearance of a clean-shaven Santa Claus. Most of his officers and men found him friendly and fair, but on infrequent occa-sions he went on long drinking bouts during which he became irascible and gave way to violent temper outbursts. He despised Custer and had ever since the day he reported for duty with the 7th and, according to his story, had to spend two or three hours listening to his command-ing officer boast tediously and shamelessly of his many past exploits. Benteen's dislike had deepened into hate when Custer had failed to make any attempt to find the missing Major Joel Elliott and his de-tachment during the Washita attack. He had written an anonymous letter to a newspaper about the abandonment of Elliott and his men, and then admitted his authorship and faced down Custer when the latter had called a meeting of his officers to promise to horsewhip the letter writer if he found out who he was. Benteen always referred to Custer's book, *My Life On the Plains* as "My Lie on the Plains." Yet there is no evidence that he let his personal feelings interfere with his duty as a soldier—and he was a good soldier.

When they had ridden off just before Benteen's column had arrived, the Sioux had left only a few warriors to keep up a long-range fire at the beleaguered soldiers. An officer made a dash back to the pack train on the freshest horse available, to have the ammunition mules brought up as quickly as possible, and to hurry the rest of the train and its protecting cavalrymen as well. Custer's whereabouts were a mystery, except that he was somewhere north of them, on the east side of the Little Bighorn. They heard gunfire, very heavy, indicating that hard fighting was underway. It was without doubt that gunfire and fighting that had been the magnet that had drawn away the hundreds of warriors who had been attacking Reno. Captain Thomas B. Weir, commanding Company D of Benteen's battalion, became impatient when Reno made no move to go out to support Custer, wherever he might be, and finally, without orders, rode with his company about a mile to the north, to a high hill (now called Weir Point). Benteen followed with three companies to give support. From the hill they could see, about four miles north, a mighty cloud of dust and smoke, and many Indians, some of whom appeared to be shooting at the ground. The scene did not quite connect into a meaningful picture in the minds of the beholders on the hill.

Reno waited for the pack train to come up; then, his ammunition replenished, he began moving the rest of the force up to Weir Point. The difficulties were tremendous, especially moving the wounded. And in the meantime, the Indians had looked up at Weir Point and seen the blue uniforms atop it, and had begun racing to attack. The leading companies were soon engaged, and Reno and Benteen quickly decided that their original position was superior. A withdrawal under fire was completed just before the full force of the attack struck.

The assault was furious, and did not slacken until darkness fell. Then the warriors withdrew, leaving a number of the defenders dead or wounded. All during the night the soldiers, about three hundred strong, worked to dig defenses, employing knives, mess plates, and any other makeshift that came to hand, for they had only three spades and two axes. Saddles and anything else that would stop a bullet were piled as breastworks. The hill was well suited for defense because its top had a saucer-shaped depression; there the animals were picketed and the surgeon established his hospital. It was a busy night for him, too.

All during the night, as they made ready for the inevitable morning attack, the men on the hill could look across the river toward the village where a mighty victory celebration went on. Great fires burned, drums throbbed, and the elated warriors yelped and chanted as they danced. Several times, sentries were alerted by someone approaching through the dark, but each time it turned out to be survivors of the debacle across the river who had been left in the woods when they had failed to hear Reno's command to mount. Fifteen had hidden successfully and most came in that night, a few not until the next day.

Dawn comes early on June 26, just past the shortest night of the year, and the immense world of sky over the Little Bighorn valley was getting gray at 2:45 A.M. when the first Indian rifle cracked and opened a fusillade that thereafter continued hour after hour without letup. There was no noisy and aimless answering fire from the hill; fire control was being rigidly enforced and most of the time only a few crackshots were permitted to shoot at the Indians.

On all sides except the east the hill fell away sharply; on that quarter natural defenses were weak and a maze of gullies and hillocks gave natural cover to attacking warriors. Captain Benteen had chosen to defend this vulnerable spot on which the Sioux were concentrating their fire and were working nearer through the abundant cover afforded by the terrain. He went to Reno for reinforcements; during his absence an especially bold warrior dashed in and counted coup by touching the body of a dead cavalryman. Such were the opportunities for concealment afforded by the broken nature of the ground. Benteen put into practice the old adage about the best defense, and ordered his men to charge the Indians. They scattered the Sioux in front of their position, and returned without a single casualty.

Benteen urged Reno to order a general charge on the Indians to clear them from positions they were gradually pushing closer to the entrenchments. Reno agreed and led the charge, four companies strong, which went down the western slope of the hill whooping and cheering, scattering warriors who were gathering for their own assault. The cavalrymen returned to their defenses completely untouched; they had forced the Sioux and Cheyenne back and rendered them considerably more cautious.

Thereafter, the warriors kept up a more or less token fire. Thirst became the great enemy on the hill; for the wounded, water was becoming a matter of life or death. Volunteers crawled down to the river with canteens, kettles, and other vessels while sharpshooters stood up to keep under cover any Indian who tried to interfere with the operation.

Soon after midday (June 26) the pressure began to ease. Down in the Indian camp, scouts came in with news that led to earnest conferences among the chiefs, and then to the dismantling of tepees and preparations for moving. The besieged men on the hill realized only that something was going on among the Indians; they had no way of knowing that the enemy was beginning to withdraw because scouts had reported the approach of Colonel Gibbon and his column.

Late in the afternoon, the grass in the valley was set afire, and behind the rising clouds of smoke the Indians began moving out, possessions packed on ponies, tepees rolled up and lashed to travois, thousands of men, women, and children on horseback, and additional thousands upon thousands of ponies. Officers watched in awe from the hill. It was no straggling, savage rabble but a precision movement. Each of the bands moved as a unit, and the soldiers on the hill compared the river of horses and humans to a cavalry division on the march. By dark, the last of the encampment had disappeared from sight, headed in the direction of the Big Horn Mountains.

The band on the hill buried their dead (there is no agreement on how many died on the hill and in each phase of the fighting, but the total losses of Reno and Benteen in the two days of fighting were somewhere between forty and fifty killed and at least fifty wounded), and moved their position somewhat to be nearer the river and its water, and to get away from the stench of dead horses. With the Indians gone, several men still hiding in the woods rejoined their comrades. The main subject of conversation was the whereabouts of Custer, and there was widespread cursing of the commanding officer because it was almost universally believed that he had deserted them to go off on some chase of his own. No one suspected that there might be a much more calamitous reason for his disappearance.

6. A VICTORY TOO COMPLETE

That same night, June 26, Terry and Gibbon were camped about nine miles away, down the Little Bighorn. During the day, Lieutenant James Bradley, in charge of Gibbon's Indian scouts, reported back to the column that his men had come on Crow Indians up ahead who had

been scouts with Custer's regiment; they told a story of a great battle
in which the pony soldiers had all been killed. No one believed the
story in its entirety, but it was accepted that hard fighting must have
taken place, and Gibbon had pushed his infantry as fast as possible
during the rest of the afternoon and long into the lingering June twilight.

The next morning at daybreak they took up the march and soon
closed the remaining nine miles. The approaching column was sighted
from afar by Reno's men, who were unable to make out whether it was
soldiers, or Indians returning, but as it neared, it became identifiable
as an Army column. Lieutenants Hare and Wallace were sent out to
cross the river and learn who was approaching. When they discovered
General Terry riding with Gibbon at the head of the column, they
galloped up to the general, reined in their horses, saluted, and both
spoke at once, "Where is Custer?"

Terry did not know the answer, but it came a short time later when
he and Gibbon, and their staffs were standing on the hill talking to
Major Reno and his officers. Lieutenant Bradley rode up; with his
scouts he had been working through the hills on the east side of the
river and had sighted objects that shone white in the distance. Approaching, they had been horrified to find that they were naked human
bodies, lying among the carcasses of many horses. Bradley had counted
197 dead.

The annihilation of Custer and the five doomed companies has
woven its spell ever since, not only for its drama and tragedy but for
the element of mystery. More than two hundred rode out, and not one
came back to tell what happened. The Indians who fought that day
told their stories only long afterward and reluctantly—and they could
not throw any light on what went on in the minds and hearts of the
commander of the 7th Cavalry and his men. There is much that is unknown and unknowable, a situation that is a rich seedbed for the
growth of legend. But there is no deep enigma about the general path
that led the five companies to death and immortality. It is mainly in
details of the picture that the mystery lies and will remain forever.

After having sent Reno to attack the lower end of the huge Indian
camp, Custer followed him for a short distance, apparently meaning
to support him as he had promised. But then he turned off the trail
and went north, more or less parallel to the river. He seems to have
changed his mind about supporting Reno when Captains Cooke and

Keogh returned from seeing Reno to the river and brought word that the Indians were not fleeing, as he had thought, but were attacking. Then, beyond any doubt, Custer made the decision to attack the Indian camp in its flank—probably at its lower end to nip the enemy between his force and Reno's.

Custer had known that Reno was desperately engaged and needed help. During the first ten minutes of Reno's fight, when he had halted his charge in the face of the hundreds of warriors confronting him and had dismounted his men, Lieutenant Varnum had somehow found a moment in the chaos of combat to raise his eyes to the river bluffs opposite, about half a mile away. It was a brief glimpse—he was too occupied for much gazing—but he saw, clear and unmistakable, Company E of Custer's column. He sighted only a portion of it through a break in the bluffs, but there had been no doubt. How could he be sure at that distance it was E Company? Because of Custer's custom of coloring the horses; Company E was the Gray Horse Company. If Varnum saw Custer, Custer saw Reno under attack.

Custer had become completely aware that a large village lay across the river. He had sent Sergeant Kanipe back to hurry up the ammunition supplies in the pack train for the battle he was preparing, and then, for a better look, rode to the top of a high hill. With him were not only his adjutant, Cooke, and Trumpeter John Martin of H Company, his orderly trumpeter, but also brother Tom, commander of Company C, and nephew Autie Reed (the Custers were together whenever possible).

Even though the trees hid much of the camp, it stretched some three miles long, and he could not have escaped an impression of its great size. But size did not faze Custer; he dangerously underrated the fighting ability of the Indians, and at the same time, had convinced himself that the 7th Cavalry was invincible—at least, when it was under his leadership. The camp half a mile or so across the river and below represented no possibility of defeat but another step on the ladder to fame.

There were few signs of activity in the camp: women here and there tended cooking fires, children played their games among the tepees; a few dogs slept in the sun. Custer spurred his horse down the hill and rejoined his command with the jubilant announcement that the Indians had been caught napping. The command took on new life and galloped ahead—still north and parallel to the river—for about another mile before Custer called Martin to him. "Orderly, I want you to take a message to Captain Benteen," the colonel said, as nearly as his order can be reconstructed, for Martin's command of English was poor. "Ride as fast as you can and tell him to hurry. Tell him it's a big village, and I want him to be quick and bring the ammunition packs."

At this point, Lieutenant Cooke, recognizing the danger of Martin misunderstanding the message, halted the trumpeter before he could gallop away and wrote down on a page of his memorandum book the message which Martin later handed to Benteen: "Benteen—Come on. Big village. Be quick. Brink packs. W. W. Cooke. P. S. Bring pacs." Martin was the last survivor of the 7th Cavalry to see Custer alive.

From that point on, everything must be pieced together from circumstantial evidence and what light the Sioux and Cheyenne threw on the event long afterward. There is no way of knowing whether he meant to strike the village in the flank and was thrown back by the sudden attack of Indian forces, or whether he was planning to cross the river and hit the lower end of the camp, where the Cheyenne tepees stood. Whatever his plans, they go no further, for the somnolent camp had been an illusion, and soon after Martin had left, a mass of yelling warriors pounded over the rise from the river and struck like a thunderbolt.

Custer got the battalion on a ridge, the first one of any size back of the river. His five companies, about 225 cavalrymen and several civilians (no one, not even the Army's own records, can say for certain exactly how many men were there), stretched along a front of about three-quarters of a mile. The first mass of warriors had struck from the southwest; they were led by the great and dour Hunkpapa chief, Gall, and had just turned from throwing back Reno's attack to meet this new threat. Gall's men hit Lieutenant Calhoun's Company L at the southern end of the line first and then swept on to Keogh's I Company; these two units were simply overwhelmed by superior numbers and wiped out where they stood, so that bodies of officers and men lay in platoon formation as they had died.

The ordered line of battle was knocked apart as new hundreds upon hundreds of warriors, Crazy Horse's Oglalas and the Cheyennes of Two Moon came in a solid mass from the northwest after fording the river at the lower end of the camp. The bodies of the officers and men of the remaining three companies were found grouped more or less by

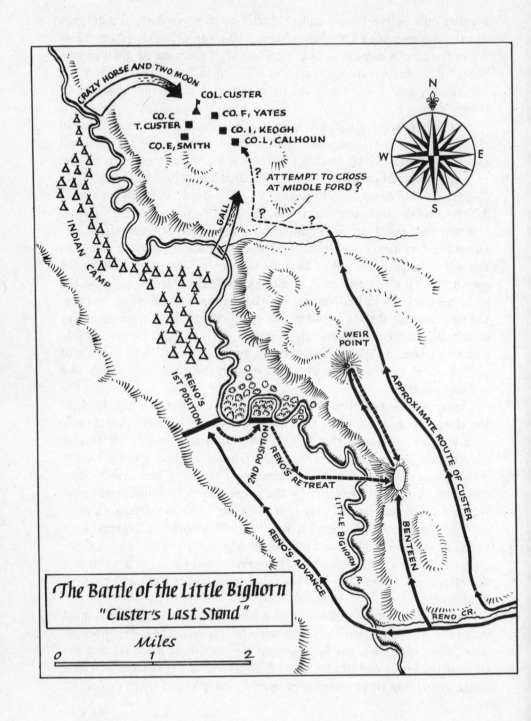

CRAZY HORSE AND TWO MOON

COL. CUSTER

CO. C
T. CUSTER

CO. F, YATES

CO. I, KEOGH
CO. L, CALHOUN

CO. E, SMITH

ATTEMPT TO CROSS
AT MIDDLE FORD ?

GALL

INDIAN
CAMP

N
W E
S

WEIR
POINT

RENO'S
1ST POSITION

APPROXIMATE ROUTE OF CUSTER

2ND POSITION

RENO'S RETREAT

RENO'S ADVANCE

LITTLE BIGHORN R.

BENTEEN

RENO CR.

The Battle of the Little Bighorn
"Custer's Last Stand"

Miles

0   1   2

companies, but beyond that there was no semblance of formation, indicating that the field had been broken up into a swirling, milling nightmare of dust, smoke, yells, and curses in which war had often been reduced to its most elemental form of one man against another in hand-to-hand combat.

The battle was fought on foot by the cavalry and by most of the Indians because of the rough terrain with its hills and gullies. Some of the cavalry horses had been shot and used as breastworks but the Indians had stampeded most of them; many of the men were firing from prone positions to present as poor a target as possible, but their situation was hopeless with bullets and arrows coming from rear as well as front. And the hopeless odds kept increasing as Sioux warriors who had been fighting Reno kept streaming across the river.

George Armstrong Custer, who had dreamed of leading the 7th Cavalry to new glory for it and for himself, was at the northernmost point on the ridge. His adjutant Cooke was near him, and so were Boston Custer, who had hoped to cure a bronchial condition in the West, and nephew Autie Reed, who was being shown the fun and excitement of Indian-fighting. Also at the last were his brother Tom, Lieutenant Smith, and Captain Yates, with almost half a hundred enlisted men, who had rallied to their commander.

There were fifty-one of them in the little knot of men standing by Custer, a little cluster of frantically fighting men that dissolved and grew smaller almost by the minute. Custer did not stand to the last with revolver in one hand, saber in the other, long golden locks streaming in the smoky air, as decades of saloon art have portrayed. The revolver was almost certainly in his hand, but the cavalry carried no sabers in 1876, and just before leaving Fort Abraham Lincoln, Custer had had the horse clippers run over his head, shearing his hair almost to the skull.

There, on the ridge, Custer's luck, which its possessor had had in such abundance and had so badly abused, at last choked off. A bullet took Custer in the temple, another in his breast. Either would have been fatal.

The Indians stripped off his clothing and left him naked, but they did not scalp him. In the afternoon, Lieutenant Bradley, who had discovered the battlefield, led Captain Benteen and two other officers of the regiment back to the field to identify the body of Custer. They found him lying in an attitude of perfect composure, with a look of repose on his face as though he were asleep rather than having ended his life at the height of violence. After they had left, Bradley asked the three officers if they had noted Custer's death wounds; the wounds, though in plain sight, were so inconspicuous that none of the three could say where Custer had been shot.

Later, when the story reached the outside world and rumors began to multiply, among the most persistent were accounts of horrible mutilations of those who had fallen by the Little Bighorn. Lieutenant Bradley, who had some knowledge of this macabre subject, felt called upon to put the record straight in a letter to the Helena, Montana, *Herald* about a month after the battle. Wrote Bradley, in part: "Of the 206 bodies buried in the field, there were very few that I did not see, and beyond scalping, in possibly a majority of cases, there was little mutilation. Many of the bodies were not even scalped, and in the comparatively few cases of disfiguration, it appeared to me the result rather of a blow with a knife, hatchet, or war club to finish a wounded man, than a deliberate mutilation." *

The only bodies that had suffered deliberate mutilation were those of Major Reno's men who had fallen near the village and had been set upon by the women and children. Scalping, yes, but even that was not universal, as Lieutenant Bradley pointed out. Most of the dead had been stripped of their clothing, but not all. The dead were buried in shallow graves where they had fallen. The difficulties of identifying naked bodies were great, especially after they had lain in the hot sun for two days, and eighteen were unaccountably missing: four officers and fourteen men as near as it was possible to tell. Their bodies were never found—but not one of them ever turned up alive. The Indians removed their own dead, as usual. Estimates of their losses range widely, but they appear to have come off rather lightly.

One living being, and one alone, was found on the field of battle. Comanche, the horse of Captain Myles Keogh, commanding officer of Company I, was grievously and almost mortally hurt with seven

* A favorite story was that Captain Thomas Custer had had his heart cut out by a Sioux named Rain-in-the-Face; this tale gained credibility because it was told by Rain-in-the-Face himself, who bore a special grudge against Tom Custer because the latter had once arrested him on Colonel Custer's arbitrary orders in a rather involved matter arising from the Yellowstone Expedition of 1873. Rain-in-the-Face was a big-mouth and a brag-hard; Lieutenant Bradley, in the same letter quoted above, denies the truth of his account of the removal of Captain Custer's heart. Yet Elizabeth Custer later presented the story to the world as the unvarnished truth in *Boots and Saddles,* and biographers of Custer are presenting the limp and tired story even today.

wounds in its body but it was still alive and strong enough to be led some twenty miles to where the Little Bighorn joined the Bighorn River. The *Far West* had been able to follow Terry and Gibbon that far, and the horse was put aboard, with the wounded from Reno's command. Comanche survived his wounds and was, by regimental order, placed on the retired list; no one was ever permitted to ride or work the animal. The horse was led in all 7th Cavalry reviews and parades, and died, full of years, at Fort Riley, Kansas, at the age of thirty.

The *Far West* had to wait at the mouth of the Bighorn to ferry the troops over to the north bank of the Yellowstone; then it set out down the Yellowstone to the Missouri and on to Fort Abraham Lincoln under forced draft with its load of wounded and its heavy cargo of news. The 700-mile trip was made in fifty-four hours, a record never again equaled. Captain Marsh, skipper of the sternwheeler, paused at Fort Buford on the Missouri long enough to take aboard a large amount of crape with which he draped his boat, and thus appropriately dressed out in keeping with her doleful mission, the *Far West* swung into the Fort Lincoln landing at 11 P.M. on July 5.

The telegraph operator at Bismarck, J. M. Carnahan, spent twenty-two hours without relief sending the basic dispatch of the disaster, and then settled down for another sixty hours without rest, with his finger on the key tapping out dispatches for newspaper correspondents. The country was quick to condemn one side or the other. Grant said that Custer had sacrificed his men. Terry and his staff had no doubts that the tragedy had occurred because Custer had disobeyed orders, and Terry said so in a confidential report. With characteristic dislike of saying anything derogatory about a man, he prepared another report for release to the public which made no mention of disobedience, but an enterprising newspaperman posing as a War Department messenger got the confidential report from General Sherman and printed it in full. On the other hand, very soon Reno and Benteen were being accused of pusillanimous conduct, and in some quarters, of deliberate refusal to support Custer because of their personal dislike of the man.

As the accusations continued over the months, Reno demanded a court of inquiry, which finally met in January of 1879, and after two months of intensive hearings, returned its findings which, while hardly acclaiming Reno as a hero, did absolve him of cowardice. It had also been the opinion of virtually every surviving officer of the regiment that if Reno had not retreated when he did, the battalion would have been wiped out. The enlisted men of the regiment gave their own vote of confidence: nine days after the battle a petition signed by 236 who had fought under Reno and Benteen was submitted to the President; it asked that Reno be promoted to lieutenant colonel of the regiment, and that Benteen be promoted to major to fill Reno's position. The men said in their petition that the two officers, "by their bravery, coolness and decision . . . saved the lives of every man now living of the 7th Cavalry who participated in the battle . . ." The petition, of course, was not acted upon. General Sherman returned it with the explanation that promotion in the United States Army depended on seniority, not heroism.

The disaster (Custer's Massacre, it inevitably became, although it was no massacre but a battle in which Army troops were outguessed and outnumbered) profoundly shocked the nation. When Captain Judd Fetterman had led his command into an ambush and got it annihilated in much the same fashion, the national mood had been one of soul-searching amid a widespread feeling that greedy white men had been largely to blame for driving the Indian to defend his dwindling heritage. There was little such feeling after the battle of the Little Bighorn. The news reached the country on July 6, in the midst of the celebration of the nation's centennial, and it was a harsh discord amid all the patriotic rodomontade about past glories and the predictions of limitless bright futures. It was unthinkable that a people so favored by destiny should be thus humiliated by savages. The Sioux and Cheyenne had made two serious mistakes: they had won far too overwhelmingly, and they had won at the worst possible moment.

General Sheridan combed his command for troops to reinforce both Terry and Crook. General Crook had waited in his camp on Goose Creek ever since June 19 following his defeat at the Battle of the Rosebud. He at last set out on August 5 marching north down Rosebud Creek again, his force enlarged to 2,100 men, including 225 Shoshone and 25 Ute scouts. Among the white guides was none other than Buffalo Bill Cody, gathering publicity between theatrical engagements.

Three days later, General Terry with a force of 1,600 left the Yellowstone and started up Rosebud Creek. It was expected that these two mighty forces would catch the overconfident Sioux between them and grind him to powder. Instead, they came together in a great cloud of dust and confusion without having sighted a hostile Indian.

The campaign was almost equally sterile of results during the rest of the summer. After a couple of weeks during which their commands operated more or less together, Crook and Terry separated again. General Terry went back to the Yellowstone and worked toward the east where he accomplished nothing. Crook also headed east, but farther south than the ground covered by Terry. He was a great believer in cutting loose from hampering wagon trains and depending on pack mules and what his men could carry in their saddle bags. This time he cut it too fine, and the rations his column carried gave out completely; the journey became known as the "horse-meat march." As cavalry horses gave out, they became food for the column; it was a choice between that and starvation. The weather added to the misery with rain pouring down most of the time, and great portions of the route were through difficult badlands. Men who had struggled to the limit of endurance sat down and broke into tears because of their inability to continue—but all somehow found the strength to go on.

Crook's course took him more or less directly east into present North Dakota till he was due north of the Black Hills; then he headed directly south. At a place called Slim Buttes in northwestern South Dakota, just north of the Black Hills, the column found and attacked the village of Chief American Horse, which they captured. The Sioux defenders sent an urgent appeal for help to Crazy Horse a few miles away, but reinforcements reached the attacking Army force at about the same time more Sioux warriors arrived, and the troops remained in possession of the village.

This was the only victory of the entire expedition, indeed, the only passage at arms with the Indians since Custer's defeat. Several men on each side were killed, including American Horse himself, and the village was destroyed, but the mountain had labored to bring forth a mouse. The Indian Wars produced certain statistics: one was that it cost the government $1,000,000 to kill an Indian; another, that the cost of keeping a regiment fed, clothed, and otherwise maintained on the plains for a year was $2,000,000. These figures should be highly suspect—they are too nicely rounded, for one thing—but they do indicate that fighting Indians was no bargain basement matter. The campaign of Crook and Terry proved that fact; the government had spent many millions of dollars to kill several warriors and burn a number of tepees and buffalo robes at Slim Buttes.

Sheridan disbanded the Bighorn and Yellowstone Expedition and

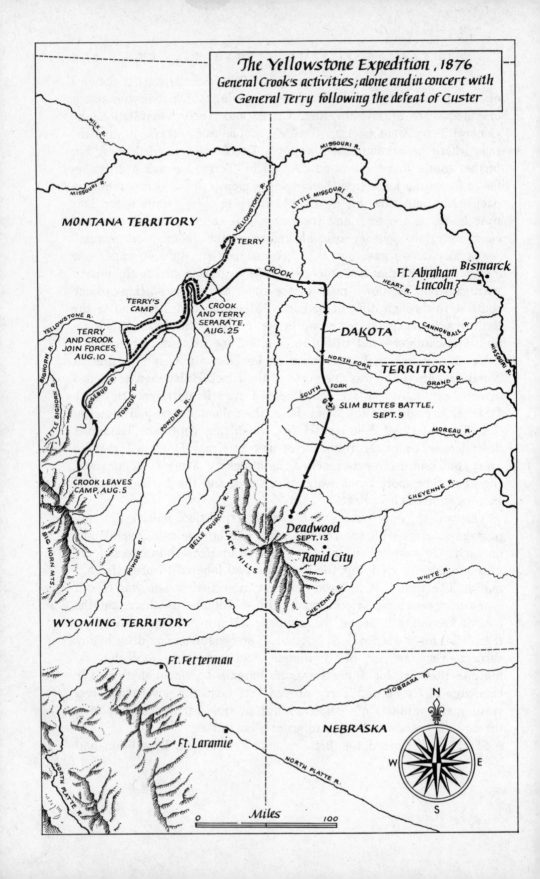

organized a new one, the Powder River Expedition, to carry the fighting to the hostiles into the coldest months of the year. On the surface, it appeared that the honors during the campaign just past had gone largely to the Indians. They had defeated Crook on the Rosebud, wiped out Custer, and repulsed Reno, and had been hit themselves only at Slim Buttes. But the Army could afford to absorb its losses; the Indians could not. The big battles had used up much of their ammunition; the hostiles had driven much of the game from their hunting range by burning the grass to impede Army movements; and many of them were becoming discouraged by being constantly pursued. Agency Indians who had joined the hostiles in the spring drifted back to the agencies again; the price of freedom and defiance was proving too high. But Crazy Horse, Sitting Bull, Gall, and most of the other nontreaty chiefs and their bands were still prepared to fight for their free way of life.

The Powder River Expedition got under way in November. Crook's forces moved north once again from Fort Fetterman but this time something new had been added: his column included Sioux and Cheyenne scouts, recruited at the agencies. Crook was a strong advocate of employing scouts from the tribes he was fighting; he had used the system successfully against the Apaches, and he argued that there was a powerful psychological effect when the hostiles saw that even their own tribesmen were fighting against them. What it might do to the self-respect of the men used as scouts was another matter, although Crook was sincerely convinced that the system helped to civilize the Indians.

While Crook moved north, establishing his headquarters on the site of Old Fort Reno, a new army commanded by Colonel Nelson A. Miles moved down from the Yellowstone River. On November 25, Crook's cavalry, led by Colonel Ranald Mackenzie (he who had routed the southern Indians two years earlier in Palo Duro Canyon in the Texas Panhandle), fell on the camp of Dull Knife and his Cheyennes, killing many, destroying their village, and driving the rest north where they joined Crazy Horse.

Colonel Miles had already clashed with the Hunkpapas of Sitting Bull and Gall in October; a council had been arranged but it broke up and ended in a battle. Miles had been successful, however, in persuading several of the important Hunkpapa chiefs, with hundreds of their followers, to surrender and come in to the reservation. He harried and hunted the hold-outs relentlessly, his fur-clad soldiers moving even when temperatures were far below zero. Sitting Bull and Gall, with a small band of followers, fled into Canada in February. Most of the band drifted back over the next few years; Sitting Bull himself was to return in 1881 to end his exile.

Crazy Horse now became the main target of the hunt. Colonel Miles had found his camp in January and several running battles had been fought in snow and cold; the warriors succeeded in holding off the pursuing soldiers until the village escaped. Miles lost the trail and went into camp, but the Indians were in a bad way, exhausted and near starving.

General Crook was no longer in the field. He was certain that he could get Crazy Horse to surrender without another campaign, and using Chief Spotted Tail as his emissary, he sent word that if Crazy Horse would give up, he would see that the Oglala chief was given a reservation in his own land, the Powder River country. Crook had a good name among Indians as a man who kept his word. Other hostiles trickled in but Crazy Horse remained out as spring advanced. Sheridan was pressing for more fighting before a 2,500-man reduction in the Army went into effect on July 1. Much of the public was demanding action; Colonel Miles was unhappy at the prospect that Crook would have the honor of receiving the surrender of the great Sioux leader. But Crook insisted he could bring in Crazy Horse without fighting, and on May 6 the chief, with his followers, came in to Camp Robinson in northwestern Nebraska, near Red Cloud agency. They arrived, not as a beaten people, but some eight hundred strong, riding in a procession with warriors in paint and feathers, carrying shields and weapons, and singing war songs. Crook allowed them this last salve to their pride before they were disarmed.

The rest of the story is a familiar fabric of broken promises and unprincipled robbery. Long before the fighting had ended—in August of 1876—a commission arrived on the Great Sioux Reservation, and by the old combination of bribery and threats forced a new agreement on the reservation chiefs of the Sioux and Northern Cheyennes and Arapahoes. What was then being accomplished by force was dubiously legalized. The unceded Powder River country was taken from the tribes, so were the sacred Black Hills and adjacent lands, about a third of the Great Sioux Reservation. The agreement was made with the chiefs only, ignoring a clause of the Fort Laramie treaty which stipulated that the treaty could be changed only by vote of three-quarters of the adult males of the tribe. That clause had been put in precisely to block the favorite trick of government commissioners of gaining the consent of a few amenable and compliant chiefs to an agreement and then blandly declaring their decision binding on the entire tribe.

The Cheyennes who had surrendered—the bands of Hog, Dull Knife, Little Wolf, and Standing Elk—were sent to Indian Territory to join their brothers, the Southern Cheyennes. The government could claim that they had elected of their own free will to go south, but it was only after they had been fast-talked with a rosy picture of what they could expect, and promises had been made about food and other annuity goods that would not be kept. The cost of the government's perfidy was going to come high, but it would be the Cheyennes who would foot most of the bill.

General Crook had promised Crazy Horse that he would help obtain a reservation for him and his band in the Powder River country—on the Tongue River, he had said, which Crazy Horse especially loved. The General found himself unable to make good on his promise. He traveled to Omaha, Chicago, and Washington petitioning at the seats of the mighty, but everywhere he was frustrated by indifference, bureaucratic lethargy, or a spirit of vengeance that precluded any generosity toward a defeated Sioux chieftain.

That summer the Nez Percé Indians from Idaho were fighting their way across the mountains and heading for Montana. Crook sent a message to Crazy Horse, asking if the chief would lead his warriors against the western Indians. After a long council, Crazy Horse replied that he would, and added that he would keep fighting until all the Nez Percés were killed. The interpreter distorted this to say that the chief would fight until all the whites were killed.

There were many Indians on the agency jealous of Crazy Horse and his prestige and eager to do him harm, but his friends came to Crook with the truth about the distorted translation. Crook started for the agency to talk to the chief; on the way another trouble-maker met him with a warning that Crazy Horse planned to kill him if he showed up. Crook canceled his visit, instead sent soldiers and Indian scouts to bring in the chief. Crazy Horse was on the point of leaving the agency but permitted himself to be taken back without resistance. However, he began to resist when he saw that he was to be locked up in the guardhouse of the fort, and was stabbed by a soldier with his bayonet and mortally wounded.

Crazy Horse was killed on September 5, 1877. Indian Bureau officials and Army officers feared for a short while that his death might precipitate violence among his followers, but the spirit was gone from the Sioux, and nothing happened. So, in October, General Crook was ordered to conduct the Sioux to their new agencies on the reduced reservation. The Indian Bureau, through inertia and indifference, had failed to make provision for either food or transportation during the move. By improvising, by making use of worn-out cavalry horses, and by other makeshifts, Crook was able to accomplish the move without any noticeable hardship, and the Indians were settled in their new locations.

And so, as 1877 ended, in all the Great Plains, from Canada south, there was no longer a free tribe or a "wild" Indian. It had not taken long; in 1840 the boundary of the permanent Indian Country had been completed and the Great Plains were to belong forever to the Indians. A mere thirty-seven years later every solemn promise had been broken and no bit of ground large enough to be buried in remained to any Indian that could not—and probably would—be arbitrarily taken from him without warning.

IX

The Last Small Wars

1. "I LOVE THAT LAND MORE THAN ALL THE REST OF THE WORLD"

THE company guidons still snapped in the wind when cavalry patrols passed on the plains just as they had for years, but there was a difference. The patrols no longer really expected trouble. There would be no ambush ahead; there was no chance that they would come on the burned wagons and the scalped bodies of a party of emigrants. Their main call to action was likely to be a request from an Indian agent to round up and escort back a few tribesmen who had wandered off the reservation. The Army on the plains had changed from fighting force into jail warden.

Custody of the Sioux had been returned to the Indian Bureau again, now that the war was over, and the Army had relinquished control. But the military was always close at hand. There were Army posts on almost all the reservations, most of them nearly within shouting distance of the agency and ready for any trouble. The chances of further trouble would appear remote, but while most tribes now settled down to empty and frequently hungry existences, a few last flickering fires of resistance born of desperation were to break out during the next several years. Then, and only then, would it all be

301

over, and the white man would at last have conquered and caged every Indian, from sea to shining sea.

The year after the Little Bighorn, it was the turn of the Nez Percés —or rather, a band of nontreaty Nez Percés—to face the United States Army. The Army never fought a more unjust war, nor did it ever oppose so superior a type of Indian foe. If any people deserved well of the United States, they did, and in the end they got less than nothing.

The Nez Percés are a people of the Pacific Northwest, who originally lived in the region where Washington, Oregon, and Idaho meet, in the valley of the Clearwater River and in part of the valleys of the Salmon and Snake. It was—and is—a magnificent country of deep canyons, ridges, evergreen forests, and grassy meadows carpeted in season with flowers of many colors and kinds. They had lived here for hundreds of years, hunters of deer, bear, mountain sheep, and lesser game, eaters of salmon which the rivers supplied bountifully, dwellers in semipermanent lodges. Then about 1760 they acquired the horse, and it worked the same revolution in their lives as it had with so many other tribes. They became superb horsemen, and were deeply influenced by the horse-and-buffalo culture of the Plains, to the extent that they actually became buffalo Indians to a degree, crossing the Continental Divide and traveling three or four hundred miles to the nearest buffalo ranges in Montana on hunting trips. They adopted the tepee and a seminomadic way of life, and many other attributes of the Plains people, although in other ways retaining their old culture.

Lewis and Clark came through Nez Percé lands in 1805 on their famous trip to the Pacific, and again on their return when they stopped with the tribe for several weeks while waiting for the snow to melt in the mountain passes. The Nez Percés were hospitable hosts, and it continued to be their claim through succeeding decades and increasing provocations that they had never killed a white man.

At the Council of Walla Walla in 1855, when treaties were made restricting the tribes of the region to reservations, the Nez Percés managed to retain about half the country they claimed, partly because no one was yet interested in such wild and remote country, partly because the government wanted the backing of the powerful Nez Percés in negotiating with other tribes. White indifference to the country disappeared when prospectors came looking for gold, and the

Indians, after turning them back for a time, were at last persuaded to let the gold-hunters in—under proper restrictions, of course.

There is no point in detailing the betrayal of the Nez Percés once the whites had an entering wedge. The prospectors spread beyond the limits set for them; settlers followed although it had been a clearly stated part of the agreement that no farmers should enter the Nez Percé lands; Indian fences were torn down, their pastures taken over and they were driven off lands they were farming. When the Nez Percés demanded that the government enforce the 1855 treaty, there was a cry of outrage at such impertinence. The government did at last intervene in 1863 to set things right—which it accomplished by a new treaty taking away three-quarters of the Nez Percé lands. The remaining reservation lay entirely in Idaho on the Clearwater River; the lands in Washington and Oregon were outside the reduced reserve. Despite gaining so much land, however, whites only increased their depredations against what remained.

Two-thirds of the chiefs present at the council had refused to sign the treaty, saying there was no point in a new agreement when the government had not honored or enforced the old one. One of the non-treaty chiefs was known as Joseph, a name he had taken long ago when he had become a Christian. A good and long-time friend of the whites, he now tore up his New Testament and swore to have nothing more to do with white men in whom no trust could be placed. Joseph and his band were more fortunate than many of the nontreaty Nez Percés who were living on land where they were now being pushed around by settlers, because Joseph's home was in the country of the Wallowa River in the northeastern corner of Oregon, a region no white man had yet become interested in. The band was still living there in peace in 1871 when Joseph, very old, died, leaving two sons, Ollikut, a great athlete and warrior, and Hinmaton-yalatkit (Thunder-Rolling-in-the-Mountains), better known as Young Joseph. Young Joseph, the elder son, became Chief Joseph on his father's death. "I buried him in that beautiful valley of the winding waters," Joseph later said. "I love that land more than all the rest of the world."

Love it he might, but keep it he could not. The time came, as inevitably it would, when settlers began moving into the area. They and state officials set up the familiar anguished cries for soldiers to come and take Joseph's band away to the reservation. For a time the Federal government resisted the pressure and set aside part of the Wallowa country as a reserve for "roaming Nez Percés" by presidential order in 1873, but minds were changed two years later and the entire region thrown open to homesteaders.

Chief Joseph, however, continued to maintain that the land belonged to him and his people. His father had not given it up, neither had he parted with it. Old Joseph, in his last days, had told him never to sell the land. "This country holds your father's body," he told his son. "Never sell the bones of your father and mother."

A five-man commission was sent to talk to Chief Joseph. Two members were Army officers, three civilians. One of the officers, whom the Nez Percés were to have considerable to do with very soon, was Major General Oliver O. Howard, who had lost his right arm at Fair Oaks in the early part of the war, and had commanded a wing of Sherman's army during the March to the Sea during the last part. Howard was a man of pinch-nosed religiousness. During the war he liked to bring cheer to the boys in the hospitals by appearing among them on Sundays to distribute religious tracts, homilies, and fruit. He was much interested in helping the recently freed Negroes (he was instrumental in founding Howard University for Negroes) but his heart did not go out in a like manner to the Indian in his time of trouble.

Joseph made the commissioners uneasy. He was a man of quiet dignity and commanding presence. He was confident, calm, intelligent, capable of expressing himself with a logic the five white men found difficult to answer. Moreover, he nettled them because there was no trace of obsequiousness in his manner. He acted with the quiet assurance that he was the equal of the white men to whom he was talking—and as every Indian ought to be taught, no red man was the equal of any white. He denied the commissioners' contention that the Wallowa country had been signed away by the Nez Percés in the Lapwai Treaty in 1863. His father had not signed the treaty, said Joseph, and the Wallowa belonged to his father. "If we ever owned the land we own it still, for we have never sold it," Chief Joseph said. "In the treaty councils, the commissioners have claimed that our country has been sold to the government. Suppose a white man should come to me and say, 'Joseph, I like your horses, and I want to buy them.' I say to him, 'No, my horses suit me, I will not sell them.' Then he goes to my neighbor and says to him, 'Joseph has some good horses. I want to buy them but he refuses to sell.' My neighbor answers, 'Pay me the money and I will sell you Joseph's horses.' The white man returns to me and says, 'Joseph, I have bought your horses and you must let me have them.' If we sold our lands to the government, that is the way they were bought."

But in spite of Joseph's logic—or perhaps because of it, for the commissioners resented being put on the defensive by an untutored savage —the five whites decided that Joseph's band should be removed to the Lapwai reservation, by force if necessary, and there receive about sixty plots of twenty acres each (they had about a million acres in the Wallowa country). Just about six months earlier, the other officer on the commission, Major H. C. Wood, had made another investigation of the Wallowa question and had decided that the right was all on Joseph's side, and General Howard had rendered a similar opinion. The truth and right could vary from month to month where Indian policy was involved.

Joseph bowed to the inevitable. He selected land on the reservation on May 15, 1877, and then was given one month by General Howard to bring his band in. Joseph asked for more time. The stock was foaling and calving at that season; the animals were still scattered in dozens of secret valleys and it would take time to round them up. Even more serious, the Snake River, which the band would have to cross—women, infants, aged—was half a mile wide and raging with melt waters. One month, Howard repeated. If the band delayed one day beyond that time—only one day—the troops would be there to drive them in.

The band was in no position to resist—it had only 55 men of fighting age—and the thing was somehow accomplished. Stock was rounded up, although hundreds of head were missed in the haste, and the crossing of the Snake was made without loss of human life, with the very young and the very old of the band towed on rafts through the swift, wide current. More livestock was lost when several hundred head were swept away in the river, and white settlers hanging around the edge of the band like jackals were able to cut out and stampede a large number of horses.

After the crossing, the band stopped to camp for the ten days or so still remaining before they had to come on the reservation. Other non-treaty bands, likewise ordered to settle down, joined them, and the encampment became a lively and cheerful place, considering the circumstances. But some tempers were thin. During a parade two days before the deadline date, someone became irritated by the antics of a young man named Wahlitits who was clowning on a horse, and made a waspish comment to the effect that he had not been such a big man when it had come to avenging his father's murder two years before.

Wahlitits's father had died at the hands of a white man who had squatted on his land while he had been away; when the Nez Percé had returned and protested, the white man shot him. The dying man made his son promise not to take revenge, but now, burning from the taunt made at the parade, Wahlitits set out the next day with a cousin and another youth to take belated vengeance. They were unable to find the guilty man but they killed four others, at least two of whom well deserved it. They returned to camp, recruited another fifteen or twenty firebrands, and set out on a carnival of raiding and murder. With the help of liquor which they found and dipped into heavily, they killed fifteen more white men, plundered homes, and assaulted women.

The Nez Percés had always claimed they had never killed a white man, but now they had done in a good number of them, and rather messily, in a few hours. The encampment was shocked at the news, and broke up rapidly as families left to disassociate themselves from the murderers. Many went south, to the canyon of White Bird Creek, a stream emptying into the Salmon River. Joseph had been away from the encampment when the raids had taken place, but he knew that neither that circumstance, nor that none of the murderers were members of his band, was likely to be taken into consideration when retribution was dealt out. He stayed for two days with his wife who had just given birth to a daughter, then the three joined the others at White Bird Canyon.

General Howard, at Lapwai on the reservation, got the news on June 15, and at once sent Captain David Perry with two companies of the 1st Cavalry after the Indians. On the way Perry was joined by eleven volunteers, to give him a total of about 110 men. As the force neared the Indian camp at White Bird Canyon, the Nez Percés sent several men with a flag of truce to meet it, but they were fired on. The Indians were outnumbered; they had only about sixty to sixty-five men, some of them old, some still in sorry condition from too much stolen whiskey the night before, about a third armed with bows and arrows, many of the rest with old muzzle-loaders. But fighting a battle which they improvised as they proceeded, they routed the troops, cut them into sections, pinned one group of nineteen men against a rocky wall and wiped them out, and killed thirty-four and wounded four, while suffering only two wounded themselves.

The Indians picked up sixty-three badly needed rifles and large amounts of ammunition from the battlefield. They behaved in a very un-Indianlike manner by leaving the bodies of the enemy unmutilated, unscalped, and completely clothed.

General Howard moved more cautiously now. He called in more men from posts throughout the entire Pacific Northwest while reserves were brought in from as far as Atlanta, Georgia, to stand by in case the war spread. The Nez Percés picked up some strength, too. Two competent warriors, Five Wounds and Rainbow, returning from a buffalo hunt in Montana, met the fugitives and joined them with their small bands. General Howard, through a stupid act, gave them more recruits. A prominent chief named Looking Glass was camped on the reservation with his band, completely divorced from all the violence that had been occurring. Nevertheless, when wild-eyed settlers brought stories that Looking Glass was preparing to join the hostiles, Howard, without investigating, sent a Captain Whipple with two companies of cavalry against Looking Glass's village. Nor did he direct Whipple to investigate before he took action, so Whipple did not hesitate to launch an attack when he found a peaceful camp. Only three or four Indians were killed in what was a completely treacherous attack, but the village was destroyed. The infuriated Indians thereupon left the reservation and set out to join the hostile force.

While Captain Whipple was making his ill-advised raid on Looking Glass's camp, General Howard had been decoyed across the swollen Salmon River and led on a chase through the rugged, almost trackless country south of that river. Then the Indians doubled back, leaving Howard to flounder about in the wilderness. The Nez Percés headed north to a new camping place on the Clearwater River at the mouth of Cottonwood Creek, annihilating on the way a reconnoitering party of ten men sent out by Captain Whipple. At the Clearwater camp, they were joined by Looking Glass and his still-angry band, giving them just under 200 men, and about 450 women and children.

By July 11, General Howard, with his army reinforced and increased to 400 soldiers and 180 scouts, teamsters, and packers, had caught up with the hostile band, who were still camped on the Clearwater, and took them completely by surprise by opening fire from the bluff across the river with a howitzer and two Gatling guns. However, before Howard could get his attack underway, Toohoolhoolzote, chief of one of the nontreaty bands, an elderly man but a noted warrior, dashed across the river and up the bluffs with only twenty-four men to hold the soldiers off until reinforcements could follow and swing around Howard's flanks and rear.

In spite of a numerical advantage of six to one, and despite his possession of artillery, the chagrined General Howard soon found himself completely surrounded and besieged, with his forces drawn up in a hollow square. For more than a day, the Indians kept up the close siege, sometimes coming near enough for hand-to-hand fighting. Then, tiring of the battle, they broke it off, after first giving the camp plenty of time to move on. They had lost four killed and six wounded, the Army thirteen killed and twenty-three wounded.

After traveling a safe distance to the east, the Nez Percés camped to take stock of their situation and decide their future course. They had fought their battle on the Clearwater as five separate bands, each under its own chief (Ollikut, Joseph's brother, had led the Wallowa band), and with no clear idea of what they were fighting for except to defend themselves. Now it was decided that the only course open to them was to leave Idaho Territory and go east across the mountains. There they could join their friends, the Crows, on the buffalo plains in Montana. Chief Joseph objected; he wanted to continue to fight for his beautiful land, to the death if need be, but he was overruled. The Nez Percés, in their naïveté, believed that their fight was only with General Howard, and that if they crossed the mountains beyond his jurisdiction there would be nothing more to fear. Looking Glass was named war chief for the united band, and the march began, over the difficult Lolo Trail across the high Bitterroot Mountains. Besides its aged and infirm, its children and infants, its sick and wounded who had to be carried through, the band was driving a herd of two to three thousand horses. Yet they made it, through a trail so blocked by jack-straw tangles of fallen trees and boulders that Howard's forces, following behind, had to be preceded by a crew of forty axmen.

The band passed over the high point of the Bitterroots and were moving down its eastern slope into Montana when they found their way blocked by hastily built fortifications manned by about thirty-five regular Army infantrymen and some two hundred volunteers, under the command of Captain Charles C. Rawn. Chief Joseph, Looking Glass, and old Chief White Bird rode forward to parley. They explained that

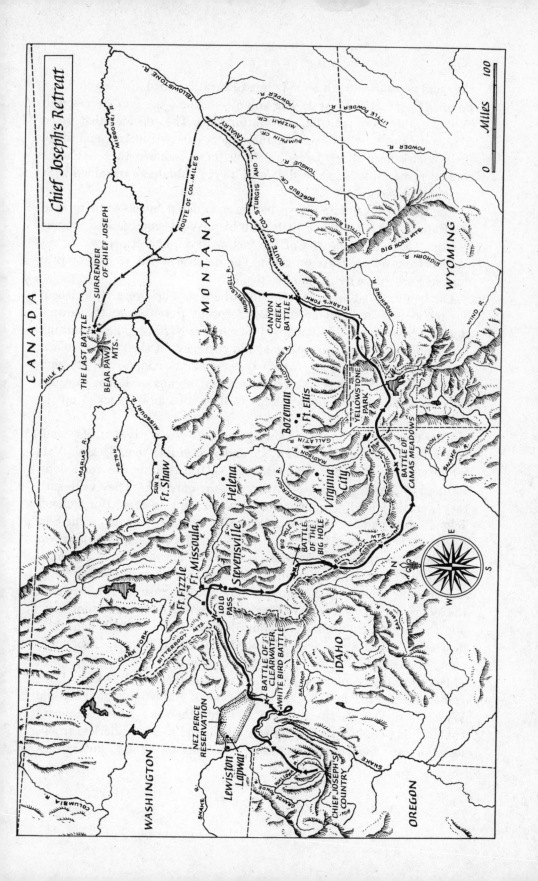

they had no quarrel with anyone but General Howard and would harm no one if permitted to pass. The volunteers knew the Nez Percés well and favorably from their buffalo-hunting trips. They decided that, since they were there only to defend their homes from Indians, and since their homes needed no defending from these Indians, they might as well go home. Most of them did; only thirty volunteers remained with Rawn and his regulars.

The unhappy Captain Rawn had been ordered by Howard to hold the Indians but he could do little with his depleted forces. The Indians swung wide around the end of the fortifications, and Rawn wisely refrained from opening fire on them. The defense works were promptly dubbed Fort Fizzle by the public.

The band moved on to Stevensville where supplies were replenished, not by looting and pillage, but by decorous purchase in the town's stores. These strange Indians, who could easily have taken anything they wanted, quietly paid with gold and currency for their sugar, coffee, and tobacco, and at prices which the merchants had raised sky-high for the occasion. There was, however, no buying of liquor because the chiefs had told the town fathers to have all supplies locked up till the band had moved on.

Now they turned south, following the Bitterroot River to its head, then crossed the Continental Divide and passed into the Big Hole Valley just south of it, where at last they set up their tepees for a long rest and to repair some of the ravages of the hard trip. They were sure they were in friendly country now, with nothing to fear. But Colonel John Gibbon had come by forced marches from Fort Shaw on the Sun River, gathering men from other posts as he came, and at dawn on August 9, he attacked the sleeping camp with approximately two hundred men. There was no warning. The shot that killed a solitary horse herder came almost at the same instant as the crash of rifle fire into the lodges and the whoops of charging soldiers. Women were shot without hesitation; children were gunned down; even babies had their heads crushed with a kick or a clubbed rifle. Such, at least, is the testimony of an officer who took part in the campaign.

But despite the overwhelming surprise of the attack, some of the Indians recovered and began to fight back, rallied by doughty old White Bird. One sharp stroke of luck fell their way; the lieutenant commanding Gibbon's left wing was killed, and as the leaderless troops lost purpose, the Indians opposing them organized a counterattack that continued until it had rolled up Gibbon's entire force, which was now giving too much of its attention to plundering. The marksmanship of the Nez Percés was taking a heavy toll (their accurate shooting, unusual among Indians, was remarked in every engagement). Gibbon was soon on the defensive and besieged; Chief Joseph had taken charge of getting the camp packed up and moving, and the weary, never-ending flight was on again.

When a detachment of soldiers attempted to set up a howitzer, a handful of Indians drove them off, seized the cannon, and, since they did not know how to use the weapon, wrecked it. Gibbon, running out of food, water, and ammunition, was saved only by the arrival of General Howard. He had lost thirty-three dead and thirty-eight wounded, including himself. He claimed the Indians lost eighty-nine, and this appears to be correct, or very nearly so, but most of those dead were women, children, and aged. The Nez Percés later said that only twelve warriors died, but they included some of the best, among them Rainbow and Five Wounds.

The Nez Percés buried their dead before withdrawing; Howard permitted his Bannock Indian scouts to dig up the bodies to scalp and mutilate them. This barbarism, coming on top of the savage slaughter of noncombatants, shocked the Nez Percés, who had been fighting by all the rules of so-called civilized warfare. Howard became the most despised man in the world as far as they were concerned, not completely logically, for it was Colonel Gibbon who had been guilty of killing the women and children.

Looking Glass was displaced as war leader because he had let the camp be taken by surprise, his place taken by a chief named Lean Elk who had recently joined the band; he had been buffalo hunting and was camped in the Bitterroot valley with half a dozen lodges when the fugitives came by shortly after the affair of Fort Fizzle. But the stories going out to the country—and the public was by now intensely interested in what was occurring—all credited Chief Joseph with the military leadership of the band. General Howard, recalling Joseph's astuteness in council and his leadership in peace, assumed that he was continuing to guide the Nez Percés in battle. So the legend arose of a rude military genius in the northern mountains, a redskinned Napoleon, maneuvering his outnumbered warriors so skilfully as to confound, confuse, and defeat, time and again, the trained troops of the United States.

The truth is somewhat less exciting. Joseph was not a war chief, and although he took part in the fighting once or twice, he usually took charge of the camp to see that it was struck, packed for traveling, and on its way, with women and children taken care of. It was an important and necessary function and not to be denigrated—most tribes had peace chiefs and war chiefs—but it lays to rest the myth of the master tactician in moccasins. The Nez Percé victories were due, not to any unusual brilliance in battle, but to a combination of bravery, determination, and the rare ability to stand fast when caught off-balance and then recover and take the initiative. That, along with overconfidence and some fortuitous (for the Nez Percés) mistakes on the part of their white foes.

The fleeing band paralleled the general line of the Continental Divide, which swung in a great arc toward the east. General Howard was pushing them hard. To slow him up and give the fugitives some respite, a group of warriors, whose leaders included Ollikut, made a raid on the night of August 20 on the horse and mule herd of Howard's column at a place called Camas Meadows. The Army camp was alerted by an alarm in time to save its cavalry mounts but the mules were run off, and Howard was held up several days while he gathered new pack animals in settlements in the surrounding regions.

The fugitives passed on into Yellowstone Park, then only five years old but already attracting a considerable number of hardy tourists. They barely missed one party containing General William Tecumseh Sherman, but swept up another, shooting and almost fatally wounding one man. The timely arrival of Lean Elk saved the rest of the party from injury and the women from molestation (the young Nez Percés had become much less forbearing toward whites since the affair at Big Hole).

The flight continued, through Yellowstone Park and the northwestern corner of Wyoming; then the Indians swung northward where more trouble awaited. Part of the 7th Cavalry, commanded by Colonel Samuel Sturgis (who had been on detached duty when almost half the regiment died at the Little Bighorn), tried to head them off, but the Nez Percé band found its way through mountainous country which had been considered impassable for men with horses and came out behind Sturgis on Clarks Fork of the Yellowstone River.

The decision was made to continue the weary journey on to Canada. They had discovered that there was to be no haven among the Crows as they had planned. The embarrassed Crows had explained to Looking Glass and other emissaries who had gone to them that they were not only at peace with the whites but were working for them as scouts. However, when Army commanders in the area shortly afterward tried to enlist them as scouts against the Nez Percés, an unusual number of them proved to be busy elsewhere. Those who did agree to serve showed an amazing ineptness.

Sturgis and his companies of the 7th picked up the trail again, and caught up with their quarry, after a pursuit of perhaps seventy-five miles, at Canyon Creek, a small tributary of the Yellowstone, not far west of the present site of Billings, Montana. The attacking cavalry was stopped by warriors protected behind rocks and ravines while the rest of the band retreated up the creek canyon; then the Indians fought a rear-guard action as they retreated. By nightfall Sturgis, with four dead and a number of wounded, gave up the chase; no Nez Percé was known to have been killed although at least three had been wounded.

The band, exhausted, slowed down now that pursuit appeared to have been left behind. Their course took them north across Montana, as far as a low range called the Bear Paw Mountains which rose from the plains in the northern part of the Territory. There, only thirty miles from the Canadian border, the fugitive band made camp to rest and to hunt and lay in a supply of dried meat and buffalo skins against the coming winter.

Once again they had reckoned without the telegraph. Colonel Nelson E. Miles was hurrying up from Fort Keogh on the Yellowstone with six hundred men: parts of the 2nd and 7th Cavalry and the mounted 5th Infantry, along with a considerable number of Cheyenne warriors. Another day and the Nez Percés would probably have made it to Canada, for most of the pack animals already had their burdens lashed on and the band was making ready to move again when Miles's scouts sighted their lodges on the morning of the last day of September.

Colonel Miles ordered an immediate attack, hoping to smash the Nez Percés with a single charge. But he had begun the charge a good four miles away, and the Indians had that much warning; old White Bird quickly posted his men in front of the camp, and as the onrushing battle line of troops came within range, it met a withering fire which killed two officers and twenty-two men, and injured another four officers and thirty-eight men. The charge stopped as though it had been poleaxed, and the men took shelter behind rocks and in gullies. But they did not retreat; the camp remained under fire.

White Bird had only 120 men against Miles's six hundred; the 2nd Cavalry which formed Miles's right wing extended so far beyond the Nez Percé defenses that it met no opposition and swept on toward the horse herd, most of which it captured. The pack horses, standing ready to go, had been started on their way by women and children as soon as the troops were seen approaching; about fifty warriors went along and beat off attempts of the cavalry to pursue and capture the pack train. When the soldiers gave up the pursuit, many of the warriors turned back, too, and slipped into the camp.

Two brave leaders, Chief Toohoolhoolzote and Ollikut, were among the good men who died in the first confused fighting. Chief Joseph and his twelve-year-old daughter had been with the horse herd when the attack came. He told the girl to catch a horse and join those who were cut off from the camp. Then he galloped his horse through the line of soldiers, unharmed, though his horse was wounded and his clothes pierced many times. His wife met him at the entrance of his lodge and handed him his rifle. "Here is your gun. Fight."

The battle quickly settled down to a siege. The next morning, October 1, heavy snow fell and the storm continued for two days; although it added to the discomfort of both sides, it brought fighting almost to a halt. Colonel Miles, attempting to win by deception, tricked Joseph into his camp with a white flag on the pretense of wanting to negotiate, and then seized the chief. The Indians countered by capturing an officer; an exchange of prisoners restored the situation as it had been.

On October 4, General Howard arrived with more troops, making the situation of the Nez Percés hopeless. Negotiations were begun through two treaty Nez Percés who had come with Howard as interpreters. The few remaining chiefs were told that Howard would treat the band with honor if they surrendered, and would send them back to the Lapwai reservation in the spring, when the mountains were clear of snow again. Looking Glass and White Bird wanted to fight on, but Chief Joseph insisted that they must make their decision for the freezing women and children crouching in the pits that had been dug for shelter from Miles's howitzer.

Just as the council broke up, brave Looking Glass fell dead, struck in the head by a chance bullet. For four months, and over a trail 1,300 miles long, the Nez Percé band had fought and fled, to be caught only thirty miles from freedom. A short distance still remained for Chief Joseph to travel, the ride from the camp to the hill where General Howard and Colonel Miles were waiting, but for him it would be the longest part of the journey. He had already sent his message of surrender ahead with Captain John, one of the Nez Percé interpreters, who had carried it to General Howard and repeated it with tears in his eyes: *

Tell General Howard I know his heart. What he told me before I have in my heart. I am tired of fighting. Our chiefs are killed. Looking Glass is dead. Toohoolhoolzote is dead. The old men are all dead. It is the young men who say yes and no. He who led the young men [Ollikut] is dead. It is cold and we have no blankets. The little children are freezing to death. My people, some of them, have run away to the hills, and have no blankets, no food; no one knows where they are—perhaps freezing to death. I want to have time to look for my children and see how many I can find. Maybe I shall find them among the dead. Hear me, my chiefs, I am tired; my heart is sick and sad. From where the sun now stands, I will fight no more forever.

About two hours later, Joseph rode over, with several of his men walking beside him. He dismounted and handed his rifle to Howard, who motioned that he should give it to Colonel Miles. Thereafter, he was treated as a prisoner of war.

Chief White Bird escaped to Canada that night with a handful of followers. A number of those who had gotten away on the first day also made it to safety across the border, but some had been killed by hostile Assiniboines and Hidatsas. A few more than 400 were captured of about 650 who had started on the long trip; probably close to 200 died during the flight or on the plains. But Joseph's fears that his own children might be dead were groundless; of his six children, only the baby born on the eve of the long journey remained with him at the time of the surrender, but all were later found safe.

* There are two versions of the manner in which the famous message was delivered. The one given here was contained in the *Report of the Secretary of War, 1877,* and would appear to have the ring of authenticity. Another and more dramatic description of the event later became current: it had the saddened Joseph making his speech directly to General Howard and Colonel Miles. This version also seems made of sound metal since it was the story recounted by Charles E. S. Wood, who, as Lieutenant Wood, had been General Howard's aide and was present at the surrender. However, when he wrote of the event he had become a professional author, and probably was tampering with history to increase the dramatic effect.

The captives were taken to Fort Keogh, a logical place to hold them until they could be returned to Idaho in the spring. But soon an order came from General Sheridan to send them to Fort Abraham Lincoln. It would be too expensive, he said, to maintain them at Fort Keogh through the winter. Colonel Miles, after making a futile protest, put most of his prisoners on flatboats to make the long trip down the Yellowstone and Missouri without military guard or escort except for one enlisted man on each boat. The able-bodied men and some of the women marched overland with Miles and his troops. All arrived safely.

When Miles arrived in Bismarck with the overland contingent of Nez Percés, a remarkable thing occurred. Bismarck, it will be remembered, was still a frontier community, and most of its people were convinced of the basic rightness of Sheridan's dictum, "The only good Indian is a dead Indian." * Not only that, it was at Fort Abraham Lincoln, near Bismarck, that the 7th Cavalry had been stationed. Many of the townspeople had had friends who had died only a year before with Custer.

Bismarck would, in short, seem an unwise place to bring a group of Indians who had lately been at war with the Army. But as the column rode through the main street, with Chief Joseph on horseback beside Colonel Miles and the rest of the Nez Percé following, enclosed by a protecting square of soldiers, crowds of townspeople surged out into the street, and against the cordon of troops. However, there was no hate and no violence intended; they carried food, and broke through the square of troops to give it to the Indians. Only when the people had exhausted all their gifts was the column able to proceed on to Fort Lincoln.

Two days later an even more remarkable event occurred. The good ladies of Bismarck were hostesses at a dinner at which Chief Joseph and the other chiefs were guests of honor. But these were the only two bright spots in their treatment by white people since their war began, and would be just about the last. Two days after the dinner, they were on a train, headed for Fort Leavenworth, with Indian Territory as their eventual destination. Colonel Miles and General Howard protested this

---

* Sheridan appears not to have made his deathless remark in quite these words. At Fort Cobb in Indian Territory, in January, 1869 during the Washita campaign, a Comanche named Turtle Dove introduced himself to Sheridan, adding, "Me good Indian." "The only good Indians I know are dead," the General graciously replied, according to the man who overheard and recorded the exchange. The quotation was revised into the more serviceable one the world knows.

betrayal of the promises made by Howard to the Nez Percés at the time of the surrender, but the higher powers in Washington felt under no kind of obligation to honor the promises. General Sherman, while refraining from talking about extermination in this case, announced that the Nez Percés must be suitably punished to discourage other tribes who might feel moved to defend their rights.

The Nez Percés were settled in a low, malarial part of Indian Territory, especially deadly to these highland people whose resistance to disease had been lowered by their recent hardships and suffering. Within a few months, more than a quarter of them were dead. They got along fairly well after they became somewhat acclimated to their new surroundings, and even prospered in a small way through their skill at stock raising, but they remained hopelessly homesick for their mountains. Strong public sentiment had been aroused by their magnificent retreat and by the way they conducted themselves during it, and the public was not permitted to forget their story. Colonel Miles (brigadier general after 1880), a firm friend of Joseph since the end of the war, regularly recommended that the Nez Percés be permitted to return.

A few widows and orphans were allowed to go to the Lapwai reservation in 1882, and the rest were sent north three years later. Slightly more than half went to Lapwai; the rest, among them Joseph, were for some reason sent to the Colville reservation in northern Washington to live among the several small tribes there. None of Joseph's six children returned north with him; he had buried them, one by one, in alien soil, victims of the climate and disease of the south.

Chief Joseph, during the rest of his life, asked to be permitted to returned to the Wallowa country, of which he had said, "I love that land more than all the rest of the world." But where the rest of the country had come to admire Joseph, the ranchers in his former home opposed his return, and the government supinely gave in to their wishes. Joseph died, still grieving for his lost country, in 1904. Charles Erskine Wood, aide to General Howard during the Nez Percé War, wrote what might be Joseph's epitaph: "I think that, in his long career, Joseph cannot accuse the Government of the United States of one single act of justice."

2. "A NUMBER OF INSUBORDINATE,
CUNNING, TREACHEROUS INDIANS"

The Bannocks of southeastern Idaho went on the warpath, briefly and futilely, in 1878, the year after the Nez Percé lunge toward freedom. Their bill of particulars is long but the cause of their hopeless uprising can be reduced to three words: they were hungry.

During the great period of treaty making on the plains and in the mountains in 1867 and 1868, the Bannocks accepted a reservation on the upper Snake River, being careful to reserve all rights to an area called Camas Prairie. The camas is a plant of the lily family which covers entire meadows with its blue flowers in spring; its onion-shaped root-bulb, when baked, formed an important part of the diet of the Bannocks as it did of most of the tribes of the Pacific Northwest. The Camas Prairie was an especially extensive and prolific source of this foodstuff.

After the treaty was signed and the Bannocks had moved onto the reservation in 1868, the usual things happened. The government was late with the annuities it had promised, and when it did send them, the amounts were less than had been agreed on in the treaty. To keep from starving, the Bannocks went after buffalo. They were part-time horse-and-buffalo Indians, and at one time bison had ranged as far west as the headwaters of the Snake in their own country, but now the buffalo ranges were farther away each year, and it required some nine months for a hunting expedition to cross the mountains to the plains and return. Nevertheless, it was a choice between that or going hungry, and even their agent encouraged the hunts because with part of the tribe gone, the food annuities went further among those who remained on the reservation.

Even so, it was not enough. Food was so scarce one year that the agent reported that the people came begging because their children were crying for something to eat. Under these circumstances, the food supplied by the camas roots became even more important than usual, but white settlers were encroaching more and more on the Camas Prairie, using it not only to pasture horses and cattle, but as a feeding ground for large herds of swine which uprooted and destroyed the camas plants.

Trouble came in the spring of 1878. The Bannocks had been on very short rations because there had been no buffalo hunt the previous winter; like all other tribes in the region they had been ordered to stay on their reservation of fear they might join the hostile Nez Percés. The food rations were stretched thin to go around. Then, when spring came and the tribe moved to Camas Prairie, they found settlers there herding their hogs and cattle, as they had done for several years. Only this time, Chief Buffalo Horn, who had led the Bannock scouts against Chief Joseph's Nez Percés, had had enough of it. He ordered the herders off Bannock land. Before they could get off, two were shot and wounded by a pair of irresponsible young Indians.

The war that followed was confused, but was uniformly disastrous to Bannock arms. Some of the tribe returned at once to the agency to remain clear of the conflict; the rest headed west and north, hoping to enlist the Paiutes, Umatillas and other tribes of the region in the conflict. No one joined them; on the contrary, the Umatillas offered their services to the Army. The Bannocks, defeated and their leaders killed, turned east, and in small groups tried to find refuge among friendly tribes. A few got as far as Wyoming Territory across the Continental Divide, where they were attacked by Colonel Miles, and a number were killed when a cannon was turned on their lodges; others were slain when an Army unit ignored their attempts to surrender and met them with heavy gunfire.

The war was over by October. Nine soldiers and thirty-one civilians were listed by the Army as having been killed. Seventy-eight Bannocks were reported to have died, but it was probably more because the Indians had undoubtedly carried off many of their dead and wounded whom the Army knew nothing of. There was no talk by Sherman either of extermination or of removal to Indian Territory. The principal punishment was to keep the captured Bannocks, about six hundred, at Fort Simcoe, Washington, for periods up to two years before permitting them to return to their own agency.

General George Crook had been on the Bannock reservation a year before the outbreak, and to enlighten his professional colleagues about the situation, wrote an article which appeared (in the *Army and Navy Journal*, June 29, 1878) shortly after the start of the trouble:

. . . I was up there last spring, and found them in a desperate condition. I telegraphed, and the agent telegraphed for supplies, but word came that no appropriation had been made. They have never been half supplied.

The agent has sent them off for half a year to enable them to pick up something to live on, but there is nothing for them in that country. The buffalo is all gone, . . . and there aren't enough jackrabbits to catch. What are they to do?

Starvation is staring them in the face, and if they wait much longer, they will not be able to fight. They understand the situation, and fully appreciate what is before them.

The encroachments upon the Camas prairies was the cause of the trouble. These prairies are the last source of subsistence. . . . I do not wonder, and you will not either that when these Indians see their wives and children starving, and their last sources of supplies cut off, they go to war. And then we are sent out to kill them. It is an outrage.

The last of the Bannock hostiles had not yet surrendered before there was new trouble, this time on the Great Plains again. At the close of the Sioux War, the defeated Cheyenne band of Chief Dull Knife, as well as a smaller number of other surrendered Cheyennes, had been sent south to join their southern kinsmen on the Cheyenne-Arapaho reservation in Indian Territory. The Indians had been misled about what they would find in the south, and about how they would be treated when they got there. Dull Knife claimed he had been promised that they could return north if they did not like their new home, and it is very probable, in view of the usual practices of government commissioners, that such assurances were given with no intention of abiding by them.

The Cheyennes did not like their new home. They suffered from malaria and other illnesses. They were hungry most of the time because the Indian Bureau did not send the food that had been promised— their agent said he received rations enough to feed them only nine months of the year—and there were no buffalo to hunt as there were on the northern plains. Perhaps hardest of all to bear, they were acutely homesick.

By 1878, after a year and a half in the south, they had had all they could stand, and a band of them, under the leadership of Dull Knife and a warrior chief, Little Wolf, decided to go home. Little Wolf had told the agent that they were not going to remain; the agent called troops from near-by Fort Reno, and a cordon was placed around the

Cheyenne camp. Yet one September morning, daylight revealed to the guard that the tepees were empty.

Flight across the plains was not the same matter of escape through empty distance it had been ten years earlier. Three railroads now cut across from east to west, lines along which troops could be moved rapidly. Telegraph lines had proliferated. Ranchers and homesteaders were numerous, and every one of them was ready to report the passage of a band of Indians. It would be next to impossible to get through without being seen and pursued.

There were very nearly three hundred Indians in the band when it started north. Perhaps seventy were warriors, the rest were women, children, and old men—although it was a very old man who did not fight when the time came. Many were without horses. But they trudged on north, skillfully hiding their trail where a white man would consider it impossible to do so, turning at bay to fight when troops caught up with them. They fought four battles of importance, beating off troops and suffering only six killed; their wounded the medicine men treated, often with results that made Army surgeons shake their heads in wonderment later.

They tried to avoid contact with homesteaders and ranchers, but they needed horses and they needed meat, and usually there was no other source than the horses and cattle of whites. Sometimes the owners tried to stop Indians from making off with their animals; then there were exchanges of gunfire, and white men were killed—and the Western newspapers spread stories of great massacre and bloodshed. It was an unhappy situation for both Indians and settlers.

General Sheridan's entire Division of the Missouri hastily mobilized its manpower to block the northward march of the Cheyennes. Nevertheless, the Indians crossed the Atchison, Topeka & Santa Fe, they crossed the Kansas Pacific, and at last they passed over the Union Pacific, where troops were spread out in a great net to snare them, but were unable to prevent them from slipping through.

After crossing the Union Pacific, the Cheyennes split into two groups, both heading into the sand hills of northwestern Nebraska. One band, under Little Wolf, settled down to winter on a stream called the Lost Chokecherry. The others, led by Dull Knife, were moving through a heavy snowstorm near Camp Robinson in the extreme northwestern corner of the state when they suddenly found horsemen looming up

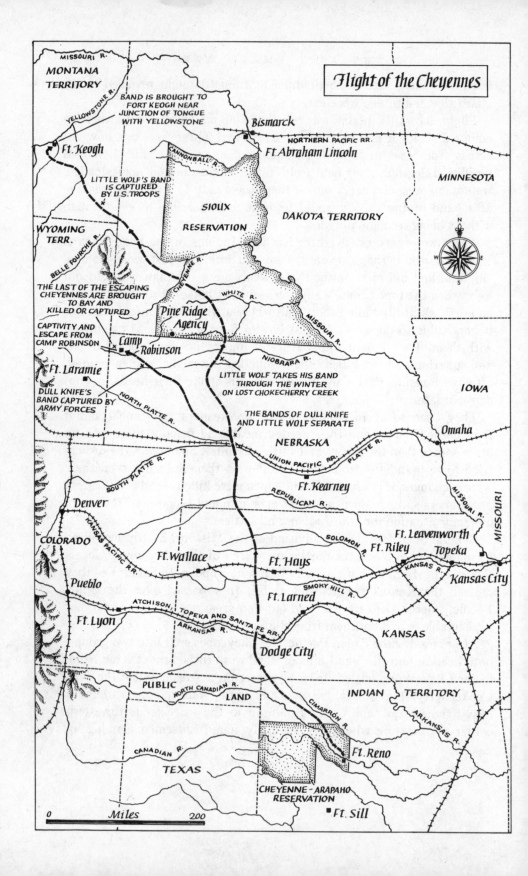

Flight of the Cheyennes

MONTANA TERRITORY

MISSOURI R.

BAND IS BROUGHT TO FORT KEOGH NEAR JUNCTION OF TONGUE WITH YELLOWSTONE

YELLOWSTONE R.

Ft. Keogh

Bismarck

NORTHERN PACIFIC RR.

Ft. Abraham Lincoln

MINNESOTA

LITTLE WOLF'S BAND IS CAPTURED BY U.S. TROOPS

CANNONBALL R.

SIOUX RESERVATION

DAKOTA TERRITORY

WYOMING TERR.

BELLE FOURCHE R.

CHEYENNE R.

WHITE R.

THE LAST OF THE ESCAPING CHEYENNES ARE BROUGHT TO BAY AND KILLED OR CAPTURED

Pine Ridge Agency

MISSOURI R.

CAPTIVITY AND ESCAPE FROM CAMP ROBINSON

Camp Robinson

Ft. Laramie

NIOBRARA R.

DULL KNIFE'S BAND CAPTURED BY ARMY FORCES

NORTH PLATTE R.

LITTLE WOLF TAKES HIS BAND THROUGH THE WINTER ON LOST CHOKECHERRY CREEK

IOWA

THE BANDS OF DULL KNIFE AND LITTLE WOLF SEPARATE

Omaha

SOUTH PLATTE R.

NEBRASKA

UNION PACIFIC RR.

PLATTE R.

Denver

Ft. Kearney

REPUBLICAN R.

KANSAS PACIFIC RR.

MISSOURI R.

COLORADO

Ft. Wallace

SOLOMON R.

Ft. Leavenworth

Ft. Riley

Topeka

Ft. Hays

KANSAS R.

Kansas City

Pueblo

SMOKY HILL R.

Ft. Larned

MISSOURI

ATCHISON, TOPEKA AND SANTA FE RR.

Ft. Lyon

ARKANSAS R.

KANSAS

Dodge City

PUBLIC LAND

NORTH CANADIAN R.

INDIAN TERRITORY

CIMARRON R.

ARKANSAS R.

CANADIAN R.

Ft. Reno

TEXAS

CHEYENNE - ARAPAHO RESERVATION

Ft. Sill

0   Miles   200

out of the whiteness ahead. They had run into two companies of the 3rd Cavalry by pure chance in the obscuring snow; the soldiers were as surprised as they were, and Captain J. B. Johnson, commanding, was happy to see Dull Knife raise a white flag rather than prepare to fight.

During the next two days, as Johnson parleyed with Dull Knife and his chiefs about what should be done with them, the military forces were gradually increased. The Indians had been certain that now they were so near their old hunting grounds, they would be permitted to remain, and the situation became tense when Johnson indicated that it was not quite as simple as that. At last, faced with overwhelming Army strength that now included artillery, the Indians were induced to give up their weapons and to move on to Camp Robinson. They gave up only their oldest guns, however; the best ones were secretly taken apart and hidden under the women's clothing.

At Camp Robinson they were quartered in an empty barracks. They had wanted to join the Sioux on Pine Ridge agency (the former Red Cloud agency), just across the Dakota border not far to the northeast, but the Army decided otherwise. For a time, their captivity was a light burden. They were allowed to roam in the near vicinity of the fort, hunting grouse, rabbits, and such other small game on the river bottoms as they could bring down with bow and arrow, which they were permitted to use. The main restriction was that they all must be in the barracks each night; their future liberties would depend on observing that rule.

But, although they had been treated with kindness, the sword hung over their heads. They knew that someone in Washington was making up his mind what should be done with them, and they were afraid of being sent back to Indian Territory. They knew only that they did not want to go back to the empty land in the south. "We will not go there to live," Dull Knife said. "That is not a healthful country, and if we should stay there we would all die. We do not wish to go back there and we will not go. You may kill me here, but you cannot make me go back."

After two months, the easy-going captivity came to a sudden end. When the prisoners were first brought to Camp Robinson, and before they had been counted, one woman escaped and joined the Sioux on Pine Ridge agency. In time, her lorn husband, a warrior named Bull Hump, found the separation too much to bear, and went off to the agency to see his wife. He was found and brought back within a few days, but as a consequence, all the prisoners lost their privileges of moving freely around the post, and henceforth were locked in the barracks.

In the meantime, the Cheyennes had become the focus of attention of do-gooders, of Indian-haters, of people sincerely concerned with helping the Indians, of revenge-seekers, of a host of the other types who appeared from all directions whenever Indians became involved in controversy. The magnificent flight of the Nez Percés was only a year past, and the public had become more acutely aware of the injustices being done to Indians. Not all the voices raised in defense of the Cheyennes and their right to remain in the North spoke with Eastern accents. Even the editor of the Omaha *Herald,* in the frontier state where the Cheyennes were at that moment imprisoned and where Indians were not loved, appealed to the Indian Bureau not to take the plucky little band back south. For, said Editor Miller, it would mean hauling them back trussed up like cattle. "It means starvation for them. I implore you for justice and humanity to those wronged red men. Let them stay in their own country."

There were, of course, other voices. Kansas authorities were demanding the surrender of the Cheyenne men, to stand trial for the murder of ranchers and homesteaders. And Lieutenant General Philip Henry Sheridan, deploring the tears shed for the Cheyennes, was certain that unless they were severely disciplined, all Indians would break loose from every restraint. "The condition of these Indians is pitiable but it is my opinion that unless they are sent back to where they came from, the whole reservation system will receive a shock which will endanger its stability."

At Camp Robinson, the temperature dropped lower and lower: to zero, to ten below, to as low as forty below zero. There are degrees of cold that one who has not experienced them cannot quite imagine; they are not merely uncomfortable but dangerous and potentially deadly to those not properly protected. While the cold hung so deep, the long-expected word came through; the Cheyennes were to be sent back to Indian Territory, and immediately.

The order came as no surprise because it had long been more than rumor that the Indians would be returned. It was the impossibly bad timing of the move that upset the military authorities. General Crook, commanding the Department of the Platte in which Camp Robinson was located, telegraphed the Indian Bureau to send a man to take charge of the move. If the Indian Bureau was going to insist on moving the Cheyennes in the iron-hard depths of winter, Crook felt it should assume the responsibility. The Cheyennes themselves, who had already sensed that they were going to be shipped back south, were told definitely and finally, on January 3, 1879, that they would have to get ready to move. Their answer, as it had always been, was that they would not go back to Indian Territory; they would prefer to have the soldiers kill them than to die slowly in the south.

Captain Henry W. Wessells, Jr., commanding officer of the post, went in to the prison barracks with an ultimatum: agree to go south or go cold and hungry. Once again they gave the same answer, that they would rather die than return to Indian Territory. They were given no more food or firewood. They bundled up in their ragged blankets and kept tiny fires going by burning the crude furniture; the few scraps of food they had saved were carefully doled out to the children.

A few days later, Wessells gave the screws another turn by ordering water withheld, even drinking water. He offered to take care of the women and children if they would come out, but the Cheyennes disdained even to answer. To quench their thirst somewhat, they scraped the thick frost from the windows. At that time there were 149 Cheyennes in the barracks, less than a third of them males between the ages of eleven and eighty.

On January 9, Captain Wessells called Dull Knife and two other chiefs, Old Crow and Wild Hog, to a council. Only the latter two came; the Cheyennes would not let Dull Knife out of the barracks for fear of treachery. Their suspicions were completely justified; after trying to get a surrender agreement out of Old Crow and Wild Hog and receiving only a scornful reply, Wessells had the two chiefs seized and put in irons. An alarm reached the prisoners in the barracks, who at once prepared to defend themselves against an expected assault by troops. The rifles were taken out from hiding places under floor boards, and men without guns armed themselves with the women's household knives with their worn-down blades, and even with pieces of board for clubs. With such weapons, they stood ready to resist Army rifles.

The attack did not come, nor had Captain Wessells any intention of attempting to drive the Cheyennes out by force. He was so confident that his campaign to starve and freeze the Indians out was going to succeed that he was perfectly content to wait. In his assurance, it did not occur to him that hungry, desperate people might be driven to extreme measures. The Cheyennes had been forced to just such extreme. They had decided that same day that it was far preferable to die like free people in the open air than miserably like caged beasts.

About ten o'clock that night, they made their desperate try for freedom. Warriors of the Dog Society leapt from the windows first to shoot the sentries and cover the escape, deliberately giving up their lives to delay the first pursuit and give the others a few minutes start. Wessell's refusal to believe that the imprisoned, hungry Indians could be dangerous also gave them a few minutes; he had declined to post any extra guard in spite of the trouble of the afternoon, although other, less sanguine officers sat up waiting for the disturbance they were afraid would come. But there were no enlisted men waiting at the ready, and some of them actually set out in pursuit in their underwear, even though the temperature was far below zero. They suffered acutely before they were ordered back to camp for warm clothing.

The Indians headed for the bluffs some two miles distant from the post, leaving the way strewn with their dead and wounded. When warriors fell, women and young boys picked up their guns and tried to fight on. A lieutenant stumbled into a pit and found himself with two Indians who set upon him with knives. Despite a bright full moon, it was not possible to make out much in the hollow except that he was in mortal danger; he shot the Indians with his pistol and then found they were both women. There were, without doubt, instances of the indiscriminate killing of men, women, and children that had been such a common feature of Army attacks on Indians, but they appear not to have been so much in evidence during these bloody minutes. Perhaps it was that the sympathies of the soldiers had been with the Cheyennes in their simple, understandable pleas not to be sent back south. In any event, attempts were made to obtain surrenders where possible, and wounded were brought in to the post hospital.

Most of the crimes against the wounded seem to have been the work of the traders and other civilians at the post who soon arrived with wagons and followed the path of the flight, clearly marked by dark bundles easily visible against the moonlit snow. The dead they stripped of their garments and sometimes scalped; there were dark indications that more than one dead person had been only wounded when these body-robbers came on him.

The mass of the Cheyennes reached the bluffs at last, at a point they had noted at some time in the past; it was an inconspicuous break in the cliffs which provided a way to the top for people on foot. There was no other way up anywhere in the vicinity, and for men on horseback it was necessary to travel six miles to find a way to the top. The pursuit had to be given up for the night; the Cheyennes had gained that much time—at a terrible cost.

By daylight, some thirty dead Indians had been brought into the camp, and perhaps thirty-five wounded, along with a number of uninjured prisoners. More dead were found after it became light, and more living, too, who were killed, or wounded, or surrendered half-frozen and filled with the hopelessness of resistance. Warriors had to be shot out of caves; elsewhere, women gave up, saying there had been enough killing.

The main body of the escaped Cheyennes, after gaining the top of the bluff, had pushed on westward during the night and next morning, covering an unbelievable seventeen miles in the bitter cold, hungry and weak as they were, some of them carrying children, some of them wounded. Then, when troops from the post did catch up with them, they did the completely unexpected: they circled about and lay in ambush for the column. Two soldiers were shot down and several horses; the Cheyennes were in a strong position on a timbered hill and could not be dislodged by an attack. At night, Captain Wessells left a line of decoy fires around the Cheyenne position and took his troops back to Camp Robinson, because so sure had he been that he would bring the Indians back at heel that he had come without camp equipment or rations. The Cheyennes were not fooled by the decoy fires; that night they cut up the dead cavalry horses and had their first food in days, then moved on.

The cavalry column picked up their trail again the next day, and found and besieged them, only to have them slip away again at night. This went on day after day, the intrepid little band always managing to find a position virtually impregnable to direct attack before their pursuers caught up with them, and always gliding like ghosts through the Army picket lines at night. But time after time there was a price to pay: a man or woman killed here, another there, someone wounded. And constant hunger and cold, the cold that could freeze fingers and toes, hands and feet, of those whose necessary errands or carelessness exposed them to it.

At last, on January 21, twelve days after the breakout, the end came.

The band, now shrunken to thirty-one persons, was brought to bay about forty-five miles west of Camp Robinson, near the head of War Bonnet Creek. They took shelter in a washout in the bluffs, digging in deeper for better protection. Wessels, greatly reinforced on this last day, carefully surrounded the pits before calling on the Indians to surrender.

He was answered by a scattering fire, and the death chants of the Cheyennes.

He ordered an attack on the Indian positions. The soldiers charged to the edge of the pits; only the exhaustion of the Cheyenne's ammunition saved the lives of many soldiers, so closely were they grouped as they fired down into the holes. As they sprang back to reload, three men leaped out of the defenses and charged the troops—three against three hundred. Two were armed with knives, the third with an empty pistol. They were dropped in their tracks.

The soldiers fired another volley into the heap of dead and dying in the defense pits, and then it was over. Seventeen men were dead; one still lived, but only for a matter of a few hundred heart-beats. Six women and children were dead, another woman dying. All but two of the remaining seven women and children were badly wounded but would live.

These were the people who had wanted only to go home.

Dull Knife had been much sought by questing troops, who neither found his body nor were able to get any information about him from those who were captured. In the flight, he and his wife, his son and his son's wife, a young child and a youth, had become separated from the main party. They had hidden in a cave for a number of days, almost starving, until it was safe for them to strike north for Pine Ridge agency, living on rose hips, roots, and moccasins tops as they traveled. At the agency they were taken in by a half-breed interpreter and cared for until the day when it was no longer necessary to hide.

At Camp Robinson, the inevitable court of inquiry had convened to sift through events. There were a number of loose ends still dangling. What had happened to Dull Knife? Where was Little Wolf and his band? What was to be done with these people now—those who remained? What about the continuing demands from Kansas that the men be returned there to stand trial for murder? The Army was not happy; the affair had been handled very messily, which is to say it had been done with too much publicity. Indignation was nationwide; protests against military brutality came from everywhere. The figures were damning: 149 had broken out of the barracks; now only 78 were known to be alive, and many of these were wounded, crippled with frozen hands or feet, or sick. Sherman's brittle temper cracked when a newsman asked him, soon after the escape from the barracks, for more details on the massacre. "Massacre!" the prickly General snapped. "Why do you call it a massacre? A number of insubordinate, cunning, treacherous Indians."

But the voices of national conscience, already raised against the treatment of the Nez Percés, now moved even the ponderous bureaucracy of the Indian Office—to a degree. It was ruled that women, children, and a few badly crippled men could go to live among the Oglala Sioux on the Pine Ridge agency. They were loaded into wagons and taken north, fifty-eight of them, arriving at last without hindrance in the northern country to which they had set out when they left Indian Territory—but arriving as widows, orphans, and cripples.

Seven men of the band—all who appeared whole enough to stand trial—were taken to Kansas, along with their families. Defense funds poured in from across the country; lawyers offered their services without cost. But the case against the seven never went to a jury; it was soon dismissed by the court for lack of evidence. Nevertheless, they were sent on south to Indian Territory with their families, but the voices of indignation found them out even there, and the Indian Bureau soon permitted them to go north again.

While the prisoners at Camp Robinson were going through their time of trouble, Little Wolf and his band remained in their winter camp on the stream named the Lost Chokecherry in Nebraska's Sand Hills. They had settled in for the winter shortly after they split away from Dull Knife's band, and had spent the cold months in all the careful concealment of hunted animals, livings in pits in the stream bank, keeping their fires small and burning only fuel that would send up no smoke, always staying to the windswept ridges when they hunted or scouted—to avoid leaving tracks in the snow—and somehow the troops endlessly patrolling the great reaches of prairie never came upon them.

In March, they started on their way again, and on the twenty-fifth of the month, when they were just west of the headwaters of the Little Missouri River in the extreme southeastern corner of Montana Territory, the band, 112 strong, met strong cavalry forces under Lieutenant

W. P. Clark. It was not a surprise meeting; Northern Cheyennes living in the region had met Little Wolf and told him that Army forces were in the vicinity. The Cheyenne leader placed his people on a strong defensive position; then, when the cavalry forces appeared, he went out alone to talk to Lieutenant Clark, an old friend for whom he had scouted two years earlier, and an officer the Indians trusted completely. Clark could promise him only that he would do all he could to see that they were permitted to remain in the north—and for a mere lieutenant, that would be nothing, because even generals had not been able to keep promises made to Indians.

But Little Wolf accepted his assurance for want of anything better. He and his people rode along with the cavalry to Fort Keogh, where the Tongue River empties into the Yellowstone, and when they arrived there was no locking them up in barracks. They were back in the Powder River country where they wanted to be, and such was the public temper after what had happened to Dull Knife's band that not the Indian Bureau, nor Sherman nor Sheridan spoke of returning them to Indian Territory. They were permitted to remain where they were; later, the Tongue River Reservation was established for all Northern Cheyennes, to include portions of the valleys of both the Tongue and Rosebud. Here Dull Knife and most of the battered survivors of his band eventually came, and here were gathered the Northern Cheyennes who had never been sent south.

It was not, however, quite as they had dreamed it. Very soon the buffalo were gone in the North, too, and the Cheyennes found themselves not only idle and purposeless a good part of the time, but sometimes hungry when the government annuities failed to arrive. But that was the way it was with all Indians now, and if nothing else, they were home.

3. GHOST DANCE AND GATLING GUNS

And still the unnecessary and bloody little wars continued. In 1878, Nathan Meeker, a single-minded and arbitrary man, was appointed agent for the White River Utes, one of the three bands of a tribe whose reservation covered most of western Colorado. Meeker, a theorizer on agricultural subjects, looked on his position as an ideal opportunity to put some of his ideas into action, and he immediately proceeded to do so, attempting in the process to turn the Utes from hunters into farmers almost in a matter of weeks.

As Meeker became more and more demanding and high-handed, the Indians became more resentful. The explosion came in September 1879 when, after long and shrill demands, Meeker prevailed upon his superiors to have troops sent in for his protection. The Utes took the arrival of soldiers as a declaration of war, ambushing and besieging the column and killing eleven. At the same time, the agency was destroyed; Meeker and nine other white employees were slain, and Meeker's wife and daughter, and the wife of another employe were taken captive and handed around among the Indian men for a number of days until released.

The war, if such it can be called, was over as quickly as it had started, and Meeker's dreams and ambitions had been wrecked and his life taken by his own stubborn refusal to understand the customs and point of view of the Indians. But for Governor Frederick Pitkin of Colorado, the war was an unqualified success. He had been trying with indifferent success for some time to work up convincing atrocity cases against the Utes as an excuse to take their lands from them; now at last he had something spectacular to work with. He made the most of it.

"My idea is that, unless removed by the government, they must necessarily be exterminated," a reporter for the New York *Tribune* quoted Pitkin. "I could raise 25,000 men to protect the settlers in twenty-four hours. The State would be willing to settle the Indian problem at its own expense. The advantages that would accrue from the throwing open of twelve million acres of land to miners and settlers would more than compensate all the expenses incurred."

The attitude of the frontier toward the Indian could not have been stated much more cynically: land was everything; the rights of Indians nothing. There is no way of knowing how much of what Pitkin was saying was bluster and bluff, but the Federal government, probably remembering when Colonel Chivington led other Coloradans to do some exterminating, took no chances. The Utes were removed from the state, their great reservation turned over to white settlers. It made no difference that only one of the three bands of Utes had been involved in the affair, and only part of that band. All were moved to Utah, to share the reservation of the Uintah Utes there, each family on an individual piece of land. A portion of the southern band was permitted to remain on a small reserve in the southwestern part of Colorado, on arid land no white man could possibly want; they were granted this special favor because of the pleading of their chief, Ouray, who had always jumped through hoops for the white men.

That was almost the end of the Indian wars, but not quite. In the spring of 1885, a small group of Chiricahua Apaches, the stubbornest fighters of all, fled from their reservation under the leadership of their renegade chief, Geronimo, and disappeared into the almost trackless mountains of Arizona and Mexico. General Crook, who knew the Apaches as no other white man did (and who was convinced that every one of their outbreaks could be laid to white harassment, cupidity, and larceny), persuaded most of the hostiles to surrender after a strenuous ten-month campaign. Then he resigned as commander of the Department of Arizona in vigorous protest because President Cleveland and the commander of the Army, General Sheridan (he had succeeded Sherman in 1883), repudiated the surrender terms Crook had granted and, in a shameless breach of faith, had the Apaches sent to Florida for imprisonment for an indefinite period.

General Nelson Miles replaced Crook. There were only thirty-three Apaches still at large, and thirteen of them were women, but Miles chased them futilely for more than five months; he finally caught them only by adapting Crook's strategy and sending a couple of Apache scouts into the mountain to find and parley with them. Because Geronimo and his ragged handful of followers were weary and tired of fleeing, they agreed to give themselves up.

Less than three dozen Apaches had been hostile when General Miles induced them to surrender, yet the government gathered up the entire Chiricahua band, 498 in number, and sent them into captivity in Florida. These were people who had remained at peace when a minority of the band had followed Geronimo into the mountains. Among them were the scouts who had fought so hard for General Crook; their number included even the two scouts who had risked their lives at General Miles's request to go into the mountains to establish contact with Geronimo. All were sent into exile, and treated in no way different from those who had actually been hostile.

For those interested, it may be noted that the Chiricahuas never did return to their native Arizona. Many friends—chief among them General Crook until he died in 1890—worked for them, while they sickened and died in the lowland climate. In 1894 they were at last sent to Fort Sill in Oklahoma Territory, but not till 1913 was the unjust sentence of exile completely lifted. Even then, those who wished to return to the Southwest (many had farms in Oklahoma by then and remained there) were permitted only to join the Mescalero Apaches on their reservation in New Mexico; they were not allowed to go back to Arizona.

But that is looking ahead; no Indian in the years around 1880 knew what was going to happen to the Chiricahua Apaches forty years hence, and no one cared. They had their own troubles of the moment. Civilization was blotting out the last remnants of the old ways of life everywhere in the West, and in few places more thoroughly than on the Great Plains. There were still great spaces where a man could raise his eyes and still see nothing but grass and horizon—there are even today, although one must search well to find them—but with each passing year the open plain was giving way to cattle herds, sod shanties, plowed fields, and the sky-pointing towers of windmills.

Nothing did more to break up the open character of the plains than barbed wire. Fencing had been one of the unsolvable problems of living in a treeless country until Joseph F. Glidden of De Kalb, Illinois, devised a wire fence with barbs for use around his own farm. It worked so well he started a small factory in 1874 with five boys stringing barbs on wires; by 1880 he had a huge factory in De Kalb with 202 machines turning out 600 miles of fencing every ten hours. As fast as it was produced, this barbed wire was being strung over land where herds of buffalo had grazed less than ten years before.

The semblance of the old plains disappeared last in the North. Even while homesteaders were laying up blocks of sod to make their shanties in Kansas and Nebraska, and the cattlemen were fencing off the high plains with barbed wire, the Sioux were still hunting buffalo in the Dakotas and Montana. The last of the southern herd had been killed in Texas in 1878, except for a few scattered buffalo it did not pay the hide hunters to go after. The next spring the professionals moved up north with their hide wagons and their Sharp Fifties and commenced the final slaughter.

The last remnant of the great, brown living blanket that had once grazed the plains from Canada to Texas was now concentrated in Montana, and, to a lesser extent, in northwestern Dakota Territory. And there the professional hunters went to work with a skill that had been drawn fine with several years of practice. The grass to the north of the herd was burned over to discourage the beasts from migrating northward into Canada. The buffalo, surrounded on all sides, were helpless before the hunters, whose equipment now included telescopic sights. A hunter could lie, with his gun on a good rest, and wipe out a small herd from a distance; all he had to do was to keep knocking down the animal that became nervous and tried to lead the herd away.

The northern herd was much smaller than the huge masses of buffalo that had ranged in the south. It melted away under the guns of experts who seldom wasted a shot or spoiled a hide; the clumsy amateurs of the early days in Kansas who wasted more than they marketed were missing. "I saw buffaloes lying dead on the prairie so thick that one could hardly see the ground," a hunter described the scene created by the industrious killers along the Little Missouri in the winter of 1881–82. "A man could have walked for twenty miles upon their carcasses."

By the end of 1883 about all that did remain were the carcasses. The incessant shooting had driven the animals out of their normal migrating pattern, and a herd of about ten thousand wandered eastward across Dakota where the hunters made short work of most of them. But a thousand or more evaded the hunters, and were located by the Sioux. Sitting Bull led his band out from Standing Rock agency to hunt the buffalo as they had in days past. They found the herd about midway between Bismarck and the Black Hills, and in two days of hunting in October, wiped it out to the last animal. It was the last time a band of Indians ever rode out to hunt buffalo.

It was also just about the last time anyone hunted buffalo. The season was very nearly over at the time of Sitting Bull's hunt, and after the hide men had outfitted and gone out at the beginning of the next season, their first impression was that the buffalo had wandered farther from their accustomed range than usual. It was only after they had searched as far west as the Rockies, among the stinking carcasses and bones that marked their deeds of prowess of former years, and had found no buffalo, that it came to them that the Great Slaughter was over. No hides came off the plains in 1884; the carcasses disintegrated, and for years homesteaders earned an extra dollar now and then by gathering bones and hauling them to the nearest railroad station.

There had been a time when it was an article of faith that the civilizing of the Plains Indians would follow close on the annihilation of the buffalo—and a civilized Indian was universally understood to mean one who had given up everything of his own culture and had become an imitation white man. Once the buffalo were gone, it had been believed, the Indian would be forced to give up his roaming ways and settle down to feed and clothe himself by the sweat of his brow as a farmer, a herdsman, or a laborer. There were a couple of things wrong with this theory. One was that the former nomadic tribes had no experience in farming, and although the government promised implements, seeds, and instruction every time a treaty was made, it produced precious little that was tangible.

What was even more to the point was that almost all tribes, former farming peoples from the east and from the tall-grass prairie as well as the one-time horse-and-buffalo tribes, had been put on land that could by no means be called the best. Dohesan, a Kiowa chief, remarked acidly that if the President was so eager to have Indians raise corn, he should have given them land that would grow corn.

But even yet the land greed of the settlers was not satisfied. The biggest prize remaining was Indian Territory, the last piece of the old and forgotten permanent Indian Country. In the beginning, it had been the land of the Five Civilized Tribes until the government had taken the western half away from them on the thin pretext that it was punishing them for treason during the Civil War; the vacated western part was used as a dumping ground for unwanted tribes that were in the way of the tide of settlement elsewhere. All this has been detailed in earlier pages. However, after the other tribes had been brought in, a large tract of land in the center of Indian Territory remained empty. These "Unassigned Lands" began to be irresistible to settlers as early as 1879, and organizations of land-seekers, who came to be called "Boomers," persistently moved in and were ejected by troops. When they transferred their efforts to Washington and began speaking the loud, clear language of votes, Congress listened and soon opened the Unassigned Lands to white settlement. The result was one of the most fantastic episodes in American history, when a pistol shot at high noon on April 22, 1889 set off tens of thousands of men and a good number of women from the Kansas border by wagon, horseback, railroad train (a line ran south through the lands), and even on foot to stake out claims.

Before night, the entire Unassigned Lands, almost two million acres, had been claimed and entire cities had been platted. Once the camel's head was in the tent, the rest of the beast quickly followed. The next year, the entire western half of Indian Territory, along with the Panhandle to the west, which was part of no state or territory, was organized into the Territory of Oklahoma. The Indian reservations were sold during the next several years and the land opened to settlers some of it by land rushes, some by lotteries. The eastern half of the former Indian Territory, the lands of the Five Civilized Tribes, continued to bear the old name for a few years more. Then the tribes, although they were operating as strong, effective nations with their laws and governments, were coerced into giving up their free existence. The result was the extinguishment of the last part of Indian Territory, which was merged with Oklahoma Territory.

But this, again, is moving ahead of the story. A great deal of other Indian land was taken in smaller bites, a nibbling away by "adjusting" reservation boundaries. Scores of such changes were made during the decade of the 1880's by simple presidential decree. Some of these adjustments, let the truth be said, were for increased efficiency in administration and two or three did correct minor injustices, but most of them seemed to end up leaving the Indians with less territory, or edging them onto land that was more rocky, sandy, or hilly.

There were few ways in which these were good years for Indians. Hunger was often with them; deprived of most ways of obtaining their own food, they had to depend overmuch on the annuities that were usually late in arriving and short in amount. Children were often virtually kidnaped to be sent away to boarding school, or sometimes rations were withheld from parents who refused to let their youngsters be taken. Disease was prevalent, fostered by malnutrition and exposure. Even the fact of being an Indian was a cause for shame as both agents and missionaries often tried to root out symbols of the old culture: tribal dances, Indian clothing, even the traditional way the men wore their hair.

In a time of misery and hopelessness, people who can see no way out of their troubles and woes are prone to look to some higher power for help, and the voice that now spoke to the unhappy Indians came from Nevada, from a messiah named Wovoka. This young man—he was about thirty-five—was a Paiute; he had never been outside the narrow limits of mountain-girt Mason Valley (about fifty miles southeast of Reno). When his father died when he was a young boy, he had been taken in by the family of a rancher named Dave Wilson, and so had come to be called Jack Wilson by all the whites in the valley (he had, several years before becoming famous, adopted the name of his grandfather, Kwohitsauq or "Big Rumbling Belly," which is undoubtedly a perfectly good Paiute name, but mercifully did not replace his boyhood name, Wovoka or "Cutter," in general use).

Wovoka received his inspiration from on high in 1888 during an eclipse which occurred while he was ill with a severe fever. The event, which he considered supernatural—"the sun died"—had a powerful effect on a mind disordered by fever. He was taken up into heaven where he not only saw God in a long white robe but all the people who had died in the past, now forever young and happy and engaged in their old sports and pursuits. God directed Wovoka to go back and teach his people to put aside war and love each other, and that they must also live in peace with the white men.

But the heart of the revelations was that the earth was to be regenerated and returned to the Indians, including all the dead of the past who would come back in all the beauty and strength of their youth. The Indians were given a special ceremonial dance, which required five successive nights to complete; the oftener they performed the dance, the more they would hasten the coming of the millennial future.

Wovoka, whose beliefs were a strange blend of Indian religion and the Christian theology he had learned from the Wilson family, apparently never claimed to be other than a prophet, although he had received certain small powers from God, such as songs by which he could produce fog, snow, a shower or a hard rain, or sunshine (once he had offered, for an annual fee, to keep Nevada supplied with rain but was ignored, a short-sighted act by a state which can use a great deal more precipitation). But rain-making and such were minor matters; it was the vision of the return of the Indians' old days of glory that won him his following as soon as he began preaching his doctrine. His own people, the Paiutes, danced, and soon Paiutes went out as missionaries to spread the new gospel to the tribes beyond the mountain valleys.

And the tribes, in their unhappiness, listened eagerly, because here was exactly what they wanted to hear. The Arapahoes and Cheyennes, both northern and southern, the Bannocks, Sioux, Shoshones, Utes and other tribes sent delegates to talk to the messiah; they returned full of wonders to start the dance—which the whites had named the Ghost

Dance because it was to help bring back the dead—among their own tribesmen.

The Ghost Dance religion spread over most of the West, with the exception of the Columbia River country and much of the Southwest. Each tribe practiced it with its own variations, just as there are differences of liturgy among Christian denominations, but all believed in the same basic thing: the world made young again and returned to the Indians, with the dead come back to enjoy the good life. As they danced to bring the new day nearer, the excess of their emotions sent many of them into trances in which they saw visions—and this appears to be much of the hold it had over many of them, almost like a narcotic—and from their visions they built most of the simple, chanting songs which they used in subsequent dances. They are songs without much meaning today, but others are still all too clear, as when the Arapaho dancers sang:

> My Father, have pity on me!
> I have nothing to eat,
> I am dying of thirst—
> Everything is gone!

White people anywhere in the vicinity of Indian reservations became nervous at the activity and chanting and interpreted it as a war dance, but the usual talk of troops and protection usually disappeared rather quickly when investigation showed how little the white community had to worry about. The Ghost Dance was no war dance; the full participation of women should have indicated that to the most suspicious white observer. After all, why should they fight when the world was going to become theirs only for believing and dancing—and in as short a time as a year or two, according to Wovoka?

There was one place where the Ghost Dance did take on a slight martial note. Among the Sioux, where the new religion happened to coincide with a number of causes of unrest, "Ghost shirts" magically impervious to white men's bullets were worn, at first only in the dance, but later beneath the outer garments at other times.

The catalogue of misery and despair of the Sioux had grown very long by 1890. There was of course, the passing of the buffalo and the growing scarcity of deer and other game which deprived them of food and clothing, and except for what the poor land of their reservation would produce, put them at the mercy of government annuities. Then,

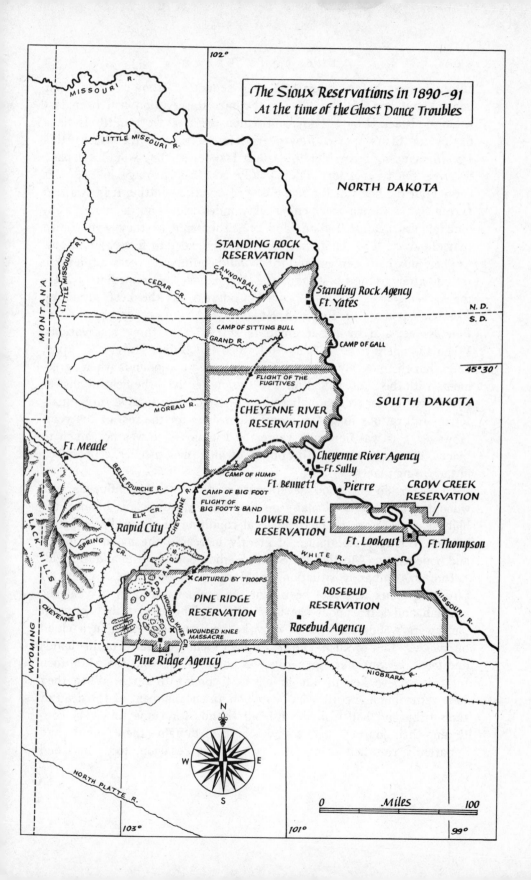

only the year before, they had been separated from more of their land. About one-third of the Great Sioux Reservation had been lost when the Black Hills and adjacent regions were taken from the Indians during the Sioux War. A few years later, settlers in the Black Hills were demanding a corridor to eastern Dakota so they would not have to cross the reservation. They finally got their passage in 1889; it carved out the heart of the remaining reservation, cutting it in two and taking half its area, an opening sixty miles wide—no danger of rubbing elbows against Indian land on either side as they went down that alleyway. The remaining land was divided into five reservations.

The Sioux had been assured they would continue to receive the same rations after giving up so much of their lands, but immediately after the agreement had been approved, Congress cut the beef ration by 2,000,000 pounds at Rosebud Reservation, by 1,000,000 pounds at Pine Ridge, and by lesser amounts at the other three reservations. When the agent at Pine Ridge informed the Indian Bureau in April, 1890 that the monthly beef issue was only 205,000 pounds when agreements with the Sioux called for 470,400, he received the helpful answer that it was better to give half rations all year than to give three-quarters or full rations for a few months and none for the rest of the year. However, this was one case where the Indian Office was not much to blame. The fault rested with Congress which then, as ever, economized in the wrong places.

In both 1889 and 1890, severe outbreaks of measles, influenza, and whooping cough caused many deaths. Agency physicians blamed the high death rate on the poor physical condition of the Indians due to hunger. Whatever the cause, it greatly increased the mood of gloom and hopelessness affecting the Sioux. So did poor harvests and drought.

Into this unhappy situation, in March of 1890, came a group of returning Sioux who had been sent the previous autumn to visit the messiah and learn about the new religion. The stories they brought back were wonderful indeed. Wovoka had come to earth in a cloud of smoke to talk to them, and had shown them nail marks on his hands and feet; the very next spring he was going to wipe out the white men for being so wicked to him at his first coming to earth. When they were returning home, they had come on an encampment of the dead of their tribe and had visited with old friends for some time. On continuing their journey, they found a herd of buffalo (these buffalo had apparently returned from the dead for the occasion, too), and had killed one and feasted on its meat; head, hoofs, and tail were left lying as Wovoka had instructed them, and as they walked off, had reassembled into a new buffalo. This appears to be the most outrageous kind of fabrication, but many visitors to Wovoka came back with tales no less fantastic; apparently in their extremely suggestible state of mind the difference between reality and illusion all but disappeared.

The delegates made their report at Pine Ridge agency and a council was called to discuss these marvels, but the agent, Colonel Gallagher, arrested three of the delegates and threw them in jail for two days. This attempt to nip the Ghost Dance before it got started failed because very shortly another delegate, Kicking Bear, arrived after having tarried on the trip home to visit the Northern Arapahoes on their reservation in Wyoming, and now brought the exhilarating information that the Arapahoes had not only taken up the dance but were able to see and talk to dead family and friends during their trances.

The story produced wild excitement. Red Cloud announced that he was accepting the new religion. The famed chief was considerably older than when he had closed the Bozeman Trail, but his leadership was still accepted by most of the six thousand Oglalas on Pine Ridge Reservation. The first dance was begun a few miles from the agency, with some of the returned delegates serving as priests and leaders.

But while the Ghost Dance religion was promising a glorious hereafter, the present was looking more and more grim. Agent Gallagher, who had earlier written the Indian Bureau that his charges at Pine Ridge were getting less than half the beef they were supposed to, was writing more letters as the summer wore on, reporting that the Indians were suffering from hunger. The Bureau received warnings from other sources as well that the Sioux were becoming increasingly restive, but no more food arrived, and in the summer the Pine Ridge Indians rebelled and refused to accept the half-ration. They eventually took it—they had not much choice—but Gallagher decided his job was a hopeless one and resigned.

He was replaced in early October by one D. F. Royer. Few men less qualified have held the post, even in a service known for the general sorry level of its appointees. He was described as "destitute of any of those qualities by which he could justly lay claim to the position—experience, force of character, courage and sound judgment." The Indians quickly took his measure and dubbed him Lakota Kokipa-Koshkala, "Young-man-afraid-of-the-Sioux." From the first he had

no control over his Indians; before he had been there a week he had
stood by helplessly while a handful of them had released a prisoner
from the jail. Before two weeks were up he was reporting that more
than half his six thousand Indians were dancing, and that he was afraid
troops would be needed because the situation was entirely beyond the
control of the Indian police at his disposal.

The Sioux were dancing at the other four reservations, too, but the
agents there, better endowed than Royer with judgment and courage,
remained calm and tried to stop the dancing, though with only partial
success. The fervor with which the Sioux were accepting the Ghost
Dance religion was a measure of their need of it.

Agent Royer became more and more frightened by the strange chanting and dancing going on a few miles from his agency. He wrote to the
Indian Bureau on October 30, saying that the situation could be saved
only by the arrival of six hundred or seven hundred troops; within a
week he was sending daily telegrams asking for permission to come to
Washington to explain, but was told that the place of an agent during
a crisis was at his post. At last, on November 15, he was directed to
report the situation to the commander of Fort Robinson in northern
Nebraska, the nearest Army post. Royer, by now in a state of near-
panic, had sent off a message saying that the Sioux were wild and out
of their heads, and that at least a thousand soldiers were needed to
cope with the situation. But Royer was not speaking completely from
hysteria, for the agent at adjoining Rosebud Reservation reported that
his Indians were so engrossed in their dancing as to be beyond the
control of himself and his police.

The old formality was observed, of transferring jurisdiction over
the Sioux from the Interior to the War Department. The Army at once
began moving units into the region, most of them into the area around
the Pine Ridge agency, until within a matter of days it had almost
three thousand men in the field. On the appearance of the troops, a
large number of the Sioux, almost two thousand, living on Pine Ridge
and Rosebud reservations fled to an area called the Bad Lands on the
western edge of Pine Ridge, a place of hills, canyons, and weirdly
eroded tablelands which provided a hiding place where an army might
not find them. Within a short time, as more refugees joined them, their
numbers increased to at least three thousand. The escaped Indians,
some of them rebellious but most only frightened, were declared to be
hostiles, although the last thing most of them wanted was to engage

in hostilities with Army forces. The movement to the Bad Lands had been almost entirely a stampede caused by panic at the appearance of the soldiers.

Things became quieter on the reservations with so many troops around. Most of the Ghost Dancing ended or was reduced to a much smaller scale; the main centers where it continued were at the camp of Sitting Bull on Grand River in Standing Rock reservation, northern-most of the five reserves, and at the camp of a chief named Big Foot on the Cheyenne River. The Indian Bureau, feeling that it should get some use out of all the troops on hand, asked its agents to submit lists of trouble-makers who should be arrested and removed, with the help of the military if necessary. Among them, four of the agents produced a total of about fifteen names. The fifth agent was Royer; all by him-self he came up with a list of sixty-four which was a "conservative estimate" and to which no one paid any attention.

As it turned out, most of the men honored by being included on the list were in the Bad Lands at the moment, but the one considered the most potentially dangerous of them all, Sitting Bull, was within easy reach. There is not much doubt that the great medicine man was a center of mischief during most of the time since he had reached the agreement with the government that had let him return from Canada in 1881. Except for joining Buffalo Bill Cody's Wild West show for a season and touring the country, he had remained on or near the reser-vation, brooding on the past and feeding his hate of white men. Toward the last he refused even to come in to the agency. He was a matter of concern to the authorities because he was a rallying point for all con-servative and dissident elements among the Sioux. When the Army took control of the Sioux reservations, it moved quickly to arrest the famous medicine man, and as its deputy it called on William F. Cody. It was believed that Cody had a great deal of influence over Sitting Bull, supposedly the result of friendship engendered by shared experi-ences in show business, and he was given authority to reach surrender terms with the Sioux leader or, failing that, to arrest him and bring him in by force. Cody arrived at Fort Yates on November 28, but the scheme was called off when Agent James McLaughlin of Standing Rock heard of it and urgently protested.

Wait until the weather got colder, said McLaughlin. Then Sitting Bull and his band would not be so likely to bolt and join the hostiles in the Bad Lands. McLaughlin also felt that the arrest should be made by his own Indian police, who were trained, dependable men, and not as liable to arouse opposition as white soldiers. The agent got his way; the arrest was deferred until December 12 when orders came to Colonel Drum commanding Fort Yates to make arrangements with McLaughlin to take Sitting Bull in. The two decided to arrest the famous chief on the twentieth, when most of the Indians would be at the agency collecting their annuities and Sitting Bull would have few potential defenders.

But on the afternoon of the fourteenth, a messenger came from the Indian school near Sitting Bull's camp, saying that Sitting Bull had just received an invitation to come to Pine Ridge because God was about to appear there. The medicine man was even then making preparations for the trip, the informant said.

It was then sundown, but McLaughlin and Colonel Drum made plans to arrest Sitting Bull the next morning. The agent already had police watching the Sioux leader's camp; more were assembled by hard-riding couriers until forty-three men, under the command of Lieutenant Bull Head, approached the camp at daybreak. Two troops of cavalry, about one hundred men, with a Hotchkiss gun (a rapid-fire gun that shot two-inch explosive shells), rode more than thirty miles from the fort during the night to be within supporting distance of the police.

Indian police had been first authorized by Congress in 1878, and eventually they were used on a majority of reservations, although to varying extents. Those on the Sioux reservation were, in general, well-trained men with excellent morale. But Agent McLaughlin had miscalculated in thinking that an arrest by them would be less offensive to Sitting Bull than one by white soldiers. For the police represented the most progressive element among the Sioux, those who had accepted the white man's way completely. Sitting Bull and those around him were the most conservative element; the medicine man himself was an apostle of the good old days and looked with scorn on all Indians who cooperated with the white authorities.

At dawn on December 15, these two opposed forces confronted each other. The police surrounded Sitting Bull's house; then Lieutenant Bull Head and several others entered to find the prophet asleep on the floor. When he was awakened and told he was a prisoner, Sitting Bull agreed rather mildly to go with them to the agency, but as his followers began to gather outside, calling on him to resist, he started to berate the police for breaking into his house and waking him. When his seventeen-year-old son, Crow Foot, taunted him as a coward, he abruptly refused to go, and called on his people to rescue him.

By that time, the police outside had been backed up against the house wall by more than a hundred threatening men, and as Sitting Bull was brought outside and the police attempted to clear a path, one of the followers shot Bull Head in the side. The police lieutenant was walking beside Sitting Bull; as he sagged, mortally wounded, he turned and shot the Sioux Chief in the side as another policeman, Red Tomahawk, behind Sitting Bull, shot the leader through the head. The entire situation exploded into a deadly, close-quarter combat, in which the training of the police more than made up for the difference in numbers. They drove their attackers off and held the house until the cavalry came up to their relief about two hours later.

Six policemen were killed or fatally wounded, while their assailants lost eight, including Sitting Bull and his son, Crow Foot. Sitting Bull died in his fifty-sixth year, a great man, not only a valiant fighting leader, but a famous prophet and medicine man. In the end, however, the gift of prophesy faded; during his last years his visions were increasingly of the past.

Next after Sitting Bull, the most dangerous leader among the Sioux outside the Bad Lands was assumed to be a chief named Hump, head of a band of about four hundred, whose camp was on the Cheyenne River. Dancing had been going on at his camp on the Cheyenne River for several weeks, and civil authorities considered him so sullen and hostile that it would probably be dangerous for anyone even to attempt to talk to him. To cope with this problem, the Army had a Captain E. P. Ewers transferred from Texas because Ewers had been in charge of Hump and his band in former years and had gained their confidence.

Captain Ewers cheerfully disregarded the dark warnings and left Fort Bennett on the Missouri with a lieutenant as his only companion. They rode sixty miles west on the plains, where they were met by Hump who had heard Ewers was coming; the chief greeted the captain like the old friend he was. When it was explained to the Sioux chief that the military authorities would like to have him take his people to Fort Bennett to get them away from hostile Indians who were causing trouble, Hump immediately answered that he would do anything that General Miles wanted. He not only brought his band to the fort, but at once enlisted as a scout and did valuable service for the

Army in getting fugitives from Sitting Bull's band to surrender rather than join the hostiles in the Bad Lands. The case of Hump was a classic example of how little the so-called Indian experts often really knew about their Indians, and of how much could be accomplished by a man the Indians had learned to trust.

With Sitting Bull dead, and Hump on the side of the angels, Chief Big Foot was next on the list of supposed trouble-makers. The chief and his village on the Cheyenne River were being watched by Lieutenant Colonel E. V. Sumner with one troop of the 8th Cavalry. Big Foot had voluntarily assured Sumner that he meant no trouble and was not going to run away. The relationship between chief and officer appears to have been relaxed and friendly. When Big Foot came in mid-December to bid good-bye because he and his people were going to the agency for their annuities, Sumner did not send an escort, and when orders came a day later from General Miles's headquarters to arrest Big Foot, he demurred. Big Foot was keeping his warriors under control, he reported, and if he were arrested and taken away from them, trouble might occur. Besides, he could always arrest the chief on his return from the agency if it still seemed advisable.

But very shortly afterward, Sumner received word that Big Foot's band had camped and had been joined by some refugees from the camp of the late Sitting Bull. He immediately set out in pursuit but had traveled no more than a dozen miles or so when Big Foot met him and informed him that he was still friendly. Then why, asked Sumner, had he taken in these other people, knowing they were refugees from their own reservation (there appear to have been thirty-eight of these dangerous characters). Because, replied the chief, they had come to his people tired, hungry, footsore, and almost naked; they were his brothers and his relatives, and he had given them shelter and food; no one with any feelings could have done any less.

It was a good answer, and it is hard to understand why Sumner did not accept it at face value. On the contrary, he now considered Big Foot's and his band as having had outlawed themselves. They were brought back to their village, and Big Foot was informed that he and his people would be taken under escort to the agency the next day. The chief not only protested the removal because he had done nothing wrong, but added that there would be trouble forcing the women and children away from the camp again because they had suffered from hunger and cold during the previous few days when they were traveling.

But Colonel Sumner was adamant. And since it was fairly plain that he was going to have to use some force, he sent out a call for additional units of the regiment. Word that more troops were on the way was carried to the Indians, and that evening Sumner was informed that the entire band had fled, and were headed in the general direction of the Bad Lands, probably meaning to join the hostiles already there.

Except for the few military units engaged in controlling potential trouble-makers in the north, the great body of troops was operating against the Indians in the Bad Lands. Almost three thousand of them were there, under the immediate command of General John R. Brooke, although General Miles was in over-all command. It was the general strategy of the two men to avoid bloodshed if at all possible, and Brooke had thrown a strong wall of troops to the north and west of the hostiles' stronghold. With these he maintained a steady pressure which gradually forced the Indians toward the east and Pine Ridge agency.

Most of the Indians were weary and cold and ready to give up anyway; some of them never had had any real chip on their shoulder but had fled only from fear. Along with military pressure, General Brooke got word to the Indians that he would protect their rights as far as he was able, and this helped swing the balance toward surrender, even though the Sioux had scant faith left in the government. The hostiles began moving in, and on December 27, the entire body left the Bad Lands to go to the agency. There had not been a single battle except for a fight between hostiles and Cheyenne scouts; the only engagements between troops and Sioux were two or three very minor skirmishes. But the book had not yet been closed on the uprising, if such it can be called.

Big Foot and his people, fleeing south, had nothing on their minds except to get away from soldiers. They passed very near several ranches without committing any depredations, and once went directly through a pasture without taking even one of the horses or cattle there. At the edge of the Bad Lands, they sent scouts to make contact with the Indians camped in the stronghold, but no answers were received to their signals for the hostiles had already gone and were on their way to the agency. It was then, on December 28, as the band was proceeding along the edge of the Bad Lands, that it was intercepted by

Major S. M. Whitside with four troops of the 7th Cavalry, about two hundred men.

Big Foot was ill, too sick with pneumonia to ride on a horse, and was being carried on a travois. He got to his feet, had a white flag raised, and asked for a parley. Whitside refused, insisting on nothing other than unconditional surrender, and the Sioux chief, with only about one hundred cold and hungry warriors, was in no position to resist even if he had been of a mind to. The band was conducted by the cavalry to a place called Wounded Knee which was only a post office and a few scattered Indian houses near Wounded Knee Creek. There they went into camp as directed by Major Whitside, while the cavalry set up its tents nearby.

General Brooke, when informed of the capture, sent Colonel George A. Forsyth, commander of the 7th Cavalry, with four more troops of the regiment to reinforce the guard around the Sioux. A company of scouts also joined the guard, and a battery of four Hotchkiss guns, making a total of 470 men to keep a watch over about 340 Indians, of whom only 106 were warriors.

Forsyth provided a tent warmed with a camp stove for the sick Big Foot and sent his own regimental surgeon to attend the chief, set a strong cordon of troops around the Indian camp, and made plans to disarm the Sioux in the morning. It was General Miles's intention either to return the band to their own reservation, or possibly to remove them entirely from the country for a while until the excitement had died down a bit—he had not yet made up his mind which.

Colonel Forsyth, whom the combined workings of promotion, rotation of duty, and happenstance had brought to command of the 7th Cavalry, was the same man who had been in command during the epic defense at Beecher Island twenty-two years earlier. There had been a great deal of campaigning on the plains for him in the years since; after the next morning it was always to be a debatable question whether he had grown as much in judgment during that time as he had accumulated years of experience. Note, too, that a number of the 7th's company commanders—among them Captains Wallace, Varnum, Moylan, Edgerly, and Godfrey—were men who had stood on the hill with Reno and Benteen at the Little Bighorn to beat back the Sioux charges, and a desire for revenge may still have smoldered in some of them.

The next morning, December 29, Forsyth made ready to disarm the Sioux. Their lodges had been set up on a flat piece of ground a short

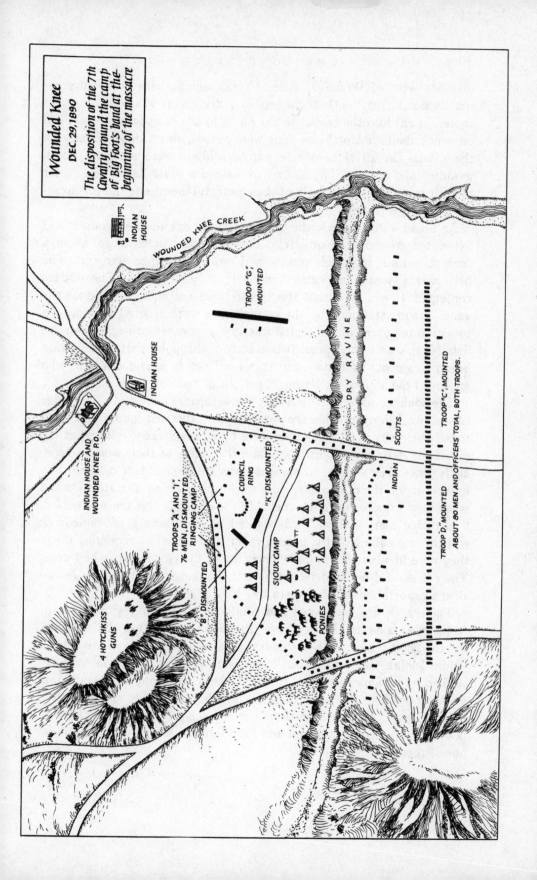

Wounded Knee
DEC. 29, 1890

The disposition of the 7th
Cavalry around the camp
of Big Foot's band at the
beginning of the massacre

INDIAN HOUSE

WOUNDED KNEE CREEK

INDIAN HOUSE

INDIAN HOUSE AND
WOUNDED KNEE P.O.

TROOP "G"
MOUNTED

DRY RAVINE

SCOUTS

TROOPS "A" AND "I"
76 MEN, DISMOUNTED,
RINGING CAMP.

COUNCIL
RING

"K" DISMOUNTED

"B" DISMOUNTED

SIOUX CAMP

PONIES

INDIAN

TROOP "D," MOUNTED

TROOP "C," MOUNTED
ABOUT 80 MEN AND OFFICERS TOTAL, BOTH TROOPS.

4 HOTCHKISS
GUNS

distance west of Wounded Knee Creek, which there flows approximately north. Just south of the tepees, a dry ravine running from west to east opens into the creek; to the north of the camp was a slight hill on which the four Hotchkiss guns were posted, and trained directly on the camp. On all sides of the camp, soldiers were stationed, both mounted and on foot. The Sioux had hoisted a white flag in the center of their camp as an indication of their peaceful intentions and a guarantee of safety.

At about eight o'clock the warriors came out of their lodges and sat on the ground in a semicircle. They were instructed to go, about a score at a time, into their tepees, and return with their weapons. The first twenty went, and came back with only two guns. The officers conferred. It was plain that this method was not going to produce the guns. Troops stationed by the council ring were ordered to move up to within ten yards of the seated warriors, and other enlisted men were detailed to search the tepees. It is exactly at this point that the situation began to get out of hand—and it is hard not to blame Forsyth, who approved the action, for letting it get out of control.

The soldiers acted like bully-boys, overturning beds and other lodge furnishings, shoving aside the women who protested loudly and tried to bar their way. The Sioux men were becoming greatly agitated at the sounds of strife from their tepees and the voices of their women, especially since they did not know what was going on. Most of them had knives under their blankets, and were approaching a state of mind when they were ready to use them. In the midst of this tense situation, a medicine man, Yellow Bird, walked about, blowing an eagle-bone whistle, and calling on the men to resist because, as he reminded them, they were invulnerable to bullets because of the Ghost shirts they wore. The officers did not understand Sioux; the dangerous trend of Yellow Bird's exhortations passed them by.

The search was completed and produced about forty guns, most of them antiquated and worn pieces. But one weapon they did not find, for the good reason that it was being carried under his blanket by a young Indian, name unknown but probably Black Fox, who was described by a Sioux witness to the event, later testifying in Washington, as "a crazy man, a young man of very bad influence and in fact a nobody, . . ." But for a brief moment he was a very important somebody as he pulled out the gun and fired into the line of soldiers, killing one of them.

The line of troops replied instantly with a volley at point-blank range, killing possibly as many as half the warriors. The rest of the Sioux men threw off their blankets and drew their knives or, in some cases, pulled out old-fashioned war clubs, and grappled with the soldiers in hand-to-hand fighting. At almost the same instant, the Hotchkiss guns on the hills opened fire on the camp, pouring their two-inch explosive shells at the rate of nearly fifty a minute into the women and children gathered there. This, too, must be weighed when the question of whether Forsyth showed good judgment is considered. Afterward, it was pointed out in his defense that he had separated women and children from warriors during the search for arms, to prevent just such a thing as did occur. Nevertheless, the Hotchkiss guns on the hill were trained from the beginning on the camp where there were women and children only, and if Forsyth did not know this, he should have.

The murderous fire was augmented by the weapons of the outer cordon of troops who surrounded the entire camp; they began shooting, killing many Indians who attempted to flee. Within a matter of minutes, some two hundred Indians and sixty soldiers lay dead or wounded, and many of the tepees had been ripped apart by explosive shells and were burning above helpless wounded. A good number of the soldier casualties appear to have been victims of their own comrades' bullets since troops were firing from four sides with rather blind enthusiasm.

The 7th Cavalry had a splendid record, but all witnesses agree that from the moment it opened fire, it ceased to be a military unit and became a mass of infuriated men intent only on butchery. Women and children attempted to escape by running up the dry ravine, but were pursued and slaughtered—there is no other word—by hundreds of maddened soldiers, while shells from the Hotchkiss guns, which had been moved to permit them to sweep the ravine, continued to burst among them. The line of bodies was afterward found to extend for more than two miles from the camp—and they were all women and children. A few survivors eventually found shelter in brushy guillies here and there, and their pursuers had scouts call out that women and children could come out of their hiding place because they had nothing to fear (one wonders how these Sioux scouts could have found the stomach to stay at their work); some small boys crept out and were surrounded by soldiers who then butchered them. Nothing Indian that lived was safe; the four-year-old son of Yellow Bird, the medicine man, was playing with his pony when the shooting began. "My father ran and fell down and the blood came out of his mouth," he said, "and then a soldier put his gun up to my white pony's nose and shot him, and then I ran and a policeman got me."

Dr. Charles Eastman went out with the burial party later and commented on the way a number of women had pulled their shawls to cover their faces as though to hide the sight of the soldiers raising their guns to shoot them. Dr. Eastman spoke with admirable restraint and detachment; although he had made his way quite well in a white man's world, he was a full-blooded Santee Sioux whose family had been dispossessed from Minnesota after the uprising there.

No one knows how many Indians died on that miserable field, because by the time anyone could count the bodies, some had already been removed. But the number was very close to three hundred, about two-thirds of them women and children. The sound of the firing had been heard very clearly at Pine Ridge agency, almost twenty miles away, and in time survivors reached the agency with their stories and their wounds. Some of the Indians who had come in from the Bad Lands to surrender rode out to Wounded Knee, where they found the troops scattered about the field, hunting down the few refugees. The Sioux attacked the cavalrymen, driving them in toward the center, where the troopers collected their dead and wounded, as well as about fifty Indian prisoners, almost all wounded, and then marched through to the agency.

The dead were buried on New Year's Day, 1891, by a detachment sent out for the purpose. A blizzard had swept over the Dakotas after the massacre, and the bodies were found partially covered with snow and frozen into the grotesque attitudes of violent death. In spite of the snow and cold, a number of women or children still lived, though most died later of wounds or freezing, or both. A long pit was dug, and the bodies were tumbled into this, most of them naked, for there were many souvenir hunters along with the burial party, and an item in great demand were the Ghost shirts. There was no ceremony; the several missionaries in the area who had been preaching Christianity among live Indians could not be bothered with dead ones. The Roman Catholic priest alone had a good reason for not being there; he had been stabbed while ministering to the troops during the massacre and was in critical condition at the time of the burial.

The effect of the massacre on other Indians was immediate. Those camped at Pine Ridge agency, who had just come in from the Bad Lands to surrender, went hostile again. They attacked the agency itself, they attacked small troop detachments and wagon trains, and they killed one unfortunate herder near the agency who thereby gained the distinction of being the one white civilian slain in all the uprising. These Indians, even with the provocations they had, had somehow lost the will to fight after so many years of going down bloody for lost causes. Their attacks were half-hearted, and after their first anger had burned out, many of them began looking for ways to break away from the main hostile band.

General Miles moved his headquarters to Pine Ridge agency, and followed his former strategy of trying to avoid armed clashes; a cordon of troops was thrown around the hostiles again, and they were nudged and pushed toward the agency. It was over, for good and all, on January 16, 1891, when the hostiles surrendered. General Miles had them set up their tepees, 724 in all, just west of the agency, and from the Army's commissary supplies he issued beef, coffee, and sugar. It was their first full meal in several weeks.

So, abruptly, the history of the Indian wars of the West ends around cooking fires with hungry Sioux gnawing on ribs of grass-fed beef. There is very little epilogue. The Ghost Dance died at Wounded Knee, as far as the Sioux were concerned. When the Ghost shirts proved as impotent as everything else they had ever put their faith in, they quickly dropped the entire religion of the Ghost Dance. Skepticism proved to be as contagious as the first enthusiasm, and other tribes throughout the West soon followed suit. Although some tribes continued to dance for a year or two, final disillusionment set in when the bright world peopled by friends from the past and covered with restored buffalo herds did not appear as Wovoka had promised. The dance became a game for children, where it was remembered at all.

There was never any more fighting by Indians after the uprising on the Sioux reservations. The strength of the tribes everywhere was gone. They were broken up; apathy, hopelessness, hunger, and disease became their constant companions. Nor had the rapacity of their white neighbors lessened, for they have since lost three-fifths of the land they still possessed shortly before Wounded Knee—and what they have managed to keep is largely sand or rock that no white man has considered worth taking from them.

It is not completely coincidence that the Sioux who fell at Wounded Knee died at the close of the same year in which the Superintendent of the Census announced that the frontier, until then a dominant fact of American life, had ceased to exist. The Indian of the Old West was a creature of the other side of the frontier, the dwindling side, and when it finally pinched out, there was no place left for him. He became in truth the Vanishing American, and it was a long time before any bright spots began to appear on his future. There still are not anywhere near enough of them.

But that is another story entirely. This one began on the Great Plains, when uncounted buffalo grazed over grass that had never been marked by wagon wheels, where the great tribes fought and hunted, secure in their own strength. It has ended, after many years, broken promises, and tragedies, at the edge of a mass grave in Dakota. Indians have gone down many paths to defeat, along many ways filled with pain and heartbreak, but none so much so as this long, last trail.

Bibliography

Athearn, Robert G., *William Tecumseh Sherman and the Settlement of the West*, Norman, Okla., 1956.

Beal, Merrill D., *"I Will Fight No More Forever,"* Seattle, 1963.

Billington, Ray Allen, *Westward Expansion*, New York, 1949.

Bourke, Captain John G., *On the Border with Crook*, New York, 1892.

Brady, Cyrus T., *Indian Fights and Fighters*, New York, 1904.

Brown, Dee, *Fort Phil Kearny*, New York, 1962.

Bryant, Charles S., and Abel B. Murch, *A History of the Great Massacre by the Sioux Indians in Minnesota*, Cincinnati, 1864.

Carrington, Margaret I., *Absaraka, Land of the Crows*, Philadelphia, 1868.

Clapesattle, Helen, *The Doctors Mayo*, Minneapolis, 1941.

Clark, Dan Elbert, *The West in American History*, New York, 1937.

Crook, General George, *His Autobiography*, as edited and annotated by Martin F. Schmitt, Norman, Okla., 1960.

Custer, George A., *My Life on the Plains*, New York, 1876.

Custer, Elizabeth Bacon, *Boots and Saddles*, New York, 1885.

————, *Following the Guidon*, New York, 1890.

————, *Tenting on the Plains*, New York, 1887.

Ellison, R. S., *"John 'Portugee' Phillips and His Famous Ride," Old Travois Trails*, Vol. II, No. 1, 1941.

Emmett, Robert, *The Last War Trail: The Utes and the Settlement of Colorado*, Norman, Okla., 1954.

Finerty, John F., *War Path and Bivouac, or the Conquest of the Sioux*, Chicago, 1890.

Folwell, William W., *A History of Minnesota* (Vol. 2), St. Paul, 1924.

Freeman, Winfield, "The Battle of the Arickaree," *Kansas Historical Collections,* Vol. VI, pp. 346–67.

Gard, Wayne, *The Great Buffalo Hunt,* New York, 1959.

Godfrey, General Edward S., "Custer's Last Battle," *Century* Magazine, Vol. XLIII, January, 1892.

Graham, Colonel W. A., *The Story of the Little Big Horn,* 5th edition, New York, 1962.

Grinnell, George B., *The Cheyenne Indians,* New Haven, 1924.

———, *The Fighting Cheyennes,* New York, 1915.

Guthrie, John, "The Fetterman Massacre," *Annals of Wyoming,* Vol. 9, 1932.

Hagan, William T., *American Indians,* Chicago, 1961.

Haines, Francis, *The Nez Percés,* Norman, Okla., 1955.

Heard, Isaac V., *History of the Sioux War and Massacres of 1862 and 1863,* New York, 1864.

Hebard, Grace R., and E. A. Brininstool, *The Bozeman Trail* (2 vols.), Cleveland, 1922.

Hodge, Frederick Webb (editor), *Handbook of the American Indians North of Mexico,* American Bureau of Ethnology, Smithsonian Institute, Washington, D.C., 1912.

Hoig, Stan, *The Sand Creek Massacre,* Norman, Okla., 1961.

Jones, Evan, *The Minnesota,* New York, 1962.

Josephy, Alvin M., Jr., *The Patriot Chiefs,* New York, 1961.

Knight, Oliver, *Following the Indian Wars,* Norman, Okla., 1960.

Lavender, David, *Bent's Fort,* New York, 1954.

Lowie, Robert H., *Indians of the Plains,* Garden City, N.Y., 1963.

McConkey, Harriet E., *Dakota War Whoop,* St. Paul, 1864.

McLaughlin, James, *My Friend the Indian,* New York, 1926.

Madsen, Brigham D., *The Bannock of Idaho,* Caldwell, Idaho, 1958.

Meacham, Alfred B., *The Tragedy of the Lava Beds,* Washington, D.C., 1883.

Mellor, William J., "The Military Investigation of Colonel John M. Chivington Following the San Creek Massacre," *The Chronicles of Oklahoma,* Vol. XVI, No. 4, December 1938.

Miles, General Nelson A., *Personal Recollections and Observations,* Chicago, 1897.

Mooney, James, *Calendar History of the Kiowa Indians,* 17th Annual Report (1895–96), Part 1, Bureau of American Ethnology, Smithsonian Institute, Washington, D.C., 1898.

———, *The Ghost Dance Religion and the Sioux Outbreak of 1890,* 14th Annual Report (1892–93), Part 2, Bureau of American Ethnology, Smithsonian Institute, Washington, D.C., 1895.

Murray, Keith A., *The Modocs and Their War,* Norman, Okla., 1959.

Payne, Davis P., *Captain Jack, Modoc Renegade,* Portland, Ore., 1938.

Paxson, Frederic L., *History of the American Frontier,* Boston, 1924.

———, *The Last American Frontier,* New York, 1910.

Richardson, R. N., and C. C. Rister, *The Greater Southwest,* Glendale, Calif., 1934.

Riegel, R. E., *America Moves West,* New York, 1947.

Rister, Carl C., *Border Command: General Phil Sheridan in the West,* Norman, Okla., 1944.

———, *Border Captives,* Norman, Okla., 1940.

Royce, Charles C., *Indian Land Cessions in the United States,* 18th Annual Report

(1896–97), Part 2, Bureau of American Ethnology, Smithsonian Institute, Washington, D.C., 1899.

Sandoz, Mari, *Cheyenne Autumn*, New York, 1953.

Satterlee, M. P., *A Detailed Account of the Massacre in 1862*, Minneapolis, 1923.

Seymour, Flora W., *Indian Agents of the Old Frontier*, New York, 1941.

Van de Water, Frederic F., *Glory-Hunter: A Life of General Custer*, New York, 1934.

Vestal, Stanley, *Sitting Bull*, Boston, 1932.

Webb, Walter P., *The Great Plains*, Boston, 1936.

Wheeler, Colonel Homer, *Buffalo Days*, Indianapolis, 1925.

Wyman, Walker D., *The Wild Horse of the West*, Lincoln, Neb., 1945.

Index

Index

371
10-07